KU-684-370

PENGUIN BOOKS

LET OUR FAME BE GREAT

'A courageous young journalist illuminates one of the world's
most ethnically and culturally diverse regions. His travels and
historical back-stories show that contemporary brutality in
Chechnya is nothing new, and reminds us of the fate of whole
nations such as the Circassians, scattered to the winds by
Russian imperialism' *Financial Times*

'Bullough should be congratulated on his brave and tireless
investigations into an under-reported region of the world'
New Statesman

'A beautifully written piece of reportage intertwined with historical
narrative. He has been up and down Russia's North Caucasus, across
its plains and into its river valleys, and has returned with tales told
by locals themselves: of carnage and heroism, of glorious pasts and
the uncertain present on the periphery of an authoritarian state'
The Times Literary Supplement

'Bullough tells a brilliant story . . . most importantly, it is
critical to understanding modern Russia, with its worrying
collective amnesia' *Spectator*

'Lively and impassioned . . . a tragically neglected corner of
our world' Orlando Figes

'Oliver Bullough's book is a painstaking, sensitively reported
effort to knit together their lost history . . . wonderfully told'
Sunday Times

'Powerfully written . . . a revelation' *Independent*

'[Bullough] teases out memories, reminiscences and family sagas. The majority of the stories are frankly heart breaking. The Caucasus, now thoroughly Russified, may be a realm of physical beauty but it is also one of human tragedy. Bullough's book means that while the peoples of the Caucasus have had neither fame nor glory at least their stories may be told'
Will Gourley, lonelyplanet.com

'Documenting a great historical tragedy unknown to most, Oliver Bullough's new book is a fascinating and groundbreaking work . . . a really important document'
Thomas de Waal, opendemocracy.net

ABOUT THE AUTHOR

Oliver Bullough was born in 1977 and grew up on a sheep farm in mid-Wales. He studied modern history at Oxford University and moved to Russia in 1999. He lived in St Petersburg, Bishkek and Moscow over the next seven years, working as a journalist first for local magazines and newspapers, and then for Reuters news agency. He reported from all over Russia and the former Soviet Union, but liked nothing more than to work among the peoples and mountains of the North Caucasus.

He moved back to Britain in 2006, and has spent the following years travelling for and writing this book. He now lives in east London. He likes to travel, to take photographs, to watch Welsh rugby, to cook and to read.

Let Our Fame be Great

*Journeys Among the Defiant People
of the Caucasus*

OLIVER BULLOUGH

PENGUIN BOOKS

PENGUIN BOOKS

Published by the Penguin Group
Penguin Books Ltd, 80 Strand, London WC2R 0RL, England
Penguin Group (USA) Inc., 375 Hudson Street, New York, New York 10014, USA
Penguin Group (Canada), 90 Eglinton Avenue East, Suite 700, Toronto, Ontario, Canada M4P 2Y3
(a division of Pearson Penguin Canada Inc.)
Penguin Ireland, 25 St Stephen's Green, Dublin 2, Ireland (a division of Penguin Books Ltd)
Penguin Group (Australia), 250 Camberwell Road, Camberwell, Victoria 3124, Australia
(a division of Pearson Australia Group Pty Ltd)
Penguin Books India Pvt Ltd, 11 Community Centre, Panchsheel Park, New Delhi – 110 017, India
Penguin Group (NZ), 67 Apollo Drive, Rosedale, Auckland 0632, New Zealand
(a division of Pearson New Zealand Ltd)
Penguin Books (South Africa) (Pty) Ltd, 24 Sturdee Avenue, Rosebank, Johannesburg 2196, South Africa

Penguin Books Ltd, Registered Offices: 80 Strand, London WC2R 0RL, England

www.penguin.com

First published by Allen Lane 2010
Published in Penguin Books 2011
1

Copyright © Oliver Bullough, 2010

The moral right of the author has been asserted

All rights reserved.
Without limiting the rights under copyright
reserved above, no part of this publication may be
reproduced, stored in or introduced into a retrieval system,
or transmitted, in any form or by any means (electronic, mechanical,
photocopying, recording or otherwise) without the prior
written permission of both the copyright owner and
the above publisher of this book

Typeset by Jouve (UK), Milton Keynes
Printed in England by Clays Ltd, St Ives plc

ISBN: 978-0-141-03774-5

www.greenpenguin.co.uk

MIX
Paper from
responsible sources
FSC
www.fsc.org   FSC® C018179

Penguin Books is committed to a sustainable
future for our business, our readers and our
planet. This book is made from paper certified
by the Forest Stewardship Council.

Contents

Maps

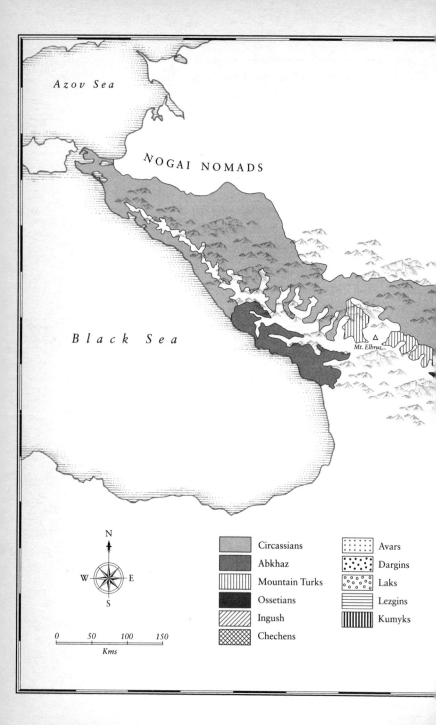

Azov Sea

NOGAI NOMADS

Black Sea

Mt. Elbrus

N
W E
S

0   50   100   150
Kms

Circassians

Abkhaz

Mountain Turks

Ossetians

Ingush

Chechens

Avars

Dargins

Laks

Lezgins

Kumyks

Mountain Peoples of the Caucasus, before the Russian Conquest

KALMYK
NOMADS

COSSACKS

*Caspian
Sea*

GEORGIANS

AZERIS

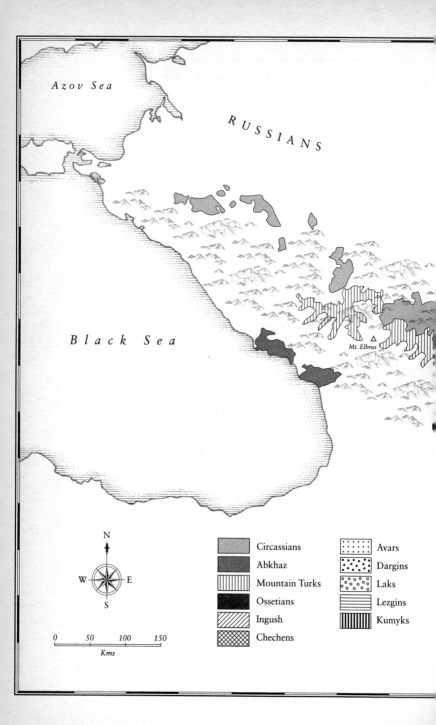

**Mountain Peoples of the Caucasus,
present day**

RUSSIANS

GEORGIANS

AZERIS

*Caspian
Sea*

Author's Note

The North Caucasus is an area of great ethnic diversity, with dozens of native languages and dialects, none of which had a written form until the twentieth century.

As such, for centuries it was only described in the languages of foreigners: Russian, Turkish, Arabic, Georgian, Armenian, Persian, Greek and Latin. These have in turn been passed on to us through English, German and French, all of which have their own ways to transliterate the alphabets used by the others.

Thus, names are spelt in a bewildering variety of ways. The capital of Abkhazia, for example, can be Sukhumi, Sukhum, Sokhumi, Sukumi, Sookom, Soukum, and that's before we start on how to spell its name in Abkhaz. Many of these spellings have a political dimension. Anti-communist exiles have often refused to use the Soviet-created Cyrillic system for Caucasus languages, and employ complex Latin-based scripts of their own.

None of the imposed methods look satisfactory. They are full of superscripted letters, apostrophes, dashes and mysterious marks that convey minute but important varieties of pronunciation. To stick with Abkhaz, a student would need to master fifty-eight consonants – by turns bilabial, labio-dental, alveolar, alveolar-palatal, palato-alveolar, retroflex, velar, uvular and pharyngal, as one classification has it – before he could begin to speak like a native. And Abkhaz is relatively restrained. Neighbouring, but now extinct, Ubykh had eighty consonants.

The Caucasus traveller and historian John F. Baddeley explained in his epic *The Russian Conquest of the Caucasus*, which was published in 1908, how Dagestan – at the opposite end of the mountain chain – was even more complex.

'The Avar language, like many others in the Caucasus, is extremely difficult of pronunciation to Europeans, in proof of which it may be mentioned that the "tl" so frequently occurring on the map is the only rendering the Russians have been able to find for four different sounds or clicks; while their "k" represents no less than six,' he wrote.

While researching this book, I puzzled over how I would fit this complexity into the familiar twenty-six letters of our alphabet. A system could presumably be created to harmonize all the different systems into one, but it would be a lifetime's work, and I am a journalist, not a linguist.

My revelation came when visiting the tomb of a Sufi holy man, born in Dagestan, but buried in Turkey. He and his family members were clustered together in an attractive building that doubled as a prayer-hall for pilgrims wishing to visit his grave. His own headstone was written in Arabic script, but three of his descendants had been commemorated in modern Turkey's Latin alphabet. The name he had passed down to them was spelt, on three adjacent graves, in three different ways: Serafuddin; Serafeddin; Serafetdin.

I puzzled for a while over how I could manage when even his family could not agree, then decided simply not to bother. If they did not care, it seems perverse to spend too long worrying about it. As a result, I have not even pretended to use a unified system of spelling, but have tried to create a book that is easy to read, in which names do not baffle the reader with clusters of consonants, strange apostrophes and clumps of ugly vowels.

I come to the Caucasus via the Russian language, so I have used the Russian version for most names, transliterated in the same simple system most British journalists employ. For people in the book who would have written in Arabic (primarily the nineteenth-century leaders of Chechnya and Dagestan), I have used a version of their name closer to Arabic, with the letter 'j' instead of the Russian 'dzh', for example.

I have also tried to use the form of spelling most likely to be familiar to readers. For example, I have called the capital of Chechnya Grozny, the Russian version, rather than Dzhokhar, as some separatists insist. In such cases, the decision on which name to use is as much political as linguistic, and I mean no recognition or rejection of the locals' positions by the choices I have made. I had to call the places something, and came down on the side of familiarity.

I know some readers will be offended by some of the choices I have made, and will feel I have sided with their opponents. I just hope they will take comfort from the fact that their opponents are almost certain to have been offended by something else in the book.

On a separate note, I apologize that throughout I have used the word 'Caucasus' as a rather clunky adjective as well as a noun: as in 'Caucasus peoples'; 'Caucasus wars'; 'Caucasus cultures'; 'Caucasus languages'. This at least is not my fault. I blame the German eighteenth-century racist Christoph Meiners, who gave his anthropologist colleague Johann Friedrich Blumenbach the idea to randomly assign the origin of the 'white' race to the south Caucasus.

To this day, the word 'Caucasian' remains a racial category and is thus not available to describe things and people actually from the Caucasus, which is extremely annoying.

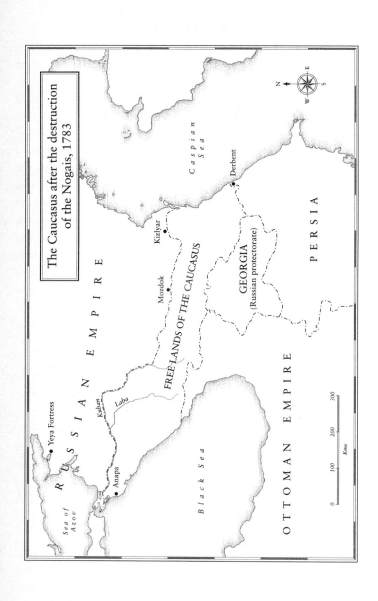

The Caucasus after the destruction of the Nogais, 1783

Introduction
Let Us Live in Freedom

Russet and gold marshes choke the river Yeya. Its muddy waters merge into the stagnant pools that bubble and ooze through the reeds of its estuary.

Driving along the causeway from Yeisk towards Azov in a Hungarian-made Icarus bus, I failed to notice that I'd crossed the river at all. Only when the marshes ended, and the bus had climbed the tiny elevation to the steppes proper, did I realize I had passed the site of a battle that doomed the peoples of the Caucasus mountains to two centuries of carnage.

This muddy land, where Russia stares at Ukraine across the waters of the Azov Sea, is a strange place to look for the gateway to a mountain range, since all around the horizon is a flat line ruled dead-straight against the sky. To the west are the sea's turgid, grey-brown waters. To the east are the broad steppes that stretch to the Sea of Japan. And here is an in-between land of mud and reeds that struggle to lift themselves out of the water.

Yet in these marshes, in 1783, Russia opened its path to the south, to the land of the mountains. Here it finally extinguished the power of the steppe nomads that had held it in subjection for so much of its history. The muddy waters swallowed up the last descendants of the terror from the east that – according to Russian folklore – had held it back, kept it backwards and poor. The nomads had ruled the steppes by raiding and skill for as long as Moscow had ruled Russia, but the Muscovites had finally outgrown them. With the horse lords killed, Russia was free to fulfil its destiny: to march to the warm waters of the Black Sea and beyond.

Above the marshes on the north bank of the river is a tiny village, which still bears the name Yeya Fortress – Yei Ukreplenie – given to it by the advancing Russian army. To this fortress, in early July 1783, came thousands of the families that made up the Nogai horde, the last free descendants of the armies of Genghis Khan in Europe. The Russian General Alexander Suvorov had summoned them to swear allegiance to their new ruler, Catherine the Great, and the steppes were covered by their tents. Over three days of feasting, he cajoled, he persuaded, he charmed and he threatened, until eventually he had the agreement of the Turkic-speaking nomads. They would transfer their loyalty from the defeated Khan of Crimea to the great empress from the north.

According to the little museum in Yeya Fortress, in the course of the feasting Suvorov treated them to 500 barrels of vodka, 100 bulls and 800 sheep. A picture on the wall shows the scene. Oriental princes in pointed hats, beards and fur-trimmed caftans are interspersed with clean-shaven Russian officers in their full dress uniforms and epaulettes. In the distance, giant cauldrons steam over an open fire, while musicians play for a Russian and a Nogai dancing energetically together.

The picture is one of friendship and conviviality. On the far right, a Nogai man is upending a jug into his mouth. The white-haired Suvorov himself is raising his glass in toast, while another Russian is embracing a nomad lord, as they all sit on sumptuous carpets spread on the fresh turf.

Lyudmila, the museum's director, insisted on showing me the rest of her exhibits. She proudly pointed out jars of sunflower seeds, lentils, maize and wheat from the long-defunct collective farm. Photographs showed happy workers parading down the streets that still bear their communist names: Street of the Second Five-Year Plan, Street of the Soviets. As we looked out of the window, a long-legged girl cycled through the dust of Lenin Street, chased by her squealing little sister.

On that lazy August afternoon, as flies buzzed in the sunlight and swallows darted in the blue, it seemed nothing bad could ever happen here, as if time had stood still since that merry afternoon in the eighteenth century when Suvorov persuaded the Nogais that their future lay to the north.

But the picture was deceptive, like a photograph of a rock concert before it is suicide-bombed.

Suvorov had a surprise for his new friends. After they swore their allegiance, he told them that the first order of their sovereign empress was that they should gather up their belongings, cross the Volga and resettle on the plains south of the Urals. They must retrace the westward journey their forefathers took centuries before and leave Europe behind them. There was no place for headstrong and troublesome nomads on Catherine's steppes, and Russia's hard-working and obedient peasants had another use for the black earth, perhaps the richest land in the world, on which they grazed their horses.

To the nomads, the rule of Crimea – which itself had been annexed by Russia earlier that year – had always been light if felt at all. Government for them was a question of tribute, not of obedience. This order shocked, dismayed and then angered them. The rank and file rose up and killed the leaders who had signed this treacherous pact. Suvorov was suddenly faced not with 6,000 dinner guests, but with 6,000 armed, angry and warlike opponents. They marched on the Yeya Fortress, determined to avenge the insult and secure their lands.

But Suvorov was ready for them. Perhaps this was the outcome he had wanted all along. As would so often prove the case in the battles with its southern neighbours – the Chechens, the Dagestanis, the Circassians and the other mountain peoples – over the next 200 years, Russia's disciplined troops could easily destroy any angry mob that charged against them. Reinforcements arrived and pinned the Nogais back against the marshes of the river.

Where now the rushes whisper to each other, the cows blink against the flies, and the falcons hover, the Nogais were pushed back. Their ranks breaking under the strain, they began to sink into the mud, to feel the helplessness of their position. Their sudden attack had failed, and now they were trapped.

Even the great nineteenth-century Russian historian of the Caucasus, Vasily Potto, whose five volumes trumpet the achievements of his country's armies, allowed the Nogais some sympathy here.

'The Tatars were pushed into the marshy river and, seeing no salvation, in a fit of helpless anger, destroyed their own treasures, slaughtered their wives and drowned their infants.'

The destruction was terrible. Suvorov sent back to the Russian lines a living prize of 300,000 horses, 40,000 head of cattle, 200,000 sheep, as well as uncounted numbers of women and children – who were perhaps shared out as the animals were among the victorious soldiers.

But the group at the feast had not been the whole Nogai nation; others had been grazing their herds or camping elsewhere, and they rose up to avenge the massacre. Towards the end of August, a new mass of tribesmen attacked the Yeya Fortress, besieging it for three days before once more being beaten off. And now the Russians pursued them. Chased across the steppe southwards, the Nogais crossed the river Kuban and tried to flee up the river Laba into the mountainous land of their neighbours, the Circassians. The Russians left the valley choked with their dead.

In 1838, an old man called Mansour told an English traveller he met on the southern bank of the Kuban of how the raid had changed the complexion of the land. 'My beard is not yet white, still do I remember the day when, instead of yonder castles, there was nothing on the opposite bank but the huts of the Nogais – a people whose customs and religion were in unison with our own – with whom we could trade, associate, and war, it might be, all on a neighbourly footing, as we would do among ourselves; but these the Muscof [Muscovites] chased them from their rightful homes, driving some of them across the Kuban, where they found refuge among ourselves, and the rest to the devil or Krim Tartary [Crimea]. In their place they established these Cossacks – giaours [unbelievers] like themselves – and whose way of life is to us an abomination,' the old man said.

After this second suppression, the Nogai nation was truly no more. Although they had long since lost the dread reputation their forefathers had earned when Genghis Khan's armies were unrivalled between Korea and Ukraine, their military strength had still been formidable. They had traded with Russia for years, and were largely dependent on it for their commerce. As early as the sixteenth century, Russia was buying 50,000 horses from them a year. But the fact remained, while they roamed and raided lawlessly across the steppe, no Russian peasants could hope to settle, plant crops and live peacefully.

Suddenly, with them gone, to the south of the Yeya was an empty space, ready for settlement. And to the south of that space loomed something quite new for the Russians: a mountain range. Without the Nogais to plague them, the Russians, children of the forests and swamps of the cold north, could march onwards to warm lands of wine and feasting. By destroying the Nogais and winning the steppes, they had opened the door to the Caucasus mountains, and, after the Caucasus mountains, to the lands of Georgia and Armenia, and to Turkey and Persia too. And perhaps after that, they might march to India itself, the greatest prize of all. Russia had discovered its destiny, and the Caucasus peoples were standing in its way. For them life would never be the same again.

These peoples who lived to the south of the Nogais had, over the millennia, developed an astoundingly complex patchwork of free communities, of princes, of lords, of slaves and of freemen. The nomads had effectively secured their frontier so, on the northern slopes of the Caucasus mountains, where few armies had ever been, they had been free to develop in their own way untroubled by outside interference.

They had traded with the Turks, the Genoese and the Greeks. Turkish slave-traders had purchased their sons and daughters to serve as mercenaries and concubines in the Ottoman Empire. Some embassies had gone back and forth to Moscow, and occasionally an army had appeared from Persia to be defeated and sent scurrying home again. The religions of the Russians and the Turks had taken root here and there, but in the main the highlanders had been left alone to live their lives untroubled by the outside world.

In its isolated bubble, the Caucasus had become perhaps the most ethnically complex place on earth. Whole language groups exist here with no relations outside the region. The Circassian language is related to no other, save for neighbouring Abkhaz and now extinct Ubykh. The origins of Chechen and Ingush fascinate linguists. The two million people in Dagestan, on the shores of the Caspian Sea, speak forty different languages. By comparison, there are just sixty-five languages native to the entire European Union.

An ethnic map of the region looks like an oil stain on a puddle. The yellow of the Circassians juts up against the light blue of the mountain Turks. The dark blue of the Ossetians touches the browns of the Chechens and Ingush. Then the purple of the Avars heralds the whole rainbow of the peoples of Dagestan. This Babel was a world apart, with its own traditions, many of them dating to long before the arrivals of Islam and Christianity. It governed itself without much interference from anyone.

No organized power had ever tried to conquer the northern slopes of the Caucasus, since no organized power had ever had a secure route there before. To the west, where the Black Sea washes the mountains' roots, the cliffs plunge straight into the water. A single traveller would struggle to pass from south to north here, let alone an army. Very few genuine passes traversed the high mountains, and those that did were threatened by savage tribesmen, vicious weather, wild beasts and avalanches. Only to the east, along the Caspian shore, could foreigners hope to pass into the North Caucasus: and there the Dagestani and Chechen warriors were more than a match for almost any invader.

But suddenly, with the destruction of the Nogais, a whole new route was created: across the steppes, from the north. The mountains that had served as a wall to defend the highlanders from the aggressive south became a trap that blocked their retreat.

The Russians swept across the newly conquered steppes quickly. The Cossack colonizers built their fortified villages in the river valleys, and – together with the regular army – they were fighting the tribes all along the range within less than a decade. If the Russians expected it to be an easy fight though, they were mistaken. Over the next two centuries, their armies would defeat Napoleon and Adolf Hitler, as well as almost every single one of their neighbours, however mighty. No one resisted them for as long as these supposed savages in the valleys of the Caucasus.

The outside world did not notice the clashes on the marshes of the Yeya in 1783, since it had other things to think about. The Americans were building their democracy, while the French were preparing to build theirs. The British were spinning textiles and digging coal. Communications within Russia were notoriously bad, so it is possible that few Russians even realized the significance of what had happened. But had anyone noticed the little campaign, they would have gained a sneak preview of how the Russian army would fight all the tribes to its south.

Like the Nogais, enemies would be slaughtered if they did not submit. Like with the Nogais, the slaughterer would be honoured. Suvorov received the Order of Vladimir First Class, and has streets still named after him in Moscow and St Petersburg. He went on to fight in Poland, Turkey and Italy, and died having never lost a battle. Few of those battles would be as easy or as brutal as these ones had been, however.

And as with the Nogais, the slaughter would be forgotten by its perpetrators. No one I spoke to in Yeya Fortress knew their little village had once witnessed a battle that decided the future of Russia. In the larger town of Yeisk, a bargain-basement holiday resort an hour's journey along the coast in the rickety bus, the museum staff reacted with disbelief to the suggestion. The only hint that Suvorov might have done something morally questionable was a quote attributed to him on the museum wall: 'Never has vanity, especially that fuelled by momentary passion, directed my actions, and I always put aside personal ambition when it came to serving the nation.' Perhaps here he was apologizing for the destruction of the Nogai nation: 'I was just doing my job.'

For the Nogais are gone. A few villages in the foothills of the mountains remain. But here, in their heartland, no trace survives. I left Yeisk the next day, heading south on a bus towards the distant Black Sea coast, and looked for a Turkic name or a felt tent, anything that might suggest a nomad influence.

There was nothing.

In fact, there was less than nothing. It took me a while to spot the absence, but by the time we had reached the foothills of the Caucasus range, I had realized what was wrong. Where the Nogais had herded horses, cattle and sheep, these Russians farmed only wheat, sunflowers and maize. In the 300 or so kilometres between Yeisk and the hills, whence Suvorov took the hundreds of thousands of stolen livestock, I saw only two cows, a gaggle of geese and one pig. Where the nomads moved their tents with the herds, now the Russians are huddled into compact villages of two or three thousand people, their right-angle streets identical to every other settlement along the highway. The Russian-language village names showed the curse of the colonialist by being either crushingly dull – Sandy, Jolly – or totally over the top – Progress, the Bright Path of Lenin, the Revolutionary Wave. The very culture of freewheeling movement and lordless life was extinguished with the nomads, to be replaced by the blind obedience of the Russian state.

But not every nation would vanish as readily as the Nogai, although Russia was equally merciless to all those who did not accept its troops with the bread and salt of friendship.

The Russian troops of Alexander II – hailed today as the great reformer of the tsarist empire, but for the Caucasus tribesmen the biggest murderer of them all – could only defeat the Circassians by driving them en masse from their lands on the Black Sea coast.

In what was the first modern genocide on European soil – fifty years before Turkey's Armenians were butchered, ninety years before the Holocaust – perhaps as many as 300,000 Circassians died from hunger, violence, drowning and disease when Russia expelled them from their lands on their final defeat in 1864. Scattered pockets of their descendants still cling to the slopes of the North Caucasus, but the vast majority of the nation now lives in Turkey, Israel, Jordan and elsewhere in the Middle East. What was once their country is now home to Russians, Armenians, Cossacks, Ukrainians and all the other loyal nations of the empire.

Eight decades later, Joseph Stalin – a communist who learned the lessons of his tsarist oppressors well – crushed the mountain Turks and the Chechens by ripping them from their homes and dumping them on the steppes of Central Asia. Tens of thousands of them died too.

In the 1990s, those same Chechens – far from being cowed by their treatment – fought a war more terrible than anything even the Caucasus had seen before. Grozny, their capital, was destroyed block by block. The fighting became so savage that children were targets for both sides. Tens of thousands of Chechens, tired of war, disgusted by the brutality, fled Russia with just a suitcase to seek peace elsewhere. They now live in France, Norway, Poland, Austria and throughout the world.

Through the horrors and joys of their shared history, and in the dozens of countries where war has driven them, the Caucasus nations have mingled and traded and fought, creating a rich shared culture of folklore, music, dance and costume.

That folklore includes a corpus of poems passed from generation to generation. They describe the Narts, the mythic ancestors of all the Caucasus nations. The stories are told in many different languages, but remain essentially the same. In one such tale, their god sends a swallow down as a messenger, and gives the Narts a choice.

'Do you want to be few and live a short life but have great fame and have your courage be an example for others for evermore?' asked the swallow. 'Or perhaps you would prefer that there will be many of you, that your numbers will be great, that you will have whatever you wish to eat and drink, and that you will all live long lives but without ever knowing battle or glory?'

Throughout the chronicles, the Narts delight in holding meetings and discussions to decide the correct course of action. But in this tale they do not do so. Without hesitation, they tell the swallow to take their answer back to his master.

'If our lives are to be short, then let our fame be great! Let us not depart from the truth! Let fairness be our path! Let us not know grief! Let us live in freedom!' The swallow took that answer away with him and, so the story goes, 'their fame has remained undying among people'.

But, in truth, their god did not keep his side of the bargain. Despite what he promised them, their lives have been cut short, fairness has passed them by, they have known endless grief, and their fame has not been great.

Like the Nogais, many of the peoples that listened to the tales of the Narts around their winter fires were to face slaughter, and have their fate forgotten. Who now remembers the Circassians? Or the Balkars? Or the Karachais? Or indeed the Nogais?

With a few honourable exceptions, the world has responded to the slaughter in the mountains with blank indifference. The Circassian exodus attracted headlines at the time, but the nation's fate has drifted out of history. While the deliberate destructions of Turkey's Armenians and Europe's Jews are remembered and taught in schools as bleak warnings of humanity's inhumanity, the Circassian genocide is not even known about in the land where it happened.

In Neal Ascherson's otherwise wonderful book *Black Sea*, for example, which traces the interaction of nations around the great inland sea, the Circassians do not appear even once in the index. He finds room for such diverse subjects as Pol Pot, Boudicca and Queen Elizabeth I of England, but a nation that once controlled the entire north-eastern coast of the sea that is the book's subject does not warrant a single mention.

Likewise, taking another book at random from my bookcase, Philip Longworth's *Russia's Empires* details at some length (in a chapter called 'The Romantic Age of Empire') how Russia subdued the Caucasus, but without mentioning that a major military tactic had been depopulation on a national scale.

Likewise, Stalin's destruction of the mountain Turks – divided by the Soviets into the Balkar and Karachai nations – has passed largely unnoticed. The deportations were perhaps overshadowed by the horrors that were happening elsewhere in 1943–4, but they are indicative of the approach of the Soviet Union to its subjects, and deserve far greater publicity than they have received.

The Chechens, meanwhile, have been victims of geopolitics. Some of their own leaders have been stupid enough to employ terrible brutality in the cause of their attempt to gain independence. The world has been able to effectively brand the whole Chechen nation as terrorists, and has been happy to avoid grappling with the dreadful strategy Moscow has followed in suppressing their self-rule. Ignorance has bred indifference, which in turn has bred deeper ignorance.

A friend who worked for a Western television station in Moscow once told me how an interviewer had been flown in specially to speak to the then president, Vladimir Putin. The interviewer – who was apparently quite well known in his own country – glanced down the list of questions prepared for him by the local staff, saw one about the plight of the Chechens, and crossed it out.

'I asked about them last time,' he said, simply, when asked why. In the years between the two interviews, possibly as many as 10,000 Chechens had died in a war waged by Putin's army.

I was musing on all this, on the mountains and on the fate of the Nogais, as I wandered out into the marshes along the Yeya river down tracks the cattle had made in their quest for food and water. Flies buzzed around me, and birds rose up complaining from almost at my feet. I sat at last on a patch of cropped grass and listened for a while. I thought that if I cast my mind back I might be able to imagine the cheers of the Russian soldiers, the cries of the tribesmen, and the screams of the dying women and children.

I heard nothing except the flies and the birds.

The day was hot, and after a while I eased onto my back. The sun glowed red through my eyelids, and I thought about the giant mountain range away to the south. It would not take me long to get there – just a day or two by bus, if I did not stop on the way – and I wondered what awaited me.

I had seen horrors beyond my imagining because of the Caucasus. I can still, without closing my eyes, see before me the butter-pale, serene, long-eyelashed face of a dead teenage boy, one of the 334 victims of the Beslan school siege. I can still feel the revulsion of picking through the snow, trying not to step on scraps of fat-edged flesh that were all that remained of a Chechen woman who had blown herself up, along with five passers-by, in central Moscow. I can still remember the shock of seeing bombed-out Grozny, with its crumpled factories, and shattered tower blocks, for the first time.

The memories of those outrages were close around me as I lay in the marshes. They always are. But that was not what I was thinking of. As I lay there, I replayed something that had happened earlier, the first time I ever saw the mountains, one early morning in 2003.

I had visited a Chechen refugee camp where civilians who had lost their homes existed in ragged, khaki tents in a field of mud and stones. I called on a Chechen woman who lived in one of these tents – in size, no bigger than my living room in Moscow – and she had told me about her life, how she cooked, tended, cleaned and mended for twelve children who had nothing to do all day but play in the mud. The children were not all hers; some were the orphaned children of her sister, others of her cousin. She lived without a husband, and I got the impression that he was dead too.

She had had no stove, just an open gas flame which she used to boil water for washing clothes and cooking pasta.

The load she was bearing would have broken a lesser woman, but she shrugged it off. She could even laugh at the idiocy of a humanitarian organization which had called at the tent a fortnight before. She had not been home at the time, so they had asked the children what the family needed. As a result of the charity's generosity, the tent now boasted a large television for everyone to watch while she washed their clothes by hand, juggled sauce pans on the gas flame, and tried to keep mud off the bunk beds.

I had left her tent shaking my head at the wonder of her, and walked back towards my car. Glancing upwards as I walked, I was stunned to see the full majesty of the main Caucasus range suddenly emerge from the clouds. Where just a moment before had been a dirty grey blur, there was now the brilliant white clarity of the highest mountain range between Canada and Central Asia.

The slopes shone as they soared up to sharp point after sharp point, and the range receded into the west where Mount Elbrus – the highest peak in Europe – was perhaps just visible.

That was what I remembered as I lay in the sun on the marshes and felt the grass stems tickle the backs of my ears. I remembered that woman and those mountains, and the unbreakable spirit that made them both rise gleaming and pure.

Their fame is not great, and their stories have not been told, but truly they deserve to be.

To learn their stories, I would have to travel far from the mountains. I would labour across the steppes of Central Asia. I would squat outside the internment camps of Eastern Europe. I would wander through the cities of Turkey. First of all, though, I would sit and drink tea on a warm, fragrant morning amidst the olive trees and gentle hills of northern Israel.

PART ONE

The Circassians, 1864

1. Are You Not a Circassian?

That same sun eased down on me a few weeks later, as I drove along one of Israel's immaculate roads and gazed up at a church crowning the brush-covered lump of Mount Tabor to my left. Idar Khon, a 44-year-old retired lieutenant-colonel in the Israeli army, was at the wheel, but there was nothing military about the atmosphere.

I had phoned him, without warning, that morning. The man I was supposed to meet had been called away, and had given me Khon's number. I had been apprehensive about calling this unknown officer, but need not have worried.

'Well, I don't actually have a driving licence at the moment,' he had said, pausing for effect, and then laughing, 'but I'll come down and get you in half an hour.'

He was better than his word, and was outside my hotel in his Japanese SUV within fifteen minutes. We drove together up the hill towards his village, surrounded on all sides by the dense cultivation that makes Israel look so lush. And after ten minutes or so a sign told me we had arrived. It was written, like all signs in Israel, in Hebrew.

But there was another, more familiar, alphabet alongside the boxy Hebrew letters: the Cyrillic. In a script that could be welcoming visitors to any place in the Russian Caucasus, it told me we were entering the Circassian village of Kfar-Kama.

This village is one of the southernmost outposts of a great Circassian diaspora that spreads from a couple of villages in Kosovo, through the great cities of Turkey, and on into the arid and difficult lands of Syria and Jordan. Here, in Israel, was the end of the chain, a chain created after Russia expelled almost the entire Circassian nation from its home in the hills that fringe the north-eastern shore of the Black Sea in 1864.

Witnesses at the time testified to the desolate conditions of the refugees, who were crammed into leaky boats, ferried across the

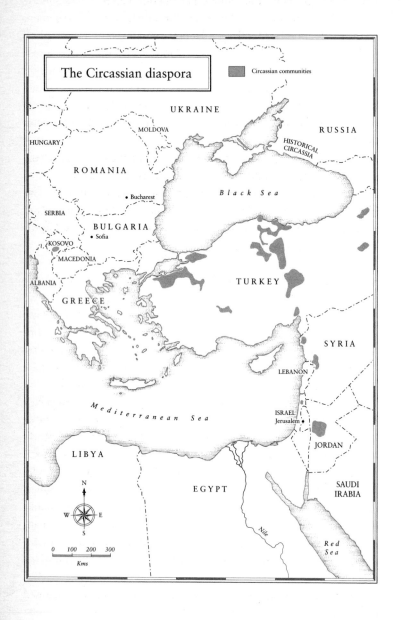

The Circassian diaspora

Circassian communities

UKRAINE

MOLDOVA

HUNGARY

RUSSIA

ROMANIA

HISTORICAL
CIRCASSIA

• Bucharest

Black Sea

SERBIA

BULGARIA

• Sofia

KOSOVO

MACEDONIA

ALBANIA

GREECE

TURKEY

SYRIA

LEBANON

Mediterranean Sea

ISRAEL
Jerusalem •

JORDAN

LIBYA

EGYPT

SAUDI
IRABIA

N

W   E

S

Nile

Red
Sea

0   100 200 300

Kms

Black Sea from their mountain home, and dumped to shiver and die on the open beaches of the Ottoman state. Perhaps 300,000 of them were dead before that doddery old empire organized itself enough to find them places to live. It gave them land that no one else wanted, land that was threatened by disloyal nations or anarchic nomads on the edges of the vast Ottoman state that stretched from modern-day Bulgaria to North Africa and the borders of Iran. Hence, the Circassians found themselves spread in a long line ending in Kfar-Kama in Galilee.

I had come to the village to see how much of the Circassians' culture had survived their destruction and dispersal. Nineteenth-century travellers, who had wandered through their Caucasus valleys before their defeat and marvelled at the resistance of this outnumbered nation, had admired their openness, their moral fibre, their impulsiveness and above all their generosity.

Khon, a handsome man with short grey hair and an open face, was a credit to his ancestors. He clearly cared far more about hospitality to a guest than about the Israeli traffic laws. He barely flinched as we passed a police car on the way into the village, and he welcomed me warmly to his clean, airy home. He would, he said, teach me about the Circassians' culture and, over a long morning of tea and conversation, while the breeze lazily stirred the curtains and the sun beat down, he did so.

Eventually, it was time for lunch. His wife Dina, a radiantly beautiful woman with a headscarf and a broad smile, put out food for us and their children and we sat and chatted. With lunch over, Khon and I took our time over cups of tea, while the children hared around the house, enjoying their after-school freedom.

Khon was deep into a description of *habze*, the Circassians' code of conduct, when their nine-year-old sprinted round the corner into the living room, slipped on the carpet, and slammed the side of his head into one of the chairs. It sounded painful and he screamed with the shock of it. He sobbed into his mother's arms as she comforted him.

Khon, however, barely looked over his shoulder, and just snapped out the words: 'Wu adiga ba?'

In English, that would be: 'Are you not a Circassian?', but the question has far more force in the original. In fact, I could not think of an English phrase which even came close to its spirit. It is a rhetorical question that suggests someone has shamed himself. The boy was crying. Circassians do not cry. Therefore the boy could not be a Circassian, and had shamed himself before his ancestors.

The doings of those ancestors are endlessly recounted in tales of the Narts – the legendary giants that lived in the Caucasus before people – which bear lessons in how men and women should behave. Savage punishments are meted out for minor indiscretions, such as criticizing a wife unfairly, or being overproud. The true heroes of the tales are those who persist in doing the right thing – caring for the poor, saving the weak, and so on – even when their foolish neighbours mock them for it. Where Western children swap tales of Robin Hood or Tintin, Circassian children all over the diaspora will tell of Setanaya or of Sosruquo, born when a shepherd was so overcome with desire for Setanaya that he ejaculated across a river onto a rock.

Sosruquo, even when a child, could beat any Nart in a fight, outshoot them, and outdance them, yet would refuse riches, presents or praise. As an adult, he would likewise refuse praise for brave deeds or great feats of strength, crediting instead his neighbours or his horse.

These were the virtues Khon was trying to inculcate into his boys, although he was not always very consistent about it.

Under the stern rules of traditional habze, no father can touch his child, and brothers should never be in the same room as each other. Khon was earlier quite happy to pick up his angelic golden-haired daughter and bounce her around before lunch with the jokey words: 'This is not habze'. He had his two sons wedged up against him on each side while he did it, and they clearly adored rather than feared their father.

Nonetheless, he guided me though the principles of habze with a steadiness and certainty that showed he truly believed in them.

The cornerstone of habze is respect. Respect for the Circassians must be earned and awarded. In order to earn respect you must respect others in turn, and that reflects itself in many ways. True Circassians, for example, must never interrupt when an elder is speaking – a trait which, incidentally, makes them terrible translators.

I later heard the apocryphal story of a young man who was standing near the fire in a house when an elder started to speak. The elder had a lot to say, and took his time about saying it. The young man was unable to move while he was speaking and thus ended up with severe burns. Several Circassians told me this story, or a closely related version of it, as a model for how young people should behave. It would have been disrespectful to interrupt the old man by moving during his speech.

Elders, on the other hand, must behave honestly and respectfully to the young. Another apocryphal story that I heard at around the same time relates how some Circassians were choosing a new leader for their group. Several elders were presenting themselves as candidates, and the group was discussing their merits. One of the elders showed signs of wanting to go to the toilet, so a young man quickly ran into the toilet ahead of him and dirtied it. When the elder returned, the young man checked the toilet and found it to be clean. He then told the assembled men that he would back the choice of this old man, since he had the dignity to be humble. His choice was then ratified by the group. Respect, the story showed, is for the Circassians a two-way process. This is not a society that celebrates aristocrats or slaves, but free men who appreciate they are part of a community.

Likewise, Circassians must respect members of the opposite sex, and Circassian women enjoy much greater freedom than in the Arab communities of the Middle East.

Several Circassian men boasted to me that they had kidnapped or 'stolen' their wives, in order to force them to marry them. At first I was shocked, but the situation was not in fact what it sounded like. Far from being effectively the rape of an unwilling woman, Circassian bride-stealing is a strategic step taken to force her unwilling parents to agree to her getting married. The stealing is ritualized, and accompanied by a volley of gunshots to alert the parents that it has happened. The couple would never be alone together, and the groom's uncle would normally be employed as an emissary to sound out the prospective in-laws.

If they relented – which they almost always do – and agreed to the match, she would return home immediately, and the wedding would be prepared. If they did not agree, she would go to live with the groom's uncle until the wedding.

Khon was in fact one of the most recent people in Kfar-Kama to steal his wife, and many of the villagers were sad that, under the influence of Islam and with more tolerant parents, bride-stealing and the slight whiff of scandal it generates was dying out.

'It is all very easy now, so there is less and less kidnapping. The last case was a year and a half ago, when they decided to get married they wanted to do everything properly, but the mother of the girl said she was too young at only twenty years old and that her grandmother had only died two years before. That night, gunshots were heard. There are lots of weapons here, you see soldiers with weapons, but we do not use them. So if you hear gunshots that means someone has been kidnapped. Then they told the mother the girl had been kidnapped, by SMS I think, and she said okay, they could get married, and everything was fine,' said Zoher Tahawha, curator of the village museum.

The most famous Circassian trait, however, and the cornerstone of habze, is hospitality. Circassians must respect their guests, and treat them as a member of their own family – a trait I exploited shamelessly.

While travelling through the Circassian communities – from Kosovo, around Turkey, to Israel, Jordan and then to the Caucasus itself – I rarely had more than one phone number to call for help in any of the countries I visited. Sometimes I would not even have that. Still, everyone I met would put me in touch with a friend or acquaintance in the next town or village. And people gave up sometimes several days in a row to show me their communities.

In the afternoon, Khon took me to talk to his friends, and they too greeted me like a long-lost brother.

We sat, the four of us – Khon, me, and his friends Ali and Gerchad – and discussed habze in the delightful warmth of an Israeli afternoon, cups of coffee on the table in front of us and the breeze stirring the folds of a Circassian flag – a green rectangle, with three golden arrows crossed below twelve gold stars.

'Just to begin to understand the Circassians you have to be such a philologist,' said Gerchad. 'There are no histories of us, so you have to be able to read English, Arabic, Turkish, French, Russian, Circassian and more. If you can't read all of these you will not get a complete picture. Besides, I don't think anyone could write down habze anyway.'

Habze, they told me, is about obedience and loyalty. Look at the Circassians, they said. The whole nation fought for the army of whatever state they found themselves in. I thought back to the conversation with Khon in the morning. I had asked him if, being a Muslim, he was not troubled by serving in the Israeli army.

'When the British were here,' he had replied, 'we served the British as policemen. Then in 1948 some younger men moved into the Israeli army. I did not plan a career in the army, but I am from Rehaniye, a small village. There is no factory, and all there was was the police or the army: what we call security jobs. I did not enjoy the war, fighting the Palestinians. We have a problem because we are Muslims but we are a part of Israel, and so we do our best to be part of the community, but we do not like the war between the Palestinians and Israel.'

This loyalty to their new homes had been a characteristic of the Circassians ever since the tragedy of 1864. Circassians fought for the Ottoman Turks until their state collapsed after the First World War.

When the sultan was deposed, they fought for the Turkish Republic against the Greeks and the occupying powers, although their leader, Ethem, received no thanks for it. He was driven out by Ataturk, who disliked rivals and accused him of being a traitor.

With the Ottoman Empire shattered, they also served their new masters in Jordan, Syria, Iraq and elsewhere. They earned a reputation as tough soldiers to fight alongside or against. One Sir Gerald Clauson wrote a memo to the British Foreign Office in 1949 about his time fighting with the Arab Legion – of Lawrence of Arabia fame – against the Ottoman state.

The Circassians in Jordan, he said, were 'the best fighters in that area, and, generally speaking, a pretty tough lot'.

He reminisced about a Circassian officer commanding an Ottoman force near the Iraqi city of Fallujah who refused to surrender until the British sent a plane over and dropped artillery shells on him. 'The gentleman sent us a message to say that honour was satisfied now that the angel of death was hovering over him and that he was willing to surrender. I saw him when he was brought in in a thick black uniform in the height of summer and thought he was one of the toughest and most attractive creatures that I had met in the course of the campaign.'

His note formed part of a memo suggesting that the Circassians might be trained up as an anti-communist force to be secretly despatched from the Middle East to fight Moscow. The idea apparently originated from émigré Circassians from the Soviet Union. The suggestion was rejected, as likely to cause severe embarrassment if the local Arab governments found out about it, but does show the regard with which the world viewed the Circassians' prowess.

The plan would probably have failed, however, for the simple reason that Circassian loyalty does not know borders. On the other side of the Iron Curtain, the local Circassians were equally loyal to the Russian state and had been since before 1864, and would have resisted insurgents. Regiments of Circassian cavalry were raised from the region of Kabarda for all the nineteenth century, and the tribesmen in their national costume regularly formed the honour guard for the emperor, as they do now for the king of Jordan.

With great irony, Alexander II – whose armies destroyed the Circassians and conquered the Caucasus – had a Circassian bodyguard in 1881 when he rode through St Petersburg. As he passed, an anarchist hurled a bomb at his carriage. The bomb bounced off, exploding on the street and fatally injuring one of his Circassian guards. This emperor, who had so uncaringly sent the Circassians into exile and seized their homeland, was now overcome with compassion for this individual. He descended from his carriage, presenting an irresistible target to another anarchist who had kept a bomb in reserve. The bomb was thrown and the emperor killed, victim of his regard for a loyal Circassian.

The Circassians fought for the tsars again in the First World War, raising the Caucasus Cavalry Division even though they, as Muslims, were exempt from conscription. Circassian regiments may even have fought each other since the Turks also employed them as cavalry, and most Circassian villages in Turkey have photographs of the volunteers they sent off to fight the Russians. In the Second World War, the Soviet Union's Circassians fought again, although – Turkey being neutral – they no longer had to fight against their ethnic kin.

The Circassians, however, are no longer the fighters they once were. Young Circassians are now – in Israel, Jordan and Turkey – more likely to study technology than to enter officer training school. The older martial qualities are slipping away, and the world offers more opportunities than Khon ever had.

But it is the lasting respect for military virtues that sustains the Circassian regard for a phlegmatic nature – for the lack of which Khon rebuked his nine-year-old. Traditionally, a Circassian should never express frustration, anger or weakness. To be seen drunk in public is shameful, and a Circassian should be able to hold his alcohol. Circassian women traditionally wore a corset from puberty to marriage, the strings of which were only untied once a day by her mother. On the marriage night, the groom would have to restrain his impatience by untying the fiendish knots concocted by his in-laws. Any man who used a knife to release his new wife showed a lack of self-control, and was publicly shamed.

Circassian women no longer wear corsets, but the tradition has been updated, according to Tahawha, who talked me through the wedding traditions used by the young Circassians of Kfar-Kama.

'People used to try to make the groom tired. His friends would often kidnap the groom, and eat, dance, play – the only sad one being the groom. They only sent him home at first light, and when his wife opens the door she has been asleep and she was not afraid of anything. Then, twenty years ago or so, they started to put obstacles in front of the groom, or burst the tyres on his car. When I got married in 2002, my friends sat with me until two in the morning. I kept telling them I had to go to my wife, but they would ask me what the rush was. I was angry, and did not know what they were doing. But afterwards I understood, they were making me tired so I would be gentle with my wife. People still do this now, although only until twelve midnight or so.'

All of this perhaps gives the impression that habze is a rather austere discipline, but that is far from the truth. Hospitality is given joyously and willingly, while loyalty and comradeship are an excuse for competitions and showing off. Nineteenth-century travellers wrote how the Circassian young men raced and fought to establish precedence.

In a strange reflection of this tradition, I made kebabs.

In Kfar-Kama, a wedding takes place almost every weekend in summer. At least a quarter of Israel's 4,000 Circassians are invited to each one and the catering is a major challenge. A dozen or so men are required to shape the mince into shish-kebabs, to skewer the marinaded chicken, and to chop the onions and other vegetables. Although, as a vegetarian, I did not look on preparing several thousand kebabs as a major treat, I could hardly turn down an invitation to take part.

Funnily enough, although the mince was clammy and the fat stuck to my hands, the occasion was a joy. Conversation was almost all in Circassian, with just the occasional comment in English to me, but the constant laughter and spirit of the occasion made me feel included and happy.

Our host, who spoke very little English, kept encouraging me to 'make kebabs with love' – a baffling comment that I only later discovered was a reference to an Israeli hummus advert. Every time he said it, a gale of laughter would sweep the room. Then the fierce competition that had developed between our table and that next door, where a group of older men were trying to match our prodigious kebab output, would resume in even deadlier earnest.

Every task was the excuse for a joke. And when I wiped my eyes after peeling an onion, there was a good half-hour of banter about whether it was or was not habze for a man to cry if he was not actually sad.

The same good-natured rivalry extended to the wedding itself, where the men competed for the most flamboyant dancing. Circassian dancing is a well-developed tradition, in which the women glide on scarcely moving feet within a circle of clapping onlookers, their hands undulating and dipping like fish in a tropical sea. The men, however, are all flash and fire. Their feet stamp, and their arms dart as they shepherd their partner around the ring. With chests out, and their heads thrown back, their dances have a primal quality: a mating display in its rawest form. That men and women dance together at all is, of course, a rarity in the Middle East and just another sign of the exceptional nature of Circassian culture in the region.

The dancing, the accordion music, and the rules of habze were common elements to all the Circassian communities I visited, even ones where the language had been lost. But, for decades, the Circassians of Israel did not know that. They had only the smallest signs that any Circassians outside their two villages survived at all.

'In my time,' remembered Khon, 'there was one radio station from Amman or Syria maybe that played one hour of Circassian music a week, this was the only thing we had outside our own community. And the whole lot of us sat by our radios and listened to this music.'

Khon visited the Caucasus in 1992 for a month and is still excited about it. 'It was a spiritual journey,' he said. 'It was more than I expected, I did not expect to ever see that we had a country. I went to the theatre, I heard people in a town speak Circassian. At last we had a chance to raise the nation up again.'

At that time, Israel and Jordan were not to sign a peace treaty for another two years, so Khon could not visit his Circassian compatriots the other side of the Jordan valley. He looked for another way to connect with the diaspora, and found it in the internet. If you searched for the word Circassian on the internet in those days, he remembered, you found nothing. And since the Israeli Circassians got the internet before any of the other diaspora communities, and they could learn from their Jewish neighbours how to mobilize a scattered nation, they hit the ground running.

They used the internet to seek out other Circassians dreaming of creating a united nation for the first time in over a century, and forged ties that have strengthened and spread in the years since.

Kfar-Kama is now home to a radio station called Adiga Radio that broadcasts over the web twenty-four hours a day. It has news in several languages and plays a peculiar selection of Circassian music in which home-made hip-hop will morph into a folk melody and back again, to an audience around the world. The radio site also allows visitors to download Circassian versions of classic films – including *Bambi*, which has been renamed *Nalbi*, perhaps because *Bambi* has an unfortunate double meaning in Circassian, although none of the locals would explain it to me. Israel's Circassians are also active in chat rooms and discussion forums trying to reach out to their compatriots across the Middle East.

This ability to expand their horizons while remaining Circassian came along just in time. Israel's Circassians were running out of non-relatives to marry and the opening of borders has allowed people to look for wives or husbands in Turkey and Jordan.

The Circassians in Israel now have a professional folk-dancing troupe, coached by a Jewish immigrant from the Russian Caucasus, and the children are well-educated about the history of their nation. But, in reaching out, they did find one problem. Despite being the smallest community, Israel's Circassians are the only ones outside the old homeland to have preserved the language completely. It is so vigorously alive in Israel that even non-Circassian neighbours in Rehaniye speak it well.

But it is hard to talk to compatriots in other countries. Young Circassians elsewhere speak Arabic, Turkish or even English.

Take Sebahattin Diyner, a stern 75-year-old in the Turkish city of Kayseri, for example. He never thought he would visit the Caucasus, and he never thought his children would need the language that he grew up speaking. He was born after all in Turkey – a Turkey where saying you were not a Turk was a political act. He was a Circassian, and his parents taught him to be proud of it. But he did not advertise it.

As the 1980s came to a close, however, change was bubbling over not only in his own country, where the economy's growth was altering society profoundly, but in the Soviet Union too. Suddenly ethnic groups that had long been part of the happy communist family under the Russian 'older brother' could look around them and explore their past.

The communities began to reach out to each other and, when they found each other, to dream of re-creating what was lost at a groundbreaking conference for the whole nation.

So Diyner was nervous when he stood on stage at the International Circassian Congress held in the Caucasus town of Nalchik in

May 1991. The Soviet Union still existed. Would the dream of forging bonds between the fragments of the shattered nation be pulled away as it had been in the past?

'There must have been 15,000 people gathered there and I addressed them on behalf of the Turkish delegation. When I was speaking people started crying. When we went out on the street, people came up to us, they wanted to know about relatives in Turkey. An old woman, she must have been eighty, just hugged me, she said she had been told a big lie all her life. The governments had lied, they had been told that the diaspora had lost its culture, that Circassians abroad lived badly. She said she felt like a mother who had found a lost child,' he remembered, seventeen years after that historic speech.

Diyner was seventy-five years old when we met in the central Turkish city of Kayseri, and at first he possessed an austere dignity. He tapped his foot up and down as he answered, leaning back in an overstuffed armchair.

Without being rude, he managed to give the impression of someone who wanted to be doing something else, rather than answering questions about his past. But as he remembered the congress of 1991, he thawed. He leaned forward in his chair, planting both feet on the ground, and began to lose himself in what had been. He talked more quickly about the people he had met and the amazing sights he had seen.

'We could talk to everyone, we had no problems, our language was identical. I met sixty people from the same family as me, people with the same surname as me. Many of them lived in the little village of Lo'okit. We have a village just near here with the same name.'

With the ice broken, he allowed me to ask more questions. I probed deeper and suddenly he just opened up. I sat in amazed silence, scribbling in my notebook as he told me his family story. He only stopped – his foot tapping again but this time in impatience – for his words to be translated into English so he could continue.

Some sixteen members of his family left the Caucasus in 1864, with his grandfather's father on the boat as a young boy. Twelve of them survived the voyage and the refugee camp. Three died of disease, while one young man had broken his leg and hurt his head climbing on board ship and died without reaching Turkey.

They arrived in Samsun, and trekked into Anatolia in search of the empty lands that the government had promised them. They reached the Uzunyayla – the 'Long Plateau' – of central Turkey, where only nomads lived, and they settled down to make it their own.

Uzunyayla is a bleak, terrible place, treeless and windswept. Villages are tucked into folds in the ground but are still dreadfully exposed. Poles along the verges mark the road when it is covered by dense snow in winter.

The Circassian country along the Black Sea could scarcely have been more different. Densely wooded, and made up of rolling hills and tumbling rivers, it provided ample farming and grazing for the nation before its expulsion. It must have been cruel indeed for Circassians to trek from their lush home to this arid and blasted land.

But on a map of Circassian communities in the Middle East, this plateau holds a special meaning as a crossroads. The Circassian villages fan south from the Black Sea city of Samsun in a line, stretching down through Uzunyayla to the border with Syria, then on into Jordan and Israel. To the east, only a handful of villages are scattered near the borders of Armenia and Iraq. To the west, however, a mass of them rings Istanbul in the regions of Sakariya, Eskisehir and Bursa. When Diyner's great-grandfather arrived here, this Circassian world was just being created. Its members were cousins and neighbours and friends. They would serve together in the Ottoman army, and trade together and enjoy each other's company. The Circassians had lost Circassia, but they were still linked in one giant community.

Diyner's grandfather left Turkey in 1911 to go to the Caucasus for a visit. He met those of his aunts and uncles who had remained behind. After staying for two and a half years, he reluctantly turned down offers to find him a bride. He had a wife and children in Turkey and they were waiting for him. But it was cruel homecoming, for he died in 1915 fighting the Russians in the First World War.

He would not have known it but he was one of the last Circassians to have enjoyed the freedom to wander through the newly created diaspora. He just saddled a horse, rode for four and a half months, and came back to Uzunyayla.

Diyner had a picture of him. It was a photograph of a painting, which was in turn taken from a photograph. It showed a young man, straight-backed and handsome with his moustache and astrakhan hat. He wore the tunic of the Circassian, with its cartridge cases in their holders across his chest and the long dagger in front of his crotch. Diyner was seventy-five years old and the very model of the secular Turk, in his checked shirt, glasses and cardigan. But he had the same moustache, the same hooded eyes and the same straight back. The resemblance was striking.

The war that killed his grandfather also destroyed the Russian empire. The communist state that succeeded it built walls that separated the diaspora communities from their homeland for more than seventy years. No one from Diyner's generation had ever been to the Caucasus, nor even dreamed that it would one day be possible.

Uzunyayla is in a way the most Circassian of all Turkey's districts. When the Circassians arrived in the Ottoman Empire, they were distributed wherever the government could afford to give them land. Circassians today like to say they were placed along the frontiers of settled agriculture as guardians of the Ottoman heartland from the wild nomad tribes. It is a pleasant myth, and has a comforting feel to it. In truth, however, it is more likely that the land used by nomads could be given away to the new arrivals without anyone significant complaining. The farmers would then encourage their nomad neighbours to settle. The line from Samsun down to the Holy Land was the line where the farming Turks and Arabs bumped against the Turkoman and Bedouin nomads, and thus the line where there was land available to give to the Circassians.

To the west, where Circassians are clumped around Istanbul, they were moved onto swampy valley floors, which they drained and turned into fertile and profitable fields. Circassians were settled in the Balkans as well, but were driven out when the states of Romania and Bulgaria were created in 1878–9, leaving just a handful in Kosovo – a community that now is all but extinct.

Hundreds of thousands of Circassians left the Caucasus. Estimated numbers vary wildly: from a probably overinflated two million, to a clearly too small 300,000. The number was probably somewhere between a million and 1.2 million, according to the latest research by historians. The death toll of their terrible journey is impossible to estimate, but the mortality rate was probably about a third.

The world's current Circassian population is hard to estimate. The emigrants' descendants today number maybe as many as four million in Turkey, although historians have not studied them and even Western histories of the modern Turkey fail to include them in their indexes. A hundred thousand or so are in Syria, and maybe 70,000 more live in Jordan, while 4,000 live in Israel and a handful cling on in Kosovo. Significant secondary communities also live in the United States, Germany and the Netherlands. The diaspora community, therefore, massively outnumbers the 600,000 Circassians who still live in the Caucasus.

There was, therefore, great excitement among these Circassians when, just a few months after Diyner's speech at the International Circassian Congress in 1991, the Soviet Union collapsed and the prospect of reuniting the nation rose in its place.

Young Circassians take great interest in the traditions of their parents. Today, in Turkey, very few Circassians below thirty or forty years old speak their own language, but they have nonetheless sought to assert their culture.

Listening to old stories, a group of young people in the early 1990s had heard an old folk tale of a woman called Elif Ketsep'ha. She, the story told them, grew up in the Balkans when it was still Ottoman land but was forced to flee in 1877–8 and ended up in a small village north of Adapazari in western Turkey. Her family died of disease and famine, leaving just her to honour their corpses. She sat every day by their graves singing the mourning songs of her people, becoming a symbol of the constancy and the tragedy of her nation.

The young, idealistic Circassians of the early 1990s found the graveyard where she had lamented her loss, and began to commemorate their nation's destruction there, choosing as their remembrance day 21 May: the date when Russia proclaimed victory in the Caucasus in 1864.

Elif's village stands a few kilometres inland from the tiny fishing port of Kefken, which also has a special place in the hearts of the

Circassians as one of the arrival sites of the massed refugees. It is a wild and bleak coast, with a few caves pushed into the low cliffs that mark the edge of the beaches. In these caves, Circassians sheltered and scratched the rocks with their names in the Arabic script they then used.

The memorial ceremony, which I attended in 2008, has become a tribute to how far the Circassians have come in uniting their far-flung nation. They had come from all over Turkey, from America, from Russia, from Israel. Many of them bore the green flag of Circassia, with its crossed arrows and stars, and they all stood together on the jagged rocks to throw flowers into the sea which formed the final grave for so many of their compatriots.

As the sun touched the horizon, an old man's voice rose in a lament joined by the quiet hum of other Circassians singing together. Hundreds of carnations arced through the air to land in the water, which heaved beneath them. Song followed song, as the purple stain of evening spread over the sea. Darkness fell and I sat on the clifftop watching as a bonfire flared up on the beach and the assembled Circassians – young and old – took a blazing torch in each hand and made a procession along the shoreline. The haunting melody of the Circassian song 'Road to Istanbul' hung in the air like a floating scrap of silk: delicate but strong:

> Our beautiful caps lie on the edge of our foreheads,
> The steeds we ride, alas, we shall also have to leave behind.
> Woe, our forefathers and foremothers are weeping over us!
> Wailing and mourning we are exiled from our motherland,
> We utter our farewells to the fatherland with bleeding hearts!

2. We Share Happiness, We Share Sadness

I sat in the bus driving back to Istanbul from Kefken musing on the amazing strength of the Circassians, and on how, after so many years apart, they had reforged the links connecting their nation together so quickly. It was only our small bus-full that was leaving the event. A horde of young Circassians remained, and they would drink and talk and dance all night at a building on the jagged cliffs. New friendships would be born, new courtships would begin, and maybe new marriages be agreed.

But, in some ways, the impression of a newly united nation was a misleading one. The nineteenth-century travellers who had been so amazed by the Circassians would have struggled to recognize some of their traits in their descendants. Circassians all over the world were often profoundly troubled by what they found in the communities of their compatriots in other countries.

It is not surprising perhaps that a Circassian who has grown up in the democracy of Israel has a different mentality to one who grew up in the communism of Russia, or the authoritarian strictness of Jordan or Kosovo. But it still came as a disappointment to Circassians – overjoyed by the new freedoms they found after 1991, and by their chance to visit the Russian Caucasus – to find their ancestors' homeland so, well, Russian.

I found Selim Abazi, fifty-four years old, in Milosheve, one of two villages in Kosovo where Circassians once predominated. He moved to southern Russia in 1993, and was joined by the whole Kosovo Circassian community in 1998 when the war with the Serbians started in earnest. He remained a fiercely patriotic Circassian, with the green-and-yellow flag tacked to the wall of his shack, but he had left the Caucasus to go back to Kosovo in 2000.

'I did not like these Russians, they are communists and we had no relations with them at all, they were scared of us. We could speak to the Circassians, but they too had become like Russians. They would ask us if we had only come to their country to find work and they would swear at us and say they did not have enough to eat for themselves,' he told me in the broken Russian he had learned in his time in the Caucasus.

'The Caucasus is beautiful, it is subtropical. But the people are bad, when they got democracy everything fell apart. There is too much alcohol, too many drugs.'

I got the impression Abazi was not being entirely open with me. He certainly never explained how he'd lost his arm, which was just a bandage-swathed stump. But his story was echoed by the few Circassians I managed to track down in the wretchedly poor Kosovan villages they had returned to in preference to the nice, red-brick houses the Russian government gave them to live in.

The graveyards were still full of Circassian surnames, the mosque – built by Circassians – stood tall, but the few old men and women left here would be the end of Kosovo's Circassian community.

Murat Cej's brother Musa lives in the Caucasus along with many other of his former neighbours, but he also came back to Kosovo when the war ended. We stood out of the rain and chatted – a translator having to help since Cej had not learned Russian during his stay – about the history of his people.

'When we first got to Russia we were so excited,' he said, with a broad smile raising crinkles all around his watery blue eyes. 'All the Circassians were asking how had we saved our language. These Circassians were very nice, but not the Russians, they did not like us. My wife, even though she's Albanian, wanted to stay there but I wanted to come back here. My father died here, and I will die here too.'

In other countries, too, Circassians had problems realizing the dream of moving to the Caucasus. Technically, as people whose ancestors originated in Russia, they have the right under Russian law to move back there. But, in fact, they struggle to do so, especially since the Chechen war has made Russian officials so suspicious of any foreigners in the southern provinces of their country.

Omer Kurmel, aged forty-five, is one of the leaders of the Caucasus Cultural Federation in Turkey. His organization, which has members throughout Turkey's large Circassian community, aims to secure Circassian repatriation. He speaks perfect English, and has an American PhD, but even his diplomatic skills betrayed a slight frustration with the difficulties Circassians face in patching their people together.

'It is not easy to get a visa now, it can take weeks. The security clearances go on. I understand that Russia is concerned about terrorism in Chechnya, but this has hit us particularly,' he said as we sat in his office in Istanbul a few days after I took the bus down from Kosovo.

'I would say not more than a hundred people from here have moved back to the Caucasus,' he said.

He said the Circassians needed to emulate the Jews and launch a movement to move back to the homeland, while accepting the fact that Russians now live there. 'When I was a teenager, like all Circassians I used to think that the Russians were bad people who had persecuted my people. But when I went to the Caucasus I saw that the local people had developed a common way of life with the Russians. The problems are because of our weakness, rather than Russian strength.'

But the Circassians face an uphill struggle. According to one report, 3,000–4,000 idealistic Circassians had immigrated to the Caucasus by 1993. It is hard to say now how many have joined them, but the number of foreign-born Circassians in the Caucasus would seem, if anything, to have shrunk since then.

Chen Bram, an Israeli anthropologist who has studied the Circassian communities in the Middle East, summed up the disappointment felt by many Circassians. They had dreamt of an ancestral homeland running with milk and honey, but instead had found a land where people 'reel under economic chaos, huge inflation and political insecurity. Moreover, the poor systems of transportation, communication and other features of modernity that affect the standard of living in the cities made an unfavourable comparison to their lives in Israel. If one adds the havoc at local airports and the horrible and useless bureaucracy in general, it is easy to understand why some of the Israeli visitors heaved a sigh of relief upon returning to Ben Gurion Airport in Israel.'

Indeed, one Israeli friend in Kfar-Kama joked to me that Israel now 'imports Circassians'.

The difference between the Circassians in the Caucasus and those in the diaspora are perhaps most marked in Jordan, where the Circassians have a privileged position. Circassians, more than the Bedouins and Palestinians who make up the rest of the population, have created a civil Jordanian identity and allied themselves closely with the ruling family. They act as a unit in the tribal law that regulates relations between communities, and hold high posts in government, the army and business.

Amman, the capital of Jordan, was founded by Circassian refugees on the site of a ruined Roman city and Circassians still provide the bodyguards for the royal family. Their property in central Amman is home to Palestinians who fled what is now Israel in a series of waves starting in 1948. Although they were initially poor, the Circassians have made money from property deals and from their closeness to the royal family, and are now Westernized and secular.

The Circassians I spoke to were fluent in English, and, despite being proud of their heritage, they came from the mould of wealthy Middle Easterners who looked to America and Europe for their culture. Before a concert and performance given by a dance troupe from the Caucasus, young and fashionable Circassians kissed each other on meeting, then stood and chatted in Arabic, their conversations larded with English phrases: 'oh my God'; 'reach common ground'; 'no way'. My friend Zaina pointed out different members of the audience, with remarks that one was engaged to an American, another one had married someone from England, and so on.

I was surprised to hear of Circassians marrying outside their community, and asked Zaina if it was common. 'Oh, it is better to marry a European than an Arab,' she said.

During my few days in Amman, I visited sports clubs with swanky swimming pools and tennis courts, and was invited to smart, air-conditioned flats on the outskirts of the dusty, sprawling city. I had come here particularly to meet a group of students whom I had heard about in Israel. While I'd been sitting with Khon in Kfar-Kama, which is just the other side of the river Jordan, he had wanted to show me quite how much the Circassian diaspora had changed since those days when he and his neighbours had hunched round a crackly radio broadcast from Syria.

Turning on his television, he showed me NART TV, a station made by Circassians for Circassians and decorated with the Circassian flag in the top corner. It showed a folk dance, and then a children's tale, then some words by a Circassian academic, then some talking in the extinct Ubykh language. It was an interesting broadcast, but then, abruptly, it went back to the beginning again. This was on loop, and full programming had not started yet. Khon, however, was excited. This satellite television station could help provide the glue required to bring the scattered Circassians together.

When I tracked down the NART (National Adiga Radio and Television) TV team, I was stunned by how young they were to carry such a heavy burden. The oldest of them, and the originator of the idea, was Nart Naghway, a 24-year-old with a quite breath-taking degree of ambition.

'As you can see,' he said, waving around the clean but messy office where his team was based, 'we are a small group, but it's going well. We do everything here, we edit, shoot, make reports. There are thirteen of us, mostly students at the university. We had this dream, but the money issue is critical. Most people make a business plan before they start a television station, but we decided to do it the other way around. We thought we'd create the TV station first.'

He had already forged contacts with Circassians in the Caucasus and in Turkey, and planned to broadcast in all the languages of the diaspora. He would also broadcast, he said, in the different dialects used by Circassians – Kabardian in the east of Circassia and for people originating from there, Shapsug for people originating from the Black Sea coast, and other dialects in between. Circassians who did not speak Circassian would also be served with broadcasts in the languages of their home countries. The sheer complexity of broadcasting a multi-national television channel in at least four languages and an unspecified number of dialects did not seem to daunt Nart at all.

'We will have Circassian lessons in English, in Turkish, in Arabic, that is the main role of NART TV, to teach the youth. We must use

modern technology to keep this nation alive. If we cannot communicate with each other face to face then we need to use the satellite.
The internet is nice but not everyone can use it.'

As if that plan was not ambitious enough, he also told me they
planned to gather archive footage from all over the Circassian community to create a resource for future generations to draw on, while
also preserving the current generation from assimilation by the nations
that threaten to swamp them. As we chatted, another man walked into
the office. He looked to be in his mid-thirties, very fit and smartly
dressed. He spoke perfect English, and handed me his business card.
His name was Yinal Hatyk and he was, much to my surprise, chief of
staff to Prince Ali bin al-Hussein of Jordan.

With easy authority, he took over the conversation from the
younger Circassians and required little prompting to tell me his story.
He visited the Caucasus for the first time in 1986 aged twenty-two.
He had gone to live in the city of Nalchik for a month along with
five other Jordanian Circassians. A few years later, he started working
with Prince Ali because King Hussein – the prince's father – wanted
his son to learn about the traditions of the people, and that included
the Circassians. The prince took the project to heart. Together they
hatched a plan to ride horses to the Caucasus, thus re-creating the
links between the old Circassian communities, and perhaps reignit-
ing old trade routes. In 1998, they rode up through Jordan, Syria
and Turkey, caught a boat across to Russia and turned west towards
Nalchik.

The then 23-year-old prince struggled to get a Russian visa for his
trip, however, and had to leave four of his horses behind in Turkey to
avoid a customs infringement. It was a disappointment for the idealistic group to strike the stifling bureaucracy of Russian rule in the
Caucasus. Hatyk was to come to know the suffocating legal culture
even better. At that time, he had the prized *vid na zhitelstvo*, or Russian residency permit. But he would not have it for long.

'For the Russians, they cannot distinguish if you are a Chechen or
a Circassian, or if you are going to fight against them or not. They
cancelled my vid na zhitelstvo, for example, on the charge that I am
a nationalist. They've made it harder for us to get visas. It costs more

money and it takes longer. There is a law that Circassians should be able to get passports, but they've made it harder. You have to give up your old passport, and you have to speak Russian. It's easier perhaps if you're fifty or sixty years old, then they know you're not going to fight them.'

I walked away from the meeting more depressed than I'd expected. The students might be trying to set up a television station, but if the Circassian population was still divided, then the chances of uniting its far-flung elements were slight. Struggling for a metaphor, I thought of the people as a pot that had been smashed, and then tumbled around in a river for a hundred years. The shards would still match in colour and pattern, but their edges would have been knocked about and chipped and scarred and encrusted. It would not be possible to slot them back together.

But enough of the pattern survived to make the culture recognizable, and people who visited the Caucasus in the nineteenth century would still have seen flashes of their familiar Circassians in what was all around me two centuries later.

In Kayseri, where I met Sebahattin Diyner, I was adopted by a young man called Aytek, who, as a friend of a friend of a friend, afforded me all the wonders of Circassian hospitality. He was a cynical and amusing man, with at times a very jaundiced view of his own people, but he loved the glory of its traditions. As we drove out to the village where he grew up, he told me about his aunt: a woman of a character strong even for a Circassian. Aged thirty, she was told that she could never climb a particular mountain while playing her accordion. Unable to resist the challenge, she set off and did so, marching up the mountain – which is a 45-degree scree slope – and down again. At the bottom, she promptly died. 'Someone had told her she could not do it, you see,' Aytek said.

That evening, he took me to a wedding to see how Turkey's Circassians – otherwise indistinguishable from other Turkish citizens on the streets – revelled in the traditions of their ancestors.

The dancing circle was if anything even more frenetic here than in Israel. The men were sweating as they competed with each other for ever more macho poses. They remained careful, however, to never shame themselves by turning their backs on their partners, who responded by looking ever more graceful and demure.

All this dancing was thirsty work, and Aytek took me by the arm and steered me out to the car park where his friends had gathered around the open boot of a car to drink Johnnie Walker Red Label out of plastic cups and discuss the action inside. The dancing partners, although they appear to an onlooker to be entirely random, were it would seem part of an important ritual. One man and one woman are empowered with the right of selecting the partners for each dance, and if a party guest is interested in a particular woman, he asks the controllers to organize a dance for him. A few dances and they are considered to be an item, or *kashen* as the Circassian word has it.

Aytek's explanation of the intricacy of Circassian wedding lore was interrupted by a succession of loud gunshots from nearby. A Turkish wedding was taking place in a hall the other side of the car park wall and the groom was being saluted by his friends. My companions could not let such a challenge pass and one guest pulled a pistol from his pocket and loosed off a volley into the night. He masked the muzzle flashes with his jacket, but the noise was loud enough for the Turks to hear. There was no response.

I was thrilled, for firing into the air is a standard celebration in accounts of Circassian life in the 1830s. And here it was, used again in 2008.

This, however, is one tradition that the Circassian community is not united in defending.

Circassian culture, like many others based on family ties, diaspora, respect and martial prowess, has been at times prone to develop into the kind of mafia clans that have marred Sicilian and Italian communities in the United States. The Circassian villages near Istanbul are well-known for their giant palaces built with the proceeds of criminal empires. In the 1990s, the area between the cities of Dubze, Adapazari and Izmit was known as the 'Bermuda Triangle' because so many pro-Kurdish businessmen would vanish and be found dead there. The mafia groups apparently take habze to the extreme. One chieftain, according to local legend, was shot in a bar in an argument that began when someone else paid the bill for him. Paying the bill was seen as a mark of disrespect, an argument began, guns were drawn, and the mafia boss paid for it with his life.

As such, the communities east of Istanbul were awash with automatic weapons and, in the 1980s, people began arriving at weddings with boxes of ammunition all ready to be poured into the air in greeting, in exuberance or in celebration of particularly impressive dancing.

Sadly, the bullets that went up also came down. Most Circassians I spoke to had at least one family member who had been killed or wounded by falling bullets at a wedding, and the situation had been getting worse.

Eventually, the community had to act, as I heard from a group of old men who were attending a wedding in the village of Balballi east of Istanbul, where most of the residents were enjoying a few dances and a small celebration. Jihan Agumba, aged sixty-five, said that he and a number of other old men had decided to rein in their younger neighbours after a mother of two was killed at a wedding five years before.

'Even before this woman was killed we had discussed what we could do to stop this,' he said. 'When we were young, not everyone had guns and shooting was very regulated. If someone danced beautifully then people would shoot to honour him. If someone who was dancing well was honoured with a shot he would stop and gesture at the shooter to show how happy he was to be honoured.'

But when more guns arrived, things got out of hand, with shooting unregulated and uncontrolled. In short, this Circassian tradition had become excessive and, thus, non-Circassian.

'The night this woman was killed, we were sat drinking coffee here and I used very strong words,' remembered Agumba. 'I said that anyone who shoots in the air should be shamed before his family, that he should be dishonoured. Anyone who serves them at the wedding should be dishonoured, we should not attend the weddings of these people, or their funerals. There were very strong words.'

We were sitting in a corner of the wedding set aside for the old men. The men – grey-haired, straight-backed and dressed in suits and trilbys – nodded at Agumba's emphatic points. Some of them even turned away from the dancing, which in this mainly Abkhaz village was more intricate and involved less obvious courtship than at the Circassian weddings. Abkhaz, though ethnically very close to the Circassians, have customs of their own and this dance appeared to have more in common with those of Ireland than those of their ethnic kin.

'These youths who were shooting were influenced by gun culture on television. They did not learn like we did how to use guns, and how to control themselves. The main thing in our culture is respect. This is like an unwritten constitution. If someone dies, all sixty or seventy Circassian and Abkhaz villages in this region send people to the funeral. It is the same for a wedding. We share happiness, we share sadness. And if someone is older than you, you respect him, even if he is two or three years older. It took time, but the young people agreed to stop shooting.'

In the nearby village of Tashkorpru, I asked the young men if they were prepared to submit to the authority of the elders like their ancestors always had. The general response was that, yes, they would stop shooting if it was insisted on, but they were not happy about it.

'I have never talked to anyone of our age who thinks it is right that we cannot shoot in the air. Probably 80 per cent of us do not agree with this,' grumbled Omer Shakoomda, a 45-year-old sitting in the village coffee house with a crowd of younger men.

'If the hosts of the wedding insist that we should not shoot then we will not shoot. We still think though that if there are thousands of gunshots it shows the amount of respect people have for that family,' said Nejat, one of his friends at the bar.

'At the last wedding I went to there was shooting. The man who asked us to stop was not really respected so people shot in the air anyway. If there is a sign saying "Please do not shoot" then people will obey it. But this is a logistical issue. If a new group arrives, they will not know you cannot shoot. It is mainly the ladies who want us to stop shooting. And groups with a lot of girls in them will leave if there is a lot of shooting.'

There was a lot of nodding around the table at this comment, and some heads were shaken in disappointment at the shame of it, but it seemed the community leaders were determined to enforce the ban. Circassians would not bring in the police – it is an article of faith that they sort out their own problems – but they had mobilized to create a regional council to sort things out. The council's development was particularly interesting, since Turkey is very sensitive to any sign of separatism, but it appeared to have been tolerated by the government so far.

Afitap Altan, a woman in her fifties who heads the cultural centre in the city of Dubze and who acts as a delegate at the council, said Abkhaz weddings were now largely shooting-free, but the Circassians still shot a little.

'You do not have the power to stop people shooting but when the elders say stop, there is a feeling that people should stop. I do not share the same ideas as the elders, but I will not argue with them. The elders will have found a compromise among themselves.'

The next weekend, she was due to attend a meeting of a thousand or so elders from the region, where they would discuss, according to the invitation, 'keeping the culture alive, making sure shooting in the air at weddings is stopped, and that no alcohol is consumed'.

'They have tried to do this outside the official societies, so that no politics is involved. The problem is though that everyone likes to speak, and if you give them the time, then all thousand people will speak,' she said.

The Circassians' tradition of natural democracy, of allowing anyone to speak who felt he had something to say, was remarked on wonderingly in the nineteenth century, and has survived over the centuries. Although the Circassians might bemoan the decline of habze and their traditions, they are clearly still alive in the modern world.

'People from Dubze are very brave, very brave. Some people think this is mafia but it is not, we are just brave. If I have a problem on the street, then it can be solved by the family but that does not mean we are mafia. If there are problems the elders will say, "You are Circassian, how can you do this?" We solve most problems without the police. It is the same if you are poor, you will not ask for money but people will help you, we help each other,' said Altan.

What she told me reminded me of something, but it was only later I remembered a story I had heard in Israel, when I had asked why there was no theft in the Circassian villages.

It turned out that there had been a spate of thefts in Kfar-Kama some fifteen or twenty years before, which had initially confused a community where people leave their doors open and are not used to things going missing. After two weeks, the villagers realized what was happening and caught the thief, who was a Bedouin.

'They did not involve the police. No, he got what he deserved. After he was released, his mouth was the only bit of him still working. We have not had a theft since,' I was told.

Circassians, I thought, are wonderful people to be friends with. But I would not like to fall out with them.

3. I Give Thee That Little Bird

Some 170 years before me, two other British men were wandering wide-eyed through the Circassian world, trying to make sense of the strange culture that surrounded them. These were John Longworth and James Bell, and they had come on a mission.

A friend of theirs and a minor British diplomat, David Urquhart, had formulated his own foreign policy and, with great self-confidence, had set out to implement it by trying to provoke a war between London and St Petersburg. The plan involved entrapping the Russians into seizing a British ship (the *Vixen*) trading with the Circassians, and thus forcing London to intervene to secure Circassian independence. Circassian freedom would ensure the Ottoman Empire would be safe from Russian expansion, which would in turn guarantee the British hold on India.

The strategic clash created by the contradictions between Ottoman weakness, British imperialism and Russian expansion was the same one that would spark the Crimean War a couple of decades later, but that does not mean the plan was sensible. It was barmy and years ahead of its time. That did not bother Urquhart, however.

The Scot was a strangely persuasive man, and his position in the British embassy in Istanbul allowed him to come dangerously close to succeeding in his warmongering. Notes of protest were exchanged between the British and Russians over the ship. But sense prevailed, the war was avoided, and Urquhart was left as a footnote to history, rather than as the great strategic visionary that he believed himself to be.

But that was not before he had sent his two friends to Circassia to be ready to welcome the British troops when they came, and thanks to them we have a clear description of what Circassia was like before the disaster of 1864 scattered the nation across the Middle East.

One of the most remarkable elements of the English envoys' accounts is how deeply entrenched in Turkish society the Circassians

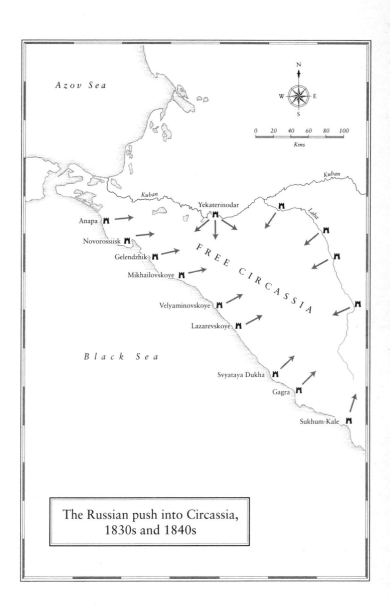

Azov Sea

Kuban

Kuban

Yekaterinodar

Anapa

Novorossiisk

Gelendzhik

Mikhailovskoye

Laba

F R E E   C I R C A S S I A

Velyaminovskoye

Lazarevskoye

Black Sea

Svyataya Dukha

Gagra

Sukhum-Kale

N
W   E
S

0   20   40   60   80   100
Kms

The Russian push into Circassia,
1830s and 1840s

were. Longworth, who was a journalist, found a large population of Circassians in Istanbul, many of them engaged in illegal trade with their homeland.

When his ship reached Sinop, a Turkish port on the Black Sea coast, his plan to visit Circassia caused something of a sensation. Inquisitive Circassians thronged around him, all wearing the shaggy hats and tunics of their national dress. Some of these men had lived in Anapa, the Turkish fortress that had changed hands several times, and had fled for the last time when the Russians finally claimed it by war in 1828. Under the treaty that ended the conflict, Turkey had ceded to Russia its claim to the northern shore of the Black Sea and the Circassians' home.

Russia had had occasional contacts with the Circassians for centuries – Moscow still considers a 1561 dynastic marriage between Ivan the Terrible and a Circassian prince's daughter as foundation to its claim to the region of Kabarda, for example – but Anapa was the key to their conquest.

If Circassia belonged to anyone before 1828, it belonged to Turkey, but the Turks had never tried to enforce their claim, which was tenuous at best. Most Circassians had never noticed that they were being ruled by the Turks at all, but could not help noticing the change of ownership. Russia launched a large-scale war to enforce the rights over Circassia that it gained in its 1829 treaty with the Ottoman Empire.

The Russian onslaught was one of the reasons that the Circassian community in Turkey was larger than normal when Longworth and Bell arrived, but its presence long predated it. The integration of Circassians into Mediterranean culture was strong, and for millennia they had been an integral part of southern civilization. Jason and the Argonauts came and sought the Golden Fleece on this coastline, perhaps in what is now Abkhazia. Other myths show how closely Greek culture was linked to the giant mountain range. Prometheus, who stole fire from the Gods to give to man, was said to be chained in perpetual torment on these mountains, an eagle pecking at his liver. According to the Bible, Noah's Ark grounded on Mount Ararat, which is to the south of the main chain, and is said to have touched on Mount Elbrus on its way. This mountain, the tallest of all the Caucasus, has a distinctive double peak created, or so the story goes, by the keel of Noah's ark when it floated by.

It is easy to forget now how closely Circassia was linked to the ancient world. Before the Circassians were swallowed up by the Russians, however, the Greeks, Genoese and Turks had traded with them for centuries, above all taking female and male slaves to serve in the harems and the armies of the countries to the south. The fame of the Circassians in these two professions was broad. For much of western Europe, the Circassian lady was the very model of beauty and grace. The men, meanwhile, were choice mercenaries. Their warrior cast, the Mamelukes, ruled Egypt until driven out by Napoleon.

The ship Bell used to reach Circassia was piloted by an engaging rogue who lived in an easy democratic way with his crew, with all sharing in the profits of the trading expedition. The risks they were taking were high, for the coast was closely blockaded by Russian ships and every visitor had to run between them, hoping that his vessel was faster than those of his pursuers.

Bell knew the risks better than most, since he had been aboard the *Vixen* when she was seized and had spent some time in captivity before being returned to Turkey. His ship bravely flew the green and gold Circassian flag – which had been invented by Urquhart – as it struggled to reach the coast through adverse winds, but fell in with two Russian warships after a week at sea. The captain was loath to lighten the ship by throwing the trade goods overboard, but some sacrifice was needed. After a brief dispute that seems to have occupied the whole crew, they disposed of the gun carriage (the gun itself was in the hold) and the Circassian flag, which clearly was yet to earn the reverence that it currently enjoys.

Although the Russians opened fire, the little boat managed to reach shore and the passengers were safe. This encounter with Russian warships became typical for anyone trying to reach the coast – Longworth had an almost identical one – and became such a cliché that comics even began to mock it. It is hard in fact to avoid the impression that the dread Russian navy was rather inept since it so frequently failed to capture visitors approaching the coastline. In

Bell's case, the Russian warships repeatedly failed to cut off their prey, sailing directly towards his ship rather than to stop it reaching the shore, thus having to change course and sail repeatedly. Their shooting also must have been slack, since they fired many times without success.

The boat used by Longworth, who arrived separately, meanwhile outpaced its chasing warship in a straight race, which suggests the latter was a sluggish vessel, and the Circassians amused themselves by taunting their failed pursuers as they fell astern.

'What are you afraid of now? Why don't you make haste, Kaffer [unbeliever]? Don't you see we are ready for you? Only come alongside, and we will give you a reception that will teach you how to terrify true believers in future,' taunted a rather ridiculous fellow passenger who had been to Mecca and whom Longworth refers to as the 'Hadji' as a result.

The reception received by the two travellers on arrival in Circassia was warm, and allowed them both to study Circassian culture to a degree never again rivalled by foreign visitors. The culture was marked by an extraordinary degree of hospitality. Every house was graced with a guest house, set aside from the main quarters of the family and kept in a permanent state of readiness. No warning was required before arrival, and a sheep was regularly killed for the English guests to eat.

Their hosts seem to have been permanently delighted by the chance of showing off their largesse, and one old man with whom Longworth was billeted at one point positively revelled in it. 'We were welcomed and waited on by the patriarch of this little hamlet, in person, to whom the duties of hospitality seemed to give new life and spirit. Indeed, it was a most pleasing sight to see him bustling beneath his burden of fourscore in the discharge of them.'

The importance of hospitality to the culture is almost impossible to overstate, and was a crucial element in the life of the nation. Without a government, organized religion or a money-based economy, the two travellers had none of the facilities for finding accommodation that they would have been used to. It was not possible to rent a room, there being no money to do so, nor to find a government guest house as was the practice on the Russian side of the lines. As such, they stopped wherever they found themselves. Anything they expressed an interest in was given to them, since the culture of hospitality included great generosity.

Hospitality was indeed taken to the extreme of the guest being sacred in every respect, and Longworth relates the story of a Circassian family that unwittingly welcomed a Russian engineer to its house. The Russian had Circassian guides, and was disguised as a Circassian, and his hosts were duty-bound to receive him with all warmth. The presence of the engineer, a man called Tornau, who later wrote memoirs of his own, was known to the Circassians hunting him. He and his guides, however, were safe within the walls of his refuge. 'They had partaken of bread and salt under the roof of a Circassian, and he and his tribe had become responsible for it with their lives: whatever their horror of a spy and a Russian, his person was sacred in the character of their guest.' The pursuit was called off and the Russian continued on his way.

Longworth and Bell were not, however, normal travellers. Hoping to fund their stay in Circassia and to find commercial opportunities there, they had taken large quantities of merchandise and presents that had to be transported with them. The average Circassian carried nothing but his weapons and a little food, so their lengthy caravans presented an attractive prospect for the impoverished men who witnessed them passing by. As guests, they could not be robbed, but the Circassians were accustomed to generosity from wealthy men, and they did not see the foreigners as an exception.

At almost every stop they were met by suitors keen to gain weapons, or gunpowder, or lead or other products, often with comic results. Many of the misunderstandings that arose may have started in the Circassian culture of giving presents, since the suitors must have been so surprised not to have been given the object they expressed regard for that they employed other means to secure it.

Longworth, for example, became very impressed by the patriotic ardour of a visitor 'whose sad and serious countenance interested me greatly'. On the first day, the tall and dark man stood by and waited on the visitor who was accommodated in the guest house in his hamlet, only sitting down after repeated insistences. On the second day, he consented to sit on the couch but remained largely silent. Longworth took his gloomy look to be a reflection of despair over the fate of his nation. On the third day, he took Longworth's hand and sighed repeatedly, increasing Longworth's respect still further. But the Englishman had completely misjudged the situation. His visitor's love for his homeland appears to have been in a distant second place behind his love for Longworth's telescope. 'The reader may judge, therefore, I felt rather surprised and disconcerted when, through the intervention of the Hadji, he all at once begged as a particular favour that I would give him my telescope, the possession of which, he said, would make his hamlet the happiest in Circassia.'

Longworth told the Hadji the Circassian could have the telescope when he left the country. The suitor then asked if, since they would henceforth travel together, he could carry the telescope. Longworth agreed and peace was restored for three days, at which point the man begged for a pistol. On being refused, he ran off with the telescope and it was never recovered. 'It is needless to add, that though I now saw clearly through the one, I was never destined to see through the other again,' he concluded.

Longworth and Bell were greatly relieved when their stocks of presents ran out, since they were then left in peace. Bell, for example, gifted three tonnes of lead to the Circassian nation, thus saving himself the constant requests that continued while he was still in possession of it.

Having arrived separately, the two men met at a large national gathering called to decide how the Circassians should respond to the Russian threat in 1837. Russian forces were in the process of building a series of coastal forts that would, in time, cut off the interior from Turkish trade and the Circassians needed a coordinated effort to rebuff the threat.

The council is a glimpse into how a truly anarchic society managed its affairs. Not all the Circassians, it should be said, lived in the same free communities described by the two travellers. To the east, in the region known as Kabarda, the tribes were ruled by princes who had already largely submitted to the Russians and who themselves took part in quelling unrest among their subjects. But here in the west, the councils ruled themselves.

That is not to say, however, that all Circassians were equal. Some came from princely families, while most were either freemen (called *tokav*s, according to Bell) or slaves. Despite these titles, however, the society was increasingly levelling itself. Longworth blamed the democratic teachings of Islam for having abolished rank, which even extended to the same fine being levied for the murder of a lord as for a commoner. But it is clear that such a fundamental shift in the way society was governed must have come from a deeper cause than just the fact the Circassians had become Muslims. Many Muslims, after all, lived in fiercely autocratic systems elsewhere. In the mountains, however, the social distinctions had been levelled.

There was still considerable nostalgia among aristocrats for the days when they had more sway, and indeed the old ways survived in full force further to the south and further inland. Bell later travelled to the south, towards Abkhazia, and observed a court case in which a prince accidentally killed one of his own cousins, rather than the slave whom he was aiming at. This would not have been an expensive mistake in the north, where the blood-prices had been made equal, but in this still more feudal environment, it was. The young prince, after three days of negotiations, agreed to pay eighteen slaves, eighteen horses, eighteen guns and eighteen sabres. This seems to have been a very expensive murder, since elsewhere Bell gives the blood-price of a noble as thirteen slaves, and that of a freeman as eleven.

Be that as it may, the Circassians first met by Bell and Longworth were democratic in their decision-making and they called their grand council for all the elders of their province shortly after the arrival of the two Englishmen and allowed them to be observers. The meeting, held beneath trees in the open air, presents a picture of a natural democracy that is wonderful to observe but hopeless in practice, and which could not possibly resist an organized aggressor. Anyone was allowed to speak and at any length, and the meeting went on for days.

'Should there be any individual fonder than others of hearing himself talk, they have a way of silencing him peculiar to themselves;

they neither crow like cocks, nor bray like certain other animals in more civilized assemblies, but adopt a method for which the form and the roomy nature of their house of meeting, *al fresco*, are most peculiarly adapted. The unfortunate orator in such cases is apt to find himself with no other audience than the neighbouring trees and bushes, the circle he had been addressing having rapidly dissolved and re-adjusted itself out of earshot, where it might be seen listening to somebody with better claims on its attention.'

The council's decision had to be unanimous, meaning the Circassians would never take action that was not agreed to by everyone, so the debates were long and tedious. This unity of purpose was both the nation's greatest strength and its greatest weakness. Elsewhere in the Caucasus, the Russians succeeded in conquering provinces by bribing or persuading local elites to side with them. This policy was most successfully used in Georgia and the Georgians never rebelled against their rule despite the deposition of the royal family that had decided to ally itself to St Petersburg.

In Circassia, however, the absence of a government meant the people could not be bought. Sadly it also meant the people could not be organized. The council attended by the travellers lasted for five days but had to keep moving to new locations to avoid bankrupting its hosts. Without a government to organize taxes and food for the dignitaries, the assembled elders were fed and housed by the local inhabitants.

While the elders talked, the younger men engaged in games of strength involving shooting in the air, throwing large stones as far as they could, or showing off on their horses. 'The principal of these [sports] is the race, or, rather, the chase, one horseman being followed at full speed by several others, whom he seeks to elude, not only by the swiftness of his horse, but by his address in dodging, winding, and availing himself of the inequalities of the ground,' wrote Longworth, before going on to describe with similarly breathless enthusiasm how accomplished the young men were with their rifles, their bows and arrows, and their pistols.

But this chaotic picture should not be interpreted as meaning that affairs between Circassians were not regulated, for they were, and in a manner that seems far more similar to that of the Bedouins of the desert than to the ways of other settled communities. Every Circassian belonged to a brotherhood or society, which fulfilled the roles of an extended family. Marriages within the society were banned so, to prevent unnecessary expense, the societies were scattered and intermingled among each other. Membership of a society meant that every member was responsible for the actions of an individual. If a crime was committed, a jury of twelve – half from the society of the victim, half from the society of the criminal – would meet to decide on what action to take.

The brotherhoods would take upon themselves the payment of fines for crimes committed by a member in the first few offences but, not wanting a drain on their resources, would take more serious action if the member was a repeat offender. Criminal cases, however, only involved those connected to the brotherhoods in question, and there were no courts or judges who dealt with cases independently. At one point, Longworth and a companion called Emin came across a fugitive wanted for murder, and the Englishman asks why Emin did not shoot him. 'God forbid . . . I should have involved myself and my connexions in a feud with his tribe. Besides, the boy he has murdered does not belong to my tribe; and if he did, we should prefer the penalty of two hundred oxen to the villain's life, which his own clansmen will, no doubt, take care to shorten for him, since they have found it so detrimental to them,' said Emin. Sure enough, the murderer was later weighted with rocks and thrown into the sea.

These descriptions are a rare glimpse into the organization of a society with no government. However, when looked at from the perspective of trying to organize resistance to the Russian invasion, the brotherhoods, and the habits of independence they encouraged, served as more of a hindrance than a help. Mobilizing the societies, and then mobilizing their members, proved almost impossible except when defending desperately against a direct attack. The Circassians would, throughout the nineteenth-century war, prove all but incapable of taking the initiative. On many occasions they dispersed rather than destroy a defeated army. The expense of an army living off the land was one that the disorganized local economy could not support.

The council attended by Longworth and Bell discussed and considered for five days, but resolved on little more than sending a letter to the Russian General Ivan Velyaminov asking him to withdraw from Circassia. The reply from the general was chilling, and instructive of the tactics that Russia was employing in its unequal battle.

Velyaminov had landed a force at the bay of Gelendzhik, which is a sheltered if shallow anchorage, that was joined by another marching overland. The Circassians, wary of the Russians' grapeshot, were confining themselves to sniping from the trees, and neither side was in a position to win a significant victory. The general, however, was arrogant in his demand for submission.

'Are you not aware that if the heavens should fall, Russia could prop them up with her bayonets? The English may be good mechanics and artisans, but power dwells only with Russia. No country ever waged successful war against her,' he wrote. 'If you refuse to listen to us, your country shall be taken from you, and yourselves treated with the utmost rigour. Be obedient, therefore, to my instructions. You must believe what has been told you, and you will be treated with lenity; otherwise, it will not be our fault if your valleys are destroyed with fire and sword, and your mountains trampled to dust! Yield, and you may retain your property; if not, all you possess, even your arms, shall be taken from you, and yourselves made slaves.'

The warning was prophetic, since the Circassians would indeed lose their country and experience their national tragedy, but a lot of skirmishing was to take place before that day.

Much of the Russian energy at this time was devoted to establishing a chain of forts along the coast that would seal off the Circassians from their allies over the sea. These forts were truly miserable affairs, often more deadly for the defenders than the attackers, but they served to warn off traders from the most important coastal sites.

Built of mud and brush, they were often cut off from all communications for the entire winter, when the sea was plagued by storms. During the winter months, the unfortunate defenders were exposed to disease and starvation as well as the ceaseless sniping of the Circassian rifles. Tornau, an engineer officer, despaired of the conditions of the forts he passed. The garrisons, he wrote, were too weak to intimidate the local inhabitants and served only as a source of slaves for the Circassians, who traded in Russian prisoners openly.

The garrison in Sukhumi, capital of present day Abkhazia, came in for particular censure when he passed through in 1835. 'The people had the look of unfortunate victims, doomed to permanent fever, from which half of them died every year. They knew this and, not exactly with a calm spirit, but uncomplainingly bore their lot, not ceasing to fulfil their difficult duty with the submissiveness characteristic of the Russian soldier.'

The appalling conditions endured by the Russian soldiers must be borne in mind when reading descriptions of the military prowess of the Circassians, who so frequently failed to capture the forts manned by these pitiful creatures. The Russian army, though justly lauded for its defeat of Napoleon, had gone sharply downhill since 1815. The freedoms that its soldiers and officers had enjoyed during those heroic campaigns had been anathema to the government, and constant drill had replaced soldiering. The army had gone from a place where aristocrats and peasants were united in a common cause to a herd of cowed conscripts lorded over by vicious martinets. The tipping point had come in early winter 1825 when Alexander I died.

Officers who had seen conditions in western Europe, and who had lived in occupied Paris, wanted to push Russia towards the European mainstream. Alexander's successor and brother Konstantin turned down the crown, and it passed to the younger brother Nikolai, who surpassed even his dead sibling in small-mindedness. In response to the proclamation of his accession, liberal officers called out their regiments to stand on Palace Square in St Petersburg, where they demanded a constitution until they were cut down by loyal troops. The significance of this 'Decembrist' uprising is often overstated, and the Decembrists were unlikely to have changed much even if they had won – Russia has a habit of reverting to autocratic type no matter who rules it – but their revolt terrified the new tsar.

Nikolai was convinced he had been spared by God, and forced the generals to come down even harder than before on any signs of subversion in the ranks. He came to believe that 'unquestioning obedience and an absence of dangerous initiative on the part of subordinates were essential to the security of his realm', according to one historian of the period.

He interfered and quibbled and altered plans drawn up for the Circassian war. At one point he was told about plans for a fort at a river crossing. Nikolai dug into his files for the results of a reconnaissance of the site three years earlier. 'After studying the drawing, he marked on it the spot for the fort, and then ordered a special messenger to gallop two thousand versts [2,000 kilometres] to the Caucasus, so the entrenchment could be built according to his wishes,' wrote the historian John Shelton Curtiss, in his book *The Russian Army under Nicholas I.*

The strict rules and mismanagement that resulted had the inevitable effect of creating flourishing circumstances for corruption. Alexandre Dumas, the French author of *The Three Musketeers*, recorded one case when he travelled in the Caucasus in the 1850s. A soldier he met told him how the men of his regiment were entitled to the meat of one bullock a day – a far from excessive amount for 400 or 500 men. On the long march from Kaluga near Moscow, their captain marched a bullock along with them. 'Whenever an official came on a visit of inspection, there were the captain's accounts, showing the purchase of one bullock a day as instructed, and there was the bullock, large as life, and ready for the men's supper tonight.' On they marched, the bullock bringing up the rear, for two and a half months. 'Perhaps we might think that at last the men had a chance to eat their beef? Not a bit of it! The captain sold the bullock and since (unlike the men) it had been well fed every day, he made a handsome profit.'

The poor food coupled with a malarial climate and constant skirmishes had a devastating effect on the Russian soldiers sent to subdue the tribesmen. Xavier Hommaire de Hell, a French explorer who travelled extensively through southern Russia with his wife Adele, noted that, in spring 1840, 12,000 men of the 12th Division went to occupy the forts of Circassia. Four months later, only 1,500 of them returned.

'The same year, the commander-in-chief found but nine men fit for service out of 300 that composed the garrison of [Sukhumi],' he wrote, adding that 17,000 men died a year in 1841 and 1842.

'Is it to be wondered that with such a military administration, Russia makes no progress in the Caucasus? What can be expected of armies in which want of all necessities and total disregard for the lives of men are the order of the day?' he asked.

The tsar raged against the corruption and inefficiency. But, in truth, what was needed was delegation of powers to men on the ground and that the tsar was not prepared to do.

His micromanagement, with its inevitable inability to react to local conditions, would have catastrophic results in the eastern Caucasus, where the war was more intense. And it was bad for morale in the west. However, it did have one unintended consequence that we can welcome: a new witness of the warfare appeared on the scene.

Nikolai Ivanovich Lorer was one of the unfortunate Decembrists who appealed for a constitution in 1825. He was not a leader of the revolt – he would have been hanged had he been – but was sent into exile in Siberia for twelve years. At the end of this period, aged forty-eight, he was posted to the Caucasus to serve as a private soldier, and arrived on the Black Sea just when the army was building its chain of forts. He was in an anomalous position. He was an aristocrat, so the officers of this force were his friends and his schoolmates, but he was forced to fight in the ranks, giving him a unique perspective on how the army worked. He took part in a massive amphibious landing at a place he called Shapsugo (Bell calls it Sashe), not far from modern-day Tuapse, where the fort of Tenginskoye was to be built.

The Russians first made a feint attack, causing the Circassians to gather, then under cover of an artillery barrage landed their troops to the north. The troops took a few small hills, much to the surprise of the Circassians gathered there, who bustled off to save their possessions and families.

The Russian victory was easy and they built their fort despite the best efforts of the Circassian snipers. But then the evil reputation of the Black Sea was confirmed. A massive storm sank a steamship and two frigates that were escorting it, leaving the army without reinforcements. The destruction was terrible. As it happens, Bell was only a few kilometres away at this time and the next few days are the only time during this whole campaign when we have two, independent witnesses to an event. According to Bell, the storm wrecked twenty-nine Russian ships on the coast as whole.

The Russians attempted to protect the wrecks near their new fort at Shapsugo/Sashe, but were driven back by the Circassians, who raided the ships for all they could find then burnt them.

Bell walked along the shore and saw the Circassians plundering the wrecks of 'small arms, damaged powder, silver coin, ship stores, bales of merchandise ... iron water-tanks, copper sheathing, bolts, bars of iron ... [which] will, no doubt, soon by transformed into swords, ploughshares, axes, knives and other necessaries'. The death toll appears to have been high. 'A creek into which the sea seemed to have made its way during the gale – surmounting its barrier of shingle – was piled full of these planks; and among them was said to be an immense number of corpses, of which the intolerable stench gave proof superabundant.'

Lorer was a thoughtful man, and his humane memoirs make touching reading. He sat in this devastating scene and looked at the thickly wooded hills rising above the little army, at the plane trees, chestnuts and hazels, and wondered what it would take to conquer them. He could see little villages in the mountains, and wished to wander up to the huts and learn more about them, but the sniper fire was so intense that the soldiers were pinned down and he could not venture far.

When a Circassian delegation, under a flag of truce, came to ask for the return of the dead, Lorer received a chance to observe the enemy, and was deeply impressed with how they conversed with the general. The conversation was one of several recorded between generals and Circassian delegations, and may be identical to one recorded elsewhere by Tornau. A story similar to Tornau's account is still quoted with pride by Circassians to this day, so it may be apocryphal but it is too poetic to leave out. The general started with a demand to know why the Circassians were rebelling against their lawful sovereign.

'The sultan,' said the general, 'made a present of you to the Russian tsar.'

'Aha, now I understand,' replied one Circassian with commendable wit, and pointed out a bird sitting on a nearby tree. 'General, I give thee that little bird, take it.'

The general's response is not given. Lorer recorded a similar conversation, which shows a similar degree of dignity from the Circassians, who appear not to have been overawed by the lofty personage they were conversing with.

'Why do you not submit to our great ruler,' asked the general of the delegation. 'And stop us having to spill blood in vain? I know that in the mountains with you is hiding the Englishman Bell, he incites you and he promises help from England, but believe me, he is lying to you, you will receive no help from anyone, and it would be better to give him up to me hand-and-foot, and you'll receive for this a lot of silver from our ruler who is very rich.'

The highlanders' leader, whom Lorer calls a prince although he is unlikely to have enjoyed the wealth that such a Russian title implies, replied with a gentle reproach.

'If it is true that your tsar is rich, then why does he envy our poverty and does not let us quietly sow our millet in our poor mountains? Your tsar must be a very greedy and jealous tsar. As for the Englishman Bell, we cannot give him up, because he is our friend and guest and he does us a lot of kindness. With us, like for you, there are scoundrels who you can buy, but we, princes and lords, will always remain honest, and you do not have enough gold and silver, to deflect us from the route of honesty.'

The Russians would not be seen off with gentle dignity alone, however, and the war continued in its brutal course. Bell and Longworth regularly saw burnt villages and hamlets on the paths of Russian attacks (although it was not clear who had set fire to the houses, fleeing defenders or vengeful attackers), and areas traversed by Russian roads had become deserted as the Circassian civilians fled into the hills.

Lorer's exile continued to be spent on excursions along the coast. The next year he took part in a second amphibious attack to build another fort, but the efforts were not subduing the Circassians, even though they appear to have throttled the Circassians' trade with the Turks. The frustration shown by the general's comments was filtering through into all the senior officers of the army, and the war was particularly brutal under the leadership of General Grigory Zass, who commanded the right flank of the army.

Brutality as a military tactic had been pioneered by General Alexei Yermolov, who was proconsul in the Caucasus from 1816 to 1827. He once famously said: 'I desire that the terror of my name should guard our frontiers more potently than chains of fortresses, that my word should be for the natives a law more inevitable than death.' He became a byword for massacre and horror, especially in the eastern Caucasus.

Yermolov was a veteran of the Napoleonic campaigns, and adored by his soldiers, with whom he shared the hardships of garrison life. But his independent spirit was out of fashion when Nikolai came to the throne. Not realizing that Nikolai's older brother had turned down the chance of ascending the throne, he ordered the army of the Caucasus to swear allegiance to Konstantin. This gaff undermined whatever trust the tsar had in him, and his position was chipped away at until mistakes in a war against Persia cost him his job. Even without his presence, however, the army maintained levels of brutality that shocked Lorer.

Lorer's equivocal position in the army, as an educated soldier, gave him access to the likes of Zass and he visited the general in his home. 'I told him I did not like his system of war, and he replied like this: Russia wants to conquer the Caucasus at whatever cost. How would we take these peoples, our enemies, except with fear and terror? They are not fit for philanthropy, and Yermolov only managed to achieve more than us by hanging people without mercy, by plundering and burning villages.'

Zass, who according to Bell and Longworth was himself feared and hated in the mountains, entered into his role with gusto. Lorer later went to tea with the general, as part of a group that included a doctor and the doctor's wife. Zass had erected an artificial mound outside his house and impaled the heads of Circassians on spikes set into it. The doctor's wife complained about the sight, and asked Zass to remove the heads before she came to tea. Zass here betrayed a mental state that surely bordered on the insane.

He agreed to take down the heads, but was loath to part with them. The visitors had not been in his house long before they noticed a revolting smell. Zass had, apparently, decided to store the heads in a box under his bed. He got out the box and showed off the heads to his appalled visitors. He would clean them up, he said, and send them to friends as souvenirs.

Zass was also, according to Longworth, in the habit of mutilating the bodies of Circassians killed in the fighting, since he knew how desperate his opponents were to regain the dead.

During their stay in Circassia, the Englishmen repeatedly complained that they were not allowed to take part in battles. They regularly heard skirmishes, but wanted to see large-scale military campaigns in which the Circassian cavalry routed their Cossack foes. They were asking the impossible here, since, as the Circassians already knew, the Russian artillery was too terrible to be braved in the field. But they finally secured permission to join an assault across the river Kuban towards the end of January 1838. The assault had been long discussed and the forces had to wait for some time before all the horsemen joined them.

Bell described how 1,500 warriors gathered together to listen to a speech by one elder, which lasted several hours. The old man wished the force to refrain from plunder, and only to destroy forts and capture ammunition. Previously the force had not known its destination, since the elders had wanted to avoid betrayal by spies, and it was only now that the old man explained the plan at length, before resigning command to a second man. A third man had been gathering support among the younger warriors for a more abrupt attack, but appears to have been satisfied with the decisions taken at this point and shelved his plan, leaving a united force ready for the morning.

Bell decided to stay on the Circassian side of the Kuban as a medic, but Longworth (together with another Englishman, called Knight, who had joined them unexpectedly) was in the thick of the action. By two in the morning, the force was reinforced and came to around 5,000 horsemen. They set off towards the river, across rough country choked with marshes, thickets, woodland and scrub.

The subsequent events were chaotic.

Longworth got lost in the dark, fell asleep in the saddle, was chased by an angry housewife whose thatched roof his horse stopped to eat, set out across country, fought his way through thorns, and finally found an acquaintance who had also lost his companions. Together, by daybreak, they found the rest of the army.

Eventually, the force was reunited and stood on the banks of the Kuban, ready to attack Russia across the frozen river. But its hopes were dashed: the ice had fractured and the attack was doomed. Instantly, the infantry which had been assigned to protect the army's rear, and about a third of the cavalry, vanished.

The remaining 3,000 or so horsemen wanted to continue the attempt, and a few individuals attempted to construct bridges over the gaps in the ice. Despite orders to the contrary by the senior commanders, who feared an ambush with no possibility of retreat, about 300 young men accompanied by the two Englishmen invaded Russian territory on the far side.

The two Circassian forces, now separated by the river, stood and looked at each other for an hour or so while messages went back and forth urging their respective courses of action as the better. After lengthy deliberations and a certain amount of prayer, the smaller force decided to press on through the forest of reeds that blocked the northern bank. It moved a few kilometres in good order into Russian territory when the Circassians came across the ambush their more cautious comrades had been dreading, and which clearly showed how deeply their plans had been betrayed to the enemy.

A causeway they would have had to cross was completely dominated by cannon, while a strong force of Cossacks and infantry waited at the far end. The Circassian force stopped now for further debate, only for the discussion to be forestalled by the most hot-headed members of the group, including the two Englishmen, who charged the guns. A mad gallop foundered halfway along the causeway in a deep bog, which came up to their stirrups and which none of the warriors could circumvent. 'Our party was compelled reluctantly to retreat and disperse with the main body on the opposite bank,' concluded Longworth. The reaction of the Russians was not recorded.

As an attack, it was a complete fiasco. But, as a demonstration of the shortcomings of the Circassians, it is rather instructive. The difficulties they faced in uniting under one leader, in maintaining a force, in keeping their plans secret, in crossing difficult terrain, and in facing down artillery are all laid bare in a single episode. The attack, like much that the Circassians did when they tried to be ambitious, was a complete failure.

The Englishmen remained in Circassia some time, but they must have already known that their hopes that Britain would fight to secure their friends' freedom were pointless. Letters were few, but when they came they painted a uniformly gloomy picture of how Urquhart's plan had unravelled. Longworth remained until June, spending much of that time bedridden with a fever. Bell stayed for another year, but eventually he too was forced to return home a broken man.

They did not vanish entirely from history, however, and were both to write about Circassia again. Bell found a new lost cause to champion, and became the British representative to the Mosquito Coast, a part of the Caribbean shore of central America that London claimed as a protectorate despite Nicaraguan and American objections, whence he wrote a letter to the London *Times* about Circassia in 1855. Longworth was to return to Circassia as an official government agent. Their actions were provoked by an event that could yet have saved Circassia from conquest: the Crimean War.

4. Three Hundred Prime-Bodied Circassians

The cause of the Crimean War was in fact more bizarre than Urquhart's peculiar plan of provoking Russia to seize a merchant ship, and ignite a world war. It started with a spat between France and Russia over who had the right to protect Christians in the Holy Land, but was really about the Russian desire to dominate the Ottoman Empire. Action rapidly moved into the Black Sea, where Russia destroyed the Ottoman fleet. The British and French navies stormed into the sea in response, forcing the Russians to scuttle their own ships in the harbour of Sevastopol.

That left Russia's Black Sea forts – its frontline against the Circassians – undefended, so their garrisons pulled back beyond the Kuban river, destroying the fortifications behind them. The Circassians had the best chance of securing their independence since Turkey had so casually given them away a generation before. They had powerful potential allies in Britain and France, who like them were sworn to fight the Russians. They had free access to the Turkish markets that had long been cut off by the Russian forts. They had the morale boost given by seeing their Russian enemies running away to the borders of three decades before. They could finally take the initiative.

They did nothing.

With the Russian evacuation of the Black Sea coast, Sefer Bey, a Circassian prince who had been friends with Urquhart, scurried back into action. The Turks despatched him to the old fort of Anapa, now once more in Turkish hands, to take control of Circassia. So began a great fiasco, despairingly chronicled by Longworth, in which all sides squabbled and disagreed and the prize of an independent, free Circassia was lost for ever.

Longworth returned to Circassia in 1855, shortly after British troops had moved into Crimea in their drive to destroy Russia's naval power in the Black Sea. He was an official agent of the British government

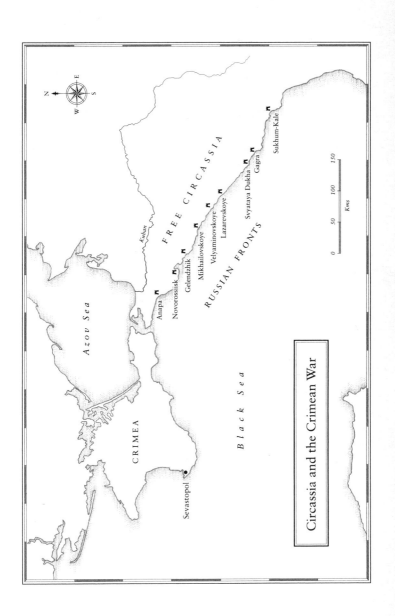

N
W   E
S

Azov Sea

Kuban

F R E E   C I R C A S S I A

Anapa
Novorossiisk
Gelendzhik
Mikhailovskoye
Velyaminovskoye
Lazarevskoye
Svyataya Dukha
Gagra
Sukhum-Kale

R U S S I A N   F R O N T S

CRIMEA

Sevastopol

Black Sea

0   50   100   150
Kms

Circassia and the Crimean War

but his trip was a sideshow, ignored rightly by historians of the terrible conflict which raged on the Crimean peninsula to the west of Circassia. But, for a historian of Circassia, his account provides unique information.

In his despatch of 2 July, Longworth was already frustrated and despairing. Sefer Bey, now called by the grander title of Sefer Pasha, was lying and wheedling to hide the truth that the Circassians had no army to speak of and no way of raising one. 'I have despatched trustworthy messengers to ascertain the truth of this statement and have found it to be a deliberate falsehood,' Longworth wrote. The relations between Longworth and Turkish officials, who claimed they were ruling Circassia on Turkey's behalf, were strained since Britain still officially aimed for an independent Circassia. These relations collapsed almost completely when British and French forces arrived to destroy Anapa's fortifications. Sefer wanted the town to be the capital of his province, whereas London and Paris saw it as a threat that must not be allowed to fall back into Russian hands. Sefer threatened to send tribesmen to oppose the landing allies. The threat did not materialize, and may indeed have been empty since Sefer lacked an army, but it was not a sign of good relations between the Western powers and the Circassians.

Longworth set out on a twelve-day trip into the hills to try and discover for himself what was happening. He came back dispirited. The social structure, and the division into nobles, freemen and slaves that had been already on the brink of collapse when he first visited two decades previously, had finally gone. The nobles of the coast, he noted, had lost all authority, and people inland were cooperating with the Russian government as and when they wanted to.

Longworth was rapidly coming to hate Sefer. 'He is the only man, I believe, who has the slightest control over them [the Circassians]; and that rather of a negative than an active character. He has neither the means nor the energy requisite to raise a Circassian force himself; but he is, in some measure able as he is, evidently disposed to prevent any recruitment on our part, making no secret of his objections on that score. As to his organizing anything out of this anarchy for administrative purposes, I consider such a thing as quite hopeless and out of the question.'

In despair, Longworth tried to meet Muhammad-Emin, a puritan Muslim leader operating inland. But the Muslim leader refused to talk to him, saying any contacts had to go via the Turks. Muhammad-Emin had a low opinion of the British, having met their ambassador during a previous stay in Istanbul. The Turks, angered by the meeting, which they had not been informed about in advance, cut off his allowance and stopped him returning to the Caucasus. Longworth knew nothing of this; he just saw his plans frustrated on all sides by men who were supposed to be his allies.

'Till the troubles fomented by ... Mohamed Emin Effendi, in the Kuban provinces, have been appeased, there is no probability of the Circassians being brought to co-operate, in any warlike operation against the common enemy,' he wrote in an angry memo to London, in which he accused Muhammad-Emin of trying to destroy what remained of the social hierarchy. 'While the lives and properties of a large portion of the inhabitants are at stake we cannot expect that they should take any interest in affairs of a political nature,' wrote Longworth in September 1855.

The whole picture at this point was confused, and it is hard to see what was really going on. But, essentially, the Turks appear to have decided to take over Circassia for good. The British and the French did not support that aim, but did not wish to block it and thus anger the Turks. The good old-fashioned Circassians, meanwhile, took the opportunity of relaxing. Ironically, in the midst of a European war, they had their first opportunity in decades for a bit of peace.

Longworth kept firing back letters to London, but his mission was a waste of time. Circassia would always have been a sideshow compared to the Crimean battlefield, although a force advancing north from Circassia could have seriously disturbed the Russian supply lines. With the degree of dissension and argument that Longworth experienced, however, the country did not even become a sideshow. Longworth took a steamer home, and Circassia was once again forgotten about.

The remaining papers relating to the case in the Foreign Office file are a severe anticlimax, detailing only Longworth's attempts to regain his expenses. They do, however, reveal how much Circassia had changed since the 1830s. The Circassians might have claimed they were resisting Russia, but the economic facts on the ground suggested something very different.

During the 1830s, Circassian leaders tried to impose a blockade on trade with the Russians, and foreign travellers in the region carried a great supply of goods that they could barter for food, horses, arms, clothes and their other necessities. Longworth, knowing his Circassia, took a similar amount of merchandise to defray his expenses on his return in the 1850s, but to no avail.

'I discovered however on revisiting Circassia that a decided change had taken place in this respect, not only on the coast but in the interior; and that although these effects were available as presents they could not be disposed of to advantage for the payment of travelling expenses, money being almost everywhere demanded in preference,' he wrote in one of the many letters that deal with his £142 9s. 7d. in expenses and a pile of missing trade goods.

The development of a cash-based economy in Circassia was a major change and goes to show how far the Russians had succeeded in taking over the plain of the Kuban north of the mountains on which the Circassians depended for food and grazing.

The Russian blockade of the coast, via those miserable little forts, had clearly been more successful than it at first appeared, for it stopped large Turkish ships stopping at many points on the coast, thereby forcing the Circassians to rely on Russia for trade goods and salt, which they had no way of producing. Presumably, in return the Russian merchants took their livestock and grain.

At this point, perhaps it is worth questioning what the Circassians would have been able to sell to the Turks anyway.

It is clear what they needed from the Turks: arms and gunpowder, which the Russians would not have sold them. But they produced very little, and with a subsistence economy and restricted trade routes their agricultural system was not geared up to producing enough to earn the goods they wanted to buy. What they needed was a high-value, easily transportable product.

They found one: their own children.

The slave business was Circassia's only significant export trade, except perhaps for the gold found by Jason and the Argonauts in ancient times. Otherwise, the Circassians sent their sons and daughters to fight and breed for the Turks and received the goods of war in return.

Bell noted the story of a young boy whom he met in November 1839, and who pretended to have a sore leg, and was repeatedly sent to different doctors to have his fictitious ailment examined. There was nothing in fact wrong with the boy, except that he was desperate to avoid being sold in Istanbul. Eventually, he had to admit there was nothing wrong with him and he was duly sent off. The case was unique. 'This is the only instance I can at present recollect, as having come under my observation, of disinclination having been shown by any male or female to being taken to Turkey, which appears to be in general looked to by Circassians as the land of promise,' Bell wrote towards the end of his stay on the Black Sea coast.

Russia was tactically torn over the slave trade. The more people that departed – and those leaving were either fighting-age men or breeding-age women – the fewer people there would be left to conquer. However, the more people that departed the more money would be earned with which the remaining Circassians could resist Russia. The Russians' policy oscillated. In the 1830s, they sought to throttle the trade. Later on they, or at least some of their officials, connived in it.

Alexandre Dumas, when he left the Caucasus through the port of Poti in the 1850s, said his ship was rammed with slaves. 'There are three hundred prime-bodied Kabardians with us at the moment, travelling steerage,' the captain said, 'mostly women and children in charge of two tribal chiefs and the headmen of the various villages.'

'What can I do?' the captain told him. 'They all have valid passports and have paid their fare. Everything is in perfect order and they never give us any trouble. Besides, the girls do not seem to mind. They all expect to marry a Pasha or join the harem of some great lord. If they complained to us we might take action. They easily could, for twice a day they come up for fresh air and exercise, but they never say a word.'

Visitors to the Caucasus, like Dumas's captain, were always rather torn over what to do about the slave trade. Westerners opposed it on principle and wished to abolish it, but also could not help remarking that the Circassians appeared to be leaving voluntarily, and that slavery was not the degrading institution that it was in, for example, the United States. In the Ottoman Empire, many high-ranking individuals – including every mother of every sultan – were slaves.

Dr Moritz Wagner, a German traveller, once sailed from Trabzon to Istanbul with a slave-trader and twelve Circassian girls. 'This Turkish trader was very richly attired in furs and silk and, notwithstanding his vile occupation, a man of very sociable manners. He informed me, among other things, that since the occupation of the Caucasian coast by the Russians, his trade had become much more difficult and dangerous, but also much more lucrative.' Wagner, who travelled extensively in the Caucasus and the Middle East, tried hard to understand why a Circassian would sell his daughter into slavery and in the end struggled to condemn it. 'The [children] go to pass a happy and splendid existence in Stamboul; the price of their beauty probably rescues the family from starvation, or procures them powder and shot to defend their independence. The Circassians are a poor people; their rugged land is wanting in almost every necessity. When we consider the extreme disproportion between our means and those of the Circassians, we ought not to wonder if they resort to desperate expedients.'

For any visitor to modern-day Istanbul, where the sultan's palace is a magnificent complex of beautiful architecture and stunning views, it is easy to understand how Wagner came to his conclusion. Any Circassian girl would dream of swapping the danger of the Russian wars and the squalor of existence in a wattle-and-daub hut for the glorious peace of one of the grandest palaces on earth.

Of course, now the giant Topkapi Palace, of which the harem is just a small part, is open to the public and no longer home to a sultan and his slave-girls. Where once the sultan strolled in splendid seclusion, thousands of tourists spill over onto the lawns, eat ice creams and queue to goggle at the jewels and treasures of the Turkish state.

In the blazing sunshine of a May afternoon when I visited, the clamour of the tourists was distracting and I wondered if I could ever recapture the mystery and serenity that must once have reigned in this magnificent enclave. Then, passing through the gate into the harem, there it was. The bright sunshine, parched foliage and brash noise of outside was replaced by a cool gloom produced by blue and white tiles and tall narrow passageways. Its deep courtyards and tiled walls all conspired to keep both the heat and the noise of the outside world where they belonged – outside.

But this tranquillity was a treacherous impression. This serene first courtyard belonged not to the women but to the eunuchs, the living wall of sexless muscle that policed these women and stopped anyone but the sultan interfering with them. As if to emphasize the point, a tour guide with a group of elderly Americans in baggy shorts and sandals passed into the courtyard, and destroyed my peaceful reverie. Her high-pitched and loud voice was to be my constant companion during my time in the harem. It was an irritation, but it served to remind me that the harem should not be romanticized by a lone traveller wandering around in peace. It was a place of intrigue and aggression, and very real danger.

'There were lives inside lives here. These were high-energy women, and they were competitors in power and energy,' intoned the tour guide, her voice fading away as I moved into another room to escape the bustle.

The girls who came here were all supposed to be from non-Muslim backgrounds, since a Muslim could not be enslaved. However, Muslims could be traded if they were already slaves, and a feudal society still technically existed in Circassia. Some Circassians were therefore already slaves, making them very popular with Turks seeking to buy light-skinned and blue-eyed girls to serve as playthings for the lords of the Golden Horn. Girls were brought to Istanbul and sold alongside slaves from the Christian lands of Greece, Georgia, Russia, Serbia, Ukraine and elsewhere.

Pushing further into the harem, I began to appreciate the intricacy of the power structures that had grown up around the sultan's throne. Access to the girls of the harem was controlled by the sultan's mother, and the system seemed to have a brutal honesty to it. People who had access to the sultan either were essentially sexless – his mother or the eunuchs – or were sex slaves. And the harem was finely designed to ensure the situation was not disturbed. The mother's room and the sultan's room adjoined each other, a situation that made clear the power that women wielded in this now extinct system.

The harem is glorious. Its bathroom is all gold taps and cool tiles, but it was a vicious world. For young women it was cold and unhygienic, with waterborne and vermin-borne diseases taking their toll on them. Nonetheless, the population of the harem increased steadily. By the reign of Abdulaziz from 1861 to 1876, when Circassians flooded into Turkey, it contained more than 800 women.

The Circassians among these women were shipped from their homeland when they were in their early teens and bought by the ladies of the large harems, to be reared and trained in upper-class ways to increase their market value. In a few years, they would be sold on, perhaps even to the imperial harem itself.

In 1843, while the Russian blockade was in earnest, a young and beautiful girl would sell for as much as 70,000 kurus. It is a sign of how terrible the fate awaiting the Circassian nation, and the sheer number of Circassians who were already flooding into Turkey, that by 1860, when the emigration had begun and the Russians had stopped blockading the coast so fiercely, this price had collapsed to just 1,500 kurus.

For the Russians, torn by their competing strategic demands, seem to have given up on their campaign against the slave trade in the 1840s. 'What do you want us to do with people who have already fled,' the Russian minister Count Nesselrode asked drily of the British ambassador.

The British and French, otherwise Turkey's best friends, were firmly opposed to the trade. But, ironically, when London and Paris took control of the Black Sea during the Crimean War, the trade boomed. Unlike the Russians, they were not tasked with coastal patrols, nor did they have a presence on the coast, and the slavers loved it. Stratford Canning, the British ambassador, was forced to rebuke the Turks for the trade's revival. 'So long as the trade is permitted or connived at, so long as preventive measures, capable of enforcement, are loosely, or not at all employed, the Turkish authorities will be justly open to censure, and incur, to their peril, the charge of acting upon principles inconsistent in spirit and effect with the existing alliance. Let them beware of producing throughout Christian

Europe, a total relaxation of that enthusiasm for the Sultan's cause which has hitherto saved his empire from the grasp of Russia,' he said.

It was a clumsy threat and a meaningless one. The Turks recognized humbug when they saw it, and knew that this Liberal government – like most British governments before or since – would never wreck an alliance on a point of principle. Nevertheless, they took steps to push the trade out of sight and blocked slaving raids on Georgia, since the unprotected families of volunteers in their armies would frequently get kidnapped – with a resulting decrease in their soldiers' zeal for the cause.

By 1855, however, the Turks felt secure enough to resume their slaving in style, and prices collapsed to unprecedented levels as the Circassian exodus began. The British were insisting that the trade be banned, but were roundly ignored and some of them were even rather embarrassed. One ambassador wrote to the Foreign Office noting that since the wife of the grand vizier was a Circassian slave, as were 'still more exalted' ladies, he would be 'guilty of gross impropriety' if he continued to insist on an embargo.

The trade in Circassian girls would only be stopped when Circassia ceased to exist. In 1891–2, long after 90 or more per cent of the Circassians had fled to the Ottoman Empire or died on the way, the imperial harem secretly sent out envoys to find blonde, blue-eyed non-Turkified girls for the sultan. But the girls had most of them been born in Turkey, and already knew a little at least about Turkish life. The harshness of their existence and the horrors of the exodus had left lasting marks on their faces, spoiling the perfect features the sultans had prized.

On top of that, the families that had been of the slave class in Circassia had now been freed. They did not want to sell their daughters back into slavery, and many would only sell to the envoys of the sultan when they learned it was for a large institution in the capital and received a promise that they could see their daughters twice a year.

In Ehud Toledano's excellent book *The Ottoman Slave Trade and Its Suppression*, he concludes that the great demographic and economic changes in the Circassians' lives, rather than the impact of Western ideas, had been behind the gradual disappearance of the slave trade in Turkey and he is no doubt right.

Nevertheless, the romantic image of the slave trade remains to this day. As the tour guide in the harem droned on in her harsh monotone, two of the American tourists whispered to each other.

'It would not be bad being a concubine. At least you'd work for the royal family,' one of them said.

'It's perfectly quaint,' the other, perhaps her husband, said in agreement.

5. The Caucasus Mountains are Sacred to Me

In this atmosphere of war, savagery, slavery and exile, it might appear that there was little room for leisure. The Russian soldiers that survived disease and ambush appeared to exist only to inflict unspeakable sufferings on their foe. Surely no civilian would come to this land of death and horror.

But, in fact, Russian tourists flocked to the Caucasus. They took the waters at the newly fashionable spa resorts like Pyatigorsk – its name means 'the five mountains' – at the foot of the high peaks of the central range. They gossiped and flirted and drank in this wild border region. They were attracted of course by the beauty of their surroundings, and by the thrill of the warfare. But above all they came because of the vision of one man: Alexander Pushkin.

Pushkin was a natural user of words and he loved teasing. In the stifling world of St Petersburg and its royal court in the late teens of the nineteenth century, these were both prized assets and a very real danger. For Russia's elite loved intrigues, and had little else to do but indulge in them. So the presence of a petulant, handsome, witty poet like Pushkin must have been a rare treat.

The age was one of relative liberty for the affluent few. Although hopes that Tsar Alexander would grant a constitution after Russia defeated Napoleon had been dashed, the ideas that the Russian officers had learned in Paris had endured. The tsar, who inherited the throne from his murdered father in 1801, had relaxed censorship and, though he was more inclined to mysticism than democracy, he did not do anything drastic to stop the spread of Western ideas. This new generation of Russians were no longer just European by geography; they were influenced by the same thoughts as their contemporaries in more developed countries to their west.

Pictures of Pushkin are endlessly reproduced in Russia. His flamboyant whiskers and his shock of hair were a legacy of an African great-grandfather who had served Peter the Great. His exotic looks just added to his appeal for the salons of the capital, and Russians began to whisper his verses to each other, giggling over the more dangerous passages, including his 'Liberty: An Ode' and one questioning the tsar's bravery.

Inevitably, Pushkin came to the attention of the secret police, and was exiled to the south to teach him the rules of service. It was to be a fateful choice. He spent just a few weeks at his place of exile – Yekaterinoslav, which is now Dnepropetrovsk in Ukraine – before catching a chill when swimming in the river, and being rescued by the family of a childhood friend. He had already thrilled what society there was in the minute town where he had been posted. At one point, he turned up at a party in transparent trousers and no underwear. Now, he was on his way to amaze the whole country.

As Pushkin and his rescuers – the Rayevsky family – trotted sedately across the steppes of southern Russia, and began to see the mighty peaks of the central Caucasus – including Elbrus, the tallest mountain in Europe – notch the skyline, the poet was inspired.

The family stayed in the Caucasus for a few months, taking the waters in the still untamed springs, where they scooped up drinks with a broken bottle or a bark ladle. They saw the local tribesmen, and marvelled at the wilderness around them.

'I am sorry, my friend,' Pushkin wrote to his brother, 'that you could not see this magnificent range of mountains, with their icy summits which from afar in the clear twilight look like strange, many-coloured and motionless cards.'

Pushkin had been reading, and had discovered the poet Byron: the English creator of the romantic ideal, and celebrator of oriental womanhood. Byron too was handsome, women flocked around him like they did around Pushkin. Perhaps Byron's poems have not stood the test of time as well as Pushkin's have, but, at the time, he was the model of masculine virtue. Pushkin was swept away.

His group travelled on from Pyatigorsk, across to Crimea, and to the ruined palaces where the defeated Muslim khan had once lived. Pushkin could flirt with his friend's sisters, he could play on the beach, and he could create *Prisoner in the Caucasus* – perhaps his first mature poem.

It is hard for a foreigner to appreciate Pushkin since his appeal lies in his ability to effortlessly exploit the beauty of the Russian language. If you can understand a Pushkin poem, which is hard even for someone who speaks Russian well, its beauty is breath-taking. But if you cannot, you wonder what the fuss is all about.

Translators of *Prisoner in the Caucasus* into English often render it in prose, since its daft plot looks even sillier in bad verse. In the poem, Pushkin created a handsome Russian officer, unlucky in love and disgusted by life, who is captured by the wild mountain tribes the Russian army is fighting. He is dragged into their village, half dead, filthy and unconscious, but his sex appeal remains undimmed. That very evening, as he sits alone in his cell, a local woman comes to him. She feeds him and, though they lack a common language, loves him wordlessly.

The days go by, her love grows stronger and she brings him honey, millet, wine and other foods of the mountains. 'It was the first time that the innocent young girl had known the joy of being in love. But the Russian had long ago lost the ecstasy of his younger days; he was unable to respond,' the poem says, as rendered by Roger Clarke's prose translation. As he sits and watches during the day, he learns a little of the Circassians' habits and the poem records some spurious ethnographic details: their hospitality, their delight in competitions. They admire the Russian for his indifference and nonchalance, and are delighted that they will get such a good price for him when they come to sell him in the slave market.

But they reckoned without their traitorous compatriot, whose love has taken a turn for the physical. 'Make love to me. No one yet has kissed my eyelids. No young, dark-eyed Circassian has crept at dead of night to the bed where I sleep alone.' The Russian tells her to forget him, that he can never love again, and she leaves in tears. Although she ceases to visit him, her love remains true. And, when her fellow villagers go off to war, she rescues him, guides him back to his people and, although he offers to take her with him, kills herself in the river.

It is hard to take it seriously now, with its assumption that all Muslim tribeswomen were just waiting for a world-weary adolescent to come and sweep them off their feet, but the poem caused a sensation. In an age without newspapers or other ways of finding out what was happening on Russia's southern frontier, this was the closest Russians came to news. The ethnographic details – made up by Pushkin, since he never spent time among the tribesmen – sounded authentic, and what tribeswoman would not want to share the bed of a brave Russian soldier?

The tone of the poem was one of glory in the army and its feats: a point rubbed home by the epilogue, which celebrated such generals as Yermolov, the butcher whose troops slaughtered their way across the North Caucasus, and Tsitsianov, as they marched under the double-headed eagle of the tsar.

'I shall celebrate the glorious time when our two-headed eagle, scenting bloody combat, rose up high against the disaffected Caucasus, when the roar of battle and the thunder of Russian drums first broke out along the foam-flecked River Terek, and our daring general Tsitsianov, head held high, himself took part in the carnage ... [A] deafening uproar in the East! ... at last it was time for the Caucasus to bend its snowy head in self-abasement: Yermolov was on the march!' the poem thunders.

Pushkin, a 21-year-old of a passionate and headstrong mindset, may not have intended serious political analysis. However, the implication is that, though the Russians killed and slaughtered their way through the hills, they brought progress. The Russians might have felt backward in comparison to western Europe. But they were European compared to the savages in the hills.

The poem was a giant success, and opened a vent for Caucasus literature that would spew out huge amounts of dross, along with one great towering masterpiece.

But this celebration of the conquest by young progressives like Pushkin was not to last, for Russia was on the brink of change. The poet's whole generation was to be shaken by the death of the tsar, the treason of the army and the retribution that followed.

Tsar Alexander died in early winter 1825 (on 1 December, according to the Western calendar, but in November, according to that still then used in Russia). He had no sons, leaving a two-week period of confusion in which his two brothers – Nikolai in St Petersburg and Konstantin in Warsaw – both refused the throne and swore loyalty to each other, without realizing it. A group of army officers, who had been plotting to create a more democratic system for the best part of a decade, decided to take control. They marched their troops onto Palace Square, the handsome space that fronts the Winter Palace in St Petersburg, and demanded a constitution. All day they stood in the freezing cold, focus of a more or less sympathetic crowd, until troops loyal to the new Tsar Nikolai I mowed them down with grapeshot.

The city was stunned, and the government's response was swift. The cobbles were scrubbed, the palace façade repaired, the bodies slipped under the ice on the river. By morning, it was as if nothing had happened. Then the conspirators were arrested. One of them, Alexander Bestuzhev, did not wait for a knock on his door. Wearing his full, gorgeous dragoons dress uniform, he walked into the Winter Palace and gave himself up as a traitor. That was the last that St Petersburg society would ever see of him. He would never dance or gamble in the halls of the great houses again. But in his verse, he would scandalize them, and do more to popularize the Caucasus than even the great Pushkin himself.

Bestuzhev was taken to the Peter and Paul fortress, the squat camp on the river Neva with its one soaring golden spire, where he and his fellow 'Decembrist' conspirators were locked up for six months of interrogation and trial. They tangled each other in a dense mesh of confessions, revealing all the secrets of their one-time secret society, and ruining the chances of change in Russia for almost a century.

The new tsar believed he had been preserved on his throne by a miracle. His own father was killed by plotters disgusted by his brief rule, and here were young, aristocratic officers confessing that they too had wanted to kill their sovereign, his brother. They had, however, been beaten to it by the tsar's death from natural causes and thus launched their premature and ill-fated rising.

'The beginning of the reign of Emperor Alexander was marked with bright hopes for Russia's prosperity. The gentry had recuperated, the merchant class did not object to giving credit, the army served without making trouble, scholars studied what they wished, all spoke what they thought, and everyone expected better days. Unfortunately, circumstances prevented the realization of these hopes, which aged without their fulfilment,' said Bestuzhev in a lengthy letter to the new tsar. He only joined the movement in 1823 and was just sixteen when Napoleon was defeated, but he did not hesitate to invoke the glory of his fellow plotters who had marched across Europe.

'[T]he military men began to talk: "Did we free Europe in order to be ourselves placed in chains? Did we grant a constitution to France in order that we dare not even talk about it, and did we buy at the price of our blood priority among nations in order that we might be humiliated at home?"'

Behind the closed cell doors, however, Bestuzhev was less defiant. He opened up all the secrets of the conspiracy. His biographer, Lauren Leighton, does not blame him for having done so although she concedes his evidence sent his best friend, Kondraty Ryleyev, to the gallows. He managed to shield his brothers but otherwise it is hard to agree with her positive assessment of him. He gained beneficial treatment for himself as a result of his betrayal. While five of his fellows were hanged – including the similarly named Bestuzhev-Ryumin – he was sent to Siberia to live in exile, before being posted to the Caucasus to serve as a common soldier.

Many of the former Decembrists had been writers, while Bestuzhev and his betrayed friend Ryleyev had published a literary magazine. Only Bestuzhev, presumably because of his cooperation, was allowed to keep writing after his disgrace. But he was forced to use a pen-name. As a writer, Alexander Bestuzhev, the dandy and the wit, was dead. Alexander Marlinsky, the daredevil and hero, was born in his place.

He had signed himself Marlinsky, a nom de plume that derived from the name of a pavilion outside St Petersburg, before but only now was the name to become famous throughout Russia. Decades later, Russians would remember thrilling over his stories, and the novelist Ivan Turgenev even confessed to having kissed the name Marlinsky on a journal cover.

None of his vast readership knew his real identity, or of his revolutionary past, but he swayed them with his lurid, romantic prose, his lust for action. For ten years he ruled Russia's literary scene, before disappearing as rapidly as he had appeared. A modern reader will share the opinion of some contemporary Russian critics, who as early as 1834 were complaining that his writing was awful. Nevertheless, you have to admire his sheer hard work and exuberance.

During his seven years of service in the Caucasus, he was persecuted, sent into battle again and again, spied on, beaten, envied and slandered. His own brother was mistreated so viciously that he went insane. Yet he constantly wrote letters to his sisters and his brothers – three of whom had also been Decembrists – and had time to effectively invent the Russian novel. He set it in the Caucasus.

His most famous work is *Ammalat Bek*, which reflected his deep knowledge of the Caucasus. On arriving in Dagestan, he had rapidly added the Turkic and Persian dialects spoken there to the thirteen or so languages he already knew, and would disappear for days at a time into the mountains, where he could pass as a local. *Ammalat Bek* is steeped in Dagestani legend, since it reflects the true story of a rebel who was captured by the Russians and sentenced to death. A Russian officer called Verkhovsky intervened to save him, and the two men became friends. But nine years later, Ammalat killed his protector, then dug up his body and chopped off his head. According to legend, Ammalat had been in love with the daughter of one of the local khans and forced to kill the Russian to win her hand. Using these raw materials, Bestuzhev-Marlinsky created an imaginative tissue of journal entries, letters, descriptions and more to tell the story of the failure of Verkhovsky, a sensitive man, to bridge the gap between himself and his Muslim friend. As a work of ethnography, it has some interesting passages, but, as a novel, it is almost unreadable. The writing is overblown, the plot is absurd and the noble heroism of the protagonist seems unlikely. Here, for example, is Ammalat's reaction to pleading with his beloved to elope with him.

'Speak not so. If the sacrifice is unusual, my love also is unusual. Command me to give my life a thousand times, and I will throw it down like a copper poull [coin]. I will cast my soul into hell for you – not only my life. You remind me that you are the daughter of the Khan; remember, too, that my grandfather wore, that my uncle wears, the crown of a Shamkhal! But it is not by this dignity, but by my heart, that I feel I am worthy of you; and if there be shame in being happy despite of the malice of mankind and the caprice of fate, that shame will fall on my head and not on yours,' cries Ammalat, provoking confusion in Sultanetta, who knows not what to do.

'Torn now by her maiden fear, and her respect for the customs of her forefathers, now by the passion and eloquence of her lover, the innocent Sultanetta wavered, like a light cork, upon the tempestuous billows of contending emotions.'

Despite the apparent impossibility of enduring such prose for long, the book sold in huge numbers, and he was able to support his whole family with the proceeds. At one point, he had 50,000 roubles, a vast sum, in assets just from his writing.

His life, however, was miserable. Holed up in the small town of Derbent on the shore of the Caspian Sea, he amused himself with seducing officers' wives, with drinking and with writing. In the process, he made himself far more interesting than anything in his books.

A later account of his life by a Russian writer tells how he used to creep out over the rooftops of the town by night, dagger in hand, and into the chambers of the local ladies. The beautiful wife of an officer, who was besotted with him despite being lusted over by the whole garrison, would visit him in secret whenever her boorish husband played cards all night. 'And so it was this lucky lady who was the object of the most tender and ardent passion of our writer, our unlucky hero upon whom fate had not seen fit to bestow the pleasures of a legal domestic happiness. This woman gave herself to him completely, without holding anything back. Neither the fear of punishment at her husband's hand for her infidelity, nor fear of obstacles and dangers, no nothing could keep her from meeting her beloved,' the account says.

One night she dressed in her husband's uniform to avoid notice as she slipped through the streets to Bestuzhev's house. But she was spotted by a Georgian junior officer who, guessing what was afoot, tried to force her to submit to him instead. She pretended to consent, stepped back, then hit him in the face and ran off to her lover, telling him all. The next day, Bestuzhev threatened to punish the officer 'in the Caucasus style' and the officer was so scared he asked for an immediate transfer.

Although many of these stories of a rake and a cad may have been spread to demean Bestuzhev's reputation among a public who still remembered his charm, wit and grace in the capital, they succeeded mainly in creating the legend of a Byronic hero who suffered unceasingly, and was irresistible to women. It was an image he did not try to restrain.

'Not by talent, but by fate I am like Byron,' he wrote in one of his many letters. 'What calumny was not cast his way? What did they not suspect him of doing? So it is with me as well. My greatest misfortunes appear to others to be crimes. My heart is clean, but my head is bespattered by disgrace and slander.'

He began to suffer from disease, being cooped up in forts where cholera was rife. In fact, it was a miracle that he survived at all, since in some of the forts the whole strength of the garrison would die over the course of a year. His hopes for freedom were raised by two promotions: the second to ensign, the rank enjoyed by the aristocratic boys sent to join the army in their teenage years.

But he was still marched unceasingly from skirmish to skirmish, until, finally, he was sent the whole way across the Caucasus to the Black Sea coast. 'Driven as I am from region to region, never spending two months in one place, without quarters, without letters, without books, without newspapers, now exhausted by military duties, now half dead from illness – will I never be able to take a deep breath ...? Who will be worse off if I am better off? Is it so difficult to throw a man a grain of happiness?'

Apparently it was; he still hoped for a pardon from the tsar but he should have known he would not get one. The tsar had turned down his case for a medal when he helped defend Derbent in 1830, and was a man who bore a grudge. None of the Decembrists would be allowed to return to their former lives. In 1837, the tsar visited the Caucasus and Bestuzhev hoped he might have a chance to personally plead his case, but it was not to be. The tsar did not stop at the fort where he was based, a request to move to Crimea was blocked and despair closed around him.

'I embrace you my dear brother. If God does not grant that we meet again, be happy. You know that I have loved you greatly. This, however, is not an epitaph. I don't think about dying, nor do I long for it to come soon. However, in any event it is best to bid you farewell. When you show this letter to mother, do not reveal this part; why worry her needlessly?' he wrote in words stripped free of his habitual posing. In fact, for once, he comes across as rather brave.

On 7 June 1837, he was part of a force sent by sea to Cape Adler to subdue the local Circassians. But the soldiers were outnumbered, and were forced to fall back. He volunteered — as was his habit — to run forward to tell the advance party to retreat. He got there just as it was cut off, and landed in the thick of a battle that was to be his last. He was seen leaning against a tree, bleeding heavily, but his body was never found.

Bestuzhev was dead, but his legend continued, especially since Marlinsky — his alter ego — vanished suddenly with no explanation given. The secret of the writer's real identity had been kept well. Legends abounded as to his fate. One writer recorded being asked if it was true that Marlinsky had changed sides and was leading the mountaineers against the Russians. Another veteran of the Caucasus wars recalled that his brother used to call him 'Ammalat'.

Alexandre Dumas recounted hearing about Bestuzhev — or Bestuchef, as he called him — when he passed through Russia in the 1850s. In the town of Nizhny Novgorod, he claimed to have met the French wife of the Decembrist Ivan Annenkov, who possessed a bracelet and a jewel which she said Bestuzhev had whittled out of a link of metal chain during their stay in Siberia. 'These two ornaments were a true symbol of poetry, because it transforms all it touches,' wrote Dumas.

He later passed down the shore of the Caspian Sea to Derbent, where Bestuzhev had lived for so long. And although he got most of his facts wrong, he did recount a fascinating version of one of the most peculiar episodes of Bestuzhev's life, which dates from the winter of 1832–3.

That year, the townsfolk in Derbent were starving. Bestuzhev, to arm himself against robbers or even cannibals, kept a pistol under his pillow to be secure while he slept. One day, as he and a friend were sitting in his room, Olga Nestertsova, the sixteen-year-old daughter of his landlady, came in to deliver laundry. She may have been his lover, for while 'frisking' (as she put it later) she jumped onto the bed, set off the pistol and shot herself.

The bullet passed through her chest, and she lived on for two more agonizing days before drowning in her own blood. While she still lived, she testified that Bestuzhev was not to blame and he was cleared by a trial, but the legend was born that he had shot her in a fit of jealous rage. Although she is unlikely to have been his only lover, if indeed she was at all, she became a symbol of truth and fidelity for the local community.

Dumas recounted hearing the story of the girl, whom he called Oline Nesterzof, while he stood looking at her gravestone, on which was carved a blasted rose and the single word 'fate'.

According to the story he heard, which had developed over the twenty years since Bestuzhev died, Olga and the poet had lived together for a year in perfect happiness. But one evening he and three friends got drunk, and Bestuzhev boasted of his mistress's faithfulness. One of his companions wagered that he could seduce her if he tried – a bet that Bestuzhev unwisely accepted. And soon, the friend returned with proof of his conquest. Dumas unleashed all his melodramatic skills to describe what happened next.

'The young girl entered the poet's chamber. No one knows what happened there. A shot was heard, then a cry; then, finally, Bestuchef came out, pale and frightful. In the chamber, Oline lay on the ground, dying, bloodied; a bullet had passed through her chest. A fired pistol was close by her. The dying girl could still speak; she asked for a priest to be found. Two hours later, she was dead. The priest swore under oath that Oline Nesterzof told him that she had wanted to take the pistol from Bestuchef's hands, and the pistol had gone off by accident. She was shot, she died pardoning Bestuchef for this accidental murder,' wrote Dumas, full of the passion of the tragedy.

The priest then supposedly testified at Bestuzhev's trial, and his testimony alone acquitted the poet of murder. But, Dumas assures us, Bestuzhev was never the same again. He was overcome by a need for danger, and would throw himself into the thick of battle. But he lived a charmed life and, despite his wish for death, he was spared again and again. Dumas was enthralled by the tale. 'Finally, in 1838, he made an excursion in the land of the Abazertskys: they attacked the village of Adler. At the moment of entering in the forest, it was clear that this forest was occupied by a mountaineer force three times stronger than the Russians. The mountaineers had, as well, an advantage in their position, because they were dug into the forest. The colonel gave the order to retreat. The retreat was sounded. Bestuchef commanded the riflemen along with another officer, Captain Albrand. Instead of obeying the trumpet call, these two forced their way into the forest in pursuit of the mountaineers. Captain Albrand returned, but Bestuchef did not.'

Dumas claimed to have received these details from a certain 'Prince Tarkanof', an eyewitness to the battle. Apparently, fifty soldiers were sent to hunt for the writer but all that was ever found was his watch.

The story shows how successful Bestuzhev's effort to present himself as a Byronic hero had been, while also showing how well the secret of his literary alter ego had been kept. Dumas clearly knew of Bestuzhev's past as a poet in St Petersburg and wrote about him as one who had written some good verses, but does not appear to have realized that he was a novelist, nor that Marlinsky and Bestuzhev were the same person. If he did, he kept it very quiet, since he went on to publish translations of two of Marlinsky's novels, including *Ammalat Bek*, under his own name. He claimed to have come across the manuscripts in Derbent, and did not feel the need to mention that they had already been published to vast acclaim in Russia. He called them *Sultanetta* – the name of the heroine of *Ammalat Bek*, and the woman for whom Ammalat killed his Russian friend – and *La Boule de neige*.

The translator of an American version of the novels in 1906 subtly condemned Dumas for it. 'In "Sultanetta" Dumas evidently struggled against assimilating the story of the Russian novelist whose romance he admits, under a somewhat specious plea, that he "re-wrote",' the translator said. By that time, the secret of Marlinsky's identity was out, but his novels had been all but forgotten. So much so that the translator did not even bother to record his name.

Bestuzhev is a writer in the unfortunate position of being more interesting for who he was, than for what he wrote. But many of his imitators do not even have that distinction. Following his lead, they produced reams of trash, which revelled in the oriental details of Marlinsky and Pushkin, often with semi-pornographic overlays.

One Elizaveta Gan wrote an erotic fantasy in the first person called *A Recollection of Zheleznovodsk*, which purported to be the memoir of a lady who had stayed at this spa resort. She enjoyed horseback riding in the wilds around the town, but was ambushed by Circassians and fainted out of fear. On coming to her senses, she had been slung over the back of a horse, and was being carried deep into the mountains. 'So my dream had come true: fate was casting me into that country which I had desired to see for such a long time – into the canyons, the refuge of the wild sons of nature. I was going to see the Caucasus in all its charm and terror.'

It was a Mills and Boon novel with a colonial twist, and you can almost see the society ladies flicking forward through the pages to the inevitable bed scene. A dark figure enters her quarters and foils her escape plan. 'Lightning flashed. I saw the prince, and his eyes gleamed more dreadfully than all the sky's lightning.' The lady saves her virtue by seizing the prince's dagger and killing herself with it, only to wake up in her own bed to find it was all a dream. Nevertheless, she refused to apologize for her over-active imagination and promised to 'keep having such dreams every night and describe them in even greater detail'.

These novels have been extensively studied by Susan Layton, whose rather dry *Russian Literature and Empire* cannot hide its joy whenever it records another erotic thriller. She describes another such book plotted around a harem love triangle in Abkhazia, in which the son murders the father and the sex slave hurls herself into the sea while lightning flashes. In a rather uncomfortable afterword, the author then goes on to lecture his audience on the importance of civilized Russians colonizing the Caucasus to stop such irrational foreign behaviour.

The dramatic setting of the Caucasus as created by Pushkin and Marlinsky was exploited outside Russia as well, with British writers joining in on the act. They could combine the standard celebration of the lusty savage with a good measure of anti-Russian prejudice, and came up with results every bit as dreadful as their Russian counterparts.

Grace Walton set *Schamyl, or the Wild Woman of Circassia* in the basic factual framework of the war in the eastern Caucasus, but otherwise seems to have imagined the mountain folk to be more or less equivalent to the townsfolk of *Romeo and Juliet*. Schamyl – her version of Imam Shamil, the ruler of the highlanders – has a son Hamed, who is staunch and fearless, a daughter Lelia, who is a 'peerless beauty', a ward Ivan, who is noble and handsome, and an aide Hassan Bey, who is sly and treacherous.

A battle separates them, threatening their total destruction, only for them to be helped by a mad woman called Wenda who appears out of the mountains and rescues them from a desperate fate. The plot twists and turns in an ever more complex web of love intrigues. Hamed ends up marrying the ward of a Russian general after he spurns an employment offer from the tsar. Lelia, who is not really Schamyl's daughter, marries Ivan, who actually is Schamyl's son. Hassan Bey gets his just deserts after trying to seduce Lelia, while Schamyl finds the wild woman is really his lost wife and the mother of Ivan.

In one exceptionally racy passage, Catherine Dubroschi – the young Russian girl who ends up marrying Hamed – is stripped to the waist and threatened with a flogging. The audience is treated to an illustration of the scene, with her perfect skin and only-just-not-visible right breast threatened by the knout. It is certainly not what you expect from Victorian literature.

The influence of Bestuzhev-Marlinsky ran deep indeed, and it settled on a young man called Mikhail Lermontov, who had holidayed at the mineral spas as a young lad. In a museum now devoted to him in Pyatigorsk is a sketch he did illustrating the story of Ammalat Bek, with a savage mountaineer shooting dead a Russian officer with a rifle at close range.

When Lermontov was aged ten, his family was taking the waters at Pyatigorsk. He fell in love with a girl he met there, or so he said a

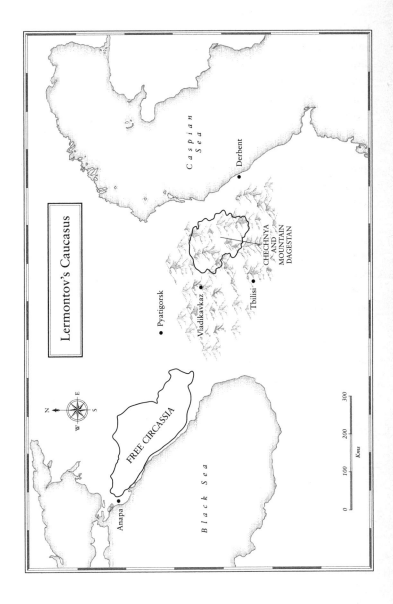

Lermontov's Caucasus

few years later, adding a layer of sensual allure to a place that already had a hold on him. 'My heart began to throb, my knees felt weak; I had no idea about anything at that time. Nevertheless, it was passion, strong though childish, it was real love. I still haven't looked like that since. They laughed at me, teased me, for they noticed the emotion in my face. I would weep silently without reason. I wanted to see her. The Caucasian mountains are sacred to me.'

As a teenager, Lermontov's fascination with the mountains endured, even after his return to the north, and his subtlety of thought quickly outstripped anything Bestuzhev was capable of. In his poem 'Izmail-Bey', written when he was fifteen or sixteen and only a few months before the Decembrist revolt, he revealed a very ambiguous attitude to Russia's conquest of the south.

'The village where his youth was spent, the mosques, the peaceful roofs, all rent and ruined by the Russians are,' the poem says, in justifying the hero's decision to turn his back on Russian service and return to the Caucasus of his forefathers. Lermontov based his poem on stories he had heard during his trips to the south, but his story is still celebratory of Russia. Disillusion would come later. For now, he believed that when the Circassians were subdued they would proclaim 'slave though I be, I serve a prince most high, a king of the world'. But even this did not go far enough for the censors, who cut it when the poem was finally published in 1843.

For the censors, after the Decembrist revolt, became even more restrictive than before. One censor called Buturlin later remarked he would have censored the gospels for their democratic tendencies if he could, and it became increasingly hard to write or think freely. Lev Tolstoy, himself destined to write about the Caucasus, studied at Kazan University at a time when the philosophy course was based exclusively on the set books of St Paul's epistles to the Colossians and to Timothy. Another great author, Fyodor Dostoyevsky, was transported to Siberia just for owning a printing press, while Turgenev was put under house arrest in 1852 for writing a kind of obituary of the disgraced satirical genius Nikolai Gogol.

It was a stifling atmosphere, and was not one that Lermontov reacted well to. Throughout his short career, he was like a wild animal kept as a pet. He would entertain with his looks, his wit and his outrageous comments, but would lash out if bored and be savagely punished for it. This explosive temperament was too much for the university in Moscow, which he dropped out of. He enrolled in the army and endured two years of training, his soul oppressed by the boredom of drill and the marriage of his childhood sweetheart to a fat man twelve years her senior. His works from this period are savage satires of society, condemning the futility of upper-class existence.

Pushkin felt the stuffy atmosphere too. Though some of his most celebrated works date from after 1825, he was subject to humiliating scrutiny. In 1829, he broke out and travelled to the Caucasus without permission, producing a travel memoir of boredom, rage and despair called *Journey to Arzrum*. As a book, it lacks the grace and beauty of his poetry, but the truth of its message is all the more powerful for that. It reflects the blank gloom of a generation in which geniuses were forced to be bureaucrats, where the life of an officer was the most freedom a man could hope for.

He stopped off at the spa towns that had entranced him in 1820, but now he thought they had been become too smart. 'Nailed up on the walls of the bath-houses are lists of instructions from the police; everything is orderly, neat, prettified,' he wrote. The Caucasus had lost its edge, this was no longer a place where a man could be free. Even the tribes were no longer noble, just savage.

'The Circassians hate us. We have forced them out of their free and spacious pasture-lands; their auls [villages] are in ruins, whole tribes have been annihilated. As time goes on, they move deeper into the mountains, and direct their raids from there. Friendship with the peaceful Circassians is unreliable: they are always ready to aid their rebellious fellow tribesmen. The spirit of their wild chivalry has declined noticeably. They rarely attack the Cossacks in equal number, and never the infantry; and they flee when they see a cannon. Even so they never pass up an opportunity to attack a weak detachment or a defenceless person. The area is full of rumours of their villainies,' he wrote in a bleak condemnation of all sides.

'Recently a peaceful Circassian who shot a soldier was captured.

He tried to justify himself by saying that his rifle had been loaded for too long. What can one do with such people?'

He continued on his melancholy progress to Vladikavkaz, the central fort that held the key to the Caucasus and which dominated the only serious pass across the mountains. Here he saw Circassians kept as hostages, dressed in rags and smeared in filth. This was the truth of the civilizing war he had praised a decade earlier. Even the magnificent pass over the Caucasus did not interest him. Indeed, it was obscured by clouds.

Most of his book is set to the south of the mountain range, where he visited the front line of the Russian war against the Turks. His return to the northern side of the mountains only takes in a couple of pages, but they are a subtle satire of the stuffy constraints of the imperial court, told as a reaction to a review of his work.

The review, told in the form of a dialogue between three companions and published in a prominent Russian magazine, was very rude about both him and his work. Instead of caring much, he mocks it by reading it out loud in a funny voice. 'The vexation which reading the article had provoked in me completely disappeared and we burst out laughing in all sincerity,' he wrote.

This despairingly sardonic world view developed further over the years as Pushkin distracted himself from his stultifying existence with flirting and dancing. After his marriage, he was awarded the lowest court rank – something he interpreted as an insult to himself, the greatest poet of his generation, and which may well have been designed solely to keep his gorgeous wife at court – and sank further into rage. In the claustrophobic world of St Petersburg, he was too big to be tolerated and finally was killed in a duel in 1837, victim of a Dutchman who had insulted his wife.

His funeral was closed to non-family members to prevent a political demonstration, but Lermontov exploded with rage anyway. Stinging with the insult that Russia's poet had been killed, and by a foreigner at that, he penned a savage attack on court hypocrisy shocking even by his standards.

'You, hungry crowd that swarms around the throne, butchers of freedom, and genius, and glory, you hide behind the shelter of the law, before you, right and justice must be dumb! But, parasites of vice, there's God's assize; there is an awful court of law that waits,' he wrote in a scintillating postscript to his poem 'Death of a Poet'.

He had gone too far. He had called the tsar's own companions 'false and worthless slanderers' and would have to pay the price. His rooms were searched. He was confined to barracks and interrogated with all the humiliating skill of the tsar's experts. The reaction was swift; Lermontov was sent to the Caucasus to serve in the dragoons, without even time to say goodbye to his friends. To him, it was a catastrophe, but the Caucasus had finally got the great writer it deserved.

If the tsar's police had intended to beat the young officer into obedience, they were to be disappointed. Pyatigorsk was home to a surprising degree of freedom. A doctor in the town lent him dangerously liberal books when Lermontov arrived to take the waters for most of the summer. He met some of the Decembrists too, including Lorer, the reluctant soldier who described the battle also witnessed by Bell in Chapter 3. It is clear from Lorer's memoirs that Lermontov's bitterness with the world was not just a front preserved for his writing.

'From the first step of our acquaintance I did not like Lermontov. I was always happy to come upon kind, warm people, who could maintain in all phases of their lives a beneficial ardour in the heart, a living sympathy for all that is lofty or beautiful, but, speaking with Lermontov, he struck me as cold, bilious, irritable, and a hater of mankind in general,' wrote Lorer, who characteristically reacted to the nasty young man by trying to be nice to him.

There was a generation gap. The idealistic Decembrists could not understand the new wave of hard cynics like Lermontov. Another Decembrist, Nazimov, who had been imprisoned together with Lorer in Siberia, was shocked by the young man's attitude to life. 'We have no purpose, we just meet, go on sprees, follow some sort of career and chase women,' Lermontov told him. And he backed up his petulant words with similarly nasty deeds. He at one point ate a whole picnic himself, without allowing any of his fellow guests to have any. When a would-be poet visited him, Lermontov listened to some of his poetry while eating his pickled cucumbers, then ran away with the cucumbers that remained before his guest had finished.

He did not do any actual fighting that year, since a trip to the Black Sea coast was cancelled when news came that his regiment had to join the tsar in Georgia. He loved the solitary trips on horseback through the magnificent central Caucasus, and he was just settling in at the headquarters of his regiment in Georgia, when news came from the court. He had been pardoned, and was free to return northwards. He took his time, staying in Tbilisi for a while and employing Bestuzhev's language teacher to help him pick up the Turkic of the mountains. But he could not stay for ever. Home once more, he received a full pardon and the right to live in St Petersburg by April 1838. His disgrace had lasted little more than a year, but it had sown ideas in his head that would burst forth in the first great novel in the Russian language.

A Hero of Our Time is a staggeringly complete work, especially when you consider it was written by a man in his early twenties who had to invent the form as he went along. Written in a structural knot that twists chronology inside out, it recounts the tale of a young man whose passions lead him to destroy everything he touches, to the bewildered consternation of older men who cannot understand his motivation.

In it, he ripped up Pushkin and Bestuzhev-Marlinsky, and mercilessly satirized the celebration of the Caucasus as a place of freedom. Instead, his Caucasus was a place of dissipation, boredom, cynical seduction, savagery and pointless violence. While stationed in a village on the Russian defensive line, the hero Pechorin seduces Bela, a wild beauty of the mountains. Pechorin is a disillusioned hero, unlucky in love, straight out of a Caucasus cliché. But Lermontov took the cliché, wrenched it into a new shape and turned it on its head. 'When I saw Bela in my home, when for the first time I held her in my lap and kissed her black curls, I – fool that I was – imagined she was an angel sent to me by compassionate fate. . . I was wrong again. The love of a wild girl was little better than that of a lady of rank; the ignorance and the naivety of one pall on you as much as the coquetry of the other. I still like her, I suppose; I am grateful to her for several rather sweet moments; I am ready to die for her – only I find her company dull,' he wrote.

Pechorin was above all bored. Everything he did was to alleviate his boredom. He was even bored of boredom. Fashionable society, he said, was so fashionably bored that it had become rather boring to be bored. 'Nowadays those people who were really bored the most tried to conceal this misfortune as though it were a vice,' he noted with a sardonic glee.

Lermontov claimed Pechorin was not a reflection of himself, though there was clearly much the two had in common, but a composite image of the whole post-Decembrist generation. He told his audience that previously they had used fiction to escape from the ghastly reality of society, but now reality had entered into fiction, and they would have to face the consequences.

'You will tell me that a man cannot be as bad as all that; and I shall tell you that since you have believed in the possibility of so many tragic and romantic villains having existed, why can you not believe in the reality of Pechorin,' he asked in the preface to the second edition. 'People have been fed enough sweetmeats; it has given them indigestion: they need some bitter medicine, some caustic truths. However, do not think after this that the author of this book ever had the proud dream of becoming a reformer of mankind's vices ... Suffice it to say that the disease has been pointed out; goodness knows how to cure it.'

In a stroke, Lermontov had killed Caucasus fiction as something that the educated elite could take seriously. His 'hero' was not honourable to Russian women and he did not rescue tribeswomen to a life of Christian respectability. Instead, he moved from being the dupe of a female smuggler – whom he had to throw into the sea to stop her killing him – to being a cynical seducer who treats all women as playthings fit only to stave off boredom.

Unsurprisingly, the tsar was not amused. 'The author suffers from a most depraved spirit, and his talents are pathetic,' he wrote in a letter to his wife, before going on to spectacularly miss the point of the novel (and, thus, rather confirm its central argument of the vacuity of the tsar's court) by praising Maksim Maksimich, an army captain who is the novel's hapless and stolid stooge. 'The Captain's character is nicely sketched. In beginning to read the story I had hoped, and was rejoicing, that he was the Hero of Our Times ... but such a hope is not to be fulfilled in this book, and M. Lermontov was unable to develop the noble and simple character [of the Captain]. He is replaced by wretched and uninteresting people, who – proving to be tiresome – would have been far better ignored and thus not provoke one's disgust.'

Lermontov, clearly, was not going to survive long at court, especially as he began to misbehave at literary salons and in public. A request to be transferred back to the Caucasus was refused. 'They won't even let me be killed,' he wrote in a letter. So he tried to arrange death for himself. Challenged to a duel, he met the son of the French ambassador in the snow with pistols. It could have been a startling echo of Pushkin's fate, since the older poet was killed by the adopted son of the Dutch ambassador, but it was not to be. The Frenchman missed, and Lermontov shot upwards.

But it was only a temporary escape. He was arrested for duelling, tried and found guilty. The tsar himself determined the sentence. Lieutenant Lermontov was sent back to the Caucasus, as an infantry officer. The tsar hoped he would 'brain-wash himself' and rewrite his masterpiece to give the dull Captain a greater part.

Strangely, Lermontov turned out to be an excellent soldier, and a brave despatch rider. There is great irony in the fact that while he made the fictional Caucasus a scene for disillusion and mockery, in truth it was the one place he found freedom. The battles he witnessed in the eastern Caucasus gave fresh material for poems questioning the point of what he was doing, but he entered into the fighting wholeheartedly while it was going on. A poem from this time quotes Kazbek, the giant mountain peak which towers over the pass to Georgia, as saying: 'Miserable men! Oh, what do they want? The earth's great plain gives room for all beneath the sky; yet ceaselessly and all in vain, alone, they war for ever, why?'

Riding a white horse, and affecting long hair and dirty clothes, he rode through the forests of Chechnya in command of a company of irregular troops, and was repeatedly praised for his bravery. He was recommended for a medal. 'This officer in spite of all dangers carried out his duties with superior courage and cold-bloodedness, and broke into the enemy entrenchments in the first ranks of the bravest,' the account said. But the suggestion was turned down in the government, and it was clear his disgrace had not ended.

After a short leave in St Petersburg, Lermontov decided to take the waters at the scene of his childhood love affair: Pyatigorsk, where his fictional hero Pechorin had fought a duel over a princess, whose heart he then broke when he became bored of her.

The cottage he stayed in is now home to a Lermontov museum. Although it is surrounded by Soviet concrete hotels and apartment blocks, it is easy to see how it would have appealed to the writer. It is peaceful and set in a garden of its own, which somehow keeps out the traffic noise and stays warm long into autumn. He received guests here, for, although he was officially in Pyatigorsk to receive treatment, he launched himself into the social scene. He both scandalized and delighted local society, which was thrilled to find itself sharing the resort with the exiled young writer.

Among the guests was one Nikolai Martynov, who had trained as a cadet with Lermontov, and who was the butt of the writer's crueller jokes.

Martynov, a retired major, had affected the dress style of the highlanders. He shaved his head, and wore a tunic and a large, ornate dagger. He was, in fact, the very kind of ostentatious officer mocked by Lermontov in *A Hero of Our Time*. His clothing prompted Lermontov, with deliberate crudity, to refer to him as 'the ferocious highlander with the big dagger'. It was a joke too far, and once more Lermontov was challenged to a duel.

It was crazy for him, already in a severely compromised position, to fight a duel at all. If word leaked out, he would lose his rank, his property and any chance of a return to polite society. But it was not certain that news would leak out. On his last duel, he had fired into the air, and apparently he intended to do so on this occasion as well. If both parties did so, then honour would be satisfied, and the matter could be hushed up.

But Lermontov was not the kind of man for that. According to the excellent account in Laurence Kelly's *Lermontov: Tragedy in the Caucasus*, the writer could not resist one more humiliation. Turning to his second, he said loudly: 'I shall not fire at this fool' and ostentatiously declined to fire. Martynov, 'goaded beyond control', strode towards him and fired his pistol at close range. Lermontov fell. He died a few minutes later.

Historians have given wildly different accounts of why Lermontov was killed. Soviet writers liked to argue that Martynov had been acting on secret government instructions to kill the poet, while another account has the hapless Martynov insulting the writer and forcing him to propose a duel. The account given by Kelly seems by far the more in keeping with his personality, however.

I like to think that Lermontov lived faster than normal people. Had he not died in the duel in July 1841, he would have died in battle soon after. He had already written one of Russia's greatest novels, as well as several of its great poems, and he was only twenty-six years old.

6. Extermination Alone Would
Keep Them Quiet

When the Crimean War ended in 1856, and the foreign troops left Circassia, the full fury of the Russian response fell on the highlanders.

And the situation looked even bleaker with the accession of a new, energetic tsar. Many believe Nikolai I, who had been so inflexible about the sites of Russian fortresses in the 1830s and stifled some of the century's greatest writers, to have been the most reactionary of all the Russian tsars, and almost any change would have been for the better. As it was, his oldest son Alexander proved a revelation. Nikolai died in 1855, during the Crimean War, his spirit perhaps broken by the dreadful performance of the Russian army he had created, and Alexander initially struggled with his father's legacy. His true potential was only shown when he had concluded peace.

Under the treaty, the Black Sea was officially declared neutral and Russia was not allowed to keep a navy there. This should have benefited the Circassians, but Alexander II's subsequent achievements cancelled that out.

The Crimean War had been a humiliation, and Russia could clearly no longer continue on its old path. In the twenty-six years of his reign, therefore, Alexander abolished serfdom – the form of slavery that tied Russian peasants to the land – reformed the army and navy, started Russia's network of railways, reformed the legal structure, introduced local assemblies with limited powers, and more.

Most important from the perspective of the Caucasus highlanders, however, was that he allowed the generals to take the initiative, and the results were dramatic. In 1859, Imam Shamil, ruler of the eastern Caucasus, surrendered. Then the whole military might of Russia was focused on the Circassians. The Circassians had no single leader to be taken in battle, and Russian officers knew they would have to find a different way to defeat them, as noticed by George Leighton Ditson, an American visitor to the Caucasus, as early as 1850.

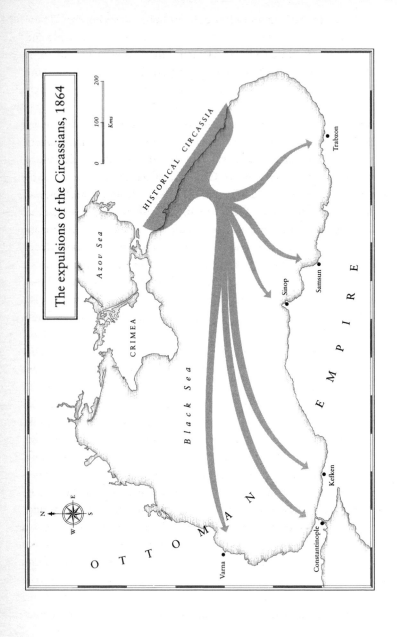

The expulsions of the Circassians, 1864

Ditson's memoirs quote a Prince Kotsohobey as saying that 'These Circassians are just like your American Indians – as untamable and uncivilized – and that, owing to their natural energy of character, extermination alone would keep them quiet, or that if they came under Russian rule, the only safe policy would be to employ their wild and warlike character against others.'

This viewpoint was encountered a couple of years later by Dr Moritz Wagner. He met a German doctor who said the soldiers were becoming increasingly exasperated with the Circassians' failure to appreciate the advantages of Russian civilization.

'It is a prevalent opinion,' said the doctor, 'among the Russians and Cossacks, that a war of extermination should be waged against the Circassians, because these people are perfectly incapable of appreciating gentleness, friendship and benefits conferred, are unsusceptible of any generous emotion, and because it is impossible to civilize them.'

Many Circassians sensed that extermination was coming. They were few, poor and starving and had no hope of military support. With the Russians in front of them and the sea behind them, they chose to take to the sea.

The editor of the *Levant Herald*, Istanbul's English-language publication, wrote to the London *Times* in January 1860 to appeal for help for those unfortunate Circassians already flooding into Turkey.

'During the past stormy season in the Black Sea above a dozen wrecks of these emigrant vessels occurred, hurrying many hundreds of these miserable creatures to death. Of those who made good the passage, thousands landed in every stage of disease and physical suffering, without a dollar to supply even their most immediate wants,' he wrote, in describing the horrors he had seen among the 20,000 refugees then in Istanbul and Uskudar. 'Gaunt visions of famishing men, women and children meet you at every turn, appealing to you in their mute passion of bitter hunger and freezing cold with a harrowing energy no British onlooker, at all events, can resist. Inside the khans the spectacle is worse. In the damp ground-floors scores of sufferers, in every stage of want-induced disease – most of them women – lie huddled together, some with no bedding whatever, and the best off with but little.'

The leaders of those Circassians who remained in their homeland begged Britain for help. Their appeal is still kept in the Foreign Office archives, a mute rebuke to the consuls' reports either side of it, with their self-satisfied handwriting, and their thick blue paper.

The paper the Circassians used is too thin for this august company, the lines followed by their exuberant Arabic script are too wobbly, and their piece of paper is too large for the ledger, and has had to be folded to fit in. Unlike all the reports from the British officials, their letter has never been properly attached to the ledger, and is just tucked between the pages. Perhaps this was some anonymous Foreign Office functionary's way of pointing out the Circassians' bad manners in being there at all.

For the message contained in their appeal was a world away from the careful prose of the urbane diplomatic reports that surround it in the file, and it is the only time we hear a Circassian voice describing the nation's doom. All other sources for the tragedy are written by foreigners, since the Circassians themselves were largely illiterate.

'It is now more than eighty years since the Russian government is unlawfully striving to subdue and annex to its dominions Circassia, which since the creation of the world has been our home and our country. It slaughters like sheep the children, helpless women, and old men that fall into its hands. It rolls about their heads with the bayonet like melons, and there is no act of oppression or cruelty which is beyond the pale of civilisation and humanity, and which defies description, that it has not committed,' the Circassians wrote, according to the translation appended to the letter.

The translation is in the same sprawling Foreign Office copperplate as the reports that fill the ledger, as if the translator could not bear to translate the style as well as the words of the outburst.

This was far from the first time the Circassians had begged Queen Victoria for help during their decades of resistance to Russia. They had previously written and declared their defiance, and their bravery, asking only for arms to help them resist the invaders from the north. But this time, their appeal was more pathetic and, at this remove, appears to be more touching. The men had given up hope and were seeking simply to save the lives of the non-combatants that lived among them. 'Many are the lives which have been lost in battle, from hunger in the mountains, from destitution on the sea-coast, and from want of skill at sea. We therefore invoke the mediation and precious assistance of the British Government and people – the guardian of humanity and centre of justice – in order to repel the brutal attacks of the Russian Government on our country, and save our country and our nation together.

'But if it is not possible to afford this help for the preservation of our country, and race, then we pray to be afforded facilities for removing to a place of safety our helpless and miserable children and women that are perishing by the brutal attacks of the enemy as well as by the effects of famine,' the letter said.

Previous letters had been signed by individual chiefs, each of whom had a personal seal – or at the very least a thumbprint – to go with his name. This time, the appeal was more direct: it is signed simply 'The people of Circassia'.

The letter is dated 9 April 1864. It is not clear how long it would have taken to get to London but it seems certain that by the time some undersecretary forgot about it in the files that have been its home ever since, it was already meaningless. Just a month and thirteen days after that appeal was handed to a sea captain and taken away, the 'people of Circassia' had lost their homeland. They were the people of Circassia no more, just Circassians.

The Russian government had sought to defeat them in their mountain home for most of the nineteenth century, and it did not plan to let them ever again pose a threat to its rule. A Russian general had once compared the Caucasus Mountains to a 'mighty fortress, marvellously strong by nature, artificially protected by military works, and defended by a numerous garrison'. The Russian army had conquered the fortress, and now it would destroy those military works, and drive that garrison out.

The Circassians received a blank choice: move to the plains and live like Russian peasants, or leave the country. Suddenly, the Circassians, so long the fighters called in to fight other people's wars, needed a mercenary army of their own. They did not get one. But they did get a Frenchman called Arthur de Fonvielle, one of a group of idealistic foreigners who came to help the Circassians at this last battle.

He did not succeed in winning the war for them, but he did write a memoir. His account of their struggle and their exile is the only one I know of that describes at first hand what happened to them.

Along with three Poles and another Frenchman, he landed in Circassia with a group of thirty Circassians and a roguish trader called Ibrahim, who affected poverty in order to gain a better price for his salt, knives, tobacco, bread and other trade goods. The Circassians in return sold him young and beautiful Circassian girls destined for the harems of Turkey.

'They didn't even ask much money for them,' noted de Fonvielle, as he waited for his little group to be led to war. The highlanders surrounded them while they waited, looking at them with wonder.

But despite the warmth of this welcome, de Fonvielle did not enjoy the lavish hospitality experienced by earlier visitors to the Circassian coast, for there was nothing to eat. The Circassians were boiling up tree leaves to make soup, and typhus was rampant, while three separate Russian columns marched towards them.

De Fonvielle, who had come to help save the Circassian nation, found himself witness to its end. Free Circassia was only thirty to forty leagues long, he wrote, and in places only three leagues between the sea and the closest Russian post. There are about four and half kilometres in a French league, meaning that Circassia was reduced to a bare rump of what it had once been.

He himself appears to have been a roguish character. His memoir, which was published in the magazine *Russian Invalid* in 1865, loves to pick out humorous events and phrases. But, as time passed, even this adventurer started to be appalled by what he saw.

In his first engagement, the memoir describes two Russian warships bombarding the shore with complete impunity. Some Circassians rush to the beach, only to be shot at themselves. The Circassians lost twenty people killed and about the same number injured, while the boat de Fonvielle arrived in was destroyed. The warship was unharmed. It was not a good omen for the months ahead.

As they set off down the coast, they discovered why the Russian army had for so long struggled to manoeuvre in these densely wooded hills. In Circassia, the hills plunge straight into the sea: often at a 45-degree angle, with the beach exposed to the storms which gave the Black Sea its ominous name. After the conquest, the Russians were to build a highway along the shoreline, but even in the twenty-first century the traveller has to twist and rise and turn sharply again to find a way through the terrain.

The Russian tactics more or less consisted of forming a line on the northern slope of the mountains, and pushing everyone ahead of them towards the summit. The crowds of refugees became thicker as the Russians progressed. And then the crowd spilled over the passes, and started to stream down to the sea. As they fled, they infected untouched communities with panic, and ate up their food supplies. Even if winter had not been coming, and the harvest had not failed, there would not have been enough to eat.

'We met several parties ... fleeing from the Russians. These unfortunate people were in the most sad state; barely clothed, driving in front of them small flocks of sheep, their only source of food, men, women, children followed silently one after another, leading a few horses, on which was placed the whole household's goods and all that they managed to take with them,' de Fonvielle wrote.

There were no bridges over the numerous rivers that cut through the hills down to the sea, adding a fresh hazard to the refugees' plight. De Fonvielle saw a party being washed away. His group saved just three of them, before itself being trapped in a storm on the beach.

Wet, cold and miserable, they finally linked up with a Circassian army of 3,000–4,000 near Tuapse, a river valley that is now a major oil export port, and battle was joined. The Russians brought up cannon, but even so were broken and fell back to their camp. Celebrations were muted, however, for this was a pyrrhic victory. The Circassian casualties were not far off one in ten, and more victories of that kind would destroy them, especially since anyone with a serious wound was almost certain to die in the cold and hungry conditions. The Circassian troops spent the night mourning every death with their traditional songs.

'There were fifteen or twenty of these choirs, and they all sang independently from the others; this terrible concert, which continued until the morning itself, did not allow us to even shut our eyes, which was appropriate in fact since we constantly expected a Russian attack.'

By noon the next day, only 500 or 600 Circassian troops were left, the others having died, been wounded or melted away. The foreigners realized further resistance was futile, especially since their feared local renegades might curry favour with their conquerors by betraying them to the Russians. 'Our retreats became every day more shameful; the fleeing by the people rose; the number emigrating permanently rose. From every place taken by the Russians, the settlements' inhabitants fled, and their hungry groups crossed the country in different directions, leaving along the way their ill and dying; sometimes whole groups of emigrants froze or were carried away by blizzards, and we often noticed, going past, the traces of their blood. Wolves and bears dug through the snow and pulled human bodies from underneath it.'

Even those few Circassians still fighting were giving up hope. De Fonvielle desperately dreamed of a hundred or so European troops to hold the Russians off, and to allow the Circassians to rally and return to the offensive. But they did not come. 'The highlanders were dying of cold, abandoning their posts and leaving just a few people to watch the enemy, and if it had not been winter, which interfered with our communications but also with those of the Russians, the country could not have been held. Every day the territory that we held shrunk more and more, the Russians, albeit slowly, moved ever forward, and it was obvious that with the first good days we would be finally defeated.'

In the circumstances, further resistance was pointless. They decided to leave to avoid falling into the hands of the Russians. And it is at this point that de Fonvielle's description became invaluable. His is the only extant description of the conditions in Circassia at this time, and he is the only man who described the panic that overcame the nation as it prepared to leave en masse for Turkey.

Ships were sailing from Turkey to the Circassian shore in relays, and would fill up with Circassians and leave again immediately, their

owners desperate to make as much money – or slaves, for some refugees were reduced to paying for the voyage with their children – as
they could from this never-to-be-repeated opportunity. A boat that
usually held fifty or sixty people, de Fonvielle said, now held as many
as 400. These refugees had just a few handfuls of grain and some water
to sustain them for the week's journey on the open sea. Returning
sailors described the horrors of seeing passengers thrown overboard,
of half of the passengers of some ships dying, and of fights between
the crews and the Circassians, but the refugees would not be put off.
They did not even build shacks on the shore to wait in. They just sat
and huddled in the snow and wind, fixated on building a better life
over the sea.

Here de Fonvielle was in luck, for a boat arrived captained by a
man he had met before. And this Yakub gave him a place that night.
Only when morning came was he able to see that 347 people were
packed aboard, with so little space on deck that the crew had to walk
on the passengers' heads to get to their places.

The voyage was desperately uncomfortable, made more uncomfortable for the Frenchman by the Circassians' resolve to throw him
overboard if a Russian warship came close. And then people started
to die. On the second day, the bodies of two women and a child were
thrown overboard. On the third day, two men and a woman followed
them. On the fourth day, fifteen people died. It is hard to imagine the
delight with which this cargo of the living dead saw the shore on the
fifth day, their water having finished two days before.

'If we had remained for another forty-eight hours on board, then
probably more than half of the passengers would have died, before
we got into Trabzon,' de Fonvielle said.

The Circassians praised Allah when they saw the shore, and de
Fonvielle recognized with pleasure the ruined fort of Akchakale,
which he had seen a few months before. The fort juts out of the coast
to the west of Trabzon (the Trebizond of the ancients), and was one
of two designated settlement sites for refugees near the town. When
de Fonvielle had last seen it, the fort was deserted save for a few fishing huts. Now, it was thronged. Smoke rose into the sky and, as they
sailed closer, they heard the sounds of the mourning songs. The camp

was full, and twelve other ships were offshore, already unloading their cargoes of Circassians onto the beach.

What de Fonvielle was witnessing, terrible though it appears from his description, was just a fraction of a human catastrophe on a biblical scale. Foreign newspapers began to refer to it as an 'exodus', as if no other word could do justice to its horrors.

The first accounts of the disaster that appear in the Foreign Office file that also contained the Circassians' petition are dated February 1864. This must have been before de Fonvielle's arrival at Akchakale, since a mere 3,000 refugees were based there, but already the situation was desperate.

'The quarters in the vicinity of the cemeteries are rendered uninhabitable owing to the careless manner in which the dead are buried, and the offensive consequences thereof; and whole families have abandoned their dwellings. The chief aqueduct which feeds the fountains of the town is tainted, a Circassian corpse having been found floating therein,' wrote a consul called Stevens in Trabzon.

By May, Stevens was writing that 25,000 people were encamped at Akchakale and at a second camp at Saradere, with 120–150 people dying every day. So far, the writers managed to retain their distant gentlemen's club style. But on 20 May came another letter, this one misshaped like that of the Circassians, which like their petition shatters the atmosphere of polite boredom. In Samsun, a town further along the coast to the west, the situation was even worse.

'Everywhere you meet with the sick, the dying, and the dead; on the threshold of gates in front of shops, in the middle of streets, in the squares, in the gardens, at the foot of trees. Every dwelling, every corner of the streets, every spot occupied by the immigrants, has become a hotbed of infection. A warehouse on the sea-side, a few steps distant from the quarantine-office, hardly affording space enough for 30 persons, enclosed till the day before yesterday 207 individuals, all sick or dying. I undertook to empty this hotbed of pestilence. Even the porters refused to venture in the interior of this horrible hole, out of which, assisted by my worthy colleague Ali Effendy, I drew several corpses in a state of putrefaction,' says the little letter written by the Medical Inspector of the Ottoman Empire, one Barozzi.

'The encampment presents a picture hardly less revolting. From 40 to 50 thousand individuals in the most absolute destitution, preyed upon by diseases, decimated by death, are cast there without shelter, without bread and without sepulture. Here, I will stop, for great as is the confidence you honour me with, a complete description of this unqualified misery might seem to you overcharged.'

By this stage, the press was beginning to pick up on the catastrophe, with regular updates in the London *Times*, despite the news distraction of the American Civil War. And stories came in from Inebolu, and then from Varna, to show that the situation in Trabzon and in Samsun was repeated all round the Black Sea coast.

An account in the Liverpool *Mercury* on 25 June showed conditions in Varna, which is now in Bulgaria but was then an Ottoman port, were every bit as terrible as in Samsun. Steamers had dumped the refugees on the shore, leaving them to live in the open air, and smallpox was rife. 'They say, "We all have had it, or have it now", and I can answer for the truth of this, for nearly every man, woman, and child is marked, and in hundreds the face and hands are quite raw with it. Since I have been here (three weeks) 300 at the lowest estimate have been buried in the sands outside the town. They all say they died of cold. We have had much rain, especially at night, and these poor wretches have had to sleep out in it with nothing to cover them but their ordinary clothes, consisting only – in the case of the women – of a sort of long dressing gown and a pair of trousers. After one of these nights the dead lie thick on the ground, the others longing, I should think, to follow them,' the letter said.

It took the Ottoman Empire several months to organize its response to the crisis, although even that was inadequate. The captain of a ship carrying Circassians to Cyprus was so brutal that the passengers revolted, causing him to have many killed and thrown overboard. Of the 2,346 embarked, only 1,362 arrived at Larnaca, while other ships reported seeing bodies in the sea off Rhodes. Circassians in Anatolia revolted too, and the slave markets were flooded with the victims.

By September, Stevens wrote from Trabzon that most refugees had now been moved from the town and from Samsun, having left 100,000 bodies in the hastily dug cemeteries.

A visitor today would never know now that Akchakale had once been a refugee camp. The fort that de Fonvielle saw from the sea is still there, with a scattering of houses and a mosque on the slopes behind and around it. But there is no monument, no organized cemetery, and no Circassian population. On the two days I was in the village, one of the beaches where the Circassians landed was dotted with white sun loungers, but there was no sun and no one to lounge on them.

I hunted local people to tell me about the events, assuming that a disaster of such proportions would have been passed down in local folklore, but was amazed to be greeted by looks of blank disbelief. A group of middle-aged men by the beach looked at me as if I was mad when I questioned them about Circassian cemeteries, while children had no idea what I was talking about.

Eventually, my translator and I sat down by the mosque to drink one of the Turks' tulip-shaped glasses of tea before heading back to Trabzon. As we sat and talked in English, a small crowd gathered to stare at us curiously and wonder what we were doing in their village. I kept being brought fresh glasses of tea, and kept explaining my interest in the Circassians. It was at this point I met Ali Kurt, aged eighty, who sat down at our table, fixed his dark eyes on me and began to talk as if he had been waiting for us to come his whole life.

'When I was a boy, we were planting nut trees and we found these bones you are talking about. These Circassians came here before I was born, they died of typhus, and they are buried on the hill,' he said, delighted by his audience of astounded fellow villagers, none of whom seemed to have heard the story before.

'It was a huge catastrophe. If you dig down just fifty centimetres you will find bones, like sand on the seashore, there are so many.'

He summoned his neighbour, and we drove jolting up a rough track that ran under the coastal highway, and onto the hills that tower above the village. Within minutes, we were looking straight down onto the mosque's minarets and the thin coastal strip where de Fonvielle arrived in 1864. After ten minutes or so, we came to the hamlet of Teke, which was not marked on my map, but which was the last resting place for many of the poor refugees of 1864.

A man with a white beard and a flat cap had joined us. He also remembered finding bones in this orchard when he was a boy, although now there was nothing to distinguish it from any other field in the vicinity, except perhaps for the lush exuberance of its hazel trees.

'I found a skull with gold teeth,' announced Ali Kurt, in a sudden upheaval of memory, before turning quiet when I asked what he had done with it. After a moment's pause, he admitted he and his father had thrown all the bones into the sea. He expected me to criticize him, I think ('What could we do?' he asked. 'There were too many of them'), but I understood.

Just the day before, I had walked along the base of the cliffs below the castle and found a small cache of bones in a crack in the rock. One appeared to be part of a pelvis, while another was half of a jawbone. I wondered about taking them back to the Caucasus with me and burying them, but in the end I too succumbed to the temptation for the quicker route, muttered a prayer or two, and threw them to the north, towards Circassia, and watched them vanish under water.

De Fonvielle landed on these rocks, probably 200 or so metres to the east of the fort, after his terrifying voyage. He buried his face in a stream that still skirts the base of the rock, although now it is choked with plastic bottles and old car tyres, and drank his fill. He had not eaten or drunk for two days and was weak with hunger, and was desperately relieved to be off the boat.

But he quickly discovered that he had celebrated too early. The Turks feared the epidemic diseases the Circassians had brought with them, and had ringed the camps with guards to stop the emigrants from escaping and infecting other areas. The situation was desperate. The refugees were sheltering under olive trees, with no houses or tents. They had almost no food, and they received rations from the government that were barely enough to live on. De Fonvielle watched as three boats loaded with bread came to the shore to feed the Circassians, but their loads were sufficient for just half of the crowd, and most of the Circassians were forced to go hungry for another day.

De Fonvielle decided he had to escape from this lethal encampment, where funerals filled the evenings of every day. 'Four men carried the dead on their shoulders and the family followed; the women went a little way behind, letting out terrible cries. This is called bewailing the dead. I heard this crying in the Caucasus, but in Akchakale there were so many dead people, that these concerts became intolerable.'

He searched the camp from one end to the other, until he finally found an old rogue called Akhmed relaxing in a shed. Akhmed boasted of a ship faster than any coastguard in the Black Sea and promised to take him to Trabzon.

At this point, de Fonvielle's wicked sense of black humour, perhaps unsurprisingly, appears to fail him. According to the text of his story, which I found in pamphlet form in a bookshop in the Caucasus town of Maikop and which was published by a Circassian firm, he wrote: 'You know they were my friends, my comrades-in-arms, but at the same time I knew that they were doomed to certain death; this thought tormented me, particularly since I knew I could do nothing to assist them.'

The ending surprised me, since it was so out of character. I would have expected a last rapier-thrust of wit to defuse the horror of his story. A de Fonvielle who gave in to gloom at this stage was not one who would have noticed the details he recorded earlier on his trip.

It was, therefore, with a sense of relief that I found a second edition of the essay: this time published as a pamphlet in Ukraine, and which had a distinctly different last paragraph. In this un-bowdlerized version, his tale ends thus:

'Slowly the cries of the Circassians were lost in the distance, and soon I could see only the red specks of their fires. Despite all the joy I felt, my heart was full of sorrow when I remember the terrible destitution of these unfortunates, whose hospitality I had enjoyed and whom I was now leaving, maybe for ever. The old smuggler was unmoved; nothing that happened around him disturbed him in any way . . .

' "These poor Circassians, how unfortunate they are!" I said to him, trying to find out how hard-hearted he was.

' "This is how the Almighty wills it," he replied in a quiet voice.

' "But they are dying of hunger and cold." '

'"Yes, the Circassian girls are going to be cheap this year in the markets in Istanbul," the old pirate answered me eventually, in a completely calm voice.'

And they could not be anything but cheap, being so plentiful.

According to official figures, slightly over a quarter of a million Circassians left Russia in that winter and spring of 1864. If we include those who left earlier and later, the best estimate I can find is that between a million and 1.2 million Circassians fled to set up a new life in Turkey, of whom 300,000–400,000 died.

The Circassians that survived were dispersed, some being sold, most being settled on marginal land where their warlike qualities could be of use to the Ottoman Empire, and all being forgotten by a world that had once praised their battles against the tsar's armies but had ignored them in their desperate hour of need. Their destruction was almost complete.

7. A Pear Tree in the Mountains

I stood at the base of the fort in Akchakale and wondered how many Circassians had looked out from this point towards the blue horizon of the Black Sea, and strained their eyes as if they could somehow reach beyond it – to the hills of their homeland away to the north. For those unhappy immigrants of 1864, the road back was closed. Their future lay to their south, in the villages that would be assigned to them by the sclerotic Turkish government.

But the world has changed since then. Turkey and Russia have both lost empires, but have developed trading links. Ferries run three times a week between Trabzon and Sochi: an ugly, wonderful Russian city on the Black Sea coast. I decided to catch a ride with one, to see what was left of the homeland of the miserable refugees.

The ferry ride was a twelve-hour exhausting journey in a baking cabin and we arrived twelve hours late. Still, as we approached Russia I was wriggling with excitement. I had left Russia two years previously and was delighted to be going back. I sat on the deck and watched dolphins bounding over the sea to examine us. They would approach exuberantly, then vanish beneath the waves again, disappointed to find just a dirty old steamer.

The first glimpses of the mountains came with evening. A line in the clouds was too sharp to be made of air and water vapour, and over time resolved itself into a dip between two mountain peaks. Patches of snow became visible, slightly yellower than the clouds behind, and soon touches of the mountain range stood out first in one place, then another, as the visibility shifted with the evening air. A high valley was quite clear for ten minutes then merged back into the haze. A mountain's shoulder emerged in its place. Gradually, the coastline itself rose out of the sea, revealing the densely furred hills of the lush west Caucasus, dotted with houses, some of them small and discreet, some of them the brutal towers loved by Soviet architects.

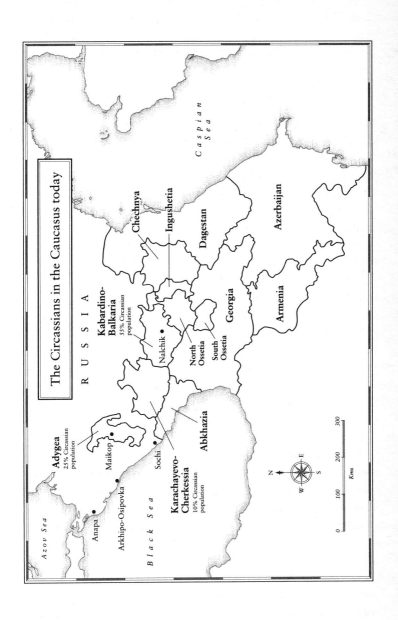

The Circassians in the Caucasus today

Although Sochi is a town that welcomes more than a million tourists a year, its impact on the coastline is less than that of resorts in some other countries. The hills remain wooded, and the tourist infrastructure is tucked away among the trees.

This is the star of the Russian tourist industry, where Stalin and other Soviet leaders chose to relax, and where they concentrated their efforts on building a holiday zone for the workers.

Sochi's use as a holiday resort was pioneered in 1872, just a few years after the Circassians left for ever. A certain F. I. Grabe, taking advantage of the combination of a temperate climate and a complete absence of people, built a villa here, and within two years fifteen other families were living nearby. The development was given a sharp impulse by the completion of the coastal road in 1891–2, which finally gave the Russians the ability to move quickly through these hills that had always frustrated their efforts to defeat the Circassians.

One Russian writer recorded: 'Sochi is our Toulouse, our Biarritz, our Bordeaux, but it stands a long way above them, because it is warmer and more picturesque.' Another, a doctor who investigated Sochi's potential as a place for treating the sick, went further. 'Sochi is not only the best corner of Russia, but of the whole world,' he wrote.

By 1902, Sochi was home to thirteen hotels, and more were being built all the time. Simultaneously, doctors built sanatoria where invalids could take the waters, and be treated with the most modern techniques.

These sanatoria were to be the drivers behind the sudden development of Sochi that followed the Soviet government's nationalization of the resorts in 1919. As it invested in industry, it also invested in holidays for the proletariat it was creating. Perhaps it did this for ideological reasons, or out of the kindness of its communist heart, but I like to think the sanatoria it built were pit-stops: where the tired, damaged workers could be repaired by skilled medical staff, before being sent back to work once more.

In the 1920s and 1930s, the Soviet Union's factories were full of danger and pollution. The workers lived cramped up, several families to a room, in damp and dirty conditions in the filthy cities or the new growing industrial towns. No human could live for long like that and stay healthy, so giving them breaks made economic and political sense.

'Centres of relaxation are organized with the aim of giving the workers and the state employees the chance of regaining their strength and their energy during a yearly regular break in the most pleasant and healthy conditions,' wrote the government in a decree in May 1921. In short, the workers would receive holidays so they could work better. They would get sunshine and balmy breezes for a week or two, then they could return to Siberia or the Arctic and eat bad food, drink too much and work too hard until next summer.

A pamphlet published in 1924 and called *Resorts of the Black Sea and the North Caucasus* praised the region for its hot springs and mineral lakes, its mud baths and its hill-walking. The only reference to the people who lived in this southern land of mountains and beaches are a handful of pen-and-ink drawings of men in the typical dress of the mountains. The implication is clear: you did not come to the south to talk to the people who lived there or to think about its history. You came to get well again in virgin territory which the Soviet Union could exploit as it saw fit. The people were picturesque details, like animals in a zoo.

The expansion in the number of holidaymakers, despite the Soviet Union's need to rebuild after the civil war that followed the proclamation of the workers' state, was staggering. In 1921, just 4,565 people came to Sochi on holiday. Six years later, the number was 21,443. By 1935, the state had given up providing exact figures, and claimed 118,000. The growth was checked by the Second World War, but took off in earnest in the 1950s, when the government stopped bothering with even vaguely specific statistics. By 1960, it said 500,000 people were coming here every year, and by the late 1980s five million were.

It was an astonishing transformation for a patch of coastline that had been home to just the Circassian tribesmen until their expulsion in the 1860s. Hotels and sanatoria dotted the shorelines, and these were the tall towers I could see from the ferry as we neared the shore. The port building is handsome, with a spire and a clock. By the time our ferry had come close enough for us to read the time, the passengers had collected their passports from the purser, gathered their belongings and headed for the stern, where we would disembark.

Apart from me, a British student called Geoffrey and a Circassian lady professor, the passengers were either Russian women or Turkish men. The split reflected the divides in the economy in the two countries.

The Turkish men were heading to Russia to work in the booming construction trade. Many of them had done it before, and the ferry was the cheapest and most convenient way to get to Sochi, where new hotels were going up all the time.

The women were a different case entirely. As we lined up on the gangplank, I spoke to two of the women ahead of me. They said they had been tourists in Turkey, and were returning to Russia to renew their visas before going back. The stories sounded flimsy. A Turkish tourist visa lasts for two months, and it seemed unlikely they could take such lengthy holidays and still want to go back for more. Besides, the towns they had visited were well off the tourist trail, too small to even be mentioned in my thick guidebook. These women were clearly not just tourists.

Then I remembered where I had seen one of them before. As Geoffrey and I had sat and drank beer in the ferry's restaurant the evening before, she had got up and done a ponderous strip-tease. She was clearly what the Turks call a 'natasha' – one of the small-town prostitutes who flooded into Turkey with the demise of the Soviet Union, and who provide to this day the raw material for the country's sex business. The two women I spoke to had been based in small towns along the Black Sea highways, presumably doing business with the truck-drivers, and never visited Istanbul or the Mediterranean coast where Russian tourists throng in summer.

The strip-teaser had been clearly seeking to drum up a little more business before she went home. I cast my mind back to the cheap hotel where I had stayed in Trabzon before we sailed, and the exaggerated cries of ecstasy that came through the thin wall from the next-door room. I wondered if any of my fellow passengers had been working there too.

We had a long wait for passport control, as is always the way in Russia, but the customs officials were friendly and the women, once they realized we were not trying to hire them, proved good company. Sochi was just the other side of a glass door, and then we were outside.

As I looked up towards the towering hotels and the neon, however, I failed to notice the threat closer to hand. Before I knew what was happening, a fat policeman had demanded to see my passport, grabbed it from my hand and marched off. Geoffrey and I had been towards the end of the queue, and the policeman had already corralled a miserable-looking group of Turkish men before we emerged. We tagged along with them and straggled after the policeman. He had a large bottom, and walked as though his trousers were chafing him, but he set a good pace and we had to struggle to keep up.

He told us to wait outside the port building, went inside with a friend dressed in civilian clothing, and began to invite us in one at a time. Geoffrey and I, as Westerners, were clearly the prized catches and had to wait until the end as one Turk after another was called in ahead of us. It was dark by this time, and the policeman's office was brightly lit. Through the window, we could see the Turks arguing over the amount of bribe they were going to pay to get their passports back. Our hearts grew heavy. After a wait of an hour, and after a Turkmen man was thrown out of the office without his passport for not being able to afford the bribe, it was our turn.

I was informed that my visa was not in order. The objections of the fat policeman, who on closer inspection strongly resembled a pig, were threefold: I had a business visa, but was in a holiday resort; I did not have a work permit, and yet I had a business visa, which meant I intended to work; the visa was issued by a Moscow company so I should be in Moscow, therefore I was an illegal immigrant. All three objections were legally groundless, but he emphasized them with an impressive command of Russian obscenities, the familiar and extremely rude 'thou' form of the verb, and a copy of the Russian criminal code, which he slapped onto the table to emphasize his points.

I attempted to argue, but he cut me off to answer a call from the window. Two women had come to ask if he would be long. We waited while he chatted to his visitors. Most of their conversation was too quiet to overhear, although from the tone it was clearly filled with female giggles and male bravado. Then he cut them off.

'Just a few minutes,' he said. 'I'm doing some business with these foreigners.'

I had no idea what right, if any, he had to enforce immigration law. I had, after all, just passed passport control so presumably my papers were in order. I did not even know what branch of the police he belonged to, since I did not recognize the three initials on his smart metal badge. But eventually, I paid the $200 he wanted, mainly because I was too tired to argue and too shocked at coming across such a revolting man. I wouldn't be surprised if he cleared $1,000 every time a ship comes in, and that would be a very useful addition to his salary indeed.

At the time, I was furious and dispirited, but after a few days in Sochi I came to realize his crass corruption was the perfect introduction to the ultimate new Russian town. His welcome could not have been more different from the generosity and hospitality with which the Circassians had greeted their British visitors in the nineteenth century, but it was certainly appropriate, for the Circassian heritage has been erased more thoroughly here than anywhere.

Sochi is a town that worships money. I rented an enclosed balcony in a grimy tower block from an old couple with pictures of Stalin on their walls. It was twenty-five minutes' walk from the centre of town, and with a view only of another tower block, but still cost triple the price of the clean little room I was to rent in central Anapa a few weeks later. The town was a mass of banks and hotels and boutiques and adverts. The adverts heaved with the transliterated English-language words that have spread across modern Russian like a fungal infection: Dizayner, VIP-shoping, Bouling, Kottedzh, Dzhiping, Rafting, Siti, Konditsioner. Every foreign word betrayed the worship of money that makes Moscow tick, and which had spread down here with the holidaymakers.

The town's wealth was reflected in its museum: far more professional an affair than those in the other towns I would visit along the coast. It was based in a graceful building in the centre of town, with two cannons out the front and a team of nosy old women manning the front desk. The Caucasus war occupied a small, delicately lit room at the start of the display, but my hopes of finding out something new about the Circassians were stillborn. Of its five individual exhibits, each of the forts that were founded in the 1830s on the territory of modern-day Sochi got one. The end of the war took up the fifth, but even that only mentioned the defeated enemy in passing, with the laconic inscription: 'after the end of the Caucasus war a mass resettlement of the Circassians to Turkey and the countries of the Middle East began.' A picture depicted a column of refugees with sheep, carts, cattle and household goods. Although they did not look happy, there was no suggestion that anyone actually died.

Next to the picture was a congratulatory telegram from Tsar Alexander II to his victorious troops. 'I thank from my soul all the leaders, the officers and the lower ranks for their excellent service, crowned by total success. I am more proud of you than ever,' it said.

The museum went on to show how Sochi developed from a rural patch of mountain into the country's premier resort town. Sochi – like everything in the former Soviet Union – has declined from its 1980s peak, of course. Its current tally of one and a half million holidaymakers a year was a long way below the five million people coming yearly two decades ago. But it has ambitions, and central to its ambitions is the greatest mountain event of all: the Winter Olympics, which is due to be held above the resort in 2014.

Circassian groups abroad objected bitterly to the first suggestions that the Olympics be held here, and they had a point. This was beyond insensitive. For the International Olympic Committee was being asked to celebrate peace and sportsmanship exactly 150 years after the Circassians' total destruction, and on the exact spot where the last Circassians surrendered.

'The Olympic flame cannot shine on a vast graveyard of nations. The Olympic spirit cannot be compatible with the spirit of a genocide. And we are sure that no Olympic sportsman would be happy to see the perspective of Olympic Games transformed into a hell for the local people,' said a coalition of twelve Circassian diaspora organizations in a letter to the International Olympic Committee before it approved Sochi's bid to host for the games.

The IOC ignored them.

'What if one of the candidates to host the Olympic Games had been Auschwitz Birkenau? Would it be of conscience and acceptable to select Auschwitz Birkenau, where 1.5 million people were systematically starved, tortured and murdered, as the Olympic host?' they asked in a new appeal.

'In a similar vein, we ask how we are supposed to accept the Olympic Games to be played in Sochi and its surroundings which became a cemetery for Caucasians as a result of Russian cruelty ... The Circassian–Ubykh nation inhabited in Sochi was almost totally massacred and more than 90 per cent of the Caucasian population in the region was either exterminated or exiled.'

Again, their words made no impact.

In Russian, the village where the games will be held is called Krasnaya Polyana – Red Glade – but in the language of the people who once lived here, variously claimed to have been Abkhaz or Ubykh, it was Kbaada. Here, in 1864, four columns of the Russian army converged on the last surviving force of highlanders, and received their surrender. The four columns paraded together and celebrated their final victory. The locals went into exile, where the Ubykh language died out on 7 October 1992 with the death of its last native speaker.

Krasnaya Polyana was deserted for a decade after their departure. Then, in 1878, a group of Greek traders crossed over the high pass into its hidden valley and saw the glorious red of autumnal bracken covering its fields, and gave it its name. A road was blasted up the narrow gorge from the sea and the village, which was the personal property of the imperial family, became one of the most prestigious resorts in Russia. Tsar Nikolai II had a cottage here (although he appears to have never used it), as did many generals and ministers.

The prestigious image has lasted to this day. Vladimir Putin, both as president and prime minister, has polished his action man image with regular skiing holidays and has used the resort for high-level meetings. The helipad Putin has used is on the very spot where the four columns paraded in 1864.

Krasnaya Polyana is a couple of hours' drive from Sochi's centre, the length of the trip depending on the heaviness of the traffic on

Resort Avenue, the main coastal highway. I visited on a beautiful autumn day, in a minibus with twelve other tourists, an Armenian driver called Rafik and an irrepressible Cossack tour guide called Valery, who started his running commentary before we had even got out of the bus station.

'You see these skyscrapers going up, cash, cash, cash, that's what they call money, it's all being done by Muscovites, and not the normal Muscovites either, these are the elite ones who've forgotten about us, who've forgotten about the people, if you look to your right you can see the famous clock on the train station.' And so he went on.

Valery wanted everyone on the bus to spend as much money as possible: lunch, honey, jeep rides, cable car rides, alcohol, souvenirs, photographs with an eagle, a bear cub or a camel. I expected him, therefore, to be rather put out when I declined any additional excursions and said I just wanted to see the sights. I had misjudged him. He was, it turned out, a keen amateur historian and declared an immediate desire to join me and to correct the errors in my historical thinking. This he did in an almost unbroken monologue, some of which I wrote down.

'These local tribes often attacked our peasants. I often argue with these Circassians. They had the chance of settling down and accepting the tsar but they refused. And you know, fifty years after the end of the Caucasus war, in 1914, they sent a delegation to the tsar to tell him how happy they were to be living under Russian laws. But sadly they did not all stay here, when the war ended, the tsar gave a condition to the local people, either move north of the mountains or leave for Turkey. They were cross with us, you see, because we wanted to abolish slavery. They did not understand this and rose up. When everyone had left these places, the animals walked around and wondered where everyone was. For fourteen years there was no one, because the inhabitants had preferred to leave their homes for a foreign land. They asked if they could come home but we said they had to give their oldest sons as hostages. They often stabbed us in the back before, they fought against us, which is why they had to leave. Circassians are like children, big children of nature, you know. I have a lot of friends who are Circassian and I say this to them. They say they invented the sabre, you know. They like to plant trees. They have this tradition that you plant a minimum of ten trees if you want to marry. And if you want to go to heaven you have to plant a minimum of fifty trees. They are just big children.'

Valery, who was sitting right next to me, gave this exhausting lecture through the public address system, as if he was still talking to a whole bus rather than just to me. Occasionally he referred to me in the plural as 'my friends' through force of habit. Meanwhile, Rafik swung the minibus through the curves up to a viewing platform giving us a panorama of the whole resort.

It was a magnificent sight, and the village will make a fine Olympic venue. The deciduous forests were dense on the slopes, and a cliff had to be fully vertical before trees failed to find a niche for their roots. As the slopes rose, the broadleaves faded into conifers and then bare rock at maybe 2,200 metres. The valley floor below was a patchwork of roofs: grey, green, orange, russet, blue, with trees in amongst them. Over to the left, the sharp higher peaks rose up towards the main Caucasus range, with glaciers and rocks and open ground.

It is astonishing that the Russian soldiers made it here at all, the passes being so high and the forests so dense. I could have stopped and looked at the view all day.

But Valery was in a hurry, and wanted me to see the zoo, which has a specimen of the rare Caucasus buffalo. We descended the hill once more, passing the new resorts being built to house big-money tourists ('... you see this cable car, that's Putin's cable car, it's beautiful, beautiful, the Turks built that, there is a new hotel, with the green roof ...') and Valery gabbled on as we drove along the valley floor to the zoo.

Although we were here to see the animals, Valery could not halt his history lecture and continued as we looked through the mesh into their enclosures. This time Rafik, the Armenian driver, joined us. Perhaps it was Valery's mention of the Turks building the cable car that had provoked it, but Rafik had started thinking about the Armenian genocide in 1915, when the Turks massacred a million of his compatriots in the Ottoman Empire. He had things to say.

'I would welcome anyone into my house,' he said, apropos of nothing, 'except a Turk. Let them recognize the genocide, then they are welcome, but not yet.' Valery, who initially looked surprised at this unexpected twist in the conversation, was vehement in his approval. He had many Armenian friends too, it transpired, and any country that did not recognize the genocide could never be a friend of his.

I had been hoping to find an excuse to ask them their opinion on the Circassian allegations of genocide, and whether it was improper to hold the Olympics on land where so many people had died. And here it was. The Turks do not recognize the Armenian genocide, I said, but then the Russians do not recognize the Circassian genocide either.

We had reached a bench under a tree, having already seen the buffalo, which stood massively in the mud. Valery turned round sharply. He stumbled at first, but soon got into his stride.

'There was no genocide, they were to blame for that themselves. They fought on the side of the Turks, this was no genocide, they left of their own accord. I have heard this talk about a genocide, but when people use their daggers to kill wounded soldiers ... well, when they were resettled, that was, well ... well, there was no genocide. And anyway, the people who lived here they left themselves, they wanted to. They had a choice, they didn't have to move to Turkey, they could have moved to the north of the Caucasus. When we pacified the people, we did not destroy them, we just told them not to attack us and then when war started between Russia and Turkey, they stabbed us in the back. So we had to give them conditions. They lived like beasts anyway, like bandits, they stole things.'

The lecture went on, but I had stopped listening. Valery was a kind, friendly man who had given up his day to show me around the village. I did not want to offend him, so I stopped asking questions and just accepted that he could not see the parallel between his own nation's crimes and those of others.

I sat on the bench, leaned back onto the tree trunk and looked up through the leaves. Valery's voice rumbled on. Hundreds of tiny pears approaching ripeness dangled between the leaves over my head.

The tree was tall, and must have been more than 200 years old considering how slowly trees grow at this altitude.

I sat and wondered about the Circassian who had planted the pip that became this tree all those years ago, and whether this tree had been one of many in an orchard, or a solitary sapling grown by accident. Perhaps he had lived nearby and tended this tree for its harvest, or perhaps he just threw a pear away when returning from the fields.

Maybe he planted nine other trees as well so he could get married. I hope that he planted forty-nine more trees though; then he will have gone to heaven.

8. Here Lived the Circassians

It is not just Sochi that is insensitive to the Circassian claims of geno-cide, but the whole coast, which – if it remembers the nineteenth-century war at all – celebrates it as a victory, not as the squalid campaign of attrition and slaughter that it really was.

A week or two later, far to the north-west of Sochi, on the cliffs above Anapa's beach, Russian tourists walked arm-in-arm along the elegant promenade. The evening sun warmed the left side of my face as I looked back into town, and gave a pleasant ruddy glow to the ugly concrete hotels thrown up for the Soviet Union's holiday-makers. Directly behind me was a white vertical slab. Its concrete sail featured a blazing sun, a woman's face and a group of four androgy-nous infants who appeared to be battling against a strong wind.

In a country not renowned for its public memorials, this one was particularly unpleasant, and a casual passer-by reading its bland inscription could not possibly imagine why it occupied such a prom-inent position. I had nothing much to do though, so I studied it, and realized as I did so that it commemorated the act that finally buried any last trace of a Circassian Circassia.

In the middle of the concrete sun, from which rays streamed down onto the back of the woman's head, were the words: 'Resorts to the Workers' with a signature and, in smaller type, 'from a decree of the Council of People's Commissars 21 April 1921'.

Without shifting my position, I could see the effects of the decree. Pink bodies lay and sunned themselves in the last glimmers of the day. Dinghies tacked round into the harbour, their captains ready for the first beer of the evening. Russian pop music boomed from a bar at my feet, where early-starting drinkers were sharing carafes of vodka and snacking on salted cucumbers and nuts.

Anapa, in the eighteenth and nineteenth centuries, was a military town. Russian forces attacked it eight times, thrice successfully, and

its possession was key to dominating both the coast and the hinter-
land. Now, old women thronged the bus station when I arrived,
offering rooms in their houses for a fraction of the cost of the big
hotels along the shore. Stick-thin women in bikinis and their sturdier
husbands wandered through the crowd. There was not a soldier to be
seen, and certainly not a Circassian.

Everything in this town is geared to mass tourism, a result of some
of the first decisions taken by the new Soviet government following
the Bolshevik revolution. In fact, the decree of 1921 is a strange one
to commemorate. Just as significant was one taken in 1919 national-
izing the whole tourist infrastructure. Anapa now has more than 600
large hotels and, though its inhabitants grumble that they are losing
custom to Egypt and Turkey, it is clean and neat and prosperous-
looking.

It is a resort for the masses, and it has erased the final signs of
Circassian culture and made what was once Circassia unmistakably
Russian.

As I wandered around Anapa, I looked out for signs of its Circassian past. The town trumpeted its history, with an archaeological
museum showing off how Greeks built a town here two and a half
millennia ago, introducing Mediterranean civilization and later
Christianity to the nomads and highlanders they traded with. But of
more recent history, there was almost nothing. The cultural museum
was closed, while a tourist booth could only offer me tickets for the
'Caucasus Legends' show, which would take place the following
Wednesday and feature the national dances of the Caucasus peoples.
I was not tempted to spend five further days in the town so as to see
it. Otherwise, there was nothing to remember the town's former
owners by except the remains of the Turkish fort that once dominated its port.

The fort was demolished in the nineteenth century by sappers who
left just one gatehouse standing. The gate now bears the name 'The
Russian gates' and stands in a delicate little park thronged by families
and snack stalls. Cannons stand around the gatehouse and children
straddled them for photographs. The gatehouse is roughly square in
plan, and its interior is blocked off by portcullises over the two

entrances. I did not at first examine the interior, being too distracted by the various shapes and sizes of the people walking by.

But eventually I walked over for a look, and saw the town had decided to commemorate those Russians who had died 'at the walls of Anapa' in capturing its fortress. The memorial was in the form of a cross-shaped military medal, bearing the words 'For service in the Caucasus' and the date 1864.

At first I could not believe what I was seeing. Perhaps the town planners who decided a reproduction of a campaign medal was an appropriate memorial were just plain ignorant. Anapa was captured by Russia more than three decades before 1864, which is when the rest of Circassia was forced to submit. The bureaucrats may not have known that, of course, and the tourists taking pictures of the cross with their phones certainly did not think there was anything out of the ordinary.

Still, there was no getting away from the fact that the Russian soldiers who died to capture this holiday resort were being commemorated not with something relevant to their battles but with a medal given out for participation in the genocidal campaign that destroyed the Circassian nation. I struggled not to interpret it uncharitably.

By marking a war memorial with the date of the Circassians' tragedy, the Russians seemed to be revelling in the completeness of their victory. No one was left here to dispute their ownership of the land. That the memorial was erected in 1996 was particularly telling, and reflected a triumphant Russian nationalism that has emerged since the end of the Soviet Union.

Once I had noticed such braying joy being taken in the Russian possession of this strip of lush, warm, sunny coastline, I started noticing it everywhere. The resorts down the coast which I visited shared the same indelicate glee that they were built on someone else's land, and a holiday I had been revelling in lost most of its charm.

To the south-west of Anapa are seven towns – Novorossiisk, Gelendzhik, Arkhipo-Osipovka, Tuapse, Lazarevskoye, Sochi and Adler – that are built on the sites of the forts built to subdue the Circassians in the 1830s. Some of the towns are export outlets for oil, but most of them are dedicated to tourism alone. Casting about more or less at random, I decided to travel from Anapa to Arkhipo-Osipovka, principally because the name is a tongue-twister and partly because it seemed to be the smallest easily accessible resort.

Arkhipo-Osipovka was founded in 1837 under the name Mikhailovskoye. The Tenginskoye fort where the aristocrat-rebel-turned-private-soldier Lorer witnessed three ships being wrecked in a storm was just down the coast from here, and this was the heart of the Circassian resistance to the Russian conquest.

The road to the town from Anapa twists and turns through the hills that line the coast. Even Soviet engineers, no slouches when it came to grandiose building projects, had failed to blast it along the shoreline, where the cliffs are simply too steep. It sometimes ducks kilometres inland before veering back on itself towards the sea once more.

Resorts and towns have sprung up wherever the road touches the sea. Our bus was forced to slow to a walking pace as we passed through the town centres, and women in bikinis and men in tight blue trunks hitched lifts to beaches or beauty sites out of town.

It is easy to see how the Russian armies struggled to master this landscape, which is choked with dense trees and scored by rocky stream beds. But, on entering Arkhipo-Osipovka itself, all historical comparison with the rugged, wild land of the Circassians became impossible.

Tanned visitors thronged the seafront, where the narrow valley, squeezed between two wooded hills, was crammed with bars, restaurants, amusements and promenades. A small artificial pond offered children rides on motorized swans, a local radio station announced popular attractions, a strip bar was getting ready for the evening, and a big wheel circled lazily.

It was a lovely place, hot and lazy, but it was cursed for me by a triumphalism untempered by empathy or concern for the people who once called this valley their own.

From the top of the Ferris wheel, you could see what a lonely place this must once have been for the inhabitants of the Russian fort here. With no port for supply ships to dock, even a small storm would have cut the defenders off from all help, while a gently sloping valley led into the heart of the dense mountains to the north. An enterprising local man has built a reconstruction of part of the fort, on a small rise in the middle of the valley, and it seems pitifully small and vulnerable when viewed from above.

This must have been something like the view seen by the Circassian force that assaulted the fortress on 22 March 1840, buoyed up by successes in capturing the forts of Lazarevskoye, Nikolayevskoye and Velyaminovskoye earlier in the year. The garrison of 440 men was in no doubt about what awaited them, and did not believe the reports of turncoat spies sent here by the Circassians to mislead them with claims they were safe. The Circassians, whose number has been estimated at 11,000 but is more likely to have been 1,500 or so, clearly were experienced by now at attacking forts and carried ladders and ropes to scale the walls with. Russian sources have very detailed accounts of what followed.

The defenders were outnumbered, and the attackers scaled the walls quickly. Hand-to-hand fighting started inside the fort itself, and immediately went badly for the Russians. They were being pushed back and defeat was going to be rapid.

Here Arkhip Osipov, one of the defenders, knew his hour had come. He had the keys to the magazine and ran towards it (stopping, the history says, only to receive a blessing from a monk). By this stage most of the officers were dead, and he was acting on his own initiative. Passing a group of surviving defenders he called out: 'Brothers, it is time! Remember me kindly! Those of you who remain alive, remember my deeds!' With these words, he threw himself into the magazine, blew it up, and wiped out the remains of the fort, most of the defenders and many of the attackers. Or so the story goes.

The Circassians took eighty prisoners, including two officers, around fifty of whom returned from captivity and told the story of Arkhip Osipov and his heroic suicide bombing.

The episode would be a small footnote in a series of skirmishes that had no long-term significance, had it not been seized on for propaganda value by the government. That this Ukrainian serf, who had served twenty years in the army and five of those in the appalling boredom and deprivation of garrison duty, should blow himself up rather than be captured was too good an advertisement for the Russian army to miss.

Arkhip Osipov was, by official decree, eternally to be named first whenever the roll-call of his regiment was read out, and his name was replied to with the words 'died for the glory of Russian arms in the Mikhailovskoye fortress'. A cross was erected to mark his feat in 1876, then the name of the village that had grown up on the site was changed to Arkhipo-Osipovka twenty-three years later in his honour. A grand, pompous memorial was erected in the garrison town of Vladikavkaz to commemorate Osipov's valour. It was topped by a Russian eagle with its wings spread and a laurel wreath in its claws.

Whether the story of Arkhip Osipov is true, or a load of imperialist nonsense, is a moot point. The fact is that the village is still revelling in its role as fore-post in occupying this land 150 years later.

I asked the family who had rented me a room if this emphasis on their military past rather than their holiday-making present troubled them, but they seemed genuinely baffled by the question. They had always been taught, it transpired, that the attackers on the fort had been Turks, themselves keen to occupy the country. That Circassians were involved had never occurred to them, and they insisted that I was wrong.

They lent me a pile of history books to help me 'understand' what had happened here and elsewhere on the Black Sea coast. The first – *An Introduction to the History of the Kuban* – was intended for quite young schoolchildren, judging by its illustrations, and is approved by the local government. It painted a troubling picture for anyone who would have liked the Circassians' fate to have been commemorated by their conquerors.

The first section of the schoolbook is a timeline. Starting with 500,000 years ago ('ancient people lived here'), it went on to mention the Scythians and the Greeks, before the one-line comment 'before the arrival of the Cossacks, here lived the Circassians'. Nothing is said of the war that the Cossacks and their Russian masters fought to take control of the land, and instead the schoolchildren are told 'the Cossacks were given the Kuban by Catherine II in gratitude for their military service', with no mention of the fact that the lands beyond the Kuban river were not hers to give.

One of the authors of the book, Tatyana Naumenko, also contributed to the *Atlas of the History of the Kuban*, which my hosts lent me as well. In it, the period 1801–60 features broad blue and green swathes on the map to mark where the Circassians lived. On the next map, which spans 1860–1917, they are gone, with no explanation.

I had become fascinated by this little bundle of historical distortion, and eagerly turned to the next item: a school-leaver's essay discussing 'literary pages in the heroic history of Arkhipo-Osipovka'. The essay, an intensely nationalistic discussion of the importance of commemorating the likes of Osipov written by my hosts' son, started with the phrase: 'Our homeland lives and will always live because millions of heroes went to death so it could live in honour and respect.' It ended with a story of a local lad who died in 2001 while fighting in Chechnya, and the quotation 'To preserve memory, and to cherish memory, is our moral duty before ourselves and our ancestors. Memory is our wealth.'

The irony of this insistence on memory in the midst of such total amnesia was too much for me. And I gave up on reading history and went to sleep.

9. The Circassians Do Not Appear in This List

Not all the Circassians left their homeland in 1864. Around a tenth of them agreed with Russia's conditions that they settle on the plain, and abandon their resistance. Among their descendants is Murat Berzegov, one of the angriest of Russia's Circassian critics. A few days after leaving the coast, I was looking for his home on the outskirts of the Russian town of Maikop, and was not having much luck.

Maikop is the capital of a Russian region partly inhabited by those Circassian families that took up the tsar's offer to move north of the mountains and not leave for Turkey. It is a nondescript town, built on a grid pattern, with its streets clearly labelled and numbered. Or so I thought, until I came to Berzegov's street, which started at house number 29, whereas Berzegov lived at number 13a. My taxi driver drove up and down the street, insisting, with ever-increasing frustration, that it had to be there somewhere.

In Russia, you pay taxi drivers by the journey, not by the distance travelled, and he was rapidly losing patience. Eventually, I paid him off and struck out on foot into a wilderness of garages and warehouses that might perhaps hide my quarry.

After a while, I came across some five-storey apartment blocks, the signature buildings of Russia. I found house number 15, then house number 13, but of house number 13a there was no sign. I asked every passer-by, of which there were very few, how to find it. I asked for Berzegov by name. No one had heard of him.

Eventually, I sat down next to a little shop in the courtyard, which had a note saying 'back in 10 minutes' tacked to the door, and waited.

Half an hour passed.

A door opened round the back of the shop, and I pushed myself up off the step I had been perched upon and went round to meet the proprietor. In a little yard, which I now saw extended to a one-storey house, a careworn but handsome woman was feeding a vast, black dog with scraps from the kitchen.

She glanced up, smoothing away a few wisps of hair when she saw me, and asked what I wanted. I asked how I could find Murat Berzegov.

'Oh, come in,' she said. 'I'm his wife. But you must excuse us, he's asleep. He has such trouble sleeping at night with everything that's going on.'

I had been looking forward to meeting Berzegov since I had first seen his name mentioned in a report from an obscure Russian news agency two years before. He headed an organization called the 'Circassian Congress' and agitated ceaselessly for Russia to recognize the destruction of his nation as genocide.

As I waited, his wife wondered that I had struggled to find him.

'You could have asked anyone you saw where Murat lives, they all know him, he's famous round here,' she said.

I had not the heart to tell her I had done just that and that no one had heard of him.

Maikop is capital of Adygea, one of the three autonomous Circassian areas within Russia. Ironically enough, it was founded in 1857 as a military base for the final push to subjugate the Circassians and was later assigned to be the capital despite being almost entirely Russian. Adygea, where only 25 per cent of the population are Circassians, has Circassian-language television, and its government building flies the golden arrows and stars of the green Circassian flag, but otherwise it is just a typical Russian provincial town, all rotting concrete and too-wide streets, and a more than usually miserable one.

The Circassians who live here are descended primarily from the Abadzekh tribe, which agreed to be resettled to the north of the mountains in 1861 and thus partly escaped the exile and death three years later that greeted their ethnic kin who remained behind. Their homeland is one of three nominally Circassian regions in the North Caucasus. To the east is Karachayevo-Cherkessia, then further east still is Kabardino-Balkaria, but the Circassians only make up a majority in the last.

The Soviets, who specialized in the politics of divide and rule, split up the Circassians into three nations. First of all are the Ady-geans, who live around Maikop; then come the Cherkess; and, on the eastern edge, are the Kabardins. The divisions are a nonsense, and their titles all derive from different names used for the Circassians. Adygea comes from the Circassians' own name for themselves, which is Adyg or Adiga. Cherkessia comes from the Turkish name for Cir-cassians, which is Cherkess. Kabardino is derived from the geographic region of eastern Circassia, which is Kabarda.

A parallel would be if a conqueror of England divided it into three states, named them England, Angleterre and Wessex, and randomly decided they were inhabited by three different nations, although they speak the same language, have the same religion and share the same customs. The splits have, however, become an obstacle to Circassians, like Berzegov, who want increased rights or recognition of their tragic past.

I walked into the little house, turned left along a panelled hall and sat in the living room, a small but comfortable place with a sofa, an armchair, piles of paper in the corner and dumbbells scattered around the floor. Berzegov's wife bustled off to wake him up, then vanished into the kitchen, from which she shortly brought the first of several trays of tea, sweets, bread and honey that punctuated the morning.

The news report in which I first heard of Berzegov described a letter sent by him to the Russian parliament's Nationalities Commit-tee. He had, in the name of his Circassian Congress, requested that Russia's parliament – the State Duma – recognize the genocide of his nation.

While I waited for him to appear, I fished out my copy of the reply he had received and sat down to read it. It is truly a fascinating insight into the bureaucratic mind.

'The Committee of the State Duma for Nationalities Issues has examined your appeal addressed to the State Duma Chairman Boris Gryzlov on the question of the recognition of an act of genocide committed, in your opinion, by the Russian Empire against the Adygean (Circassian) ethnic group, and announces the following.

'According to the data of the Russian Academy of Science's History Institute, in the Soviet period sixteen ethnic groups were repressed on the grounds of nationality, and another forty-five ethnic groups underwent partial repression. The Adygeans (Circassians) do not appear in this list,' the reply stated.

The letter, which was signed by a junior member of parliament from the Volga region of Bashkortostan and dated 17 January 2006, goes on to express a few banalities about the importance of inter-ethnic harmony for the good of the fatherland but has already made its point. It does not recognize that the massive deliberate expulsion of the Circassians, and the death from disease, starvation and violence that accompanied it, was a genocide.

The logic of the letter would not satisfy even a moderately intelligent child, since it transparently failed to answer the question. Berzegov asked about acts committed by the Russian Empire, which existed until 1917. The State Duma answered about acts committed by the Soviet Union, which existed after 1917.

On a more technical level, the reply refers to the 'Adygeans', which is one of the three Soviet-constructed nations created to undermine the unity of the Circassians. Berzegov's letter asked for recognition of the genocide committed against the Adygs, which is the Circassians' own name for themselves. It is a small but telling mistake, like referring to someone as Englandish instead of English. The fact that the member of parliament made this mistake is a clear indication of quite how little thought or research went into the committee's response.

As I finished reading the letter, Berzegov emerged into the living room, rubbing his eyes a little but otherwise looking bright and awake and happy to talk.

Berzegov is an artist and a karate coach, and of an athletic build despite his grey hair. He did not seem angry as such, but spoke with a consistent sense of outrage that never boiled over into a temper.

Since he had received this letter from the Russian parliament, he had stepped up his campaign. He set up an appeal in the name of Circassian organizations from nine different countries and sent it to the European Parliament on 11 October 2006. The parliament had promised to look at the appeal when its turn came, and he was now awaiting a response.

'After we sent our letter to the State Duma, we already started to get messages coming from acquaintances that there was no need to raise the question again,' he said. 'But we appealed to the European Parliament anyway, which meant we went outside the Russian system, and that they could not forgive. That was when they decided to do something about me.'

The appeal to the European Parliament, which was addressed to its then president, Josep Borrell, is a summary of the history of the Circassians, and how they were exiled from their homeland. It quotes the nineteenth-century Russian historian Adolf Berzhe and his estimate that of a million Circassians, 400,000 were killed in war, 497,000 deported and only 80,000 allowed to remain in their homeland.

'Russia has changed its political form several times in the 142 years since the Russo-Caucasian War, but in its relation to the Adygs (Circassians) it remains unchanged – this is the forced cultural assimilation of those of the native population who remained on their historic territory and a ban on the return of those Adygs (Circassians) exiled from the north-west Caucasus,' it concludes, in words that could not have been more different to the tale of peace and harmony laid out in the schoolbooks I read in Arkhipo-Osipovka.

When Berzegov sent this letter, the campaign against him started for real. He received phone calls late at night in pure, accentless Russian, saying that if his two sons died he himself would be to blame. Then, he said, he was abducted from right outside his house by three men who pressed a pistol into the back of his head, and told him to stop shaming Russia. 'That time they said they were veterans of the security services,' said Berzegov, with a resigned sigh. He leaned back in his armchair and awaited my next question.

There is no proof that the threats of violence against Berzegov have any connection to the Russian state, but what happened next unmistakably did.

Health inspectors, fire inspectors, food inspectors, sanitary inspectors and more started to arrive to check up on Berzegov's shop, which had sold food, drink and the everyday items that little shops sell all over the world. As soon as it opened in the morning they would arrive and start sampling.

'There are twenty-one structures, probably more in fact, that can come and check up on things. By law they can only come every three months. But if they get a complaint from a customer they can come more often. And they came so often we had to shut the shop last September. One lad has agreed to rent it off me, although I warned him what would happen. He won't last long.'

I asked him what kind of checks the authorities had conducted.

'Well, they fined us for some sausage we were selling. They say that the seller of the sausage is responsible for the taste of the sausage. But they took the sausage right from the delivery truck, they did not even wait for me to put it in the fridge before they took it away for analysis. Twenty tonnes of this sausage arrives in Maikop from Moscow every day but they only fined us,' he said.

Berzegov is clearly a stubborn man, and as these checks based on tip-offs continued, he tried to look into the allegations against him. He got hold of one letter of complaint that had been sent by a 'regular customer' of his shop. The letter was completed with all the details required by law, and Berzegov tried to find out why the writer had decided to complain about him.

The writer, it transpired, could not have been a regular customer, because he did not exist. The address on the letter could not be found on any map, there was no person with that name registered with the police, and the mobile phone number belonged to a baffled Armenian in the town of Apsheronsk who had not complained about Berzegov, had no idea who Berzegov was, and naturally did not know that he owned a shop. At this point, Berzegov realized the bureaucrats were just inventing evidence against him. Resistance was therefore hopeless, and he closed the shop down.

'This is how Russia works now. It's not about threats, they make you shut the shop yourself by suffocating you. They come and impose a fine every day, and you have no choice. If they can't find something wrong, they'll sample the air and tell you your air doesn't meet the required standards. There is nothing you can do. In a normal situation you could bribe them, but if the authorities don't like you, you can't. I can take them to court, and the court will say I was right but that will be six months later and they will already have fined me for the electrics, or for something else.'

Some Circassians, worried for Berzegov, had encouraged him to drop the political campaign and join a cultural organization that stays on the safe ground of dance, music or folklore. He said he had even been offered jobs, security and money if he would just keep his head down and join one of the mainstream Circassian groups.

'People say I am too tough, they say we should just get on with developing music and developing language, but that would be to neutralize our organization. I have stuck to my line, I want recognition of the genocide and if people want to help me they are welcome to. If they just want to play the fiddle, then they should go and play the fiddle, if they want to dance, they should go and dance. But my organization is only involved in the genocide,' he said.

'What is the point of developing the language anyway if we don't have a future of some kind? If there is no future then why bother?'

Since the end of the Soviet Union, the rise in a common sense of Circassian identity has pleased him. He said the Circassians were connecting with each other, and young Circassians realized what had happened to their nation and why they were spread all over the world. When Berzegov first came to Maikop from his home village in 1978, he said, Circassians could be stopped on the street for speaking their language as if they were foreigners. Now at least the nation had woken up.

'In my generation, we thought we had somehow just appeared as a nation in 1917. That was our understanding. As for what came before the revolution, there were only a few historians and they told us we had nothing: no history, no culture. Maybe some old people knew that there used to be a lot of Circassians here, but they couldn't talk about it or they would be accused of nationalism,' he said. 'We would sit in our village and put up the antenna and listen to Voice of America. Sometimes they would even speak in our own language, but that was the only knowledge we had that there was a diaspora somewhere.'

Although some Circassians have moved to Adygea from abroad, including a whole village from Kosovo, the numbers are few and they do not have the same rights to move back to their homeland as ethnic Russians who grew up outside Russia. Under a decree signed by President Vladimir Putin in June 2006, only people who speak Russian and know Russian culture come under the law on 'fellow citizens' which permits people whose family once came from what is now Russia to return home.

According to Berzegov, this decree is illegal, since Russian is only one of the official languages of Adygea so it cannot be insisted on. However, illegal or not, it makes any Circassian's return extremely complex, tying it up in bureaucratic obstructions that he knows only too well.

'I have always dreamed of appealing about the genocide, it has been my dream. Some people dream about a new car, a new house or a new job. I am just proud that it is my signature under that document accusing Russia. I am pleased that we have officially accused Russia of genocide, we gathered the documents. No one has ever done this before,' he said.

And he was determined to carry on, and to refuse offers or bribes or threats alike.

'I have been offered jobs, yes, but I would rather kill myself than take them. If someone else acts differently, then I won't condemn them. These authorities kill people if they want to. In the West you don't understand this, but people get killed here every day.'

With the bread and honey beside me, and a fresh cup of tea, it seemed hard to believe anything could threaten this cosy household, but Berzegov was taking the situation very seriously. He had sent his two teenage sons abroad earlier that year. He dug out pictures of them, but begged me not to say where they were.

'If I too am out of the country or dead by the time you write this, then you can say they are there, but please not till then,' he said.

The two young men looked relaxed in front of the landmarks, bright lights and taxis of the big foreign city where they had requested asylum. They smiled for the camera, with their arms round each other's shoulders. Perhaps they were seeking to reassure their dad back home.

'They will come home as soon as they have foreign passports. Then they will be safe,' he said, smiling. But I was not sure they would ever return now. They were new additions to the Circassian diaspora, living proof that the modern dreams of reunification are as unlikely to succeed as the dreams of independence a century and a half ago.

Circassians are still struggling for justice, but – then, as now – their appeals are unheard.

PART TWO

The Mountain Turks, 1943–4

10. A Red Gramophone

Osman Korkmazov was just five years old, but he had already rescued his red gramophone twice: once from two drunk German soldiers, and once from his own family. When the Soviet army came to deport him and tried to stop him taking his favourite possession with him, he knew what to do.

He started to scream.

Given the brutality of the times, he was taking a huge risk. He could have been killed outright, but he was lucky. Rather than shoot him, a kindly lieutenant called Misha befriended him, protected him and allowed him to keep his gramophone. The other inhabitants of his remote village were forced into the back of a truck, squashed together and terrified. But the little boy sat in the cab and sang his new uniformed friends 'Katyusha' – a folk song beloved of Russians.

'The truck crossed the wooden bridge across the river Koban,' he was to write more than six decades later. 'Directly after the bridge, we turned sharply to the right so the long queue of closed trucks taking all the residents of the village of Lower Teberda into exile was clearly visible.'

With the straightforward acceptance of a child, he waited for the next excitement and chatted to Misha and the driver, also called Misha. He did not realize that he was seeing the destruction of his nation, or that he would never live in these mountains ever again. He was just glad to have rescued his gramophone. It was 2 November 1943.

As he sat in the truck with the two Mishas, he told them about his life, and about his red gramophone, but of course he did not realize quite how his fate fitted into the history of the North Caucasus.

When the Circassians were conquered and destroyed by the Russians, their fellow Muslims the Karachais were largely left in peace.

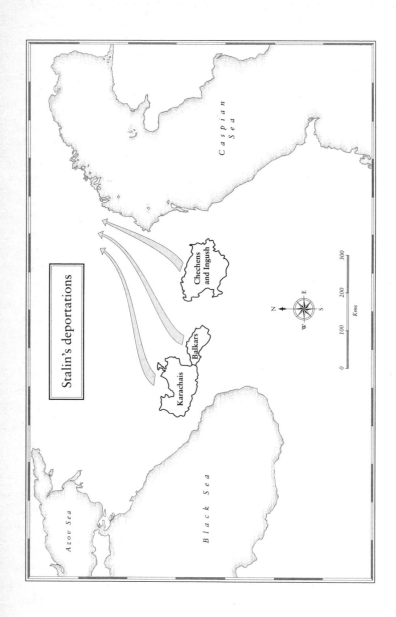

Stalin's deportations

They had submitted to Russia in 1829 and had been left to continue their untamed lives as animal herders for the rest of the nineteenth century. Occasional uprisings rocked their valleys, and some Karachais left for Turkey, where they live to this day. But only when the communist government tried to impose collectivized agriculture on them did the modern world intrude.

A series of uprisings followed, and some Karachai men fled into the hills, emerging only to steal livestock and combat the police and soldiers sent after them. Most Karachais lived peacefully, but the 'bandits' survived and clearly were fed and tolerated by the local population. Such lukewarm loyalty could not be tolerated in Stalin's Soviet Union, where the population was either mobilized or slaughtered into preserving his brutal rule.

Korkmazov's Karachai nation was the first of four North Caucasus nations that were to be stripped of their lands and dumped like rubbish onto the steppes of Soviet Central Asia in 1943–4, with the aim of ridding the inaccessible and strategic mountains of the last untrustworthy elements.

According to family legend, Korkmazov was given the gramophone as a present because 'Patefon' – a 'little gramophone' in Russian – had been his first word, reflecting a love of music that was to dominate his life. Even as a child he listened intently, enjoying sound above all as war swept around him. Born in 1938, he lived with his mother in the town of Kislovodsk – one of the fashionable spa resorts enjoyed by Russian tourists for a century already. There he learned Russian, and barely spoke Karachai – the Turkic dialect of his people.

His first full memory was also his first encounter with soldiers. He was sitting in the kitchen with his mother when the door opened, and three soldiers entered, led by an officer with a fat stomach on two skinny legs. His stomach was so large that his holster lay on it, and did not hang by his side as it was designed to do. He did not appear to have a neck, and his monstrous puppet-like face scared the young boy, who was waiting for his mother to pour him a cup of tea.

His mother stood and challenged these intruders into her home, answering them in the same aggressive tone that they used to her. This infuriated the fat officer, who reached forward and pushed off the headscarf she was wearing. She reacted furiously, he slapped her in the face and she collapsed. Korkmazov began to cry. It was an instructive beginning and, he later recalled, the end of his childhood.

'From that terrifying day I was always scared; scared for my mother and scared in general. I must have sensed the permanent threat that was all around me all the time,' he was to write.

Within days, the Soviet soldiers were gone, his mother had vanished and the town was under attack. Bombs fell all around and, with a child's curiosity, he climbed onto the wall of his yard to see them. Just then an explosion sounded nearby, blasting him off the wall and onto the ground, where he lay, his arm wracked with pain. He came to in a bed with more air-raid sirens sounding, only to be rescued by two soldiers speaking a language he did not know. He did not realize it, but the town had been occupied by the Germans. They plastered his arm, and sent him home.

So he met the second army of his short life, and, once again, the experience was unpleasant. Two drunk German soldiers stumbled into the courtyard, sending his grandmother scurrying inside. But they followed, and started hunting for food. Not finding anything, they scanned the house for valuables, and their eyes fell on the red gramophone, which sat in the corner. One of the soldiers picked it up, and started for the door. But this was more than Korkmazov could bear. With his good hand, he grabbed the gramophone's handle and began to scream. The soldier failed to separate him from it, so he picked up both of them and carried on. Luckily, a German officer who had seen the boy at the hospital was passing at the time. He angrily told the soldiers to put the gramophone down, and to let the family be. The gramophone had been saved for the first time.

'Only then did I notice my grandmother. Scared to death, she sat tucked into a niche between the wall and the stove, unable to say a word. I ran to her. My poor grandmother took me in her shaking arms,' Korkmazov remembered.

After this they were left in peace, the kind officer brought them food and otherwise they saw no one, since their neighbours had all fled. But the peace did not last long; just a few weeks after their

arrival, the Germans pulled back from Kislovodsk. They were starting their long retreat all the way to Berlin.

They were replaced by the Soviet army, and then they in turn
moved on, leaving the town peaceful but far from calm. Korkmazov's mother reappeared. She had been hiding in the forests outside
town, scared that she would be taken away by the Germans as the
wife of a member of the Communist Party, albeit a dead one. She
cried over her son, worried about his broken arm – which was by
now out of plaster – and fussed over him. But she was not with him
for long. Once more she vanished, this time arrested by the Soviets.
They would not meet again for more than a year.

For the Soviets had sent police squads in behind the advancing
army, to investigate collaborators and traitors among their own citizens. Once again Korkmazov, with the wide-eyed naivety of a child,
saw them but did not realize until later the purpose of their nasty
work. His dog Boynak, however, was not so blind. Boynak, a large
and shaggy Caucasus shepherd, was friendly to everyone, and only
ever barked at the flies that tormented him. He had befriended the
Soviet soldiers, then the German soldiers, and then the Soviet soldiers
again. But these policemen he did not like. He began to bark when
they walked into the yard. Rushing at them, he only escaped being
shot when a neighbour's son grabbed his collar and pulled him away.

'Boy, help us,' one of the two men said. 'Do you remember, did
these cursed Germans hide anything in your courtyard: bags, ruck-
sacks, suitcases? Maybe they buried them somewhere in the garden.'

Korkmazov had not seen anything and told them so, no matter
how many times they asked the question. This infuriated one of the
men, and he pulled out a pistol and screwed it into the side of the
boy's head, not so hard as to draw blood but enough to hurt.

'Speak, or I'll blow out your brains,' he shouted.

His colleague pulled him back, telling him that fear would make
the boy forget. They found nothing, but their interrogation of the
child terrified Korkmazov's aunts sufficiently to make them take their
nephew and flee. With the instinct of the true Karachais, they headed
for the mountains, their ancestral home, where they thought they
would be safe.

They packed the family's belongings as quickly as they could, brushing off the child's increasingly frantic questions about their plans. Finally, bags and cases were piled on the floor, but there was no room on the donkey for the red gramophone. Korkmazov pleaded and pleaded but the strangers who had come to guide them refused to take it. Finally, however, his aunt Dubrai relented. The gramophone was loaded onto the donkey. It had been saved for a second time.

They walked for hours, exhausting the little boy, who sat for a time on the donkey. After a short sleep, they headed off into the dawn and walked all that second day. Their journey continued more days than Korkmazov now remembers. But early one morning they reached their destination: Lower Teberda.

It was the start of a perfect summer for the boy. He was related to everyone in the village, and although their attentions were at first baffling – especially since his command of the Karachai language was poor – he soon made friends among his cousins in the high mountain valleys of his people. There were no tanks, no anti-aircraft guns, no bombs, no explosions, just the sound of the river and the talk of his family.

But the war was still felt. There were no young men in the village, since they had all been conscripted. The herding – for the Karachais were a herding nation – was done by the children. Korkmazov was among them, and they lived for the summer in a wooden hut, sleeping on cut grass, watching out for the cattle, and obeying the orders of Aimat – the daughter of his favourite aunt, Dubrai. But the summer would not last for ever, and soon they would have to descend to the village where his peaceful life was about to end.

While he had played in the mountains and watched the cattle, the secret police had been busy. Forces from the NKVD – which would later be renamed the KGB – scoured the mountains, rooting out armed men and anti-Soviet guerrillas who were fighting the Red Army. In April 1943, a decree authorized the banishment of 110 families of people judged to be bandits. Momentum was building for a solution to the unruliness of the Karachais.

The Karachais had, it was decided in a secret decree, 'behaved traitorously, joined units organized by Germans for fighting the Soviet authorities, handed over honest Soviet citizens to Germans, accompanied and provided terrain guidance to the German troops advancing over the mountain passes in the Caucasus; and after the withdrawal of the enemy they resist measures carried out by the Soviet authorities, hide bandits and secret German agents from the authorities thus providing them with active support'. On 12 and 14 October, the necessary papers were signed. The Karachais were going to pay as a whole for their lukewarm support for the government in Moscow.

'All Karachais residing on the territory of the Karachai Autonomous Oblast shall be banished to other regions of the USSR, and the Karachai Autonomous Oblast shall be abolished.'

Armed units numbering 53,327 servicemen arrived in the region. They were tasked with rounding up 62,482 people, meaning there was more than one soldier to every Karachai adult. As it turned out, those estimates were too low and they deported a total of 69,267 people. Among them were criminals, but not very many. Just 55 bandits were recorded as having been caught, along with 41 deserters, 29 draft dodgers and 184 accomplices – under half a per cent of the total deported population. The Karachai nation was paying a terrible price for the sins of the few.

Korkmazov woke up one morning to the sound of truck engines, and the shouts of male voices. When his blinking neighbours emerged into the morning light, they were surrounded by soldiers. Lorries seemed to be everywhere, and were being loaded with children, women and pensioners. A man came into the house where Korkmazov was living, and ordered them all outside. He told them to take the clothes they were wearing and food for a day, and immediately started pushing them onto the truck.

One of the old men looked out at the twin peaks of Elbrus – Europe's tallest mountain – as he pulled himself into the truck. The first rays of dawn were falling on it and had painted it red.

'Our Elbrus is crying red tears. It must be saying goodbye to us for ever,' he said tragically.

But Korkmazov had another concern: the fate of his gramophone, which had once again been deemed surplus to requirements. A soldier saw him taking it, and said it was not allowed, and Korkmazov started the screaming that saved it for the third time.

His gramophone secured, and sitting up in the front of the truck with the two Mishas, he started the long journey to Central Asia, where his people would live for most of the next two decades.

The column of trucks arrived at an empty field, crossed by railway tracks. A long train of cattle cars waited for the Karachais, but Korkmazov paid it little attention since the first Misha took him to a maize field and picked a full bag of corn on the cobs. By this time, other officers had arrived and, as the villagers climbed out of the truck, a major saw the gramophone in Korkmazov's arms.

'What is that, lieutenant?' he asked.

'A gramophone, comrade major,' replied Misha.

'I can see it's not a harmonica. Where has this gramophone come from, and since when did exiled traitors get to take music with them? Answer me now.'

'It's mine, comrade major,' answered Misha, putting it in the cab of the truck, and telling the major he had expropriated it for himself and was taking it to be mended. The answer satisfied the major, and the gramophone was saved for the fourth and last time. Korkmazov, however, was beginning to worry about other things.

'Misha,' he asked, 'what does "exiled traitors" mean, like what the officer asked you about?'

'Don't pay attention. It is just how us soldiers talk. I don't even know what it means,' replied the kind officer, whose answer calmed the young boy. Misha waited until the major was not looking, then lifted his young friend into his arms, and dashed back to the truck. He took a bullet, emptied out the lead and the powder so just the brass case remained and loaded it back into his pistol.

'There, now, pull the trigger,' he said to Korkmazov, who delighted in the feel of the gun's click. Misha then pushed the lead bullet back into the now dinted brass case. 'Take it to remember me by,' he said. Misha picked Korkmazov and the gramophone up in his arms, ran back to the wagon and loaded them onboard along with the large bag of maize.

With a last hug, he took the boy and said: 'Don't cry, all will be fine. You'll see, all will be fine. Goodbye, my little friend'. And he turned away, only to watch from his truck as the train doors were closed, and the Karachai nation was taken away.

I met Korkmazov sixty-five years later in Bishkek, one of the cities of Central Asia where the Karachai nation ended up. He was an old man by then, with nothing of the child visible in his moustache and shaved head notched with razor scars. His journey took him as an adult to Moscow, then in disgrace to the furthest parts of the Far East, then in old age back to Central Asia. He visited the mountains from time to time, but he never lived there again.

It took me some time to persuade him to let me use his account, which he has written into an as yet unpublished memoir called 'I Had a Home Once'.

He had the manuscript in front of him as he spoke. Finally pushing it aside, he described arriving in the steppes of Kazakhstan. They lived in a single room, all sixteen members of his family, to whom was added his mother, who found them in 1944, a rare happy event for by the time she came stumbling through the door, starved and unrecognizable, the tragedy that engulfed the Karachais had expanded. Like a fire that becomes larger the more fuel it consumes, it had threatened, burned and destroyed its neighbours.

11. A Dirty Animal

Khozemat Khabilayeva was a couple of years older than Korkmazov, but still just a child when her nation was scattered. Her life was saved by her dog.

She too was from a mountain village, but one far more remote than any lived in by the Karachai nation. She was from the very south-eastern corner of Chechnya, up near the border with Dagestan. This was a land that had never been governed, where the highlanders had resisted any foreigners' attempts to change the way they lived.

Now the Karachai lands were swept clean, the Soviet government paid its attention to other peoples. First came the Kalmyks, Buddhist nomads of the steppes north of the Caucasus, where the locals were accused of siding with the German occupiers. They were despatched, in late December 1943, mainly to northern Siberia, with a casualty rate more terrible than can easily be imagined.

Next came the Chechens and the Ingush, but this was an operation on a whole new scale with a whole new justification. Where there had been around 90,000 Kalmyks exiled from the barren steppe, there were more than 450,000 Chechens and Ingush being deported from some of the most rugged terrain in the Soviet Union.

The government could not pretend the Chechens and Ingush had welcomed the Nazis to their lands since, apart from one very small corner in the north-west of their autonomous area, the Germans never made it that far. Instead, a new justification was dreamed up in which the whole Chechen nation had taken the opportunity of the war to launch their own insurgency. The charges included 'active and almost universal involvement in terrorist activities directed against the Soviets and the Red Army'. The plan was codenamed, with crude humour, 'chechevitsa' – the Russian word for lentil, which is almost identical to the word 'Chechen' – and scheduled for 23 February 1944. The humour here was even cruder, since this was the official celebration day for the Red Army. While the whole country was honouring the brave troops battling the Soviet Union's enemies, the Chechens would be receiving the punishment due to traitors.

The degree of planning involved was enormous.

Even six decades later, Khabilayeva could remember how the Russian soldiers reached her village in late January. They were prepared to receive the orders to move as soon as the whole region was covered, and the Chechen nation surrounded. They came without warning, and took over her uncle's house to use as their headquarters. It was divided from her own family's home by just a wall, and they could hear the rumble of the Russian voices all day and all night, but could not understand a word of what they said.

'Maybe they were not actually Russian. They might have been Kazakhs, we did not know what nationality they were. Almost all our men were at the front, and none of us spoke Russian except my teacher. She was my cousin and director of the school. She's still alive in fact, though she's been paralysed for five years,' Khabilayeva told me.

On the evening of 22 February 1944, her father – who, as an invalid, was not at the front fighting the Germans – invited ten of the soldiers in the village to share their supper. It was a simple meal of milk, the delicious potatoes that grow in the high mountains, and cottage cheese. The soldiers seem to have appreciated it. On leaving, they made signs that he should put food in a bag and leave it by the door. The family did not know what was going on, and only later understood they were being warned about what was about to happen to them.

Early the next day, perhaps three in the morning, before it was light, the soldiers came back for her father. They entered the room roughly and took him out of the house without a word. Khabilayeva had another sister, just six years old. They sat there with their mother, and their newborn sister of ten months, and they wept for their father. They were sure they would not see him again, and cried for him as if he had died. They sat in the dark, the four of them, and cried together.

Then the dog began to bark, heralding the return of the soldiers, who gestured them to get out of bed. Khabilayeva's mother was still crying. She seems to have had a difficult time since the birth of her third child, and was incapable of organizing things for her other daughters – a task that Khabilayeva adopted for herself. She quickly dressed herself, then her smaller sister.

'I did not cry, I did not cry. I took my sister and we left the house. I did not cry then, but every 23 February now I remember our home and I cry,' she said, a sort of blank despair on her face as she said it.

The family dog was called Khola, and he was maybe three years old. A Caucasus shepherd like Korkmazov's Boynak, he was large and shaggy, lethal to wolves that attacked the flocks but gentle with those he loved. He was with her and her sister as they left their family home for the last time. The two girls looked out on the mountains of Chechnya. To their north, densely wooded hills stretched away towards the plains of Russia. In all other directions, the hills rose into a high tangle of naked peaks.

Although on the map Khabilayeva and her neighbours were less than a hundred kilometres from Grozny, there were no roads, and no trucks to carry them. The ninety-six families in her village would have to walk to the nearest point where they could be picked up and shipped off.

The soldiers were prepared, and had marked out the path for them with two wires, parallel and twenty metres apart, which served both as markers for the deportees and as telephone wires to link them to their base. As they were walked away, she looked back at the village of Khindoi, which she was not to see again.

'You could not go to either side, to the electric wire, or they beat you. There was a lot of snow that year, and there were three children with no shoes. They were barefoot, I saw this myself, but they survived,' she said. 'In fact, I heard that one of them had died just two years ago.'

The villagers had walked about half a kilometre from their homes, which were still visible, when they were stopped once more. The soldiers separated out the older women and one old man, and took them aside. The man – his name she had forgotten, but she remembered that people said he was 110 years old – had been to Mecca twice in the years before communism arrived.

'He told us not to worry about him. It was the will of Allah. He told us that the first time he was in Mecca, the Muslims there cried for the Caucasus, they said there would be war there, but they prayed for us. Then he told us not to forget each other, not to forget Allah, that Allah would help us. This old man, he spoke for five minutes. Then we had to walk further, and he was left behind with ten women. One of them had a wooden leg. They must have had orders to kill those who could not walk far,' she said.

'This woman with the wooden leg she cried out not to leave her, that they would kill her, but we walked on. We entered a gorge where a stream was, and before we were halfway through we heard it: da-da-da-da. They had shot the old man and these women.'

All over Chechnya at the time, people were streaming from the villages to the collection points. They did not know that on 29 January, after the soldiers had arrived in Khindoi even, the head of Stalin's NKVD secret police – Lavrenty Beria – signed an 'Instruction on the procedure of resettlement of Chechens and Ingush'. Beria was already in Grozny by 20 February, by the time Khabilayeva's father was preparing to host the soldiers.

With such a high-profile controller of events, there could be no one left behind. With snow on the ground, a tight schedule and a homicidal boss, it is not surprising that the officers decided it was better to kill people than to delay the plan. In a way, Khabilayeva and her fellow villagers were lucky. In the even more remote village of Khaybakh, the soldiers decided they could not evacuate everyone. So they drove the villagers they felt were not transportable – probably 500 of them, perhaps more – into a barn and burned them alive. There were to be no Chechens left behind.

The first night, Khabilayeva's villagers came to a village she called Kielo-Yurt, which may have been what is now called Nokchi-Keloy. They got there at around ten in the evening, having walked since first light. The children managed to squeeze into the empty buildings, but the adults were left outside. It was cold but Khabilayeva and her sister had their dog Khola for company. He lay down with them, his fur keeping them warm.

The second day saw them walking on to the village of Day. That was little more than fifteen kilometres away, but it was a terrible journey for young children, especially for those with bare feet. They had slept little the night before, had walked solidly for two days, but on arriving at their new stop they were forced to sleep outside. There was nowhere inside for them, but at least the children had maize straw to lie on and the dog to keep them warm. Their parents had to stand up for a second night.

On the third day, they descended into the valley of the Argun river, where transport was awaiting them and their long walk was at an end. This had been the collection point for much of upper Chechnya, and the toll had been appalling. Bodies lay in the snow. Khabilayeva remembered seeing them, the victims of typhus that was raging among the weakened women, children and pensioners being herded down from the heights.

'My mother knew nothing, she just cried. She looked for her sisters and found her oldest sister, whose sons had carried meat down. But our mother was still crying all the time, just crying. And the families were separated on the trucks, half a family there, another half somewhere else. That was where we had to leave our dog behind,' she said.

Khola, their faithful companion in the mud and snow for three days, was desperate to get on board the truck with them and, in an incongruous show of compassion, the Russian officer said he could. But Khabilayeva's father, who had been returned to his family now the soldiers deemed resistance impossible, refused his daughters permission, since dogs are dirty animals under Muslim custom. Khola's presence would pollute the Chechens in the sight of Allah and make them unable to pray. The girls were forced to leave him behind.

'That dog had come with us all the way,' said Khabilayeva.

'He took nothing from us, he didn't eat for those three days, he just walked with us and helped us. Someone had dropped a carpet because they could not carry it, and he took it in his teeth for us. He found a big jar of oil as well and we took that with us. When I lay down with my sister, he lay on us, he kept us warm. After my father said we could not take him, he was outside the truck. He was jumping, and jumping. He jumped for hours, barking, trying to go with us. That dog was like a person.'

She lowered her head and cried now for the first time since our conversation began. Her face was hidden by her white headscarf, but I could see the wet marks on her hands as she dashed the tears away. After some time, she resumed her story.

'I have used that name Khola for two other dogs since then, but I always remember him alone. He jumped and jumped, he barked for us, but he could not get in. Then the truck reversed. It went backwards. He was killed.'

The trucks carrying the villagers of southern Chechnya pushed down the Argun gorge to the plains, where they could meet the railway and the third phase of Khabilayeva's deportation began. The cattle cars that would carry them were divided in two by a horizontal floor to allow more people to be packed inside. A hole in the floor acted as a toilet, but no one would use it, being too ashamed to do so in public. This shame has been one of the enduring legends of the Chechen deportation, and many young Chechens today will tell you how their female ancestors were so ashamed to use the toilet that their bladders ruptured. I have never met someone who claims to have seen a case of it, but many Chechens have told me that this happened.

An American academic called Michaela Pohl asked some medical experts if it was possible for someone's bladder to rupture through refusal to urinate, and they said it was not. They said spontaneous incontinence would set in before that stage. Nevertheless, Pohl was told by a 63-year-old deportee that a fellow passenger had died of a ruptured bladder, almost as if it was something to take pride in.

'Former deportees clearly valued this memory and referred to it often, not only when describing the terrible hardship of transport, but when asked about the upbringing of young people more generally, and to emphasize the strength of their traditions even during the worst circumstances,' concluded Pohl.

Khabilayeva was lucky. She said she simply refused to use the hole in the floor as a toilet, instead waiting for the train to stop. At stops, which were frequent enough for the girl to survive from one toilet break to the next, the guards would give them food, including the first herring that Khabilayeva had ever seen. They travelled for twenty-six days, sitting on the upper level in their carriage, the family below them being the one with the barefoot children and another woman with her son, who was all dressed in red. He was quiet and never spoke. It turned out, after three or four days, that he had died quietly, a victim of the typhus that had raged among the quiet columns of hopeless highlanders. His mother had managed to secretly sew him into a shroud without anyone noticing.

'She asked my father and others to take him away, further from the train. My father said they found a hole in the ground and covered him up. The mother did not cry after that, knowing he was in the earth,' said Khabilayeva, again pushing tears away.

'For us, it is only men that do the burying. And she asked them to take him away. "Please take him away," she said, this mother said. I still cannot forget this, how can I forgive what those soldiers did to us?'

The train stopped in the steppes for forty-one days after that, leaving the deportees to more or less fend for themselves with no instructions and no hope. They had almost nothing to eat, just grass for days at a time. There was orach, a herb, which people ate.

Khabilayeva's father said they should not eat it if it was pink, because it was dangerous. It is not clear how he could have known that, for orach is a plant that only grows in near-desert and not in the high mountains of his home. He was right though, for it can be poisonous. But people did not listen to him; they were so hungry they would have eaten anything.

After a while, they moved on to what is now the city of Almaty, which the deportees were expected to build into a proper capital for Kazakhstan. Behind them the lowland homes of the Chechens and Ingush were taken by foreigners, by Russians, Ossetians, Armenians and other favoured nations. The mountain villages were left empty.

Here in this new land, they had nothing. They had been taken in wintertime to a country that did not want them and did not know how to feed them.

'I saw how my cousin, my second cousin, died of hunger,' said Khabilayeva, her eyes hard now and remembering, the tears gone. 'This was a month after we arrived at our destination, he was eleven years old. We used to know the time from the sirens of the factories. He asked me when the siren would be, and I said soon. He went to sleep and just died there, with all this green stuff coming out of his mouth. His father had died in the camps in 1937, they sent him to the north because he was religious.

'We children, we went everywhere and collected salt or whatever and sold it. The salt came from the railway wagons, and we collected it from the corners where it was left when the wagons were swept out. In the summer we would collect grain in the fields, then in 1946 we started to plant maize. And there would be fish brought in on the trains, and bits would be forgotten in the corners of the cars. We survived, we worked, despite being children. I worked from the age of ten.

'My father was assigned as a street cleaner, but he was ill with his kidneys, so I worked for him. I worked every day, I would not let him work. I never learned to write then, and never have.'

So we finished our conversation and Khabilayeva sat there with me drinking tea. She is still in Almaty, a city she built and which is now the financial centre of Kazakhstan – a whole new state. She has a house that she built herself, and her children live around her. She still wanted to go home, she said, but the Caucasus was a dangerous place. And besides, she could never really go home, because the Chechens have never been allowed to return to Khindoi. Her village died the day its people left and, sixty-four years later, she was one of the few people who knew it had ever existed.

12. Three Little Boys

Even before Khabilayeva's nightmare trek was over, Beria looked for more work to do. He was in the Caucasus still, and his gaze settled to the east once more: on the Balkars.

The Balkars were ethnically the same as the Karachais. They too were Turkic herders tucked away among the highest mountains of the range, but they lived to their east. The tsarist conquerors had assigned them to a different region from their kin, and this was a distinction that had persisted under the communists. Soviet bureaucrats, who liked to fragment nations as far as possible so as to make them easier to control, decided to make the administrative division into a national one, and declared nonsensically that the Balkars were a different nation to the Karachai. Perhaps they hoped that would make them easier to rule.

Despite this distinction, however, the Balkars were to share the same fate as their fellow Turks, whom they followed into exile.

'The enemy elements in Balkaria have not stopped their active anti-Soviet work and after the regions of the North Caucasus were cleansed of the Germans, they have found support from the Balkar population. In connection to the forthcoming end of the operation to deport the Chechens and the Ingush, I think it would be advisable to use part of the freed-up troops and security forces to organize the deportation of the Balkars from the North Caucasus,' wrote Beria to Stalin on 24 February 1944.

He had agreement just two days later. The State Defence Committee issued an order on 5 March, and the operation commenced within three days. The whole scheme, from conception to completion, took just twelve days.

I met Tokai Makhiyev, along with two of his oldest friends, at a wake just outside the city of Nalchik in the central Caucasus in 2008. The whole extended family had gathered to mourn his nephew in a ceremony that takes place fifty-two days after a death, not forty days after like everywhere else in the Caucasus. Despite this difference, the Balkars share the culture of hospitality common to the whole Caucasus, and the table was laden with tripes, with mutton and with little steamed parcels of meat in pastry. When I told them I was a vegetarian, bread and honey were placed at my elbow.

The Makhiyev family had lived in the village of Belaya Rechka just outside Nalchik, rather than in the mountains proper. Their village had been occupied by the German army, and he remembered how they had sheltered three Jewish families during the few weeks that the anti-Semitic troops were scouring the land for Jews to kill.

'They were children – Lyuba, Zima, Genna, Mark – and their mother's name I do not remember. We used to say they were Armenians, not Jews, so that nobody knew. They lived with us in Belaya Rechka until the Germans were thrown out, then they returned to Nalchik. They must have known that the deportation was coming because, two days before it took place, one of the women came to us and said we must go and hide with them, because we were all going to be sent away,' said Makhiyev, who was seven at the time of the deportation but a distinguished seventy-two during our conversation, pausing to sip tea.

'My mother went to her father to ask him what they should do, and he said he had lost three sons for the Soviet government, one son at the front, and two making roads through the mountains in the 1930s. He said the Soviets would not harm his family, and we did not need to leave.'

On 7 March, a handsome officer and two soldiers came into the Makhiyev house and wrote down the names of the family members, sending Makhiyev's mother into a panic. She realized that her Jewish friend's story was true, and decided they would get up early and hide with them. She got everything ready that night, and all they had to do was dress and leave.

'We got up at five that morning, and it was dark and I couldn't put on my shoes. My big brother mocked me for it, I remember that. Then there was this knock-knock-knock, and the handsome officer, he was so arrogant, with his two soldiers was back. They asked if we had a rifle, and searched everything. My mother's brother worked for the security organs, and there was a picture of him in uniform on the wall. They asked who he was, and my brother told them and said he had been in Sevastopol, but had been captured or killed, because it was occupied. They just threw us out then. It turned out this officer stole our things. He kept the key anyway,' remembered Makhiyev.

Like all the witnesses to these events still alive, his view was skewed by being seen through the eyes of a child. He retold his youth with total simplicity: the accepting nature of childhood, combined with the resignation of the elderly.

The villagers in Belaya Rechka were herded into a field, and ringed by soldiers with machine guns. One of Makhiyev's neighbours – called Bert Gurtuyev, apparently – was an officer home on leave, but that did not save him. The troops took away his pistol and packed him off to stand with the others, still in his uniform, for the rest of the day.

This day was technically a holiday. Beria had chosen Red Army Day to deport the Chechens, and had clearly decided that juxtaposing a tragedy and a celebration was too funny a joke to resist. The Balkars had been scheduled for exile on 10 March, but he brought it forward two days. March the 8th, celebrated throughout Russia with flowers as International Women's Day, is marked for the Balkars now by tears, as the day they left their homes.

But Makhiyev and the other children had no idea where they were going. Although they cried from thirst and hunger, they were excited as they looked at the trucks. They thought they might be going to Moscow, which is what one officer told them was happening. The pleasant lie kept them happy while they were loaded onto the cattle cars, and sent to follow the Karachais and the Chechens to Central Asia.

By this stage, Beria's forces had become expert in deporting civilians. Beria reported to Stalin on 11 March that the operation had been finished in twenty-four hours: 37,103 Balkars had been deported to Central Asia, 478 people of the 'anti-Soviet element' were arrested, and 288 firearms were seized.

The organization was spectacular. Most of the Balkars lived in the high, narrow valleys that plunge into the Caucasus massif. They are separated from each other by high ridges, crossable only on horse-back or with the most rugged vehicle. Every valley was swept of people individually and, although Beria had sought to get the job done by the time leaves were on the trees, the troops still had to trek to isolated hamlets where the men and boys were looking after the livestock.

Sitting at the table with Makhiyev and me was Khussein Kuliyev, who was twelve years old in 1944, and thus already doing a man's work in the mountains. As soon as his friend finished his account, Kuliyev launched into his story, about being with his grandfather in a mountain hamlet called Zhuongu.

'One morning my grandfather woke me up and told me soldiers had come. Maybe, he said, one of them was my father, who was at the front, so I ran to meet them. But my father was not there so I ran back. I was scared. They checked everything, they were on horses. The next day, my grandfather wanted to feed a calf, which had just been born, to make sure it had milk. But when we went out there were three more soldiers, and they would not let him feed it. They said gather up everything you have and they drove us off on foot. We walked for nine or ten kilometres, we did not know where we were going. I said to my grandfather that I wanted to eat, and one soldier heard me. He must have been a Tatar or from Azerbaijan, or one of the other Turkic peoples, because he understood our language and he gave me cheese,' Kuliyev remembered.

Finally they reached the lower village, and there found Kuliyev's mother and his four sisters all gathered in a field. They were loaded onto trucks then driven out of the village. But the road was bad and they had to dismount and walk over every bridge. Their aunt Fatimat had come to stay with them and as they passed through Lower Che-gem, she saw her children standing with the crowd.

'She cried out that those were her children, to let her out, but the soldiers hit her with their rifles and we just drove further. She had a three-year-old daughter who she wanted to take but they would not let her,' he said.

After the long train journey, the Balkars were unloaded in the steppes of Central Asia where factory directors or collective farm chairmen would choose those they wanted. Obviously, young adults were the most popular, since they could work and would not have children who put a burden on the schools and ate food without being productive. As such, the Kuliyev family with five children and just one adult was left unpicked when everyone else had gone.

'These collective farm chairmen, they came on camels or whatever. In the end, a Kazakh man came in a wagon and he saw us children there and he took us. He said he would take everyone. He put us in the village club to sleep. It just had an earth floor for us but it was only for one night, after that he freed up rooms for us. He was a kind man, he helped us, he gave us a metal oven, he helped us with corn. He was called Mukhash. I remember that, but I cannot remember his surname. He was a kind man.'

After the Balkars, Beria's attention moved on. Other nations would be deported – the Crimean Tatars, the Meskhetian Turks, the Soviet Greeks, and others – but they were not from the North Caucasus. Moscow's perpetual problem of governing the Caucasus had been solved. From the Black Sea – once Circassia – to the borders of Dagestan – where the ethnic map is so knotted that not even Beria could unravel it – the highlanders were either cowed or wiped out.

Moscow was, it was intended, never to be troubled by the Caucasus again. The troublesome highlanders had been kicked out of the highlands.

13. The Double-Headed Mountain

The high valleys of the Karachais and the Balkars were discovered by the outside world in 1868, when a party of Englishmen, their Swiss guide and Georgian servants slipped and stumbled down a glacier into the Upper Baksan valley. These valleys had never seen anyone like them before, although the foreigners themselves had had an indication they were about to enter a world where normal rules did not apply before they even crossed the watershed. As they toiled up the slope to the pass out of Georgia, they passed four men hurrying eleven cows down from the clouds. These, it transpired, were men from the Georgian village of Lashrash who, 'according to custom, had been on a cattle-lifting expedition over the pass, and were now returning with their unlawfully-gotten booty, stolen from one of the herds belonging to the Tartars of the Upper Baksan'.

Douglas Freshfield, the writer of those words, had reason to be apprehensive about what he would find beyond, especially since his porters were mainly Georgian – the traditional foe in cattle deals of the people they were about to meet.

But he need not have worried. He was shortly to arrive in one of the most traditional pockets of Caucasus culture, where hospitality was strong and even in the 1860s the hand of the Russian government was rarely felt. His group was made welcome in the village of Urus-biye, and treated with great kindness.

His party was not here just for fun, however. He too wanted to conquer the Caucasus, but to do so not with weapons but on foot. He had already achieved the first ascent of Mount Kazbek – the great bishop's mitre that dominates the road from Russia to Georgia – and now he would attempt Mount Elbrus, the tallest mountain in the Caucasus, and thus the tallest in Europe.

Freshfield, perhaps the foremost mountaineer of his day, was bored of climbing in Switzerland. The peaks had been conquered and the

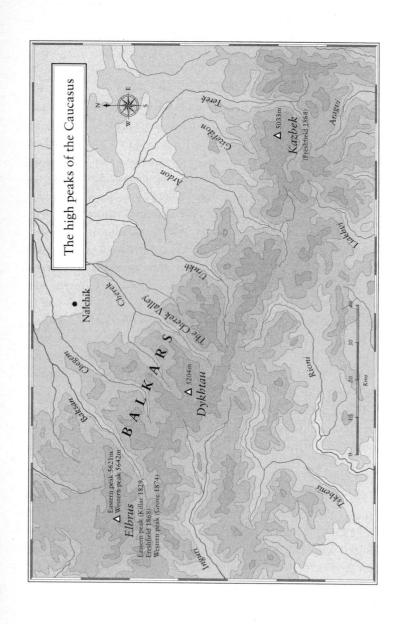

The high peaks of the Caucasus

Elbrus
Eastern peak: 5621m
Western peak 5642m
Eastern peak (Killar 1829,
Freshfield 1868)
Western peak (Grove 1874)

BALKARS

Nalchik

Baksan
Chegem
Cherek
The Cherek Valley

Dykhtau
5204m

Urukh
Ardon
Gizeldon
Terek

Kazbek
5033m
(Freshfield 1868)

Ingur
Tskhenis
Rioni
Kms
0 10 20 30 40

Liakhui
Aragvi

N E S W

mountains were getting crowded. On coming to the Caucasus, he found a new landscape of soaring peaks, tight valleys blocked by glaciers, villages of strange, burrow-like homes crowned with defensive towers, and lush green grazing for the cattle of the highlands. Here there were no other tourists, and here were villages that had never seen a western European before. Freshfield was stunned by the lost world he had found.

He engaged in an ambitious and risky trek from Kazbek, along the southern slopes of the Caucasus into the Georgian region of Svaneti, which is legendarily lawless even today. Crossing the pass into the land of the Turkic cattle-herders now called the Karachais and the Balkars, he approached his new foe – Elbrus.

In fact, his group scaled the great double-peaked mountain with little difficulty, except for the extreme cold, for it is not technically demanding. Their only major annoyance was a flock of sheep that resented their tent and spent the night assaulting it. On arriving at the peak, they saw a view they felt no one had seen before.

'Light clouds were driving against the western face of the peak, and a sea of mist hid the northern steppe – otherwise the view was clear. Beginning in the east, the feature of the panorama was the central chain between ourselves and Kazbek. I never saw any group of mountains which bore so well being looked down upon as the great peaks that stand over the sources of the Tcherek and Tchegem,' noted Freshfield, before the cold drove his party down to the plains again.

On their return to Urusbiye, they were heroes. Much of Freshfield's book *Travels in the Central Caucasus and Bashan* is a complex account of precise routes he took and gripes against the inaccuracy of the Russian map, but occasionally he allows himself to talk about the people he met. This was one of those times.

'Several minutes passed before the story was fully understood: our burnt faces, and the partially-blinded eyes of the two men who had accompanied us, were visible signs that we had in truth spent many hours on the snowfields, and the circumstantial account and description of the summit given by the porters seemed to create a general belief in the reality of the ascent,' he wrote with pride.

'The scene was most entertaining. The whole male population of the place crowded round us to shake hands, each of our companions found himself a centre of attraction, and the air rang with "Allah"-seasoned phrases of exclamation and astonishment, mingled, as each newcomer entered, and required to hear the tale afresh, with constant reiterations of "Minghi-Tau!" – a familiar name, which sounds far more grateful to the ear than the heavy-syllabled Elbruz.'

The villagers, he assured his readers, said no one had ever scaled Elbrus before so British people everywhere could take pride that here was yet another natural obstacle ground under an English-made hobnail boot. It was a triumph for the empire that was delving into the unknown hearts of all the continents on earth.

The only trouble with his glorious achievement is that it was not true. He was not the first man to stand on that peak and exult over the view. A local man had beaten him to it almost four decades earlier as part of a Russian expedition to the lands of the Turkic herders in 1829.

The mission was led by the Russian General Georgy Emanuel, commander of the Caucasus Line, who was desperately trying to prevent an uprising by the tribesmen of the central part of the mountain range. Russia was locked in the war with Turkey that would eventually win it the Black Sea fortress of Anapa, but at the time the result was not certain.

Emanuel feared that if the Turkic mountaineers in the central Caucasus rose up, they would connect the warring Circassians to the warring Chechens and threaten Russian control over the whole of its southern frontier.

Short of troops, but determined to prevent such a disaster for the tsar's army, the general had a great idea. He would take a scientific expedition to Elbrus – collect animals, gather a few rocks, measure some heights and distances, march about – and thereby show the local tribesmen the Russian flag.

He set off, according to a contemporary biographer, from Pyatigorsk in late June. Arriving at a bridge over the river Malka, which is about halfway to the mountain, his small force of soldiers and scientists was met by a deputation of tribesmen. Ostensibly here to show respect, the elders – the biographer said – were in reality concerned that the Russians would destroy their homes in retaliation for destruction caused in the war against Turkey.

The tribesmen had fortified their villages, and retreated into the heights with their weapons, while the delegates worriedly sought to find out the general's intentions. The general was apparently quite a politician and assured them they had nothing to worry about.

'Since they had already sworn allegiance to Russia, then he counted them Russian subjects, and he would have to answer before the Emperor if he even thought of doing them any harm; on the contrary, they, with their kind bearing and humility for all this time, had earned the right of friendship and protection from the Russians; his arrival with a few scientists only showed a desire to know their country, collect plants, stones, animals, and that he, taking advantage of the kind disposition of the Karachais, wanted only to come to Elbrus, which no one had yet reached, and would not even step into their houses,' Emanuel's biographer wrote.

A few presents cemented the good impression, and instead of being greeted with war, the Russian expedition gained many new members who decided to come and have a look at the mountain as well. A week of bad weather delayed their plans, but eventually, on 9 July, the expedition was encamped at the very foot of Elbrus and the assembled Cossacks and 'Circassians' (this word is likely to have meant 'highlanders', rather than people who were necessarily ethnic Circassians) were told that he who arrived on the summit first would receive the princely reward of 400 roubles.

The group of academicians and their guides reached the edges of the snows in the afternoon of that day and settled down to sleep on the mountainside. They started out the next day at three in the morning, and toiled further upwards. But they started to suffer great discomfort, as is hardly surprising since they can hardly have been in condition for scaling a 5,642-metre mountain and lacked climbing equipment of any kind.

'The thawing snow, the stones and cliffs which were impossible to avoid, and the sun rays reflected off the snow, made continuation for the academicians difficult at a height of 14,000 feet and even impossible; they had, they thought, still 1400 feet till the very top,' the biographer's account relates. They were very much mistaken. 14,000 feet is equivalent to almost 4,300 metres. If their height measurement was correct, they were still more than a kilometre below the summit, rather than the 400-odd metres they calculated.

One academician called Lents, together with two 'Circassians' and a Cossack resolved to go still higher, but they too halted before the summit, resolving to turn back. This left one man, identified as just Killar, to push on alone.

It is he, and not Freshfield, who can claim to have first set foot on the mountain's summit.

'At 11 a.m. he found himself on the very peak of Elbrus. General Emanuel, watching from the camp with his telescope, first saw Killar, standing on the summit of Elbrus, and all those around confirmed it with their own eyes. Cannon fire alerted the whole camp. While Mr Lents, who did not have the strength to go further, collapsed from tiredness, Killar managed to return from the summit, and arrived in the camp a whole hour before the academicians,' the book claims.

Brave Killar received his 400 roubles from the general, plus some fine cloth for a new tunic and the honour of the first champagne toast at luncheon. The mountain was, it would seem, already conquered before Freshfield came near.

Killar's claim of glory has been much mocked, mainly by British writers, but it is essentially believable. The length of time it took Killar to climb from the night's rest spot to the summit – eight hours – is similar to the time taken by Freshfield, although whether the conditions were really sufficiently clear to allow Emanuel to see a lone man on the summit is a different matter.

But the controversy does not stop there. Emanuel's biographer, Prince Golitsyn, identifies Killar specifically as a Circassian from the region of Kabarda, but this has not stopped Turkic tribesmen claiming him as ethnically one of their own. He is variously identified as Chilar Khashirov (if he was a Circassian) or Khilar Khachirov (if he was a Turkic tribesman), or even Kilar Heshire (by Circassian historians in exile who dislike the Russified surnames used in the Caucasus today).

It is hard to blame Freshfield for overlooking his claim. The account quoted above is from an obscure volume called *Life-Sketches of Cavalry General Emanuel* and was published in Russian seventeen years before the Englishman visited the Caucasus. Besides, the event does not appear to have remained in local memories, since he does not report anyone mentioning it.

However, there is a twist in both Killar's and Freshfield's achievements, which is that Elbrus has two summits. Freshfield, we know, ascended the eastern peak, which is lower than its western brother by just twenty-one metres.

The account of Killar's ascent does not specify which peak he climbed but later in the book it records that one of the expedition's achievements was fixing the height of Elbrus's eastern peak at 15,420 feet. Had the western peak been visible, they would have measured its height as well. And if the western peak was not visible, the general could not have seen Killar ascend it. It would seem, therefore, that Killar also only managed to scale the slightly smaller eastern summit of the two-headed mountain.

Incidentally, the height the book gives for the eastern peak is too low, but does chime with the climbers' estimate that their altitude when they stopped was 14,000 feet, and that the amount they had left to climb was 1,400 feet. They may have been using faulty equipment which miscalculated their height by 900 metres, and, if so, Academician Lents reached a heartbreaking 5,200 metres before turning back.

Anyway, be that as it may, both conquerors of Elbrus climbed the smaller summit, so the mountain was still, even after the Freshfield expedition, technically undefeated. And it would remain so for another six years. Fortunately, therefore, for Freshfield, he did not allow himself to relax but continued exploring the region and taking notes. He blazed the trail for the eventual conquest of Elbrus, and was the first Westerner to visit the valleys to the east of Elbrus, home of the Turkic nation later to be dubbed the Balkars.

'[T]he natives of this and the upper valleys next to the east consider themselves a distinct race from the Tcherkesses [Circassians], who dwell on the verge of the steppes, and in the mountains to the westward. The people here claim to be the old inhabitants, and to have been dispossessed of their ancient supremacy when the hordes of Tcherkesses from the Crimea inundated the country. Their language is Tartar [Turkic], and their religion, as far they have any, is Mahommedan; the princes seemed, however, to be very broad and tolerant in their views,' wrote Freshfield in *Travels in the Central Caucasus and Bashan*, now a mountaineering classic.

He had certainly found a more challenging venue than Switzerland. Where Switzerland was close to the rich cities of western Europe, and thronged by visitors in summer, these high valleys and mighty peaks were completely unknown. And the peaks were truly enormous. Elbrus is 800 metres taller than Mont Blanc, the highest point in the Alps. It stands north of the main chain of the Caucasus and dominates the whole northern side. To the south, the peaks are scarcely less staggering and technically far harder to climb. They include Dykhtau, of 5,204 metres, and, further east, Kazbek of 5,033 metres.

The valleys that burrow into this vast massif of rock are narrow and inaccessible, meaning their inhabitants were scarcely bothered by the outside world, despite having technically submitted to Russia in the year of Killar's ascent of Elbrus thirty-nine years previously.

'The imperial sway of Russia does not press hardly on these mountaineers,' wrote Freshfield, 'who pay only a light house-tax, are exempt from conscription, and are too remote to be exposed to those petty restraints which a once-free people often find the hardest to bear.'

Power was still in the hands of the traditional chiefs, and the communities seem to have shared the easy democracy of the mountain Circassians, rather than the more structured government of their neighbours on the plains.

'Their local government has been generally described as feudal; it seemed to us that patriarchal would be the more fitting word. The princes are the recognised heads of the community; they live in a house four times the size of any other in the village, they are richest in flocks and herds, and on them falls the duty of entertaining strangers; but their word is not law, and they can only persuade, not compel, their poorer neighbours to carry out their wishes,' said Freshfield, who had ample opportunity to see how these 'princes' – in reality, just headmen – behaved, since they welcomed him and his companions to their villages and gave them beds for the night.

It is something of a mystery where these Turkic highlanders come from. As seen above, they themselves claim to be the original inhabitants of the country, and that the Circassians and others came from elsewhere and stole their best land.

One old Balkar man I talked to on a visit of my own to the high Caucasus told me his people were the ancient Etruscans, who had spread from here to pre-Roman Italy without, mysteriously, leaving any traces in between of their passing. Another Balkar told me in all seriousness that Shangri-La or Shambala, the pure land of the Tibetan Buddhists, was at the foot of Elbrus and that the traditional Turkic religion had given rise to several of the faiths of Asia.

The Karachai-Balkars are now Muslim, and proudly so, although Freshfield reported that substantial elements of folk beliefs clung on in their villages. He and his companions had to tell their welcoming committee, when they descended the mountain, that there was not, in fact, a 'gigantic cock' on top of Elbrus who welcomed the sunrise every day by crowing and flapping his wings, while guarding a treasure against all intruders. 'We could not even pretend to have had an interview with the giants and genii believed to dwell in the clefts and caverns,' he added.

Turkic peoples are scattered all across the former Soviet Union, from the Tuvans of Siberia via the Kyrgyz, Kazakh, Uzbeks and Turkmen of Central Asia, the Tatars and Bashkirs of the Volga, the Kumyks and Nogais of the plains north of the Caucasus, the Tatars of Crimea, and the Azeris and Meskhetians of the south Caucasus. Most of them, with the stark exception of the mountain-dwelling Kyrgyz horse-herders of Central Asia, lived traditionally on the plains and it is odd that Turkic tribesmen should have ended up as the owners of the highest portion of the Caucasus.

It seems most likely that they were pushed into hills by war, or else followed their herds to the lush mountain meadows where there is plentiful grazing for cattle, sheep and horses in summer.

John F. Baddeley, a British traveller, journalist and entrepreneur whose knowledge of the Caucasus was unrivalled by any foreigner at the turn of the century, recorded a number of legends that give a possible explanation as to how the Turkic peoples came to be here. The prominent Aideboloff and Abayeff families were, he said, founded by two brothers who came from the east with the armies of Genghis Khan, but killed a prominent man and had to flee to the mountains. Misaka, the founder of the Misakoff family, meanwhile, had quarrelled with the Kumyk people of the plains of northern Dagestan and also fled.

A more romantic story clung to the origins of the Balkarokoff family, which, we hear, was founded by a Circassian called Anfakho who settled in the Upper Baksan valley. His family lived there quietly until one descendant, called Akhtougan, got ideas above his station. He rode to the Dagestani town of Tarku, where a ruler called the Shamkhal enjoyed supreme power, and waited for a celebratory dance, from which he stole the Shamkhal's daughter. Fleeing into the Baksan, he was unnoticed for two years. Eventually, however, the fruits of his victory began to pall and he wanted recognition of his royal connections.

He returned to Tarku and, with commendable cockiness, sought reconciliation with his unwilling father-in-law. The Shamkhal was outraged, and ordered him seized. Akhtougan slew the guards sent to trap him and fled back into the Baksan, but he knew pursuit was close behind and that his hideaway must have been discovered. He called for Svan masons to come over the mountains and build him one of their traditional defensive towers. This they built in record time, by employing unusually agile oxen to carry stones on their horns along planks laid between the cliffs and the upper storeys.

When the Shamkhal's army arrived, Akhtougan was safe in his new tower and had his marksmen shoot all the invaders' horses but leave the soldiers unharmed. This display of aggressive leniency rendered the Shamkhal helpless. He was forced to agree to a treaty and the marriage of his daughter to the arrogant thief.

It is a nice story, and paints a picture of the Turkic valleys being a refuge from the rulers of the plains. Place names suggest the valleys were once more ethnically mixed, but they had certainly become entirely Turkic-speaking by the time of Freshfield's visit.

The climber, on conquering Elbrus, led his party to the fashionable spa resort of Pyatigorsk, where Lermontov was killed. He was not impressed by the luxury and dissipation of the holidaymakers, and his group rapidly left, passing south through the garrison town of Nalchik and up the gorge of the Cherek into the high valleys once again.

Freshfield claims the honour of having been the first western European to visit the Cherek valley, and he probably was. It is an extraordinary gorge, guarded by cliffs a thousand metres or more high, and threaded by a stream that slams into the rocks with uncontrolled rage. When Freshfield entered it, the only passage was via a narrow path which rose and fell as it sought to find a way through the narrows. The gorge opened out eventually, extending its flanks into gentle slopes of grass and crops. Along the streams were villages, which this story will visit again. He called the main village Muchol, a name that had become Mukhol eighty years later, when the Soviet troops deported the highlanders from their valleys for their imagined treason, but otherwise was little changed.

The houses were made of heavy stones, and may better be described as manmade caves. The back wall and floor were dug out of the hillside, while the front wall was made of heavy stones laid without mortar. Massive logs supported a roof of packed earth fully two feet thick, with grass growing on it lushly. From above, the houses looked like peculiar terraces, with wicker-work chimneys sticking out of them. From below, they looked above all like burrows. The people exploded out of their houses in wonder, however, when the party of mountaineers appeared. 'The male population surrounded us in the street; the womankind, being the property of Moslem lords, were obliged to content themselves with what they could see from the house-roofs. Their dress consists of a loose crimson robe, with a cap, from which a row of coins hangs down over the forehead. There was certainly one pretty face amongst them, and there may have been more, but no second opportunity of seeing any of the beauties occurred during our stay,' he wrote.

Among the locals was a religious scholar who had been on the pilgrimage to Mecca and who affected Turkish dress. The villagers brought ample supplies of food and cake to the visitors, who had a room to themselves fitted out with the 'brightly-painted trays in which Easterners delight, and pegs, on which hung sheepskins, swords and guns, with the other necessary equipments of a Caucasian when away from home'.

Freshfield normally showed little interest in the people he met, but was clearly won over by the villagers in Muchol, which they left 'carrying away with us pleasanter recollections of its inhabitants than of those of any other village we had halted at. At Uruspieh we had, it is true, received almost equal kindness; but there the princes were imbued with a tinge of Russian manners, in contrast to which the patriarchal simplicity of Balkar was the more striking.'

Leaving the village, the climbers trekked up the valley towards Georgia, passing guard huts set up to protect the flocks from thieving Georgians who might cross the mountains, then turned east and passed into the land of the Ossetians and out of the scope of this chapter.

On the publication of his book in 1869, Freshfield started something of a craze for visiting the Caucasus. Climbers from Italy, Hungary and Germany as well as Britain came to follow the trail that he had blazed. The slopes never became thronged, like those in Switzerland, but the books written by the pioneering visitors began to resemble modern guidebooks. One of Freshfield's later works warned climbers against hiring the son of a particular man who lived in a house with a green roof, for example, and some of the chiefs appeared again and again, becoming stock characters in the accounts.

Fortunately, however, among the climbers was one who had more curiosity about the inhabitants of the valleys than just their use as porters for exploring the peaks. Florence Grove, who arrived in the Caucasus in 1874, wrote an immensely readable account called *The Frosty Caucasus* which gives us some of the best information on the tribesmen that we have.

His group too crossed over from Georgia, but it crossed first into the Cherek valley, which had so impressed Freshfield at the end of his trip. They too encountered two Georgians at the pass, although these had been obliged to kill their – presumably stolen – bullock, since it was unwilling to slog over the pass. The cattle-rustling seems not to have been affected by the passing of six years of Russian rule since Freshfield first climbed these peaks.

The group's first encounter on the northern side of the mountains was with the herder assigned to guard the cattle and sheep from such Georgian raids. Since most of the party was Georgian, and they had crossed over from Georgia, it is hardly surprising that Grove should record a frosty reception. This only deepened when the porters killed a sheep. Since it had been killed by a non-Muslim this made the herder worry that it might pollute his hut, so he begged them not to allow the meat to touch the walls or fall into the fire. '[T]he guard looked on with an expression such as a Presbyterian might wear when gazing at a Ritualist service,' Grove noted with characteristic humour.

His group passed on down the valley the next morning. 'For naked grandeur of mountain form the Tcherek valley is probably unequalled in Europe,' he wrote. Further down the valley was a stone bridge with a door on it, another precaution against cattle theft, and here the guard was more friendly, feeding them with bread cooked in the embers, and fresh milk. They passed on towards the villages visited by Freshfield, and Grove's reaction was even more enthusiastic.

The unusual houses, tucked into the hillside as they were, astounded him. 'I doubt whether anything stranger can meet men's eyes than these houses when seen for the first time. Deserted cow-sheds, vast empty dog-kennels, the home of some animal constructive like the beaver, but on a much larger scale; anything but the habitations of men do these strange hamlets seem to the traveller. They usually appear at first to be completely empty, why I cannot tell, for there are plenty of people in them; but perhaps it is because they are so utterly unlike the dwellings of human beings that the eye does not look for men, and therefore of course does not find them,' he wrote.

'On nearer approach, however, numbers of men, women, and children are found, and the traveller discovers to his astonishment that these poor sheds are inhabited by a well-to-do and orderly race, remarkably handsome, stately in bearing, self-respecting, partly civilised in their ways and sometimes very richly clad.'

The welcome from the village chief was rather cold, since their Georgian guide Paul had failed to produce the piece of paper putting them under the protection of the Russian government, but they were still treated with all the stately honour due to a guest, and were lent ponies to explore the gorge below the village, which filled Grove with raptures. On their return to the house assigned them by the chief, however, they were to have the first encounter with the extreme curiosity that was to mark their visit. When they walked back into their room, it was thronged with visitors, who found every single thing they did fascinating.

Many of their visitors wore the long tunic, shaggy hat and silver-headed cartridge cases that are the national dress of the Caucasus. They were all armed, often with pistol, dagger and sword, but remained good-natured in their scrutiny of the foreigners.

This curiosity lasted for the whole trip. In the next village of Bezengi, one old man sat next to Grove while he wrote in his notebook. He first of all took off the visitor's hat to examine it thoroughly, then watched his pen for a long time as it wrote, moved on to test the texture of his tweed jacket and then checked his hobnail boots. The next day, though rainy, was the same. A crowd gathered to watch them all morning. Grove's clearly good-natured response to everything seems to have been a hit with the highlanders, and he was greeted warmly wherever he went. Although he found the throngs who gathered to watch them irritating, he was philosophical about it, imagining what would happen if a Turkic tribesman in full national dress turned up in an English village. 'I do not think that in Central Africa the inhabitants could have shown more curiosity; but with all this inquisitiveness, which made them almost take the things out of our hands to examine them, these singular people were not wanting in dignity, or in the feeling of what was due to strangers. They pawed everything we would let them paw, but they asked for nothing; and so we found it in other places. During the whole of our journey on the northern side, I do not recollect a single instance of a Caucasian's asking for any of the things we carried with us,' he wrote.

He was limited in what he could say to the villagers, since many of them did not speak Russian and he did not speak Turkish, which meant his chances of finding out the condition of the valleys were very limited. However, he did have the translator Paul, who helped him understand one man who was vociferous in his complaints about the government.

'The Russian Government does not deal justly with us. It is now confiscating much of the property of the proprietors,' said the stranger, before spoiling the impression of a noble fighter for liberty by revealing that the substance of his complaints was that the government abolished slavery in the mountains in 1867. 'I say that the rights which men in a country have always possessed should be respected by the Government, and the Russian Government does not respect ours. Formerly we had slaves of our own who did our work for nothing; now this is not allowed, and we have to pay men to work for us.'

It is easy to mock such a complaint, but it is the first recorded sign of growing disquiet in the mountain valleys, which was to swell over the next decades as misgovernment and brutality became the staples of Russian rule under both the tsars and the communists. The highlanders were used to being left alone, and were now gaining all the benefits of the corruption and violence inherent in the Russian system.

That was all in the future though. As Grove passed on through the valleys, he told anecdotes of curiosity, filth, rain, mutton and hospitality, before recounting how they climbed the higher, western peak of Elbrus.

His expedition was almost certainly, therefore, the first to climb Europe's highest mountain, although he was very modest himself, estimating that the two peaks were actually almost the same height.

His trip was nearing an end, but he remained full of respect and liking for the Karachai-Balkars, despite their tireless ability to keep talking all day. 'Strong, healthy men as most of them are, well capable of doing a long day's work without the slightest distress, it is wonderful how they loiter on a journey, and what frequent and protracted halts they make. Most irritating, too, is their procrastination,' he noted. 'It will be seen then that, though the Caucasians are not always to be relied on, and at times try the traveller's patience largely, the good much predominates in their character, and I think that those who have sojourned among them cannot fail to carry away a most pleasant remembrance of this simple pastoral race, untouched as yet for good or evil by the great forces of Western civilisation.'

But those forces were in fact touching them, little by little. When the English historian and traveller Baddeley visited the valley of the Cherek in 1902, the guards against cattle raiding had been added to by a government sanitary inspector, and cattle needed certificates and documents before they could pass the checkpoint. In such a remote point and without oversight, it seems unlikely that the guard would have been of great honesty and the bribes paid to him are likely to have been a de facto tax on sending cattle by the traditional route to Georgia. Russian government had arrived in the high Caucasus.

Freshfield made a similar point about the deficiency of Russian administration in the central Caucasus. 'There is no competent local authority to which to appeal in case of difficulties,' he said, in *The Exploration of the Caucasus*, in which he bemoaned the failure of the Caucasus to find its true place as a mountaineer's paradise. 'While the old chieftains have lost much of their feudal or patriarchal authority, the new *starshinas* or village mayors, appointed by the Government, are in the more remote districts treated with very scant respect by their communities.'

The last couple of decades in these valleys before the 1917 revolution have been little studied, although one local historian called Zhilyabi Kalmykov has done some research. His narrative tells of how the reforming possibilities of the Russian rule over the North Caucasus ran out of steam rapidly, as bureaucratic inertia replaced military necessity after the Circassian nation was destroyed in 1864.

The government imposed headmen on every village, and ran courts centrally with their judges being part of the local administration. The system was intended to be temporary but lasted for almost twenty years. The judges were 'officials and officers, not knowing the languages of the people and not having even the smallest understanding of the cultures and shariat of the people itself'.

The court used Russian law to resolve criminal cases, which was baffling for the tribesmen, who were used to controlling punishment themselves. Baddeley knew a respected merchant called Toterbek Mourzaganoff, who had three shops and would mediate in murder cases to fix a degree of compensation that had no connection to any investigation by the official court.

'Russian legal decisions and punishments had no effect whatever on the demand for blood or the amount of blood-wite exacted under customary law ... the Russian Courts, no matter what their merits, in matters relating to blood-vengeance failed to satisfy the native idea of justice. The slayer was sentenced to imprisonment or penal servitude, perhaps even for 20 years, but *he lived*, while his victim lay rotting in the grave, his spirit in anguish because unavenged,' wrote Baddeley.

The Russian courts were not even efficient. Between 1908 and 1910, the number of unresolved cases in the Nalchik region – which covered the Turkic highlanders' eastern valleys – increased by 726. Some cases had not moved for two, three or even more years. And the legal system was ever more restrictive.

These highlanders, used to being able to wander wherever they wished, now could not visit another village without a permit from their headman. They could not take produce to market without a piece of paper certifying the amount, type and destination of their goods. Whole villages were also held responsible for crimes committed on their territory and even, in the case of the mountain villages, on the roads leading to them.

If normal police methods did not find the thief, and if the villagers were not prepared to surrender him, then soldiers, dragoons or a *sotnya* of Cossacks would be billeted on them for two months or more. The troops would behave as if they were at home, costing the already far from wealthy villagers substantial sums that they could not afford. The visiting troops were also unlikely to hurry to catch the criminal since they were receiving everything they needed for free.

The inevitable result was dissatisfaction with the Russian authorities, which bubbled over into opposition to the starshina or headman appointed by the government. The headman, assisted by an assembly of all the richer members of the villages, controlled the distribution of land and the permits allowing people to trade and travel, and did not have to pay any tax. It is hard to imagine a system better designed to breed corruption, and it was massively unpopular, even after 1906 when the government made the headman position elected.

In 1909, villagers in the Chegem valley – where both Freshfield and Grove remarked on the peculiarities of the houses – refused to elect a headman, in protest against the government. The authorities sent in the police 'flying squad', which had been set up to deal with bandits, and forced the villagers to hold their elective meeting. They also fined them for 17,000 roubles' worth of back taxes.

With traditional authority fading away, and the Russian government unpopular, the conditions were ripe for a revival in robbery in the high valleys. The valleys were so full of hiding places, and so hard to police, that bandits could rest secure against anything but a full-scale military invasion.

True authority would not be stamped on them until the 1940s, when the Soviets finally lost patience with a people who refused to bow down before foreign rule, and sent them into exile.

14. I Always Fought against the Class Enemies

Ismail Zankishiev was born into this world, where the old ways of the mountain Turkic life were falling apart. The Russian rules and institutions allowed the rich to consolidate control over the pastures and herds that had been the common wealth of his people. His family lived in the village of Kunyum in the Upper Cherek valley, and his father Musa may well have been among the crowds that welcomed the British mountaineers to the village in the 1860s and 1870s.

But by 1895, the year of Zankishiev's birth, the Caucasus had failed to become a global climbing destination to rival the Alps, and social tensions in the valleys were becoming more obvious. The number of people in the North Caucasus increased steadily over the next few years, mainly through natural population growth. Tensions rose in the villages, where demand for land was intensifying, and young men were not able to set themselves up as independent households. The injustice of a political system whereby a local trustee dominated land distribution, allowed or disallowed private trade, controlled tax payments and summoned the police must have been obvious even to a child.

The young Zankishiev took the first opportunity he had to rebel against it.

That chance came in 1917, when the tsar's government collapsed in St Petersburg under the strain of three disastrous years of the First World War. The Russia the tsars had created began to collapse too, and authority collapsed nowhere so totally as it did in the Caucasus. Bits or all of the mountain range were variously claimed or controlled in the next few years by the Caucasus Mountain Republic, the Caucasus Imamate, the Soviet Union, the Russian Empire, the Russian Republic, Turkey, Germany, Britain, Armenia, Azerbaijan, Georgia, as well as a bewildering number of even-more-micro states that sometimes did not even exist on paper.

'South Russia, since the fall of Rostov, had become remarkable for the number of "governments" in its territory and the consequent lack of any real government,' wrote one sardonic journalist who despairingly watched the blood and disease of the collapsing resistance to the Bolsheviks in southern Russia in 1920.

In the North Caucasus, the injustices of the colonial administration gave plenty of causes for conflict. Disputes raged between the Cossacks and the highlanders over attempts to undo the Cossacks' hold on the best land, between the Cossacks and working-class newcomers, who felt the Cossacks were reactionaries, and between the highlanders and the newcomers, who represented a modern world many of the highlanders distrusted. The highlanders meanwhile fought among themselves, along ethnic lines, or along religious lines, or along ideological lines, or all three. It was a bewildering period, in which various factions supported or opposed the Bolsheviks purely for local reasons, and the Bolsheviks found themselves committed to supporting religious law in one place, and to governing via the Workers' Councils in others. Some factions tried to interest world powers in the Caucasus, and the interventions of the Turks, the Germans and the British during or after the First World War raised hopes that local independent states might be secure. They were not.

An engaging, self-proclaimed ruler called Haidar Bammate even popped up at peace talks in Switzerland in 1919. His business card – still kept in the archives of the British Foreign Office – identified him as 'Ministre des affaires étrangères de l'union des peuples circassiens et du daghistan'. His attempts to lobby for the support of his union received no support at the congress, with an unnamed British bureaucrat noting sourly that it was 'quite impracticable'. A second envoy, called Abdul Merjid Tchermoff, this time 'President of the Delegation of the North Caucasian Republic', appeared later, but had the same lack of success.

The more or less fictitious states proclaimed in the Caucasus had their adherents, but eventually the Red Army crushed all opposition to its rule, leaving those who had supported it early enough in commanding positions in the 1920s. This meant a profound change for the five eastern-most valleys of the mountain Turks – the Balkars, as they would be known – which from 1921 were united with the lowland Circassians into the newly created autonomous region of Kabardino-Balkaria.

Previously political life had been dominated by rich, older men, but now the winners were young men who had fought for the Bolsheviks in the Civil War. Ismail Zankishiev, who may at this time have started to call himself by the nom de guerre 'Khutai' by which he is best known today, was among them, fighting as a Red irregular during the civil war that followed the proclamation of Soviet Power by Vladimir Lenin in 1917.

If even half the legends told about him by the Balkars today are true, he must have been a skilled guerrilla warrior. He could, it is said, shoot a soldier downhill from 400 metres through the viewing hole in the protection plate fixed around the breach of an artillery piece. It is also told how he taught his own boys to shoot by killing swallows on the wing with a rifle. Apparently, he even beat his eight-year-old son for failing to shoot his swallow through the eye, or so the story goes.

He took his uncompromising approach to parenthood with him into governing his home Cherek valley, which he dominated for much of the 1920s. He chaired the Village Council of Upper Balkaria off and on between 1924 and 1930, and appears to have exploited his position in much the same way that his tsarist-era equivalents did.

Locals who remember the time say that he requisitioned building materials, and forced local men to work for him on the construction of his new house, where he installed a mistress in a grave affront to local traditions. On another occasion a local man had kidnapped the daughter of a rich family to marry her, and Khutai terrorized those who had been involved to such an extent that they fled into the hills to become *abrek*s – a form of noble outlaw endemic to the Caucasus.

The campaign against the rich, the traditionally powerful and the religious was guaranteed to win him backing in Moscow. But it was not popular among his fellow villagers, according to documents found in the KGB files in Moscow. One woman in the Upper Cherek valley complained about stripping the vote from the previous elite.

'We cannot live without the elders and the mullahs, they gave meat and milk to the poor, and what do the communists give to the poor? We will not allow the mullahs and the prosperous people to lose their electoral rights,' the woman is quoted as saying in 1929.

But that was a dangerous viewpoint while the Soviet leadership was pushing ahead with its revolution. It wanted to collectivize agriculture and turn the conservative and stubborn peasant farmers that formed the overwhelming majority of the Soviet Union's population into progressive and pliable farmhands. Since Soviet ideology was rooted in class differences, it was important to show that even the most wretchedly poor villages were divided along class lines. Joseph Stalin, who increasingly dominated the government in the 1920s, demanded that this local bourgeoisie should be destroyed. They were known as *kulak*s – the word means 'fist' – and could be anyone, since the class of rich, capitalist peasants they represented was more or less an invention. They were said to employ others to do their work for them, and their wealth needed to be distributed to those poorer than themselves.

Often the kulaks had not inherited their wealth at all; they worked alongside their labourers like farmers all over the world, and had just been cleverer and more industrious than their neighbours in investing and building a better farm. Sometimes the kulaks were denounced by jealous neighbours, or picked at random from among the villagers. But that did not spare them from the secret police. Millions of people were 'dekulakized' and dumped in the wastes of Siberia or Central Asia to die or starve.

The Balkars were no exception, even though the already stretched dogma of Stalin's brutalized form of Lenin's tortured version of Marx's original theory could not begin to reflect the high valleys' unique conditions. Here families kept livestock in common, and lived in large extended households in the burrow-like dwellings that so stunned the climbers.

In the circumstances, with police hunting them and arrest possible for any or no reason, it is not surprising that Balkars fled into the hills where hiding was easy and the chances of survival higher than as a previously prosperous peasant farmer. It was all too much for the

Balkars to take, and the men who fled into the hills began to organize themselves. Uprisings broke out against Russian rule for the first time in these valleys, worrying the authorities.

Ismail 'Khutai' Zankishiev had lost his job as chairman of the village council by this time, apparently as part of a factional intrigue in the village, but had been appointed head of the police force tasked with stopping these would-be counter-revolutionaries.

The new head of the village council, according to a local man's version of Khutai's life, managed to restore communications with the men who had fled into the hills and arranged a meeting with them in December 1929.

But one of Khutai's allies was still working in the council, and he told his former boss. Khutai, as head of the anti-bandit department, insisted on accompanying the new chairman, a man called Magomet Zumakulov, to the meeting. At the meeting Khutai was wounded, and the new chairman was killed, as was one of the two runaways who had come to talk to them. Rumours persist that it was Khutai who shot his political rival in the back.

After the battle, the chances of the abreks returning to normal life were minimal, and twelve more men fled into the hills from the Cherek valley in May 1930. Insurrections were breaking out now from one end of the Turkic realm to the other. But Khutai's stock was at its highest, and he won the Order of the Red Banner in 1929 for his services to the Soviet state.

Details about what happened in those years between 1928 and 1931 are still hard to come by, although they must exist in the KGB archives. One ninety-year-old woman – Marisat Zhantueva, whom I met in distant Central Asia – told me how she remembered seeing men with rifles marching through her village in 1930, on their way to the Upper Chegem valley, where they intended to set up their own government. They were inspired by rumours that Turkey was planning to invade and restore traditional laws and values.

At least fifty men rose up against the authorities from the village of Dumala, she said, along with men from the two other villages that made up their village council. They rounded up the inspector and the secretary of the village council, both of whom were ethnic Russians,

and threatened to kill them. The inspector, she said, begged a neighbour of hers called Chukai Tuduev for help, but he refused. Instead,
he pulled out a pistol and killed the inspector himself.

The security forces sent in troops to crush the little insurgency,
but the Balkars had a good defensive position. She believed that more
than 250 soldiers died crossing the river, before the locals barricaded
themselves into a cave and could not be winkled out. Eventually, the
authorities persuaded the village women to tell their husbands they
would not be prosecuted if they gave themselves up. The men at first
were resistant, and pelted the emissaries with stones, but finally
agreed to surrender. The government's promise did not last long.
One man from her village, called Karakez Zhabelov, had been part of
the uprising, and he decided to take the amnesty offer. He was arrested
a week later, as the Soviet government's retribution broke.

Almost all the Balkars holding positions in the local government
were arrested and shot. Ako Gemuev was the highest-ranking Balkar
as chairman of the Kabardino-Balkaria Executive Committee, and
was unlucky enough to have been from the village of Dumala himself. His fellow villagers are said to have visited him regularly to
complain about the evils of collectivization. Those same villagers
then rose up and fought against the state.

It was enough to condemn him, and he was arrested in August 1930
under the Legal Code's notorious 58th article, which covered counter-
revolutionary crimes. His crimes came under sections 2 (organizing an
armed uprising) and 11 (actively fighting against the working class),
which bore the death sentence. Many of the leaders of the Balkar
communities, who had been young men during the revolution but
were like Gemuev now in their late thirties, were also shot.

Khutai, thirty-five by now, was a classic example. He too was
swept up in the wave of repression crashing around his people. He
was arrested in the autumn of 1930 and convicted of being part of the
Gemuev plan of organizing armed resistance to the Soviet Union.

Among his co-conspirators were the Sarakuev brothers, led by 'the
large kulak' Lukman. Doka Sarakuev, a 62-year-old who was arrested,
described how he and his four brothers were part of a family of
twenty people in total. They owned between them a house, two

horses, two bulls, twelve cows, 400 sheep and two donkeys. He complained that their property had been seized as that of a kulak even though they employed no labourers, and had no income except what they earned with their own hands.

His complaint did not save him. Some members of his family were sent to the terrible Solovki camp in Russia's Arctic, from which inmates did not normally return, while others received labour camp sentences of between five and ten years. Honest farmers, holding their property in common, were being penalized during a drive to collectivize.

Khutai appealed to the leadership of Kabardino-Balkaria for justice, and must have found it impossible to believe that he was being tried alongside the rich, old Balkars that his generation had tried so hard to destroy.

'I always fought against the class enemies, which is why they are always trying to kill me . . . Now of course I know everything will be against me, because I worked for a decade in the village council. I took land from some people, I took the right to vote from another, it is clear they will oppose me,' he wrote in an unsuccessful appeal kept in the state archives.

He was convicted and sentenced to ten years' hard labour in Magadan, a gold-mining district on the Pacific Coast where the weather was so bad and the labour conditions so brutal that the roads were said to be literally built on bones. It could have been a death sentence, but he survived.

The Balkars would be more reluctant to believe Soviet offers of an amnesty another time.

Khutai emerged from prison in the late 1930s or early 1940s, having served his time in the camps. He worked on a collective farm like any normal person, quite a step down from the heights of the revolutionary leader he had once been. But he still dreamed of returning to prominence, perhaps once again as a guerrilla leader as he had been during the heady days when the Red Flag was raised over the high valleys.

For a fresh disaster was breaking over the mountains, and over the Soviet Union as a whole. Germany invaded on 22 June 1941. Meeting little resistance, the armies pushed east and south. They wanted the oil wells of Maikop, Grozny and Baku, and the Soviet troops seemed incapable of stopping them.

The Soviet government, in a desperate attempt to save the city of Rostov, in July 1942 sent in the Kabardino-Balkarian cavalry on horses against German tanks. It was a massacre. The 115th Cavalry Division was shattered, and the traumatized survivors – mountain lads without officers or experience – fled back to their valley homes.

According to the archives, around 600 or 700 deserters hid in the mountains, perhaps fearing they would be killed under Stalin's 'not one step backwards' order, which was issued on 28 July 1942 and which counted retreat as desertion. According to a document later sent to Lavrenty Beria, head of the security services, the majority of these deserters were Balkars and around a hundred of them ended up in Khutai's native Cherek gorge.

Readers may at this point be wondering why Khutai has a reputation as a Balkar hero. He was a corrupt local government official, was imprisoned in Siberia when the leadership was purged, and tried to get himself off the hook by incriminating others on the way. Now he was out of prison he was appointed to lead a rapid-reaction force against these deserters, many of whom were people being hunted through no fault of their own. These were not the actions of a great man.

And his reputation was about to plunge even further, for he used his little force not to fight the deserters but to settle his own scores. He persecuted a local political rival: Khamid Eneyev, the new head of the village council. Eneyev, along with a deputy, was riding home one night when Khutai's forces ambushed them. As it happened, the hapless deputy was riding on Eneyev's distinctive white horse, and was killed in his boss's place. The attack had failed and Khutai, fearing arrest, fled into the hills, joining up with the abreks, or 'bandits' as the government called them, whom he had been supposed to fight.

In fact, at this point in his career, Khutai had done nothing to endear himself to anyone, but do not give up on him yet. He was to redeem himself in the eyes of his nation.

The Germans, meanwhile, were not sitting still. In October 1942, the town of Nalchik, capital of Kabardino-Balkaria, fell and the

Soviet 37th Army fled in panic before them, taking heavy losses. Units of the army were cut off in the valleys that reach down towards Nalchik from the mountains, and one of the only ways left for them to save themselves from capture was to retreat up the gorge of the Cherek and either cross over into Georgia, or into one of the parallel valleys.

The new military commander of the region, Major-General Zakharov, was concerned that the deserters hiding in the hills could threaten his army's withdrawal and on 1 November he ordered the NKVD to take deserters' relatives hostage. If the deserters had not surrendered within two days, he ordered, the hostages should be shot. The stage was set for the great tragedy that was about to engulf the Cherek valley, whence it would burst forth upon the whole Balkar nation.

The NKVD forces were not idle. Their first victims – listed as 'bandits' in the army records, but actually civilians – were two Balkar men called Taubi Appayev and Musos Khasauov. Two more herders, from the Bashiev family, were shot a little later, though it is not clear what for. Soviet troops were still streaming in retreat through the valley, carrying their weapons. For the deserters, who were now very nervous that they were about to be hunted, it was easy to take the weapons of these demoralized soldiers and use them to defend themselves.

The army managed to largely extricate itself from the gorge, but one group of five soldiers had failed to manoeuvre their anti-aircraft gun up the steep slope out of the Cherek valley. Khutai's men stopped them and, on 21 November, taking two of the soldiers with them, they dragged the gun with bulls to within range of the village council administration, where Eneyev – Khutai's enemy – was based along with his allies in the village of Mukhol. The bandits opened fire, and had their enemies pinned down all day. They failed to trap Eneyev, who fled to the local hospital when darkness fell and hid with a small Soviet force based there. Over the next four days, the two sides faced off, the bandits armed with their anti-aircraft gun and the soldiers walled up in the hospital. Five soldiers were killed, according to the military records, before the soldiers managed to retreat. The military command lost patience.

General Kozlov, head of the 37th Army, ordered that the bandits in the gorge must be destroyed once and for all, with a verbal order to Colonel Shikin of the NKVD 'to wipe the villages of Balkaria from the face of the earth, stopping at nothing'.

On 22 November 1942, Shikin passed the order on to the commander of a cavalry unit: 'Liquidate the bandit group based in the villages of Upper Balkaria. Take the most decisive measures, right up to shooting on the spot, burning their buildings and property.' On 24 November, a detachment of 152 soldiers led by a Captain Fyodor Nakin was sent into the gorge. On their way in, they detained at least six local men, none of whom had any connection to the battle in the village centre, and shot them dead.

The Cherek massacre had begun.

15. Liquidate the Bandit Group

Nakin's forces took up their positions overlooking the Cherek valley on 27 November 1942, and set their operation to cleanse the villages below them of 'bandits' for eleven o'clock that evening. The valley held at least nine hamlets. Mukhol, home to the village administration and scene of the battle over the hospital, was further down the valley. The soldiers would have to pass through Sauty and Glashevo before they could reach it.

Other hamlets overlooked the path, including the little settlement of Kurnoyat, home to eighteen families, while Khutai's home hamlet of Kunyum sat on the other side of the river, and others – such as Upper and Lower Cheget – were further off.

Nakin divided his force into two. The larger half followed the left bank of the stream towards Sauty, while a smaller group followed the right bank.

While most of the troops prepared themselves, Nakin sent two soldiers – a Russian and an Azeri – to the hamlet of Kurnoyat to start carrying out his orders. The soldiers were welcomed warmly, fed and allowed to rest. In return, they warned the villagers that terrible retribution had come and that they should flee. On their return to the main force, they both admitted they had killed nobody. Nakin, enraged, shot them both. There would be no more mercy from the Red Army.

Bagaly Temirzhanova, then a 23-year-old woman, later gave testimony to investigators describing how two men from Kurnoyat – Yusup and Kumuk Sarakuev – came running into Sauty to warn them that the soldiers had arrived and were planning to kill everyone. The two men, who were her relatives, warned the fifteen or so deserters present to flee but the remaining villagers thought they were safe. The soldiers would not bother them, they thought, as did two men who had been invalided home from the front.

The only armed men left in Sauty had departed. It was defence-less.

One deserter called Edik was left as a look-out and he told Temirzh-anova and her neighbours that the soldiers were indeed coming just as she was lying down to sleep, before moving on to warn everyone in the village. Despite her belief that the soldiers would not bother civilians, she went to her neighbour's house, where around fifteen people were gathered, all of them women or children apart from an 80-year-old man. That was when the shooting started. They had no idea what was happening until a couple more women found them in the morning, and said the soldiers were killing everybody.

The soldiers found them shortly afterwards, and started hammer-ing on the door and demanding it be opened. Temirzhanova, and a handful of others, managed to jump out the window.

'Just behind me was the son of Mustafa Temirzhanov, who was seven. It was just then that a grenade was thrown into the house. Everyone who was in the house was killed, and it ripped off the top of Mustafa's son's head and he just stayed there, hanging from the wall,' she remembered.

Sprinting from house to house, the terrified survivors desperately looked for a place to hide, but those who were still alive were too scared to open their doors and take them in.

As soon as the shooting started, the villagers instinctively gathered together in the stronger houses of the village. The village, as described by the climbers, was packed together in a warren, with connections between the houses and hidden rooms making it very hard for the soldiers to see where their prey could be hiding. A big group decided to hide in a house belonging to Teta Misirov, a neighbour, including Mukhadin Baisiev and his mother. Baisiev was at the time fifteen years old and he was already fortunate that the soldiers had knocked on their door but left without breaking it in.

When they arrived at Teta Misirov's house, around sixty people were already hidden there but with so many terrified and hungry children crying and screaming the soldiers found them quickly. When the people refused to come onto the street, the soldiers threw a grenade into the room, deafening Baisiev and killing many of the desperate villagers. The survivors decided to come out, and the soldiers sent Teta Misirov to round up other hiding parties, telling them to come to a meeting. But the meeting was a ruse, and those who had survived the grenade were shot as they emerged into the daylight.

Among those who emerged was seven-year-old Tani Mamayeva, who said the soldiers lined them all up against the wall in the courtyard outside the house where they had been hiding. Several of the older people tried to move to the side, but could not escape, and started to read Muslim prayers before the shooting started. Mamayeva herself was trapped under the body of her mother, whose long shawl covered her. She had no idea all the others were dead. Her mother, wounded but still alive, begged for water so little Mamayeva, herself wounded five times, crept out to find some. As she emerged, however, she saw that the soldiers were still hunting – although they had now turned their guns on some chickens – and hid among the dead once more. The second time she emerged, the soldiers were snacking on apples, carefully removing the peel before eating them. She hid under her mother's shawl again.

The soldiers came back to check the bodies, including that of her mother who had died of her wounds by this stage. Mamayeva stayed unnoticed under the shawl for three days before managing to escape.

The soldiers set up their base in the village, and waited for survivors like Mamayeva to emerge. Tagii Sarbasheva was one of the group that managed to jump out of the window ahead of the grenade, but was later detained. She was not killed but, as she was escorted through the village, she saw how the women in the next-door house were lined up and shot.

'We saw how they executed Kermakhan, Rakhimat, Galya and her daughter, and Mariyam, the wife of Baraz Misirov. Mariyam had her baby in her arms. A bullet hit the baby, and his little body flew about two metres, and it took off Mariyam's fingers and wounded her in the face, but she remained alive. She had the sense to pretend to be dead,' Sarbasheva remembered.

By a miracle, Mariyam managed to survive and crept to a neighbour's door. The neighbour, Khanshiyat Temirzhanova, saw her covered in blood, missing three fingers, wounded nine times and begging for water. But she had no water, for her story had been even more terrible.

On the first night, she had heard the shooting near a house belonging to her family, and her father went to investigate. He had two sons and two sons-in-law at the front with the Soviet Army and had nothing to fear from soldiers. But he was shot on sight, his brains spilling out of his skull as he lay on the ground, so never returned to tell his terrified daughters and wife what was happening. Temirzhanova and her sister Fatimat went to look for him, Fatimat leaving her own six-month-old daughter behind.

Their other sister, Rakhyimat, was desperately ill, and stayed with her year-old son in the house.

The two women saw their father dead, and began to run when the soldiers saw them. Temirzhanova stopped when ordered to, but her sister did not and was shot, the bullet shredding her right breast and killing her instantly. Temirzhanova collapsed with fear, just in time to see her mother emerge into the yard.

'They turned their guns on her and shot, and I saw everything, her neck just came in half, just like when they open a fish's belly. Without a sound, mother fell onto me and died instantly. There was a big stone nearby, and it's still there to this day, and blood from mother's wound hit this stone like a fountain, painting it red,' she said.

The blood possibly saved her from the soldiers, who may have assumed she was already dead, although one stuck his bayonet into her tunic without harming her.

When she entered the house, stepping over Fatimat, who lay in the doorway, she saw that the soldiers had killed her other sister in her bed, but that her niece and nephew had survived unscathed. They were both crying, and she could not manage to calm her niece, who was hungry and missing her mother.

Desperate, she stripped the still warm corpse of her sister and gave the little girl one last suck at the corpse's left breast – the right-hand one having been shredded by bullets – before it lost its milk. This quietened the infant for a while, but they both would need more to drink, and the only water in the house was that being used to soak a sheep-skin. She gave that to the children, but it was salty and only made them more thirsty, so after that she fed them on each other's urine.

They managed to hide, the aunt and the two orphans, until the third day, when the soldiers found them. Temirzhanova was calm, she said later, knowing that she would be killed. She opened the door when asked and walked outside, carrying her niece and nephew. The soldiers asked where her brothers were, and by a lucky chance she had a letter from the front in her pocket, and the soldiers left with it.

Five minutes later, two men talking Balkar – presumably allies of the Red Army – came and told them to hide, but she was past caring and just went home. That was the evening when Mariyam's weak voice begged her to open the door. Scared that the soldiers would follow the blood trail and track down her little group, she took Mariyam to a barn and left her there, before returning home to hide once more.

By this time, Nakin had communicated with headquarters. He had, he boasted, killed 1,200 people that first twenty-four hours, having lost just two people dead and five injured. 'The whole population has rebelled,' he reported.

The vast number of people killed – which was, in fact, exaggerated – appears to have stunned Colonel Shikin, who demanded to know who they were and what weapons he had captured. Shikin warned his subordinate not to harm women and children, but instructed him to keep killing all the bandits' accomplices.

Nakin pushed on towards the main village of Mukhol, where he sought to drive out the deserters controlling it since the Red Army had pulled out. On his way, he sacked the villages of Glashevo, where sixty-seven people were killed, and Upper Cheget. This latter was partly spared since one of the soldiers in Nakin's detachment was born there, but it was still savagely attacked.

Kabul Kadyrova, mother of four soldiers at the front, was one of the villagers murdered. She had imagined no soldier would kill a woman with four boys in the army. By this time, the deserters in Mukhol had guessed something terrible was happening, but did not know what. Khutai and a friend went to wake up Khazhdaut

Osmanov, a teacher and hence a respected man locally, to tell him the rumours about what was happening in Sauty. He visited Upper Cheget, learning for himself of the massacre that was making its way towards them.

The men in Mukhol asked Osmanov to write Nakin a letter, asking him what they needed to do to be left in peace. The answer came back that they should surrender, but they were not prepared to do so and left for the hills, leaving a look-out to see what was happening.

They joined up with residents of most of the other villages in the hills, for only those people in Sauty were unable to escape, being trapped by the soldiers who were still patrolling for them. Khalimat Misirova, thirteen years old at the time of the massacre, had already been stopped by a soldier in the village, but he turned out to be kind.

'You're Muslims, and I am a Muslim. Don't be scared of me, I'm going for water. Don't be scared of me, but we are ordered to kill everyone in this gorge,' the soldier, who was a Kyrgyz or a Kazakh, told them. He advised them to hide the best they could. Her family then went back home and her father hid the children in a potato clamp, having removed the potatoes to make room. The four children hid in the tight space, while the soldiers rampaged outside. The eight children of their neighbours also tried to get into the house to hide, but all eight – Soltan, Osman, Murat, Mukhadin, Muzafar, Aminat, Salikhat, Saniyat – along with their mother Erkekhan were shot in the courtyard.

At least sixty other people were hiding in the house, but the soldiers found them on the third day and killed them together. 'I could recount the names, but probably couldn't remember them all. There was the old man Batyrbii Misirov, his wife Nanuk, his daughter Khalimat, his sons Khizir, Mukhai, the children of Mukhai, his wife Naibkhan, his daughter Zhansurat, his second daughter Abidat, his third daughter Kyokkyoz. I've forgotten the names of the sons; there were nine or ten children in that family,' she later told investigators.

'Those four old folk who were killed in the basement, they weren't burned. The oldest was Batyrbii, the other women and children, they were all shot in the courtyard, I can't say the total, but more than sixty people. They shot them, then burned them.'

Two of the children together with her in the potato clamp argued after this, saying it would have been better to be killed since now they would be burned alive. The two got out and fell asleep where they were, and luckily were not found.

At night, she heard a voice calling them but did not react for a long time, thinking it was the soldiers hunting them again. But eventually she realized it was a fifteen-year-old boy called Yusuf who they'd assumed was dead. Yusuf was hiding on the roof and calling down the chimney. He told them the soldiers were burning the houses in the village and that they needed to get out quickly. The four children managed to climb out of the chimney, only to see the night lit up brightly by the blazing village. Misirova only had one shoe on, and the children were terribly cold as they left the village in the snow but they were eventually rescued by some fellow refugees.

Nakin had by now destroyed the hamlet of Kunyum as well, and in a report to his superiors increased his estimated death toll to 1,500. He said he had totally burned the hamlets of Sauty and Kunyum, while Upper Cheget and Glashevo were 'destroyed'.

'According to hostages ninety of the destroyed people were bandits, 400 could have carried weapons, and the rest were women and children. The artillery piece has been taken,' he wrote to Colonel Shikin on 29 November. He received a reply from Shikin that must have pleased him.

'I find your actions good, and your soldiers' actions just wonderful. If you cleanse Central Balkaria from these bastards, who instead of defending their homeland from the German occupiers betrayed it, and became bandits themselves, then you will have conducted an act of great importance. Secure the rear of our forces,' Shikin wrote.

The deserters and other men from Mukhol decided, however, to obtain weapons to defend themselves against the soldiers. In the circumstances they could not steal weapons from the Soviet troops, who were too well-armed and happy to shoot on sight. They decided, therefore, to send a deputation to the neighbouring valley and to the town of Zhentala, which was already in the hands of the Germans.

They hoped their country's enemies might help defend them against their own army.

On their way, they met Yakub Zhangurazov, a local man who had worked for the Communist Party until the war, but who had apparently changed sides to join the Germans. It seems he was now acting as a German agent and appears to have confirmed that they could obtain weapons from the Germans.

The trip, which took most of 1, 2 and 3 December, ended resistance in Mukhol and allowed Nakin to capture it – a fact that he trumpeted to Shikin on 3 December – although he did not keep it for long. In fact, General Kozlov, commander of the 37th Army, had received the report of 1,500 dead and was very concerned about it. He ordered that an investigation be conducted into the affair, but by this time the male villagers had returned to the gorge with German guns.

Nakin and the Red Army troops were considerably less brave in the face of men with guns than when slaughtering sleeping women and children, and the soldiers were rapidly driven out of the village of Shaurdat and then engaged outside Mukhol. The battle for Mukhol continued for all of 4 December, before Nakin's force retreated towards Sauty at evening-time.

The Mukhol men went on the offensive and Nakin had to consistently pretend to his superiors that secret German forces had already taken the valley to explain the fact that he had lost control of it. The Mukhol men also killed five Soviet partisans they had taken prisoner around this time, just before Nakin left the valley on 6 December.

The army had been conducting its own investigation, although it had not, it would seem, actually sent men to visit the destroyed hamlets. Three days later Seskov, a political officer in the 37th Army, sent a report on the affair to his superior. 'I consider that Nakin's unit killed many innocent people, who were totally unconnected to the bandits,' he concluded. He said the death toll of 1,500 was unrealistic and had been an attempt to show off before the high command. However, if this figure was correct then at least 1,010 women and children had been killed.

While the Soviet troops were analysing the disaster, the Balkars were left to clean up the damage. They emerged blinking from forests and caves, only to find the world would never be the same again.

Kakus Gazayeva was thirty-two when the massacre took place, and had fled her village of Shkanty for the forest when she heard shooting. She only returned to her home when she heard the Red Army had left the valley, and found her hamlet burned. She went along with her two brothers and her sister to Sauty on that first day.

Another sister had lived in Sauty and had been eight months pregnant with her fourth child, and they hurried to look for her.

'Their house was fully burned. Not far from the pile of ash, we with difficulty found among many burnt bodies the blackened bodies of Mara and her children: Ibragim, eight; Ramazan, six; Daut, three. We wrapped their remains in cloth and buried them in a common grave,' she said. 'That same day we found what had been Aslanuki Sarbashev's family, they were relatives of my husband. They were Kabakhan Sarbasheva, Aslanuki's mother; Nafi Sarbasheva, his wife; Ismail Sarbashev, six, his son; two daughters, Shamshiyat, twelve, and Nazhabat, fifteen. Every one of them had been shot point-blank in the head. As we later discovered, they were called into the yard, apparently to hold a meeting, then stood in a row and shot.'

The sad business of attempting to identify the dead continued. Bagaly Temirzhanova said they tried to find people from their clothing or personal belongings. Some bodies were burned into a powder, and the survivors swept up the powder and buried that.

'Then there were rumours that the Germans were coming. We left the village again. But the Germans did not disturb anyone, and we returned. They helped us to bury the remaining dead. They brought on sledges the sacrifices we had prepared. They did not kill a single person,' she remembered.

The 'Germans' – they were actually troops from Germany's ally Romania – were decent occupiers, and just looked on while the villagers cleared away the collapsed roofs of their houses, searching for the remains of their relatives within. In Sauty and Glashevo, the dead were buried in long trenches, since there were now too few people to dig proper graves.

It did not take the Soviet army long to realize that, with a new occupier in the valley, even one as mild-mannered as these Romanians (only one German officer ever entered the Cherek valley), they had a perfect scapegoat for the crime that had been committed. The barbarity of the Red Army could now be blamed on the foreigners, and could be hidden for ever.

On 16 December, before the Cherek valley was even recaptured, the cover-up began. The political department of the 37th Army said the deserters had German agents operating alongside them, thus paving the way for them to be blamed for crimes moved forwards in time by just a few days.

The Romanians pulled out of the valley at the end of December, provoking the villagers to once more flee into the hills in fear of retaliation by the Red Army, and the armed men to set up checkpoints at all entry points. They still, for now, controlled the valley. But storm clouds were gathering over them once more. Negotiations over their surrender continued with the Red Army, while at a gathering of the regional Communist Party one delegate urged the army to go in and crush the independent-minded villagers.

Finally, the NKVD took action. In three columns, it moved into the valley in mid-January 1943, meeting slight resistance at one checkpoint – at which one soldier was killed, and one injured – but taking over the Cherek valley with little trouble. The villagers welcomed the soldiers with red flags, but must have known their troubles were not over yet.

In the days up to 6 February, nearly all the men in the valley who had not been either conscripted or murdered were arrested. Over several days a total of 324 villagers were seized, leaving the livestock without minders, so the animals started to die as well. Another seventy-six people were arrested by the end of the year for their alleged connections to the bandits, bringing the total to 400 – which would suggest the police were operating according to a plan. They had to arrest 400 people and picked up men, women, teenagers, pensioners to meet the demands of their superiors.

On the lists of arrested people, just thirty-five were deserters; the rest were local government workers or political activists. All 400 of the arrested villagers were listed as 'bandits' in reports to Moscow, although the vast majority of them had no connection to the violence at all, and the real fighters – Khutai and his men – remained at large in the mountains, still able to move freely from place to place, secure in their knowledge of the terrain.

The Soviet government, however, did not leave the events of November to December uninvestigated. They tasked the local administration with drawing up lists of who had lost what, and how many people had been killed. Among the investigators was Baraz Mamayev, born in 1918, who had not been called up to the Red Army, because of poor health, and who was one of the few literate people left in the valley.

When the secretary of the village council was arrested by the returning Soviet troops, Mamayev was elevated to the position, and told to interview all the villagers and make lists of how much damage had been done. The summary, completed on 13 June 1943, has his signature at the bottom.

It claims to be a true account of the 'bestiality, thefts, and rapes committed by the German-fascist occupiers and their accomplices against the civilian population'. According to the report, a German major led soldiers into the gorge on 6 December and 'with active help from the traitors to their homeland, the German-fascist accomplices Yakub Zhangurazov, Battal Tabaksoev and Ismail Zankishiev', they burned houses, shot civilians and left a trail of death behind them.

The report had, therefore, changed the date of the civilians' deaths – to after the period when the Romanian unit arrived in the gorge – and it had blamed the deserters for helping them, despite those being the very people who managed to drive the rampaging Soviet Army out of the Cherek valley. It went on to give a list of the people killed in Sauty.

According to the list, the brave Soviet soldiers killed a total of 310 people in Sauty, of whom 150 were sixteen years old or younger, and slightly more than half of the children girls. A total of twenty-six of the victims were men between sixteen and sixty – the generally accepted definition of 'arms-bearing age'. Another forty men were over seventy, five of those being older than a hundred.

The female victims present more of a regular spread through the age groups, which is not surprising since most of the younger men had been conscripted, with sixteen victims being in their late teens or in their twenties, and one solitary matriarch one hundred years old.

Just a quick glance at the lists reveals family tragedies almost too terrible to contemplate. The commission recorded the patronymics of the children killed, grouping them together by father. Numbers 63 to 68 are all the children of an Akhmet Misirov: Kokez, fifteen; Seida, ten; Magomet, six; Elyas, four; Khyzyr, one; and the solitary daughter, Roza, two. Perhaps Akhmet Misirov was at the front, fighting for the Soviet Union. With a homecoming like that awaiting him perhaps it would have been better if he had already been killed.

Number 203 on the list is called Mazan Temirzhanov, a 67-year-old-man, while numbers 205 to 209 are all children with the father listed as Mazan Temirzhanov. A 67-year-old seems too old to have been their father. Perhaps he had a son with the same name who was at the front, and who lost daughters Fati, twelve, Tokui, eight, and Arzi, five, and sons Shokhai, six, and Akhmat, three.

There are 112 people with the surname Misirov on the list, and seventy Temirzhanovs, including little Osman, six, son of Makhmut, who takes up the last – 310th – place.

The hamlet of Glashevo was analysed in the same way, with sixty-three people listed by name as having been killed by the 'German-fascist grabbers and their accomplices'. Here the Soviet soldiers were a bit more restrained in their slaughter. Just nine of the victims were children, while twenty-two of them were men between the ages of sixteen and sixty. But there were still tragedies. Osman Glashev, a man from the village who presumably was at the front, lost his daughters Marzhanat, Illauka, Nazhabat and Bagaly, born in 1936, 1937, 1938 and 1940 respectively. Almost everyone on the list has the surname Glashev, which gave the name to the whole hamlet, and the family must have been almost wiped out by the attack.

There are no equivalent lists for the hamlet of Kunyum, or Upper Cheget, or Kurnoyat, or for Mukhol. And it is not certain that the lists we do have are complete either. In Sauty, for example, two daughters of the woman Mariyam – who came crawling to Khan-shiyat Temirzhanova's door leaving a blood trail – are listed as killed, but they are aged nine and five and neither of them is young enough to be the infant who flew two metres through the air after being hit by a bullet. Likewise, the Sarbashev family that Kakus Gazayeva remembered burying in Sauty – they had all been shot point-blank – does not feature on the lists at all.

Subsequent investigations did, however, give total death tolls. Published documents gave the figures 393, 373 and 458. Documents intended for internal use gave higher figures: 713 and 723. The fact that the government was not prepared to publish the true, higher figures may suggest a degree of lingering guilt among officials in the Cherek region who continued to claim the Germans had murdered their neighbours.

Each survivor also received a detailed report on the value of their lost property. One Aminat Sarbasheva and her family lost, for example, 300 kilograms of maize, 800 kilograms of potatoes, five sheep, 50 kilograms of meat, 50 kilograms of flour, a sewing machine, some cloth, two hats, two tunics, a fur coat, two pairs of boots, ten mattresses, eight pillows and ten blankets. This property's total value was 107,400 roubles, or the amount of money Sarbasheva would have earned at her 1940 salary level in slightly more than eleven years.

It is hard to imagine who the officials thought they were fooling with this drivel, even though it was supposedly confirmed by two witnesses and was signed by a whole list of officials. Sarbasheva would have known who destroyed her house and shot her relatives point-blank in the back of the head, and no amount of maize or hats or sewing machines would have made any difference. The officials compiling the reports knew the lists were a load of nonsense as well, as Mamayev – who was one of the signatories – testified to investigators in his old age.

'I heard that the Soviet soldiers killed civilians and burned the houses in the villages, although I did not see them myself; however, there were no German soldiers in the gorge at that time,' recalled Baraz Mamayev, who was explicit that the 'bandits' had done nothing against the population. 'I knew Battal Tabaksoev and Ismail – Khutai was his other name – Zankishiev well. None of them shot civilians in Sauty and did not take part in burning houses.'

But these invented reports of the massacre passed up through the Soviet command levels – where officials presumably did not know it had been committed by their own troops on the rampage – and must have shocked and outraged even higher-ranking officials. The reports were incredible, yet there it was in black and white. Balkar traitors had changed sides to fight for the Germans and had slaughtered their own neighbours.

It was a war crime that could hardly be left unpunished.

The NKVD examined the consciences of the whole Balkar population, and sent its conclusions to Lavrenty Beria in a document dated 23 February 1943. The Balkars, the report said, had welcomed the Germans to their lands. Secret organizations had existed despite the best efforts of the NKVD, and there counter-revolutionary groups had undermined the efforts of the Red Army.

'In October 1942, when part of the 37th Army retreated to the passes through Balkaria, bandits attacked particular units, exchanged fire with them, destroyed transport, weapons and goods. In the Cherek region, in one battle, several soldiers and commanders were killed and 80 people were disarmed.' 'An anti-aircraft gun' was taken.

Khutai's anti-aircraft gun seems to have been an important charge laid at the feet of the Balkars, as was the fact that the fascists allowed the 'bandits' to have their own headquarters in the Cherek region and to guard the gorge themselves against attempts by the Red Army to return. Even here, in an internal top secret document, the NKVD did not mention the real reason why the traumatized villagers were desperate to keep the Soviet forces out of their valley.

The report went on that the Germans pulled out of the mountains but promised to return, leaving Khutai to hold their territory for them. 'Fulfilling the Germans' order, the bandit organization of the Cherek region – headed by Zankishiev and his chief of staff Tabaksoev – organized the defence of the Cherek region from the offensive of the Red Army and for a month guarded the entrances and exits from the gorge. The majority of the male population of the region took part in the armed uprising,' the report said, adding that the situation was the same in the Chegem region, where the villagers had risen up against collectivization in 1930.

The NKVD said it had already arrested 845 people from among the 40,909 Balkars living in their five valleys, but a lot of 'bandits' were still hiding in the mountains and being supported by their relatives. Some of the bandits had surrendered, but others refused to do so, including Khutai.

The catalogue of treachery, crime, violence and – from Khutai – defiance required a major punishment, and the report suggested one.

'As a result of the above-listed, we think it is necessary to resolve the question of the possibility of deporting the Balkars outside the Kabardino-Balkaria region,' it said.

The Balkars were going to pay for defending their homes against murder committed by the soldiers given the task of protecting them. The deportation was at hand.

16. The 'Unnation' was a New Phenomenon

In September 1944, one of the last volumes of the *Great Soviet Encyclopedia* was published. The encyclopedia was the storehouse of Soviet orthodoxy on all subjects and, in this volume, it was the turn of the North Ossetian Autonomous Republic to be described fully, with a map which showed that North Ossetia was bordered to the west by the Kabardin Republic.

This may not seem like an earthshaking piece of information, and it was largely irrelevant to the article, but for the Turkic people of the high Caucasus, it was crucial. For it was the first step in a process of removing them from the present and the past. Until the deportation, the map would have shown the Kabardino-Balkarian Republic. Now, the reference to the Balkars was gone. It was as if they had never existed.

This method of rewriting history was perfected in the new, second edition of the encyclopedia, which was published from 1947, starting with a single volume on the Soviet Union as a whole. Under 'national composition' every people in the great sprawling communist state was listed, from the 'Russian' nation right down to the 'Assyrian' with just 20,000 people. But the Balkars and the Karachais had vanished. They had not only lost their homelands, but they had lost any public acknowledgement of their existence. They were still alive in exile, but they had ceased to exist as recognized entities.

There was, however, a chilling echo of their absence. The ethnic composition of the Kabardin Republic – the former homeland of the Balkar people – in 1933 was listed as 60 per cent Kabardin and 10.7 Russian. There was no explanation for why the figures did not add up to 100.

As the encyclopedia's second edition was completed, volume after volume rolled off the presses. Under 'B', there was no article on the Balkars. Under 'K', there was none on the Karachais. The other deported nations were ignored as well, with no articles on the Ingush, the Kalmyks and more. The article on the Kabardin Republic failed to mention the Balkars once in its entire thirteen pages, despite their having lived there since the dawn of recorded history. Robert Conquest, a combative British historian who investigated the deportations during Soviet times and came up with the above examples, likened this to something out of George Orwell.

'They are ignored almost as if they had never been – in some cases, exactly as if they had never been. There are precedents for this occurring in the case of individuals in the USSR: men ... were for decades what George Orwell christened "unpersons". The "unnation" was a new phenomenon,' Conquest wrote in his book *The Nation Killers*, published in 1970.

As far as the Soviet Union was concerned, these nations did not exist and now never had done.

But the problems faced by the newly deported and newly non-existent Karachais and Balkars in their new homes in Kazakhstan and Kyrgyzstan were very real indeed. They arrived between December 1943 and May 1944 – cruel months in a region where temperatures drop to minus forty degrees in winter – in villages and towns that could barely feed themselves, let alone strangers, during the worst war of all time.

Azret Khadzhiev, a Balkar man born in 1934, was staying with family friends on the night of the deportation so he was shipped to Kazakhstan without his parents, and ended up in a village called Khrisenko in the Pavlodar region near the border with Russia. He lived for a while with distant relatives, but they could not afford to feed him and were forced to leave him in an orphanage full of children lost in the deportations: Balkars, Chechens, Ingush and others.

'I was there for all that winter and people died everywhere. The collective farm fed us but when the wind was blowing and it was cold they could not reach us and that's when we would go hungry. People died but God helped me, and I survived. The second winter I was lucky and was taken in by distant relatives in a different region,' he remembered more than sixty years later.

According to an NKVD document written in September 1944, there were 68,000 Karachais and 38,000 Balkars in the 'special settlements' set up to receive them. The deportees lived under stringent restrictions on movement. They could not leave their designated place of settlement without a permit, and could be imprisoned if they did. Collective farms naturally kept back food for their members, and the new arrivals – already weakened by their terrible experience – sickened and died.

It is hard to pin down the early mortality rates among the settlers, but it was certainly high. In official documents, 471,871 people from all nations had been deported by July 1946, of whom 104,632 had already died. The experience naturally had a catastrophic effect on the birth rate as well, and just 7,976 babies were born in that period. That equalled a death rate of 22 per cent in two years, which testifies to the terrible conditions the settlers were forced to endure.

By 1951, more precise data had been gathered by the Soviet security apparatus. Published in an internal Interior Ministry table, it again highlighted the dreadful conditions faced by the deportees from the North Caucasus. Despite failing to include figures for 1943 or 1944, which must have been the years with the highest death tolls, the picture is appalling. In 1945, 44,652 people died and 2,230 were born. The next year 15,634 died, and 4,971 were born. The births figure did not overtake deaths until 1949, and the total number of deaths between 1945 and 1950 was almost double that of births.

In April 1949, the population of Karachais was 57,491, while there were 31,873 Balkars: a decline of 15 per cent and 16 per cent respectively on their estimated pre-deportation numbers. The scattered populations were in danger of disappearing altogether, while the restrictions on movement and work stopped them finding each other and re-establishing family or neighbourly groups.

'My relatives – my mother, my sisters – had gone to Almaty and they did not know where I was. They finally found me but then they found out they could not get permission to move me to them. You needed the right piece of paper,' remembered Khadzhiev.

'I worked in a teenagers' work brigade. I was an orphan effectively. My father had died when the war started, he was in prison and they killed him. People say this Stalin is good, but how could he take someone's livestock, send him to prison, shoot him and leave a kid like I was as an orphan? Could that person be good? I was illiterate, but a relative wrote to say that my sister and my brother lived in Almaty and had work. You could not even go to the next door village in those days. We had to sign up every month at the *komendatura*, and I did not get to Almaty until I was fifteen. I had not seen my mother for five or six years.'

The settlers had little time to remember their homeland, where their villages mouldered away with no one to look after them. But, in those high mountains, a handful of tribesmen remained – the bandits. Since they had not lived in the villages anyhow, they avoided being rounded up by the army and instead were left behind after their people vanished, like fish without a sea to swim in, lacking neighbours, friends and family.

The Soviet government sent a Balkar man called Akhiya Misirov up into the hills to persuade the outlaws to surrender, promising them an amnesty. Many of them agreed to lay down their illegal arms, although they surely knew the amnesty was illusory. Sure enough, they were sentenced to twenty-five years in prison – effectively, a death sentence in the conditions of the time – when they gave themselves up. Perhaps they had no choice since their supplies of food had dried up when their neighbours and families were taken away. But some people resolved to stay in their native hills, and to spurn the government's offer. Ismail 'Khutai' Zankishiev was among them and it is these last months of his life that created the legend that today hangs around him.

'Ismail Zankishiev, the leader of the bandit organization, is hiding in the mountains of the Cherek region with the remains of his organization. He announced that he will not legalize himself because the [Soviet Union's] signing of a treaty with England and America gives him the possibility of surrendering to the English authorities, who will apparently soon own the Caucasus,' said a report by the NKVD.

According to the stories now told about him, Khutai and a man called Shabayev moved together through the mountains, stealing cattle to eat which they would slaughter and store in natural deep freezes provided by the glaciers. They moved fast, crossing from valley to valley, exploiting the knowledge of local terrain that only they had. As the only Balkars left in their native mountains, they have become a symbol of the freedom their nation had lost. Balkars today have forgiven Khutai for his corruption and his viciousness in the 1920s and 1930s, and instead bless him for the defiance he showed.

But their every raid made them more vulnerable, since they could not avoid leaving tracks or leading their hunters directly to their hide-outs. And sure enough, in 1944, just a few months after the deportation, their luck ran out. Troops surrounded them in the high mountains, pinning them down among rocks with rifle fire. The out-laws fired back and held their assailants off, but were defenceless when their opponents brought up a mortar and began to lob shells down on top of them. Khutai and his gang, the last free Balkars in the Caucasus, died.

Since 1943, the police had taken to collecting the heads of dead bandits as proof of their demise, and they took Khutai's with them when they descended to the town of Nalchik once more. But, having deported the Balkar nation, there was no one left who could posi-tively identify him, and they were reduced to sending for someone from Kazakhstan who could confirm their victory.

A former colleague of Khutai's called Magomed Gazayev, therefore, made the long trip back to his homeland. According to the legend, he was forced to look on a grisly identification parade of disembodied heads, before he was despatched back to Kazakhstan. Among them, he confirmed, was that of the great bandit. Khutai was dead and the Turkic population of the high Caucasus had been exterminated.

The Soviet government made clear that it intended those Karach-ais and Balkars who had survived to remain in Central Asia for ever. In a secret decree from 1949, the government made clear that the exile was permanent. Any attempt to leave their allotted homes was pun-ishable by twenty years in prison, and anyone helping them to leave was liable to a sentence of five years. By cruel coincidence, the decree was dated 26 November 1948, just a fortnight before the Soviet

Union, and all the other members of the United Nations, signed up to the Universal Declaration of Human Rights.

Those included Article 9 – 'No one shall be subjected to arbitrary arrest, detention or exile'; Article 10 – 'Everyone is entitled in full equality to a fair and public hearing by an independent and impartial tribunal, in the determination of his rights and obligations and of any criminal charge against him'; and Article 11 – 'Everyone charged with a penal offence has the right to be presumed innocent until proved guilty according to law in a public trial at which he has had all the guarantees necessary for his defence'.

The government was merciless in its refusal to abide by these promises. A certain Sergeant Tappaskhanov wrote to Stalin in July 1945, asking that his sister and his brother be allowed to return to the Caucasus, where, it appears, he had found his way after being demobilized from the army. After listing the medals he won defending the nation, he described how one of his four brothers had been killed at the front, while two were missing, presumed dead. Only one other brother and his sister remained alive.

'When they were deported, they could take nothing with them, and now they live in their new place in very difficult circumstances,' he wrote.

'I already wrote you a letter in December 1944, asking that my brother and sister be allowed to move to the Kabardino-Balkar autonomous republic, but I received an answer ... that my request that my brother and sister be allowed to move to the Crimea could not be approved. But I did not ask and do not ask that they be allowed to move to the Crimea, I asked and ask that they be allowed to move with their children to Kabardino-Balkaria.'

He should not have wasted his ink. The next month, the government adopted a decree barring demobilized soldiers from the deported nations from returning to their former homes, and instructing their commanders to send them to Central Asia. Those former soldiers who had somehow found their own way to their former homes should be rounded up and sent to join their relatives in exile. Sergeant Tappaskhanov is unlikely to have stayed in the Caucasus for long and probably joined his brother and sister in Central Asia, rather than the other way round. Even those men who shed their blood defending the Soviet Union were deemed to have betrayed it on account of their nationality.

In the Soviet Union, however, even the word 'eternal' could change its meaning. Stalin died in 1953, ushering in a period of relative openness that would later be known as the 'thaw'. The Soviet dictator's butcher, Lavrenty Beria, who had personally presided over the deportations, was himself then rounded up and killed. Nikita Khrushchev took charge of the subdued state, promising to right the wrongs of his predecessor.

The first signs that something was changing for the deportees came in 1955, when their young men started to be conscripted into the army. Although the conscripted youths are unlikely to have rejoiced at the change, it meant they were now trusted to fight for the Soviet Union if the need arose, which was an important step towards rehabilitation. That year restrictions on the exiles' movement also began to be lifted, initially just for certain categories, and eventually for the whole nations.

In February 1956, Khrushchev accelerated the changes, making a speech to the 20th Party Congress condemning Stalin's 'cult of personality', and promising to redress the graver excesses of his rule. He mentioned the deportations of the Karachais and the Balkars by name as examples of Stalin's crimes.

'How can you lay responsibility for enemy actions of a few people on whole nations, including women, children, old people, communists and Konsomols [young communists], and subject them to mass repression?' he asked a closed session of the congress. Stalin, he said, had been drunk with power and no one had been able to stop his crimes.

'The Ukrainians only escaped this fate because there are too many of them and there was nowhere to put them,' he said, provoking laughter in the hall.

And then the Karachai-Balkar nation reappeared, having vanished from all official publications for more than a decade. They had not even warranted a mention in the public decree issued – two years late – by the government to legalize the deportation. The decree mentioned only the Chechens and the Ingush as having been deported from the North Caucasus, while books on state law also failed to mention the Turkic highlanders.

But in the 19 May 1956 edition of the newspaper *Sovetskaya Kirgizia* (*Soviet Kyrgyzstan*), the reader learned that the state publishing house had begun to publish the works of Karachai-Balkar poets in their native language. There was no explanation in the paper as to why these minorities should suddenly have arrived in Central Asia, though presumably its readers already knew. On 20 January 1957, Kazakh radio admitted the existence of a Karachai-Balkar dance troupe in the city of Almaty.

By that time, the Soviet government had in principle decided to allow the Turkic tribesmen to go home.

But news of Khrushchev's speech to the Party Congress had already filtered out and some 2,600 of the highlanders, anticipating their pardon, had acted on their own initiative and gone home on their own. A document from the Kabardin Republic's section of the Communist Party dated 22 May 1956 was already complaining that individual Balkars had already crept back to their homeland and were refusing to leave.

'The Balkars coming to Kabarda categorically refuse to leave the republic and affirm that only necessity, that is the use of force, can make them once again go to their place of settlement or to other regions outside the Kabardin Autonomous Republic,' the document, addressed to Moscow, said, before going on to suggest that the Balkars be put to work.

The local government tried to halt the flow of returnees, declaring itself unready for them. In June 1956 it said it did not have the money to accommodate the whole Balkar nation if it returned all at once, since the Balkar villages were destroyed and collective farms would have to build more accommodation. Only 23 per cent of their homes, the government said, remained intact.

But the Balkars kept up their pressure. A letter to the Communist Party's Central Committee in July 1956 described their desperation to come home. 'We, by the order of Beria and his gang, were called bandits, traitors, fascists, which artificially created enmity between nations. The words "Chechen", "Karachai", "Balkar" became common synonyms for the local population, which used these words to scare their children,' the letter, signed by one Zh. Zalikhanov, said.

'The longer we are based here, the more our thirst and desire to return to our homes increases ... We have a national saying: "the place where you were born is better than a place where you are satisfied".'

The government gave in. On 24 November 1956, a secret suggestion was made within the inner sanctum of the Communist Party that the Balkar and Karachai names be restored to their former homelands. By January of the next year, that had become a decree and the peoples were allowed to go home. Their nightmare was over.

But they did not receive any official apology or compensation. Instead, a veil was drawn over what happened to them and books from the period betray a remarkable amnesia about their fate, as if embarrassed by it.

The book *Sovetskaya Kabardino-Balkaria*, which was published in 1972 to mark the fiftieth anniversary of the region's creation as a communist autonomous region, hailed the local population's battle against the German army.

'When Kabardino-Balkaria was temporarily occupied by the Hitlerite forces, a guerrilla movement appeared here. The popular revengers of the republic conducted raids on the enemy garrisons, keeping the occupiers in constant action,' the book said, praising these guerrillas for killing 700 enemy 'Hitlerites' and capturing thirty-one. There was no mention of the alleged Balkar collaboration, nor of the massacre in the Cherek valley, nor of the subsequent deportation.

It was an approach used by other books from the 1960s onwards. Where once the Balkar and Karachai nations had been written out of existence, now the fact that they had been written out of existence was itself written out of existence. Some academics published accounts of the massacre in the Cherek region – two of them are listed by the dissident Aleksandr Nekrich in his book *The Punished Peoples* – but even these rare mentions squarely blamed it on the Germans, and would continue to do so for another three decades.

Soviet society forgot about the devastation visited on these little nations, and concentrated instead on building the communist utopia that was always just around the corner. But the Karachai and Balkar peoples remembered. And that remembrance would come spilling out as soon as it was allowed to.

17. Playing Stalin

Suddenly, in the mid-1980s, the Soviet system began to change with bewildering speed. For decades, the state had emphasized the common destiny of the Soviet peoples, but now the new movement towards openness allowed nations to examine their own experiences.

This allowed the Balkars and the Karachais to finally discuss what had happened to them in 1943–4, to debate who was to blame and to demand an apology. And an apology was not long coming. Even the most ardent communist had to recognize that deporting an entire nation was a grossly disproportionate punishment even if a few individuals had committed treason.

Mikhail Gorbachev, then still the leader of the world's largest country, condemned the deportations in September 1989. He was followed in November that year by the Supreme Soviet in Moscow, which called the deportations 'barbaric acts' contrary to international law. The local government in Nalchik followed suit, condemning the deportations and promising rehabilitation and compensation.

And the true facts of the Cherek valley massacre began to emerge as well. In August 1990, the local Interior Ministry's own newspaper, *Versiya*, published a searing article on the tragedy, and condemned the fact that soldiers, officially tasked with protecting the villagers, had ended up killing them.

'The leadership of the republic all these years has spent more time on the deaths of a few hundred cattle than on the genocide of a whole people. Yes, and until now the documents, related to this tragedy, are "top secret". Why? Who does this benefit?' the article asked.

But here the newspaper and the politicians were far behind the Balkars themselves. They had known the identity of their murderers all along, and had seized the opportunity afforded by Gorbachev's openness policy to erect a monument to the dead on the ruins of Sauty.

'Traveller, stop! Honour the memory of the 470 lives of children, women and old folk of this mountain village who were brutally shot and then burnt by the dogs of the Stalinist genocide – the NKVD troops in November 1942. We will save the memory of you for centuries. From Balkaria. 1989,' the monument said.

And the villagers were not prepared to leave it there. A group of people whose families came from the hamlet of Glashevo, all relatives of those killed by the NKVD, demanded a free investigation into the tragedy. The investigation was announced and they waited for a public admission of guilt. And sure enough, on 31 July 1992, Kemal Glashev – who shared a surname with fifty-five of the victims of the massacre – obtained a public admittance that their murders had been committed by Soviet troops.

This preliminary report by military prosecutors described the arrival of Nakin in the upper reaches of the Cherek valley, the murder of around 700 people, and the destruction of more than 500 houses. But it did not satisfy the villagers, for the prosecutors said no court case was planned since, in accordance with the law, the criminal case had been closed when Nakin was killed at the front in January 1943, just over a month after the massacre.

Furthermore, the prosecutors cleared the names of the captain's superiors, leaving Nakin alone to shoulder the blame for what had happened. The report even justified Nakin's actions by claiming that bandits and deserters had opened fire on his soldiers from the villages where the massacres took place.

This whitewash was not good enough for the Glashevo group, and they took their case to the regional parliament. It agreed with them, calling the prosecutors' decision to halt the case 'unfounded' and officially declaring that the massacres in Upper Balkaria were an act of genocide. The parliament also proclaimed the establishment of a separate investigative committee to record once and for all the truth of what happened.

It was a victory for the villagers, but it did not help their quest for justice. The military prosecutors were not going to be bounced into condemning one of their own, and they took another year and a half to issue a second report, which gave additional information on the massacre but confirmed that the criminal case would be closed once more, with no charges brought.

This second report's cold chronology of the events of those terrible days gives a bleak glimpse into the inhumanity of the Soviet army. Nakin, the report said, had told his superiors that he had killed 1,200 people in just twenty-four hours, but had been left to operate unsupervised in the remote valley.

The superiors, who had also died by this stage, were once again cleared of wrong-doing.

Of those superiors, General Kozlov had given the oral instruction 'to wipe villages of Balkaria from the face of the earth, stopping at nothing'. Divisional Commander Shikin, meanwhile, had passed on the instruction on paper, ordering Nakin 'to conduct the most decisive battle against banditism and its accomplices. In no circumstances should you show pity even to indirect accomplices. If there is a possibility to take hostages [the bandits' relatives], then send them to the plywood factory, but if you have to, destroy them.'

It is a chilling document, and the final whitewash and decision to heap the blame once more on Nakin has a dull, thumping inevitability.

'In the actions of Major-General P. M. Kozlov, commander of the 37th Army, no crimes are perceived in as far as the oral order to Divisional Commander Shikin "to wipe the villages of Balkaria from the face of the earth" has a figurative character, and therefore cannot be seen as an order to shoot the civilian population,' the prosecutors decided in a conclusion that astounds me every time I read it. Shikin's belated warning to Nakin not to harm women and children – which came after the captain announced he had killed the 1,200 people – got him off the hook as well.

The prosecutors, therefore, officially declared that there was no need to involve the courts and that the case was closed. Their official summary was released in March 1994, and is full of accounts of the fictional battles with bandits that Nakin's troops claimed to have fought, as if that justified their barbarity.

Fortunately, we are not forced to rely on the prosecutors' conclusions for information on the tragedy, since a small group of five Balkars had also been at work. Also in 1994, it published a tiny grey book with the simple title *The Cherek Tragedy*, based on the facts uncovered by the state commission into the events. In clear, unadorned, straightforward prose, it laid out precisely what had happened in November 1942, stripping away the accumulated lies that had congealed in the military prosecutors' reports and revealing the full horror of the Red Army's rampage. Perhaps with half an eye on the army's whitewash of itself, its authors called their book the 'first serious attempt' to uncover what had happened.

It is an excellent document, packed with archive reports, a detailed chronology and priceless eyewitness testimony which together form the backbone of my own account of the events.

Among the twenty-one eyewitnesses quoted at length in the book, many of them with grainy portraits to go with them, is a woman called variously Fazika or Nazifa Kishtikova. She was just six years old when the massacre occurred, and managed to escape by hiding under a bed when the soldiers burst in. She had been staying with her aunt Zariyat in Sauty so found herself in the heart of the tragedy, and cut off from her immediate family.

A wounded neighbour had burst in to tell the little group in her aunt's house what was happening, and they all hid in the house when the soldiers started to shoot at a sheep that was standing in their doorway. Having presumably killed the sheep, five or six soldiers forced their way into the room and ordered the inhabitants – all women and children – into the courtyard. Lined up by height with the tallest at one end and the smallest at the other, the young girl was last in line to be shot and managed to slip away unscathed before the bullets reached her.

She hid for several days, creeping out to drink water from a puddle and suffering from excruciating thirst, but survived.

When I called on her – unannounced – at her house in the suburb of Khasanya just outside the lowland city of Nalchik, it was hard to imagine her as a young girl, and harder still to imagine her as a lonely battler for justice. She was now a stout, white-haired old lady with a face scoured by the horrors she had seen. As she wandered around her spotless house, its walls decorated by carpets and a giant picture of the mosques in Mecca, we tried to communicate but repeatedly failed.

Like everyone of her generation who was a child during the deportations, she missed out on education and remains illiterate and almost entirely unable to speak Russian. Almost blind, she needed me to operate her telephone for her, and to find her daughter, who agreed to act as a translator.

For Kishtikova, whose maiden name was Ekhchieva, has a remarkable story beyond the miracle of her surviving the massacre. The state had declared what she had gone through in 1942 to be genocide, but had offered no compensation or support. The survivors like her were illiterate villagers with a distrust for the law and a dislike of the state. It was inconceivable that they would appeal for justice voluntarily, while human rights groups had other horrors to worry about.

What they needed was a sympathetic lawyer, willing to work for nothing, and that is just what Kishtikova had in her son-in-law.

'The idea to appeal to the court was mine,' the son-in-law, Iskhak Kuchukov, aged fifty-six, told me over tea in his office later that day. 'The murder of these civilians is a war crime. They closed the criminal case against Nakin, because he died. They said that an order to wipe villages from the face of the earth did not mean to kill. I was angry and just decided to see what would happen if I tried to gain her redress in the courts.'

He launched his mother-in-law's compensation case on the regional courts shortly after *The Cherek Tragedy* was published in 1994, armed with its account of events and witnesses prepared to testify on her behalf. She was appealing for compensation not because of what had happened to her, but because her father, Lokman Ekhchiev, was killed by the soldiers.

'When my mother-in-law started to tell me how she had hidden under the bed, it was interesting. That was when I decided to get involved. Then it kept not working out, and I got more involved. I was just interested to see if it was possible to gain compensation.'

It was still the heady 1990s, when activists believed that publicizing the crimes of the Soviet regime would be enough to persuade Russia's citizens to condemn it. The local parliament was on the side of the villagers, and President Boris Yeltsin himself marked the

1. The Russian army drove the Nogai nomads to their deaths in these marshes, where the Yeya river meets the Azov Sea, in 1783.

2. Three young men hold Circassian and Abkhazian flags at a ceremony by the Bosphorus in Istanbul, on 21 May 2008, commemorating the Circassian genocide.

3. Circassians from all over the Middle East gathered on the beach at the Turkish fishing village of Kefken to mark the Circassian genocide. When night fell, they li[t] torches and held a memorial procession.

4. A petition signed 'The Circassian nation', addressed to Queen Victoria and dated 9 April 1864, appealing for help against Russia: '… there is no act [o]f oppression or cruelty which is beyond the pale of civilisation and humanity, and which defies description, that it ha[s] not committed,' the letter said. It almos[t] certainly arrived in London after the final Circassian collapse.

5. Sebahattin Diyner, a Turkish Circassian who spoke at the International Circassian Congress in May 1991, holds a portrait of his grandfather in traditional dress.

6. A Circassian grave in the village of Altikesek in the Uzunyalya region near Kayseri, central Anatolia. It is written in Ottoman Turkish so must date from the first decades of the Circassian presence on the 'long plateau'.

7. Ali Kurt, an eighty-year-old Turk, stands in front of the hazel orchard where he and his father dug up the bones of the Circassians who died in 1864, just outsid Akchakale, Turkey.

8. Fragments of bone found in cracks in the rocks below the old ruined fort in Akchakale. I threw them into the sea, towards Circassia.

9. A Soviet-era monument commemorates a 1921 decree giving 'resorts to the workers', which helped start the transformation of historic Circassia into Russia's holiday coast.

10. The road up to Krasnaya Polyana, the mountain village where the last Circassians surrendered to the Russians in 1864, and the Russian army held a parade to celebrate the fact. It will host the winter Olympics in 2014, on the 150th anniversary of the genocide.

11. Khozemat Khabilayeva sits in her living room in Almaty, Kazakhstan. She and her sister were saved by their family dog, Khola, but they could not take him with them into exile.

12. Stalin, who ordered the deportation of the Chechens, the Ingush, the mountain Turks and other nations, is still admired in many parts of Russia, as this rock painting in the mountains of North Ossetia makes clear.

13. The peaks of the central Caucasus as seen from Georgia. This is the view that Freshfield and the other British mountaineers would have seen before they crossed over into the land of the mountain Turks.

14. The gorge of the Cherek valley. Freshfield's mountaineers passed up this narrow valley and were probably the first western Europeans to visit it.

15. Upper Balkaria today. Ruined houses are visible to the right of the picture.

16. A monument to the residents of the hamlet of Sauty slaughtered by Soviet soldiers in 1942. The Misirov family alone takes up almost four columns of names Ironically, Ali Misirov, who survived the massacre, went on to play Stalin in a post-Soviet film.

17. The memorial to Gazi-Muhammad, the first imam of Chechnya and mountain Dagestan, which stands just outside the village of Gimry. Pilgrims have tied strips of coloured fabric to it, which is slightly ironic since the imam devoted much of his time to stamping out such superstitions.

18. The view Imam Shamil would have seen from the site of his last stand in the natural fort of Gunib.

19. Imam Shamil is still honoured here, and his portrait stares out from a rock painting above the village of Gunib.

20. The author sits on the rock where General Baryatinsky sat to receive Imam Shamil's surrender in 1859. The site has been marked with a pavilion and a small patio.

21. Megeb, an ethnically Dargin village in central Dagestan, resembles a step pyramid.

22. Russian Cossacks march in Abkhazia, 2008.

23. Hatice Sener, a 75-year-old resident of the Turkish village of Guneykoy. She still speaks Avar, the Dagestani language of the village's founders, as do her neighbours.

24. The Dagestani influence is obvious in Guneykoy. This café has a portrait of Imam Shamil as an old man on the wall.

25. Abubakar Utsiev, the leader of the Chechen Sufis in the Kazakh village of Krasnaya Polyana, stands with his daughter on the bleak steppes.

26. Abudadar Zagayev, the only son of the sect's founder, Vis Haji, stands with one of his two wives and their children outside their house.

27 and 28. Members of the Sufi sect in Krasnaya Polyana dance their ecstatic zikr, accompanying their chant with drums, 'fiddles' and handclaps.

29. Tents in a Chechen refugee camp in Ingushetia, 2004.

30. Moscow's man in Chechnya, Akhmad Kadyrov, votes in Russian-organized elections in his home village of Tsentoroi, October 2003. He was killed less than a year later.

31. Khasan 'Dedushka' Bibulatov, the foul-mouthed and hilarious old man who underwent terrible torture at the hands of the Russian army in 1995.

fiftieth anniversary of the deportation with promises to make sure justice was done for the Balkars.

But, as Kuchukov's case ground on, the political atmosphere changed. The war in Chechnya hardened society against the appeals of Muslims from the Caucasus mountains, and the new president, Vladimir Putin, restored communist symbols and openly regretted the end of the Soviet Union.

Kuchukov, therefore, was as surprised as anyone when Kishtikova won. In October 2002, the court ruled that her father had been killed illegally and that she was eligible for compensation. For a moment, it seemed like a great victory. A victim of repression had managed to prove a specific act – rather than a mass action like the deportation itself – had occurred and managed to secure compensation for it, which was quite an achievement. But there was a sting in the tail.

'She won 10,000 roubles,' said Kuchukov with a wry smile. I initially assumed that was a monthly stipend, but he set me right. It was a lump sum. At the time, 10,000 roubles was equivalent to about £200 – two months' salary for the average Russian.

For the life of her father, and for the loss of all her father's property, with a delay of almost sixty years, Kishtikova had won enough to live on frugally for a few months. I thought back to the figures dreamt up by the 1943 investigation into the tragedy, and how one woman had supposedly lost property worth more than eleven years' wages. If that same scale was applied in 2002, Kishtikova would have been eligible for almost 700,000 roubles, with compensation for the loss of her father added on. What she had received was not compensation, it was an insult.

Only one other victim bothered to follow her lead and jump through the hoops required to win this nominal sum, and she happened to be Kishtikova's neighbour and the mother of one of the authors of *The Cherek Tragedy*. As for the other survivors of the massacre, who did not have connections to Kuchukov, they treated the state with the contempt with which it had treated them and ignored it.

Many of them still lived in the Cherek valley, and had done ever since they returned from exile, and I wanted to visit them, and to see for myself how the Balkars had recovered from their ordeal.

Getting to the Cherek valley was surprisingly easy. The gentle rolling hills of Kabarda reared up to forty-five degrees. Patches of rock showed among the grass, as if the mountains' muscles were straining to burst out of their skin. The trees became darker and more wild. And the land of the Balkars had begun. The road, which had been merrily bowling along by a stream, started to be pushed up against a cliff, and the valley ahead was choked by the gorge we were entering.

For centuries, the Balkars had been protected by their narrow valleys. Only a mule or a careful horse could have navigated the slopes leading to their homeland in the days before modern roads. No army could have passed this way without a long and agonizing march in single file, their approach overshadowed by cliffs a thousand metres high.

But now, the road has been tunnelled and cut into the cliffs, making the journey a joy rather than a struggle. The clear mountain air fizzed in my veins, and cut into my lungs in a feeling strangely reminiscent of the few weeks after giving up smoking. My body was not quite sure why breathing had become so easy.

A giant white-headed bird – an eagle perhaps, or a vulture – skimmed along the cliff opposite, wingtip-to-wingtip with its own shadow. It soared up to alight in a patch of trees clinging to a gentler slope in the middle of the bare rock. Perhaps no man had ever walked among those trees surrounded by cliffs, where the huge bird made its home. The glaciers above were a dazzling white against the blue of a perfect sky.

Amid this splendour, however, my mind kept flicking back to the days of the deportation. Although a road had been built by 1944, it had not been tunnelled out so generously, and it crawled around the cliffs rather than dodged through them. The deportation had been a logistical nightmare and I was filled with a reluctant admiration for the brains that had coordinated the destruction of this people. They might have been evil, but they knew how to do their jobs.

As we passed out of the gorge, the cliffs edged away from us, gradually easing their gradient and becoming khaki-brown. Ahead was the village I had come to visit, although it was unrecognizable as the scene of the massacre of November 1942. When the Balkars had returned, their own hamlets were in ruins. Their distinctive burrow-shaped houses had collapsed, where they had not been burned by the Red Army, and were uninhabitable.

The Soviet government did not restore the hamlets tucked up against the rocks. Instead, it built a straight street of modern houses along the valley floor. Generous though the action was, and comfortable though the houses were, the government may also have wanted to concentrate the villagers for easier control, for this was a tactic repeated in all the valleys of the Balkars and the Karachais.

A map in the museum in Nalchik illustrated the abandonment of the Balkars' villages well. It showed present-day villages with red lights, and pre-deportation villages with dots of light blue. The abandoned villages clustered in the high valleys like clumps of planets around the red star of the present-day settlement. There were red lights now on the plains too, for not all the Balkars were allowed to return to their ancestral homes in the mountains. Scattered among the Circassians on the plains, they would be less likely to take to the hills again and cause trouble.

But the ruined villages are not only remembered by blue glowing dots on a map. Their remains are still there on the hillsides, rising up in terrace after terrace of finely crafted walls. Across the rushing river Cherek from the present-day village of Upper Balkaria, and reached by a rusting suspension bridge, is what is left of Kunyum, Khutai's home hamlet. It rose up from the river bank like a maze. Each level interlocked with those above and below, but in no recognizable pattern, and I was reduced to scrambling up collapsing walls to ascend higher. There was no sign that anyone else had been there recently, and the only witness to my visit was a curious horse who watched me out of sight.

At the top of the village stood a tower. Square and tapering, it was of the kind that is far more common over the mountains in Georgia where the Svans long delighted in building defensive towers to use as bases for attacking their neighbours. I sat at its foot and wondered for a while whether this tower was the one built by Akhtougan to defend himself and his kidnapped bride against his irate father-in-law's army. But I was wrong, for Akhtougan's tower was in the Baksan valley at the foot of Mount Elbrus sixty kilometres or so to the west. Perhaps another family feud, this one lost from history, had provoked this mammoth construction.

The ruins of Sauty were below me, while tracks led into the hills where once Glashevo and other hamlets had held communities of herders. The square, blue-green patches of cabbage fields dotted the valley floor – cabbages grow particularly well at this altitude – and fruit trees spilled delicious plump plums and apples onto the roads.

Over to my right – to the south – the river flowed from deep in the mountains where the pass into Georgia crossed by the British climbers in the nineteenth century had represented safety for the Red Army soldiers desperately fleeing the Germans.

At my back were the steep slopes of the mountains. It was easy to see how the residents of this hamlet, who had been warned of the approach of the Red Army soldiers on the other side of the river in sufficient time, had managed to escape their assailants and flee into the hills. Less than a hundred metres away, a ravine dived into the mountainside, and beyond that were the high pastures and safety.

Downhill to my left, where the valley turned north towards Russia, stood the neat square houses built by the Soviets. They looked modern and more hygienic than the stone-built burrows I was sitting among, but I knew which I would rather be living in if the valley was attacked once more.

Back on the valley floor, I set off in search of survivors of the November 1942 massacre, aware that few of them would be able to tell me new information since they would be very old now, and would have been very young during the events. A son of Mariyam – the woman who lost her fingers and whose baby flew through the air after being hit by a bullet – was said to live here, but I could not find him, and ended up talking to another Mariyam whom I was directed to by mistake.

Mariyam Endreyeva, now eighty-two years old, had lived in a remote hamlet when the massacre took place, and remembered seeing refugees as morning broke.

'People came running to us and told us what had happened, and we ran with them into the hills. We were panicking, we were all panicking.

We were in the hills for ten days, while this was all going on. The children that survived came to us, they were still alive, no one knows how they survived. We lived in caves,' she told me and a small audience of family members who had gathered to hear her story.

She lay on her back in a bed drawn up in the house's living room, her bare right foot poking out from under the blanket. She spoke in Balkar, and as she spoke I had plenty of time to watch a fly which was walking steadily all the way from her big toe to her little toe, bridging the gaps in between with little jumps. When it reached the end, it dawdled for a while, then started back again.

Once Endreyeva started talking, she would not stop, and moved seamlessly into the story of the deportation and how the soldiers had sat at the end of the trucks stopping them from getting a clear view of their homes as they drove away.

As she talked, the gaps she left for translation into Russian became less frequent, and I was free to listen to the free flow of the Balkar language.

It seemed amazing that she could have lived eighty-two years in Russia and not have learned Russian, but as I listened to her talk it became increasingly clear why. The impact of Moscow on her life had been wholly negative – a fact betrayed by the Russian words that had crept into her native tongue over the years: 'soldier'; 'army'; 'komendatura'; 'registration'; 'special settler'. These were the words of repression and hate, not the words of education and enlightenment.

Her family directed me further down the street to another survivor. Abdurakhman Misirov, now aged seventy-two, a straight-backed noble-looking man, told me his own tale with minimal prompting. Like most of the survivors, he had been too busy hiding to note down details of the massacre, but he confirmed how the villagers had never believed the official story that the Germans had killed their neighbours.

'The shooting started at night, we could hear it, so close, and we hid ourselves in a haystack. There were thirty or forty of us in there. Some injured people came there too. We were there for seven days, without food, without water even. That was when they burned the village. We were scared we would burn too, so we ran away at night,' he said.

'We knew who had done this, we knew it was the Red Army men, and we had not expected it. How could we have expected it? If we had expected it, we would have run into the mountains. They were in Soviet uniforms, so we knew who they were. Even before the deportation, these officials were saying it was the Germans who did this, but we knew they were lying all along.'

He did not invite me in, and I could tell he was not comfortable talking about what had happened, perhaps because he knew that at least 112 people with his surname had not been as lucky as him and had died at the hands of those Soviet soldiers.

But before I went he told me I should look up the tale of a relative of his: Ali Misirov, who gave evidence to the commission investigating the crime, and whose incredible story was thereby saved for posterity.

Ali Misirov's account is probably the most lucid of all those given by the eyewitnesses in *The Cherek Tragedy*. It stands on its own and does not intersect with those of any other survivors, unlike many of the others quoted earlier. Born in 1918, Misirov was serving at the front in 1942, but was seriously wounded by shrapnel, and sent home on leave after his treatment. At home in Sauty, he was made secretary of the local division of the Communist Party, as one of the few literate and military-age men around. This did not apparently imply any sympathy for the communists, however, since he watched impassively as Khutai and his men bombarded the Red Army's garrison with the anti-aircraft gun they had seized from the retreating Soviets, and then saw how the troops left the valley over the high pass towards Ossetia. The soldiers, he said, had been detaining local men, which was why the bandits had decided to bombard them in the first place.

'Directly after the soldiers left, the villagers found in the basement the bodies of seven or eight of their neighbours who had disappeared earlier,' he recalled, setting the scene for what would happen later.

As a communist, he was clearly concerned that he would be killed by the advancing Germans and himself planned to leave the valley on the morning of 28 November, but was forestalled by the arrival of Nakin and his men. They started to shoot around two o'clock that morning.

'Everyone who was in the house began to run all over the place, and I, just in my underpants, jumped into the potato clamp. After a little time I looked out. The soldiers were gathering people and shooting them in groups of five or ten. Everyone. Women, children, no difference. Alibek Misirov, and he was a complete cripple, was shot without a thought. Children running away were shot in the back,' he said.

'At first I thought that the Germans had come, but then I clearly heard the Russian language, being spoken well.'

He said he had never lost consciousness at the front, but hiding in the potato store he had no idea how much time passed as he drifted into a daze. After a period – 'maybe three days, maybe five' – he came out of his hole, and walked outside. He saw a soldier, but the soldier took fright at the sight of this half-naked man wandering around in the snow and himself ran away. Misirov called the soldier back, telling him to take him to the staff building. There Misirov managed to convince them he was in the army and not a bandit, and their doctor agreed to treat him. Misirov collapsed. He lay unconscious when Nakin's troops pulled out, and was spared by the Romanian troops who briefly occupied the valley.

'All my people were killed – my wife, my son, my sister with her two children – but I did not bury them – I was ill, I did not have the strength to stand. They say that whole bodies were only found rarely, in the main there were just burnt bits, which were buried in bags, in pillowcases, or just wrapped up in cloth,' he said.

His account stops there, and the reader is left to wonder whether he returned to the army. Presumably, he did so, although he had died before I visited the mountains so I had no chance to ask him myself. Perhaps he was arrested as a bandit and sent to Siberia. We know he survived the war, so maybe he was deported directly from the front. Or he may have been one of those soldiers who were demobilized and condemned as traitors only when they had finished fighting their country's enemies. Either way, he would have had decades to rave at the horrible irony of being exposed to the massacre only because he had been injured fighting for his country.

But the greatest irony was yet to come.

In 1990, the controversial Soviet film director Alexei German, who had outraged Soviet officials with his portrayal of Red Army soldiers in a film called *Checkpoint* and who was known for his absolute perfectionism when it came to casting and props, needed an actor to play Stalin in his film *Khrustalyov, My Car*. He sent envoys to the Caucasus to find an old man who looked like the dictator.

Sure enough, they found Misirov. The man's resemblance to Stalin was uncanny, and he – who was seventy-nine when the film was released in 1998, just five years older than Stalin was when he died – played the dictator as Stalin lay shaking and spitting on his death bed.

I would like to think Misirov enjoyed acting the role of the man whose troops killed his family and destroyed his nation, since his part consisted of little more than choking, vomiting and wallowing in his own faeces. The film itself, though it veers into very self-indulgent territory, presents a horrible picture of Stalin's Moscow as a place of arbitrary arrest, random and unexplained violence, rape, cruelty and nightmarish weirdness.

It must have been a bewildering journey for Misirov to have started his adult life hiding in a potato store listening to his whole family being murdered by Stalin's forces, then to reach the end of his life impersonating the great ruler while a nurse removed his soiled pyjamas. This new Russia was surely a land of freedom.

But, as ever, the situation was more complicated than that. It might now be possible to make films showing Stalin as a frail and pitiful old man, but that did not mean the majority of Russians disapproved of what the dictator had done. As I write this, one of Russia's subservient state television channels – which never take a step without Kremlin approval – has just announced that its viewers voted Stalin the third greatest Russian of all time. Stalin had been in first place in the poll, and even threatened to win it, until a producer appealed for people to vote for someone else to avoid embarrassment.

And, despite the state commission and the definitive account of the events in the Cherek valley published in *The Cherek Tragedy*, their version had not found universal acceptance. Only 1,000 copies were ever printed and it has vanished from bookshops. My copy was given to me by a kind family in Upper Balkaria, and has a child's doodles inside the front and back covers, and several pages ripped out.

In the absence of this account of the truth, the myth of German involvement in the massacre has resurfaced.

Valery Dzidzoyev, an academic in the nearby city of Vladikavkaz, wrote an article in 2005 called 'In Search of Historical Truth' analysing whether Muslim nations in the North Caucasus had really betrayed their homeland during the Second World War. In it, he blamed the massacres in the Cherek valley on German soldiers from the Edelweiss Division, and did not mention the Red Army at all. The article was published by a research body run by the government of Kabardino-Balkaria, in clear breach of promises made in 1992 to publicize the truth of what had happened.

And this was not the only promise it has broken. After the government officially announced in 1992 that what had happened in the Cherek valley had been an act of genocide, it pledged to investigate the legality of the 1943 investigation into the killings, to check if any of the guilty parties were commemorated in street names or in monuments and to make recommendations to correct that, to erect a memorial complex in Balkaria itself, to ask the central government to give compensation to the victims or their relatives, and to ask the prosecutors to re-examine all criminal cases connected to the events.

These promises seem to have been forgotten. General Kozlov, who ordered his subordinates to wipe the villages of Upper Balkaria from the face of the earth, still has a street in Nalchik named after him. Apart from the two women who trudged through the courts, none of the survivors of the massacre, or the victims' relatives, who spoke to me had received compensation, and they did not expect to get any. There have been no further investigations into the killings.

As for the memorial complex, that has also not materialized. A bare slab of granite stands on the hillside near where Sauty once was, and bears the words 'The Place Where a Memorial to the Victims of the Genocide of the Civilians of the Cherek Region will be Set Up'. The slab is set on a plinth of rough rocks, and the words are now so faded as to be barely legible. The residents do not expect to see their memorial complex any time soon.

The authors of *The Cherek Tragedy* made a series of conclusions at the end of their book, which reflected the hopes still present in 1994 that Russia would develop democratically and peacefully.

'We must with all our strength fight against any war, before it has even started. Any war, especially in the atomic age, cannot be a means to resolve an argument,' they wrote.

The new era of freedom and equality that those authors hoped for was to prove illusory. Even before they wrote those words the Caucasus had been aflame in Abkhazia, in South Ossetia and in Ingushetia, as the new freedoms of long-oppressed nations collided with each other. The losers and the gainers of the unfair Soviet system flew at each other, in their attempts to secure what they saw as their rights.

The new Russia was to prove every bit as violent, corrupt and inhuman as the old. For the people of the Caucasus, the rule of the presidents would prove little better than the rule of the tsars, or the rule of the communists. For the most brutal war the mountains has ever seen was about to break out: in Chechnya.

PART THREE

Grozny, 1995

18. War is War, But to Behave in That Way is Not Right

Aidrus Khazaliev had been waiting to go home for all his adult life.

Deported from his native Chechnya by Stalin's troops aged just sixteen, he had lived in Central Asia ever since. One obstacle after another had stopped him returning home – the Soviet police, then difficulties selling the house, then his father's illness, bureaucratic problems, work, family – but now nothing was going to get in his way. It was 1994, the freedoms secured when the communist state collapsed were safe, and he was finally going back to the Caucasus.

'We took our children, and we had two whole wagons on the train for our things. It was in May, I remember it,' said Khazaliev, a thick-set, handsome 81-year-old wearing a white shirt buttoned up to the top, fourteen years later.

It had been a risk selling the house that he and his sons had built in Almaty, in the south of what is now Kazakhstan, but the call of his blood had been overwhelming. He wanted to go back and live out his declining years in a land where Chechen was spoken and Chechens were finally in charge.

The preceding five years had been revolutionary for the Chechen nation. After almost two centuries of oppression, war and discrimination, the Chechens had finally begun to rule themselves. The first major shift came in 1989, when Doku Zavgayev became the first ethnic Chechen to head their government since the deportation.

The whole nation was taking part in a national reawakening. Amid the ferment, Chechen historians were working to unpick the mesh of Soviet lies surrounding their ancestors. Their children had been taught that Chechnya had voluntarily joined the Soviet Union, and that the men who had fought the Russian conquest in the nineteenth century were agents of Turkey and England. A statue of their most hated oppressor, Alexei Yermolov, stood in the centre of Grozny, and their ethnic kin were excluded from senior positions.

In Checheno-Ingushetia, the legacy of the deportation still hung over the native peoples, although the overwhelming majority of them had returned home under Stalin's successor in the Kremlin. In the mid-1980s, only a third of top officials in the Communist Party were Chechen or Ingush. Russians outnumbered locals in all key positions – a political divide that extended into the economy where the oil and heavy industries that dominated Grozny were also controlled by Russians.

Young nationalists united into a movement called Kavkaz – 'Caucasus' in Russian – in 1988, and Visita Ibragimov was one of them. He was thirty-eight years old, and had only just come back to Grozny. As a young man, he had left his homeland to find work in central Russia. He had been unable to afford the 3,000-rouble bribe to secure a good job in his homeland and, without a job, he could not get a residence permit from the police so Grozny had been barred to him.

The corruption in Chechnya angered him, as did the incompetence and graft in his adopted city. As the 1980s passed by, the Soviet Union began to relax its grip on political activity, and he attended opposition meetings in Moscow and elsewhere. He began to sense that times had changed, and the balance of power was shifting, and that it was time for him to go home.

'In 1981, the Russians in Grozny would not even reply if I said hi to them on the street. Now, they would come up to me and ask how I was doing,' he remembered later.

With a Chechen running the government, many Chechens believed they were witnessing the dawn of a new age. The nationalists harnessed the anger and frustration of a generation of men like Ibragimov to demand broader autonomy and new rights.

And the Chechens began to listen to them. The version of history that the nationalists expressed – that of resistance, and oppression – appealed to national pride, and made more sense than the cant taught in Soviet schools. If the Chechens had indeed voluntarily joined the Soviet Union, why was the tsarist General Yermolov quoted as saying: 'Chechnya may rightly be called the nest of all the bandits'?

The Soviet economy was collapsing, so underemployed young people had little to do except attend demonstrations, and the

nationalist movement began to put pressure on the local government, which had declared regional sovereignty within the Soviet
Union in November 1990. A Chechen had only been heading the
region for a year, and already the first step towards independence was
taken.

Nationalists like Ibragimov organized a national congress for
November 1990. Here they would discuss and define their nation's
aspirations. Could the Chechens really gain independence? And, if
they did, who would lead them? Would it be Zavgayev, the dour
former collective farm chairman with experience of the back-room
style of Soviet government? Or would it be one of the flashy and
charismatic ideologues of the opposition? All camps were represented
in the congress, which had invited other Chechens to speak too –
including the most high-ranking Chechen in the Soviet air force,
Major-General Dzhokhar Dudayev.

Dudayev was a rare star among the Chechens. He had a Russian
wife, and had lived almost his whole life out of his homeland. But
people who expected him to have become russified during his exile
were proved wrong. Handsome, successful and gifted, the military
aviator hit the congress like a missile. It was love at first sight.

'He gave an excellent speech,' remembered Ibragimov with passion, as if the seventeen years that had passed were nothing, 'even
though he was from western Chechnya and had an accent. Everyone
was quiet and listened.'

The speech was a call to arms, appealing to the Chechens to restore
their lost independence and to throw off Russian rule. Some of the
listeners were appalled by it, but most cheered and roared. Completely seduced by the general's charm, they elected him to head the
congress's executive committee.

'Just imagine it,' said Ibragimov, his voice sunk to a whisper.
'Dudayev was such a beautiful man, and he gave this inflammatory
speech. He was a real general, a fighter. The rest of us were all the
same, we all knew each other. It is like when you are at school, you
are not interested in the girls you study with every day. Then a girl
comes from another school and you're interested. This Dudayev was
like that, he was someone we did not know. And he took charge.'

In photographs now, I can see how this general could have used his charisma to win the Chechen nationalists over.

On the cover of a book of state documents published in 1993, Dudayev is in the pilot's seat of an aircraft. Wearing headphones, a fur-collared camouflage jacket and a chunky military watch, he is giving the thumbs-up to the camera. A thin moustache – the kind that for British people belongs only on the face of Errol Flynn or a Second World War spiv – is raised up by a wry smile, which has creased the lines around his twinkling eyes. It is a picture of a handsome, dynamic, successful man. He looks like he has a sense of fun, but – since he is at the controls of a warplane – he also knows how to control and to kill.

On the back cover of the book, a young teenager is the focus among a crowd of men. His clenched right hand is raised in a defiant fist above his head, while his left hand clutches an ancient shotgun. The barrel of another gun, which looks like it may have more killing power than the shotgun, peeps out from under the jacket of the man next to him.

Other photographs inside the book show Dudayev relaxing at home, engaged in martial arts, meeting the people, talking to religious leaders. In one of them he is pictured opposite the lone wolf he chose as the symbol of Chechnya. The wolf summed up how Dudayev saw the Chechens: fierce if attacked, but only killing to eat. The wolf cannot be tamed, but is loyal to its comrades.

In all the photographs, he maintains the same unflappable quality. The sardonic half-smile suggests a man looking on the world as some kind of joke.

It is an entirely misleading impression.

As his enemies were to discover, Dudayev was erratic in conduct, but single-minded in attaining his goal. He wanted an independent Chechnya, and was prepared to shed blood to achieve it. His last post in the Soviet military had been as head of a strategic bomber wing in Estonia and he had witnessed how a small nation could throw off Soviet rule. Estonia's population was greater than Chechnya's, but its Russian minority was larger too, so the gap between the number of ethnic Estonians and the number of ethnic Chechens was only 100,000 people or so.

For Dudayev, the independence that Estonia was achieving could come to his homeland as well, even though Chechnya – as an autonomous region within Russia, not a republic within the Soviet Union – did not technically have Estonia's legal right to proclaim itself independent. Full republics, like Estonia, Ukraine, Kazakhstan and the others, had a legal right to declare independence under the Soviet constitution. It was not a right the framers of the constitution ever expected them to exercise, but it still existed.

Autonomous regions – like Chechnya, Dagestan and dozens of others – did not have the same constitutional right to independence. They were tied to whichever republic they had been assigned to by Soviet mapmakers.

The debate over whether Chechen independence was legal or not has been going on ever since, but for nationalists there is no question about it. Their land had been forcibly incorporated into a state they wanted no ties to, and they did not see why a constitution imposed on them should stop them proclaiming their rights.

Dudayev was no radical Islamist like many of the Chechens who would follow him. He loved Russian culture, and his wife wrote poems in Russian. In an interview in May 1992, he said he had read and reread Pushkin and Lermontov, and that every time he pondered their words, he understood them more deeply.

'Personally, I find it hard to imagine Chechnya without Russia,' he said.

But he had been deeply scarred by the experience of the 1944 deportation of his people. He was just an infant when the Chechen nation was taken and dumped in Central Asia. He grew up accused of being a traitor, although two of his brothers had fought in the Soviet Army against the Germans. He had struggled even to win a place at school, since he lacked official documentation and could not prove his age.

Such petty humiliations coupled with the desperate conditions the nation lived in after deportation had aroused a feeling of injustice in him, as it had in the whole Chechen nation.

This is surely the root of the desire to break free of Russian rule. Russians to this day simply fail to understand how an event like the deportation, in which 478,479 Chechens and Ingush were loaded onto trains and sent away in February 1944, created the world view of their Chechen neighbours. Between 1926 and 1939, the Chechen population grew by 26 per cent. In the next twenty years, it grew by only 2.5 per cent. The suffering that caused that statistic is indescribable.

Anne Applebaum, a journalist and historian whose book *Gulag* gives the most complete and harrowing picture of the horrors of the Soviet Union prison system, compared Russian ignorance of what had been done to the Chechens to an imaginary Germany that had forgotten the crimes of the Nazi regime.

'If the Russian people and the Russian elite remembered – viscerally, emotionally remembered – what Stalin did to the Chechens, they could not have invaded Chechnya in the 1990s, not once and not twice. To do so was the moral equivalent of post-war Germany invading western Poland. Very few Russians saw it that way – which is itself evidence of how little they knew about their own history,' she wrote.

In August 1991, hardliners rose up against the Soviet Union's reforming leadership. The freedoms of perestroika and glasnost were under threat, but the government in Chechnya hesitated to speak out. Though he was a Chechen, Zavgayev was a good Soviet functionary too. He intended to choose sides when it had become clear who had won. He was in Moscow when the hardliners rebelled, and he sought counsel while he was there. He waited two days before returning to Grozny. When he came back to Chechnya he talked, he thought, he hesitated, and he lost the moment.

Dudayev on the other hand had no hesitation about acting. He called the people out onto the streets to support the democratic movement headed by Boris Yeltsin, who was leading the crowds in Moscow against this attempt to crank back the clock.

Grozny was paralysed by a general strike, and the central squares were thronged by crowds of Chechens revelling in the destruction of communist control.

A fortnight later, they seized the Supreme Soviet and threw a Russian communist out of a window. He was the only casualty of the revolution, which also effectively ended Zavgayev's political career. Yeltsin, who had by this stage defeated the coup in Moscow, put pressure on Zavgayev to quit and Chechnya's Supreme Soviet dissolved itself.

Dudayev ignored attempts to set up an interim government, and took control himself. A hastily arranged election swept him to power with 90 per cent of the vote, and on 2 November 1991 the new parliament held its first session and declared independence.

It was a momentous time for the Chechen nation, made even better a week later, when Yeltsin's attempt to proclaim a state of emergency in Chechnya failed. Moscow sent 600 troops to Grozny, but they were surrounded by a crowd of civilians, disarmed and sent home. By June 1992, all Moscow's soldiers had left Chechnya. The Chechens were free to decide their own destiny.

In distant Kazakhstan, Aidrus Khazaliev was watching the developments with disbelief. That he could go home to a free Chechnya was a fantasy that he had never even dreamed of. He was retired, and intended to take his whole family to live out the rest of their days in peace.

While Khazaliev planned and schemed to sell his property and gather up his family, Dudayev set his stamp on things. His methods of government involved sweeping plans, which would rarely be fulfilled, and elaborate accusations against Russia. Moscow was indeed working to undermine him, but his constant jibes would have made a working relationship all but impossible to secure even if the Russians had been interested in a stable relationship.

In 1992, for example, he accused a Russian official of putting a price on his head.

'It started at five million roubles, and now the price has risen to billions. In greenbacks, it is a few million,' he said with ill-concealed relish.

In March that year, Dudayev's opponents within Chechnya sought to storm the television station, and parliament proclaimed an emergency. The television station would prove a regular target; it was blown up later in 1992, as bomb attacks and shootings became standard fare in Chechen life.

The region's status was unresolved with Russia. Russian officials mentioned Chechnya's independence in negotiations, such as in March, May and September 1992, and accepted its separation from

Ingushetia – the Ingush half of Checheno-Ingushetia, which had decided to stay within Russia. However, at the same time, Kremlin representatives tried to undermine Dudayev and his government.

This ambivalence left the door open for unique economic crimes. Dudayev had not abolished the Russian currency, and had pegged bread prices at a nominal one rouble. Since prices were uncontrolled outside Chechnya, a profitable trade in bread sprang up instantly. Chechens also enjoyed the lack of import controls, and bought consumer goods in the Middle East, flew them by chartered aircraft to Grozny, and sold them to residents of the nearby regions of Russia. Grozny became the clearing house for the whole Caucasus. Anything – guns, drugs, televisions, fridges – could be bought there.

Other, more elaborate scams sprang up too. In May 1992, a policeman in Moscow happened to notice a man drop a heavy sack, from which tumbled wads of roubles. The policeman stopped and searched the man and his accomplices, eventually finding more than six million roubles. He had, entirely accidentally, discovered the biggest bank robbery in Russian history. Since the banks in Chechnya were still officially part of the Russian banking system, they could issue promissory notes that would be honoured in Moscow. That meant someone with connections in Grozny could obtain unlimited amounts of cash by just pretending the money had been deposited in Chechnya.

When the fraud was discovered, the Moscow banks were in for another shock. Chechen 'policemen' had called after the promissory notes were honoured, and asked the banks to hand them over. The banks often had no proof that any money had been given out at all.

For well-connected Chechens, their homeland's legal uncertainty was a goldmine. Khazaliev, however, saw none of this easy money. He was in fact refreshingly upfront about the impact all this political and economic manoeuvring had on his life.

'We did not know about Dudayev, we were pensioners,' he said with an air of finality when I asked him what he thought of the general's cowboy government. In 1994, after he moved back to Grozny, he was busy getting the house he bought on the edge of the capital ready for his family. It was completed in September that year, and the family enjoyed a huge occasion of feasting and joy.

The Khazaliev family got to enjoy that house for almost exactly three months.

For while the building work was going on, Dudayev and Yeltsin were inching ever closer to violence. A bomb nearly killed Dudayev in the very month that Khazaliev arrived back in his homeland, and a Moscow-backed opposition made regular raids on Grozny from a base near the Russian border. In July, while Khazaliev's house was being repaired and made ready, the Russian government said it might have to intervene if the violence – which it was itself initiating – went on.

In November, after Khazaliev had moved into his new home, the opposition – supplied with tanks by Moscow – attempted to seize Grozny but was forced back, and several of its tanks destroyed.

Yeltsin, humiliated by the defeat of his proxies, threatened to intervene to restore peace. It was a disastrous miscalculation. The Chechens, thousands of whom had been protesting against Dudayev, rallied around their leader, who refused to stand down. It was war.

'We had to flee Grozny on 17 December,' said Khazaliev. 'We abandoned our house and fled to the village.'

Grozny had become terrifyingly dangerous. Russia's troops – 40,000 strong, but mainly conscripts with little training or idea what they were doing – took weeks to reach Grozny, often stopped by crowds of civilians or by their own disgusted officers. When the Russians finally reached the city, their tanks lacked infantry support and were vulnerable to grenade attacks from apartment blocks lining the streets.

Frustrated by their inability to reach the centre, the artillery and warplanes poured explosives into the city – one observer counted forty-seven explosions within a minute, but was so appalled that he stopped counting before the sixty seconds was up – smashing apartment blocks and the water system, and killing tens of thousands of civilians. One estimate says 27,000 civilians died in the bombardment of Grozny that winter, most of them ethnic Russians who, unlike Khazaliev, had nowhere to go.

Khazaliev crept back to see his house when the fighting had quietened.

'We went back on 13 February, and found that the soldiers had used our house. Everything was destroyed. My son had a big collection of rare records, and they were all destroyed,' he said.

The son, Ilyas, who had sat in the room with us but stayed quiet up to now, spoke out.

'If they had stolen the records it would have been better, they could at least have been used somewhere. But they broke everything,' he said. Perhaps emboldened by her son's words, Koka – Khazaliev's wife – spoke up too.

Wearing a flowery dress and a polka-dotted dark headscarf, she had sat and looked sadder and sadder as the story went on.

'They broke all of my dishes. The house was half-burned, so we were without gas or electricity with war all around. The bombing, we did not think we would survive. Then on 4 April, we went back to Almaty, and here we are,' she said.

Russia's bombing had forced them to return into the exile that Stalin had imposed on them. They had gone to a free Chechnya by train with two containers full of their property, and hearts full of hope. Less than a year later, they flew back into exile with the few things they had salvaged in a suitcase, and a leaden burden of despair they have never managed to shake off.

'It was impossible for men to walk around the town; if you were between twelve and sixty and you appeared in the town, you would be killed or disappeared,' said Ilyas, who had left the room and come back holding the three records that survived – one by Creedence Clearwater Revival and two by The Beatles.

'One half of our house was all burnt, and in the other half officers had lived and it was appalling. All 600 records were broken, and they stole all the furniture,' Ilyas added, giving way to his mother once more.

'If they could take it away, they took it, and if they could not, they burnt it or broke it so nothing remained,' she said, stern-faced and sad.

'I used to pity the soldiers when I saw them, we used to take them food because we felt bad for them. But when I saw what they did to our house, it was so unpleasant, and ...' She ran out of words for a few seconds, before starting again. 'War is war, I know, but to behave in that way is not right.

'All these young men, they wrote on the walls, they stole every-thing. They ate what was in the house but that is not a problem. But why, why did they have to be so uncultured? Russians think of them-selves as a cultured people, but they acted in this way. Please take the food, it is war. But what they did was just not nice. There was dirt everywhere, they did it on the floor and the rain and the snow spread it everywhere.'

I did not quite understand what she was saying, since she – as a Chechen woman with the sense of dignity expected of her – had spoken euphemistically. But her husband had been saving up this one great insult and, seeing that I had not understood his wife, he made things clear.

'You are a Russian soldier, imagine, you go to someone's house. They took what they could, they burnt everything, but why? Why did they do this? They used our house as a toilet, why was this neces-sary? I will never forget this, and I will tell the children what they did. Now if you go to any town, there are lists of people killed in Chechnya: Ivanov, Peskov, Siderov,' he said, listing typical Russian surnames.

'Every Russian will read these lists and hate Chechens. And why will they hate us? Because these Russians came to kill Chechens and were killed themselves.'

I had not planned to talk to them about their house in Grozny, about how they had dreamed and dreamed about going home to finally build a home in their own land. I had intended to ask them about the deportation, and about their early years in Kazakhstan. But as their story poured out of them, I forgot my carefully planned questions, and listened sadly to how one man's dreams, along with those of his wife and sons, had been crushed by politicians they knew nothing about.

I was appalled by the depth of sadness with which they had recounted how their home in a free Chechnya had became a toilet for Russia's occupying soldiers in just three months.

Despite myself though, I could not help being amazed by the appropriateness of how those Russian soldiers had acted. If divorced from the Khazalievs' own tragedy, their tale was a metaphor for everything Russia has ever done in Chechnya: the spitefulness, the brutality, the lack of justification, and the stupidity. It has, in short, used Chechnya as a toilet.

I have talked to hundreds of Chechens – politicians, poets, warriors, businessmen, officials – about their life stories, but the story of the Khazalievs' dream home moved me more than any other.

They were simply a Chechen family that wanted to live in freedom, but Russia – no doubt without even realizing what it had done – did not let them. In the same way, their whole nation has been denied the right to manage itself for the last 200 years.

'In short,' Khazaliev said, 'in my life I have seen nothing good. I have been scared all the time. It has never been calm. In 1944, I was brought here, then I went home, and there was war and I had to leave.'

He had earlier shown me photographs of his wife's relatives. They were descendants of a Chechen who in 1918 led another doomed attempt to win freedom. The black-and-white photographs showed straight-backed bearded men with the traditional, long dark tunics of the Chechen nation, with the row of cartridge cases across the breast.

'Such people do not exist any more. Their word was their word. They were friendly. There is no one like that left.'

It is true that the photographs belonged to another age. But it was an age with the same problems; the same depth of violence and oppression. And those problems started with the first encounter between Russians and Chechens, more than two centuries earlier, and have been continuing ever since.

19. A Muslim Submissive
to the Will of God

In 1721, Tsar Peter I, one of the strongest and most ambitious rulers Russia has ever had, learned that Persia was in chaos. Afghanistan was rebelling against the Persians and one of the many rulers in Dagestan – an ethnically mixed province partially under nominal Persian control on the northern slopes of the Caucasus mountains – thought he might do so too and appealed to St Petersburg for help. For the energetic tsar, both events were opportunities to gain a strategic hold over lands that could one day prove stepping stones to India, the greatest prize of all.

He was aiming, he said, to grab the southeastern shore of the Caspian Sea from Persian hands, because from there 'to Balkh and Badakshan with pack camels takes only twelve days. On that road to India no one can interfere with us.'

To secure the Caspian, he had to make sure the Turks did not fill in the gap left by the crumbling Persian empire, and so, to forestall them, he sent his army south.

His soldiers streamed along the shores of the Caspian Sea, heading for the town of Derbent, which sits on the coast at the only place where an army can bypass the Caucasus mountains, as they needed to do. They took Derbent with ease, but after that the campaign was not a great success, since Russia was not yet strong enough to challenge the Persians and Turks for mastery south of the mountains. As a result, the year would hold little relevance for this book either, were it not for one event.

A Russian cavalry detachment rode west from the main line of march to the village of Enderi, which is close to the modern town of Khasavyurt, on the borders of Chechnya. Russian-speakers were known to the locals, since Cossacks had settled along the river Terek fifty years earlier, but regular Russian troops had not been seen there before.

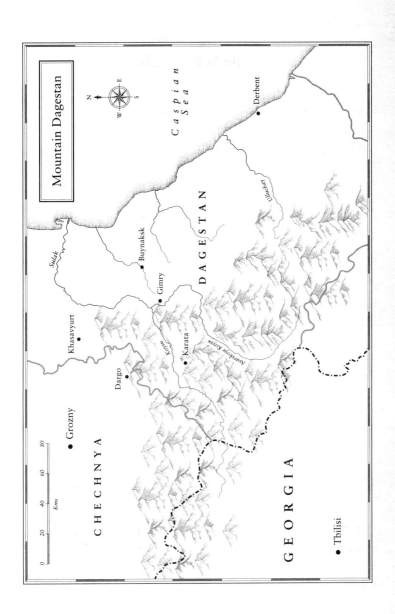

Mountain Dagestan

The Russian horsemen were wiped out.

It was a first encounter between the Russians and the mountain peoples of Chechnya and Dagestan, and it was a chilling sign of what was to come. For contacts were to become regular events. Peter's successors founded a fort at Kizlyar, north-east of Chechnya, to control the trail he had followed along the Caspian shore, and the Russians were clearly here to stay.

The Russians' presence was to have a profound impact on both sides. For this 1721 expedition was not just the first Russian incursion into Chechnya and the free mountain lands of Dagestan. It was the first incursion by any modern army. The Persians, it is true, occasionally ventured into Dagestan, but their visits were so serially unsuccessful that a Persian saying ran: 'When a Shah goes mad, he takes his army to Dagestan.'

In the decades after Tsar Peter, one such shah was Nadir, who managed to restore for a while some of his country's lost might but came badly unstuck when venturing north of the mountains. He took much of lowland Dagestan back from the Russians, but an attempt to advance into the mountains in 1741 met with disaster.

According to a legend still told in the highland villages of Dagestan, he sent an envoy to the free, self-governing community of Andalal, with a demand that it surrender.

'We are as many as stars in the sky, or fish in the sea,' said the message to the highlanders, who were supposed to be overawed by this boast of Persian might. Predictably, they were not. Their reply contained a chicken and a bag of millet.

'As it is easy for this chicken to eat all this grain, so Andalal has the power to crush your numerous forces,' the attached message said.

The story should not be taken as gospel truth, since the same man who told it to me also told me that a spiritually blessed resident of his village – Megeb, which is high in the central mountains – had kidnapped the shah's daughter and flown away with her. But Nadir was indeed defeated at Andalal in a battle seen by Dagestanis as a symbol of their unity in the face of foreign aggression.

In the absence of conquest or foreign domination, the mountain communities of Dagestan, and the forest-dwellers of Chechnya, had never created a centralized system of government of their own. They lived in free societies that governed themselves under an ancient system of customs common to all, no matter what language they spoke.

Dagestan itself is almost uniquely suited to creating a fractured society. Bleak and raw, its deep valleys plunge hundreds of metres from a high treeless plateau. The rocks of the mountains break out of the valley sides, sometimes squeezing together to make narrow gulleys, sometimes rearing up to make crags. The freebooting societies that lived in these inaccessible, tawny valleys needed protection from each other, and used the crags as natural castles on which to build villages.

To travellers along the valley bottoms, the villages are visible on the top of the slopes above, natural fortresses for some of the most warlike people in the world.

And the valleys created an ethnic mosaic also. Dagestan is home to dozens of languages, as many as forty, and the ethnic groups often live in isolated villages surrounded entirely by other nations. It is a bewildering place.

Megeb, for example, is a village of Dargins, Dagestan's second-largest nationality. Seen from the side, it resembles a step pyramid, with flat-roofed houses built on the sides of a rocky hill. Each one's walls nudge up against the back of its downward neighbour.

It is isolated in the midst of lands dominated by Avars – the region's largest nationality – and its residents moved to their current homes 600 years ago from around thirty kilometres away. They have inter-married inextricably with the neighbouring Avars over the subsequent centuries, but they are seen as interlopers in these high valleys.

Megeb residents – they are after all foreigners, and cannot be expected to know the local customs – freely admit to having a bit of a reputation for stupidity.

According to one of their legends, they once got swindled out of land by villagers from next-door Sogratl – which has a reputation for low cunning. A delegation from Sogratl came to insist that some land that had long been considered as belonging to Megeb really belonged to them. An elder from Sogratl, who was respected as a particularly honest man, stood before his neighbours and swore he was standing on Sogratl's soil.

No mountain Dagestani would break his word in a solemn oath, so the Megeb villagers shrugged, scratched their heads, admitted they must be mistaken and gave up their claim. Unbeknownst to them though, the elder had filled his boots with dirt from his village's own fields, allowing him to rightly swear he was standing on Sogratl's soil, and thus muscle in on their village's holding. (For the sake of fairness, I should point out that I did not get balancing comment from Sogratl, where villagers probably say the land was theirs all along.)

Apart from being a funny story, the folk tale shows how seriously the customs of the mountains are still respected in Dagestan. Honesty is such an important part of their culture that a villager would fill his boots with earth so he could technically tell the truth, rather than achieve the same results with just a straight lie.

Islam arrived in Dagestan as early as 733 when the Arabs conquered Derbent, and brought their new religion with them, but it took many centuries to spread. Dagestan was not considered entirely Muslim until the late sixteenth century. Chechnya was also late to Islam, and the last Chechens probably did not convert until the late eighteenth century. Some Ingush were still pagan until the 1860s.

The long absence, therefore, of a foreign ruler or a foreign religion allowed the mountain customs to continue largely unchanged into the modern age. Communities were governed by councils of elders, and land was held in common by each village. The rigid ownership of land – as in the tale of the cunning elder with his boots full of earth – could cause centuries-long disputes between rival villages or communities.

The folk traditions are full of stories of unsuccessful attempts by foreign invaders or misguided locals to make the tribes into normal peoples with normal systems of government. In one tale, as recounted by the traveller and historian John F. Baddeley, once upon a time the Ingush 'moved by some madness' gathered together to select a prince from among their number.

Every significant Ingush man came to the meeting, with the single exception of the most respected elder of the nation. Inevitably, they chose him as their ruler and summoned him to hear their decision. Three times, however, he refused to appear before them.

At last, on their fourth time of asking, he consented to come to the gathering, much to the relief of the Ingush. But their relief was not to last long, and it turned to bafflement when he arrived dressed in a beautiful silk robe, belted together with a crude, dirty girth from a donkey's saddle. One of the assembled notables finally got up the courage to ask why he was wearing such an extraordinary outfit.

'Well, why not? What is the objection?'

The spokesman for the assembly said that a donkey's girth did not befit such a beautiful garment.

'And so would a prince with the Ingush people,' replied the potential ruler, and so the attempt to establish a government failed.

The lack of rulers in the mountains, though it befitted the highlanders' ideas of honour and freedom, made it almost impossible to impose justice between communities when the tribes' customs were violated. Communities held collective responsibility for crimes committed by their members, and such inter-community crimes were frequent, since livestock was the only major source of wealth and was easily rustle-able.

Joint councils of elders would meet to deliberate on crimes committed between two communities, but their decisions could be impossible to enforce against the will of the criminal's village, leading to festering disputes that could last for centuries.

Inevitably, when serious crimes were involved, the disputes led to blood feuds, which could threaten to wipe out the entire male population of particularly unfortunate communities, despite Islam's prohibition on revenge being taken on anyone but the direct culprit. The only way out of a blood feud was the symbolic adoption of a criminal into the victim's family – murder within a family being impossible – by his touching the mother's breast with his mouth. That was, naturally, an impossible act to achieve without the acquiescence of the victim's family, so feuds dragged on and on.

The prospect of blood feuds did not stop the men of the mountain communities engaging in cattle raids on their neighbours and on the unfortunate plain-dwellers, however. Almost every man in Chechnya and mountain Dagestan was armed, mounted and ready to attack at any time.

While they prepared for war, they tended to leave the women to do most of the actual work in the villages, such as cooking, fetching water, food and fodder, milking the cows, light mowing, cleaning the house, making clothes and so on.

The men traditionally did the heavier jobs, or sat around and watched the livestock, leading to serial accusations from visitors of laziness. Baddeley wrote about how he failed to get fodder for his horse in one Dagestani village when passing through around 1900 because, as the large group of men lying in the sun told him, 'there is no woman available' to carry it.

'Muhammad said that women were camels to carry men over the desert of existence; the mountaineers of the Caucasus apparently took this dictum more or less literally and put all heavy burdens on the backs of their womankind,' he said.

Things have changed little since then. Or, as one unusually outspoken Chechen woman I know well put it: 'I have never really understood what men are for.'

It was this world of disunited, but potentially formidable, highlanders that Russia set out to conquer in the decades around the turn of the nineteenth century. Russia organized their Cossacks – originally runaways and freebooters – and formalized their links to its own armies, which marched to the mountains along the trail blazed by Peter the Great. The Cossack villages of the river Terek were linked into great fortified lines – where, incidentally, the women did the work and the men manned the watchtowers in a mirror image of the highlanders' society – and forts were added in Mozdok, Kizlyar, Vladikavkaz and elsewhere.

Russia had no foreign power to argue ownership here, as it did with the Circassian lands on the Black Sea coast, since Chechnya was unclaimed. It had a free hand to seize as much of the mountains as it could.

The highlanders' response was furious. The Russians were, as the highlanders not unreasonably saw it, stealing their land. They might squabble among themselves for land on a local level, but they could unite against true interlopers. They just needed a leader to galvanize their response, and they at last found one in a Chechen villager called Ushurma.

According to the most convincing account of his life, Ushurma was born in 1732 to influential Chechen parents in the lowland village of Aldy on the river Sunzha. His parents had migrated to the village from the mountainous region of Ichkeria, and his father had fought the Russians and taught his son to hate them.

Ushurma is said to have spent days of his youth on horseback, perfecting his martial skills, and often practised his swordplay on sheep – an expensive habit for his father, who had to compensate the owners of the outclassed livestock. His father also taught him the Koran and, aged twenty, he left to study in Dagestan, which had become the regional centre for religious learning.

According to stories passed down about Ushurma, he saw visions of the Prophet Muhammad, who told him he had to return believers to the true path. His family tried to stop him preaching, but eventually had to give way before his insistence. Speaking from the roof of the mosque, he exhorted his neighbours to live according to the rules of the Koran, and then distributed meat among them.

He proclaimed himself to be Imam – or 'leader' – and gave himself the name Mansur, which means 'victorious' in Arabic. It is under the name Sheikh Mansur that he is remembered in the Caucasus today. It is said he took it upon himself to mobilize his neighbours to oppose the Russians, provoking concern in the forts on the far side of the river.

In the centuries since, stories have accumulated around Mansur. Some claim that he could see the future, that he could fly and that he could be in more than one place at once. Russian officials became very concerned about this threat to their presence.

'On the opposite bank of the river Sunzha in the village of Aldy a prophet has appeared and started to preach. He has submitted superstitious and ignorant people to his will by claiming to have had a revelation,' wrote a Russian major-general in 1785.

The Russians despatched an expedition to Aldy that year to teach Mansur a lesson. When the 3,000 troops reached the village, they were disappointed to find it empty, so they set fire to it and destroyed

Mansur's own house to make their point. Turning for home, however, they found that the villagers had not run away at all but were waiting to ambush them in the forests lining the road. In the subsequent battle, half the Russian force was destroyed and the rest fled in panic across the river, in which many drowned.

The victory made Mansur famous across the Caucasus, and has secured his popularity to this day. A later resistance leader of the Chechens and mountain tribes described him in heroic form as being 'so tall that in a crowd of standing people it appeared that he was sitting on a horse'.

The Russians were appalled by the reverse at Aldy. The Russian major-general quoted above commented that 'it is impossible to subdue the Chechens unless to exterminate them completely' – possibly the first expression of an opinion that was to become common over the next two centuries.

Even without extermination, however, Mansur's resistance did not last. He was overambitious and his attempts to fight the Russians in the open fields failed, losing him his support in a few short months. He escaped to the land of the Circassians, where he organized their resistance for a while before being captured by the Russians in 1791. He died three years later, probably of tuberculosis, in a fortress in Russia's north.

As an uprising, his movement was a failure, but it did show the tribes what they could do if they united, and united behind the standard of Islam. Mansur's movement had laid as much weight on enforcing the rules of the Koran as it had on fighting the Russians.

Apparently, he threatened to kill himself if his father did not stop smoking, and he forced the villagers to stop drinking and to pray five times a day. All of these commands would become familiar to the mountain peoples over the next century, since the resistance leaders would all follow Mansur's lead in combining Islamic reform and battle.

The Russians realized very quickly the threat that reformed Islam posed to their rule. In a treaty with Russia in 1810, Ingush elders pledged they would not allow Muslim missionaries among them. But such agreements were no match for the forces of Islam, which had found a new driving force – Sufi mysticism.

Without rulers to convert them from above, the free communities of Chechnya and mountain Dagestan had largely been introduced to Islam by roving holy men – many of them belonging to the Naqsh-bandi brotherhood of Sufis, which preached strict observance of Islam's laws and a personal and intense relationship with Allah. Its adepts studied the Koran and obeyed their own teacher in all things.

It is unclear whether Mansur himself was a Naqshbandi. If he was not, then his movement certainly closely resembled that of the Sufis. Be that as it may, in the decades that followed his defeat, the brother-hood spread into Chechnya and Dagestan, its centre of gravity becoming the village of Gimry, a free community in the ethnically Avar lands in Dagestan's mountains. Now, if the Russians were to launch a concerted effort to conquer the free highlanders, they would find their foes organized for the first time. They might not have a unified government, but they did have a single faith.

The Naqshbandi leader in Gimry – Sheikh Jamal-Edin – opposed holy war, saying it was more important to purify individuals. But it would be ever harder to maintain the battle for a pure, peaceful inter-nal faith, if the Russians were going to impose their own legal codes and customs. Calls to wage holy war would be hard to resist, if the Russians provoked them.

All that was required was for the Russians to give a spark, and the whole of Chechnya and Dagestan could catch fire.

During the Napoleonic Wars, the Russians were largely too dis-tracted to do so. But, with the French defeated, they were able to turn their full attention to these troublesome mountains where the highlanders refused to bow down before the empire of the tsar.

And now, one of the greatest Russian heroes of the campaigns against the French was ready to lead those invincible Russian armies. Alexei Yermolov, beloved of his soldiers, had been decorated on the field by Suvorov, whose massacre of the Nogai nation in 1783 had set the tone for Russia's whole conquest of the Caucasus. Yermolov had commanded both the Russian and Prussian guards at the fall of Paris in 1814, and was the most respected soldier in the empire.

He was a man of action, and one who believed in writing his philosophy across the map. As he extended the Russian network of forts, the highlanders could have been forgiven for seeing the names given to these new Russian bases and giving up in despair.

Starting in 1817, he erected Vnezapnaya ('Sudden'), Neotstupny Stan ('No Retreat'), Zlobny Okop ('Malicious') and Burnaya ('Stormy'). And at the heart of them all was a fort that would become a city, and which the Chechens and the Russians would fight over time after time. Its name was Grozny ('Threatening'; the word is the same as that used to describe Tsar Ivan 'the Terrible').

Yermolov saw Chechnya as the breadbasket of mountainous Dagestan, and its conquest as the key to the whole eastern flank of the mountains. Apparently lacking in even the smallest remnants of humanity, he set about his task with such a degree of cruelty and such a lack of honour that his name has passed into Chechen folklore as a byword for savagery.

The Chechens were furious about the construction of Grozny in 1818, and kept up a steady sniping fire on its builders. The Chechens could not come too close, however, because of the power of Russia's artillery. Yermolov, suspecting that the tribesmen would love an artillery piece of their own, pretended to abandon one on the battle-field. When the Chechens came forward to collect it, he minced them with grapeshot.

It is a fairly typical example of the tactics by which Russian civilization was brought to these savages.

'I desire that the terror of my name should guard our frontiers more potently than chains of fortresses, that my word should be for the natives a law more inevitable than death,' Yermolov said.

His plan was simple, and spelt out by his chief of staff, Ivan Velyaminov, in words that would guide the actions of successful commanders throughout the whole Caucasus war:

'The Caucasus may be likened to a mighty fortress, marvellously strong by nature, artificially protected by military works, and defended by a numerous garrison. Only thoughtless men would attempt to escalade such a stronghold. A wise commander would see the necessity of having recourse to military art; would lay his parallels; advance by sap and mine, and so master the place. The Caucasus, in my opinion, must be treated in the same way, and even if the method of procedure is not drawn up beforehand, so that it may be continually referred to, the very nature of things will compel such action,' Velyaminov wrote.

The building of forts was part of the plan, and the subjugation of the population was another. Yermolov gave the tribesmen a choice. Either they submitted to Russia, and moved to where Russia wanted them, or they did not submit, which meant they would have to move deep into the mountains and starve. As a first step, the lands up to the river Sunzha – where the fort of Grozny glowered out over the land – would be cleared of inhabitants.

If the inhabitants refused to obey the tsar's officers, they were rebels, and thus could be massacred. In the village of Dadi-Yurt, the Chechens did refuse, and their fate has been remembered by their countrymen to this day. The Russians had already destroyed six villages when they approached Dadi-Yurt in September 1819. They surrounded the village and, when its inhabitants stood firm, it was assaulted. The Chechen resistance was stubborn but doomed.

Encouraged by singing and chanting from their womenfolk, the men fought on until they were all but wiped out. The women fought on too, often preferring to kill themselves than fall into the hands of the Russians. Only fourteen men were captured at the end of the battle and 140 women and children – many of whom were injured. It was a terrible massacre. In the short term it may have been effective in cowing the nearby people; in the longer term it succeeded only in changing the hatred felt for the Russians into near hysteria.

Subsequent years saw new 'pacifying' missions, which destroyed Chechen villages, and deepened both the highlanders' hatred and Russians' incomprehension. Unable to believe that any people could continue to resist after such punishment, some Russian officers effectively ceased to view the Chechens as human beings at all. One commander, General Grekov, referred to the Chechens in his letters as 'rogues' or 'rascals', and happily fulfilled his tasks to 'destroy villages, to hang hostages, and slaughter women and children'.

Faced with this onslaught, the Chechens were compelled to unite. In national gatherings in 1821, and again in 1824, they appointed Naqshbandis as spiritual leaders and a Chechen called Beybulat, who had served the Russians then defected back again, as military leader. Beybulat had led the assaults on Grozny which had faced the Russians' grapeshot, and his strategies of quick marches and lightning attacks on weak targets were effective. The Chechen resistance was far more successful than that of the Circassians, precisely because they fought under a single commander and submitted to the discipline of the Sufis.

The Russians, predictably, were furious, not least at their own impotence. In July 1825, shortly after the Chechens took a Russian fort, massacred its garrison and stole its guns, the Russians summoned more than 300 Chechen elders to a meeting. Ostensibly, it was to discuss the situation, but the local Russian commander took the opportunity to harangue and insult the assembled notables in their own language.

He then threatened to punish them and ordered them to surrender the daggers that all Caucasus men carried as a mark of their manhood. The first two elders called up surrendered their knives. But the third refused to do so. Grekov – he who had boasted of slaughtering women and children – struck him in the face. The elder responded by stabbing Grekov and his commanding officer to death, as well as wounding several other officers. He himself was killed, as were almost all the elders at the meeting. Any way you looked at it, it was a disaster for everyone present.

The Chechens' revolt fizzled out over the next year, perhaps because of the extreme repression Yermolov dealt out or perhaps because the spiritual and military leadership was entrusted to two different people, but their temporary successes were signs of things to come.

Next time, the tribes would be led in battle and in prayer by the same man, and he would be a fully fledged Naqshbandi from the heartland of Dagestani Islam. The Chechens would be among his best warriors, but neither he, nor his two successors, would be a Chechen. All three would be Avars, and they would shake Russia's hold on the Caucasus with the black banner of Islam and the chants of holy war.

There is no doubt that Russia's own merciless brutality in battle provoked the response that was to come, and the way the highlanders

defied that brutality in these early battles has inspired every generation, up to the present day.

Chechen rebel fighters in Grozny in 1999 sang of Sheikh Mansur,
who had been remembered in folk memory as a national hero despite
official Russian and Soviet historians saying he sold out his own
countrymen. Here are the closing lines of the song they sang, composed by rebel bard Timur Mutsurayev, whose simple recordings
feature only a voice and an acoustic guitar. His words inspired his
countrymen in their doomed battles.

> He knew no fear in the fight for faith
> And the terrible enemy trembled before him.
> He was a simple, gentle slave of Allah,
> A Muslim submissive to the will of God.
> The enemy's rumours and base slanders
> Claim Mansur was a traitor and a spy.
> However, he followed the ancient laws
> And was a firm Muslim.
> Let modernity and antiquity quarrel,
> What other hero can be compared with him?
> For it is clear to all, that this person
> Was an example in battle to all peoples.

Mansur's successors as leaders of the highlanders learned early to
answer brutality with brutality, as a Georgian family discovered to
their cost in 1854.

20. The Imam and the Princesses

In summer 1854, Prince David Chavchavadze had just taken up a post as head of the local militia protecting the lowlands of Georgia from highland attack. Since the days of Sheikh Mansur, the highlanders had become a fearful foe for Russian soldiers sent against them. The two sides rarely met in open battle, but in guerrilla war. In sniping raids, the highly mobile and skilled light cavalry of the highlanders was a threat to any settlement within reach of the mountains.

But Chavchavadze, a 37-year-old lieutenant-colonel, really had nothing to worry about. His force was more than adequate for repelling raiding parties. It might struggle to cope with anything more ambitious, but there had been no major highlander raid onto Georgia's rich plains since 1800. Worrying rumours were coming down from the hills though, so Chavchavadze had to be ready.

He pushed his militia north of the Alazani river, to the side closest to the mountains, and set his defences against any push south. He had a personal interest in stopping any mountain force from crossing the river as well, since his estate, Tsinondali, with its rich vineyards and fine mansion, was close to its southern bank.

But his duties were not a discomfort. His own family was enjoying the summer at Tsinondali, where his wife Anna and his sister-in-law, Princess Orbeliani, were holding court, and he joined them as often as he could. With the princesses were the prince's four daughters and one son, plus Princess Orbeliani's son and her niece. A French governess called Anne Drancey completed the party.

In mid-July, news came that Imam Shamil – the leader of the Chechens and the mountain Dagestanis – had massed his forces at Karata, a village whose location allowed him to attack both north into Russia and south into Georgia. The prince and his troops took up defensive positions, and were ready when the attack came.

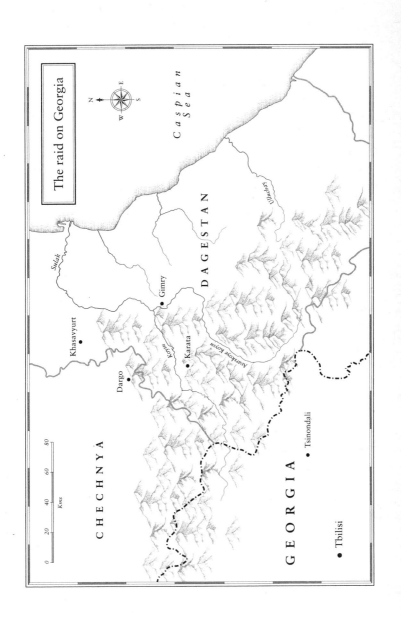

The raid on Georgia

As ever the highlanders came with devastating speed. They attacked and retreated equally rapidly, and the clashes were over within hours. The prince thought he had beaten them off and even scribbled out a note to his wife, saying that there was 'no occasion for uneasiness'. He underlined those last few words.

But it turned out he had missed the main force. A separate army under the command of Imam Shamil's son and heir, Gazi-Muhammad, had avoided the prince's force, forded the river and set to work plundering the villages on its southern bank. And among those villages was the prince's mansion, and the prince's family: a rich prize for highlanders bent on loot and ransom. The princesses hid in an upstairs room and initially thought they had escaped unharmed as the raiders concentrated on stealing fabrics and china from the bottom floors. But then one highlander tried their door, which was locked, and sounded the alarm. Men poured up the stairs.

'The door resists for a few instants ... The fury of the Tatars reaches its peak ... The door shakes under their redoubled blows ... The door yields ... Then, there is a terrible struggle,' wrote Drancey, the governess, in her dramatic account of the affair.

'A cloud of men rains onto us ... a dreadful mixture of cries of rage and desperate sobs are heard ... each one of us is picked up in the arms of one of these savages ... all resistance is useless.'

The attacking force gathered up the princesses, their children, Drancey (who cried out: 'I am French, I am French' in French, in the vain and somehow rather Gallic hope that this would stop them from kidnapping her) and the servants and rode for the hills. In their excitement, they looted the house and stole the women's clothing. Drancey was left in just her boots, her corset and her blouse. Some of the children were almost naked.

When soldiers sent by Prince David Chavchavadze reached his home, it was a smouldering ruin. His whole family was gone, and just an elderly Georgian woman remained. Marina Gaideli had nursed four generations of the family, and seen the mansion built. She sat beside its remains, half naked and inconsolable.

'David, David,' she sobbed, 'why are you not here to help your family?'

As the news of the raid spread, her shock was replicated across Georgia, and then Russia, then the world. Shamil seemed unstoppable. Even the highest families in the land were at risk of his wrath.

It was an extraordinary development. Just three decades earlier, the highlanders had been desperately resisting Russian punitive raids. Their attempts to unite had been ill-coordinated, hasty and badly led. The Cossacks and regular units had been able to ride more or less at will through the mountains burning villages, rounding up civilians and wiping out resistance.

Nikolai, the tsar whose rule started in 1825 and who was to stifle the likes of Lermontov and Pushkin with his mindless philistinism, wanted the highlanders crushed. He ordered his commander-in-chief in the Caucasus to 'tame for ever the mountain peoples, or exterminate the insubordinate'. Under this edict, Russian troops became ever more brutal, the resistance against them ever more hopeless.

It was more than the Naqshbandis could take. The official doctrine taught by the elders said that Sufis should accept the rulers of this world, and concentrate on living a perfect life by the laws of Islam. But, the younger men said, how could you live a perfect life when non-believers were burning your home, killing your neighbours, and raping your wife?

In 1829, Naqshbandis gathered in the mountains of Dagestan and proclaimed an Imam. He would lead them against the Russians both spiritually and militarily, and finally the resistance would have a focus. His name was Gazi-Muhammad, and his impact was sudden and dramatic. Over the next three years, he was to cause panic among the Russians, sacking or besieging every fort within reach. The tribes of the eastern Caucasus responded to his success, rising up against the invaders.

The jihad had begun.

Gazi-Muhammad would not be fated to lead it for long, however. The Russians – like an elephant stung by a bee – staggered around, flailing out at their maddening tormentor. Eventually in 1832, they trapped him. In the summer of that year, they destroyed eighty villages in Chechnya, then they moved into mountain Dagestan, where they intended to find the imam in his home village of Gimry: the centre of mystical Islam in the mountains.

The terrain was imposing, but the Russian generals did not care. 'Can a dog go there? Where a dog can go, a Russian soldier can go too,' said one general when questioned over paths.

To get to Gimry, they would need every bit of their surefooted-ness. Today, there is a tunnel connecting the village with the low-lands, but in the 1830s the Russians had to climb over a precipitous ridge, which was considered all but impassable. Made of a curious rock formation, it is marked by hundreds of cone-shaped outcrops, like gigantic monks at prayer carved out of stone. The ridge is so high that it affects the weather.

When I was there, the clouds were spilling over the ridge from the lowlands but vanishing when they hit the drier air of the mountains. In our mountain valley, we had a clear blue sky and perfect sunlight. On the other side of the ridge, the side of the lowlands, there was thick cloud and gloom. Once the Russians had scaled the ridge, they found a wooded gorge that descended to the head of the valley. Once in the valley though, their problems were only just beginning. They had to march across a jagged surface of moraine overshadowed by steep walls that gradually become cliffs – towards the waiting imam.

The residents of Gimry had built a wall across the gorge to stop the Russians, and at first they were successful. But they were out-numbered, the Russian musket fire was too heavy. Eventually, the brave Russian soldiers breached the rampart and the defenders fled in rout. All resistance was ended, the path to Gimry was open, except for one little house hard against the cliff on the left flank of the Rus-sian advance. It was cut off once the defenders fled, but shots still emerged from it, killing the Russians as they readied to attack. The whole fury of the assault was now concentrated on the house, and the defenders' ammunition was not endless.

The death song of the Sufis rose up as the bullets died away. The defenders prepared their knives for the end. Just then, a tall bearded figure emerged into the doorway of the house. He stared at the ranks of soldiers, took a run-up and jumped clean over them. Landing behind them, he turned, and stabbed three with his sword, received a bayonet thrust to the chest, then turned and fled into the dusk. He was safe, but the others in the house were not so lucky. Apart from one other, they died to a man. According to stories still told in Gimry, the imam was found in a posture of prayer: a hand on his beard and eyes raised to heaven.

The Russians could congratulate themselves on their victory, or so they thought.

If that bayonet thrust had only been slightly more accurate, the history of the Caucasus would be very different. For the fleeing man would be the greatest imam of all. It was Shamil, whose forces would terrorize lowland Georgia in two decades' time.

The respect in which this resistance hero is still held in Dagestan, although it has been part of Russia for a century and a half, is clearly visible at the site of the battle. A mosque has been built for visitors to pray where the first imam died.

A sign declares in Avar and Russian: 'Here, in an unequal battle with the forces of the tsarist army, was heroically killed the leader of the highlanders' struggle for freedom and independence'. Visitors have tied little strips of coloured cloth to the branches that overhang the sign to signify their prayers: a little piece of irony since the imam himself loathed such superstitions.

About ten metres up the hill are the remains of the house where the doomed defenders fired their last bullets, and between the first sign and the house, is another sign. 'Here landed Imam Shamil after his leap'. Here too are strips of cloth. Where the site of the first imam's death is holy, this is holy too. It is where the new imam lived.

If the sign is correct, it was a mighty leap: five metres if not more. Perhaps the sign is exaggerated, perhaps it is not, who can say? For Shamil is a man to whom stories attach themselves.

According to legend, he was given the name Shamil – which is a corrupt version of Samuel, and hence a Jewish name and very unusual in the mountains – after his father pledged to give his new son the name of the first person he saw. The first person he saw was a Jew, and the fierce Muslim leader would have a non-believer's name for his whole life.

Another story tells how Shamil was first called Ali or Muhammad-Ali, and grew up a sickly child. By mountain superstition, changing a child's name confused the evil spirits afflicting him, and with his new name Shamil was able to become the bravest and most nimble warrior in the mountains.

He did not take over as imam immediately on Gazi-Muhammad's death. A second imam ruled for a while, until he was killed in a blood feud, and Shamil assumed his title. The Russians apparently did not realize the threat they had left behind them, since the new imam concentrated on forcing his subjects to obey Islamic law and respect his rule rather than on fighting Russia.

A follower's account tells how Shamil, on recovering from his wounds, walked back to Gimry and was disgusted to see women sitting unaccompanied and spinning wool by the roadside: a flagrant contradiction of the Koran. The earth had barely settled on Gazi-Muhammad's grave and already the people were disobeying his laws. Shamil shook his head and walked on. As he passed the women later in the day, the situation was still worse. An old man with a stick had joined them, and this was too much for Shamil, who took the stick and beat the man with it. He then struck one of the women when she refused to leave.

Shamil was beaten twenty times by order of the court as a result, causing his chest wound to open again, but he was unrepentant. He was doing God's work. He preached that it was the duty of every believer to enforce the law. The local populace did not listen to him.

'Tomorrow we will drink wine, party and dance,' said one man. 'Then we will see how humiliated those [Sufis] will be.' Shamil attacked the group, beating them heavily, and this was too much for his neighbours. He was forced to leave his home village and retreat elsewhere.

His uncompromising faith may not have appealed to all the residents of Gimry, but it attracted young men from all over the Caucasus who wanted an imam to teach them the laws of God and the discipline of the Sufi order, and to lead them against the Russians. These men had to abide by the militant traditions of the Naqshbandi, and became known as *murid*s – or 'the committed ones' in Arabic.

As murids, they could not drink, or smoke, or indulge in luxuries of any kind. According to the legends of the mountains, however, these laws were as often as not flouted by the highlanders.

Stories today abound about individual murids who succeeded in circumventing the ban on smoking that Shamil imposed. One murid supposedly killed twelve Russian soldiers, and won the right to have a cigarette as a result. Another is said to have forded a rushing stream and carried off a particularly beautiful Christian woman on the far bank. She was to be Shuanat, Shamil's favourite wife, and her captor was allowed to smoke as much as he wanted.

Some of these stories may in fact be true, since Shamil unquestionably had a talent for dramatic and extreme gestures. He suffered from a fainting disease, which he turned to his advantage by explaining the fits he would fall into as divinely inspired. He also had an excellent network of spies and would casually drop in secret information as being something he had seen in a dream.

The most extraordinary such performance came when a delegation of Chechens sought permission to surrender. In their lowland forests, they were far more vulnerable than the Dagestanis to punitive action from the Russians.

A delegation came to the imam's village, and sought a way of persuading him to give up the fight. He had issued an order that any traitors would be killed, and anyone talking of surrender would be severely punished, so they were keen to seek out the perfect envoy to present their proposals to their ruler.

Eventually, they persuaded the imam's mother to intercede on their behalf, and she went to her son and begged him to end the torment of his subjects.

Shamil must have realized the seriousness of the situation. If even the Chechens were begging him to end the war then indeed morale must be low. If even his mother was carrying the message, then surely no one believed in the cause?

He told the crowd he would have to pray for three days for inspiration, and he vanished into the mosque. The villagers gathered and waited outside. Perhaps this time Shamil would show himself to be able to compromise? Or perhaps the Chechen delegation would be punished as the law promised?

When Shamil emerged, gaunt and pale, he had made his decision. He had communed with the Almighty, he said, and there was only one action he could take. He must enforce the law. The law stated that anyone speaking of surrender must be punished severely, and that person had been his mother. He therefore decreed a hundred strokes of the cane on his mother's back.

She screamed and begged for mercy, but he was implacable. One stroke fell, two, three, and on the fourth she fainted. At this, Shamil – the master of the dramatic – himself stepped forward, and said that the Koran allowed a son to take his parent's punishment. He stripped off his tunic and demanded that his executioner inflict the remaining ninety-six strokes on his own back.

He took the beating without a sound, stood up, and ordered the Chechen delegation to go home and talk no more of surrender. They followed his instructions, for who would argue with this madman?

And he brought them success in war too. Every year, the Russians would wait for his forces to pour out of the mountains, never sure which fort would be the target. In 1846, he even led a raid into Kabarda, the easternmost part of the land of the Circassians. The raid was not a success in military terms, but it was a striking demonstration of ambition and reach.

Russian attempts to capture him were regularly disastrous too. The year before the raid on Kabarda, a new Russian viceroy in the Caucasus received firm orders from Tsar Nikolai to destroy Shamil's capital. A force of 21,000 men – much of it led by some of the most titled officers in the army, all of them with the camp luxuries they required – set out to crush Shamil once and for all. Shamil retreated and retreated, staying tantalizingly out of reach for weeks. The Russians took Shamil's capital – Dargo – but there was no one in it, so they were no closer to reaching their objective than at the start.

It was now that Shamil's guerrilla genius appeared. Every Russian attack was unopposed, but every retreat was turned into a bloody rout. He knew the lumbering Russian column was low on supplies, and would have to send men for more food soon. When it did so, they were attacked from every side. This 'biscuit expedition' brought no supplies, and lost 556 men killed, including two generals. Over the next five days of humiliating retreat, the Russians were hounded by snipers in the forests on all sides, and lost another 295 men killed.

It was a spectacular disaster, which raised Shamil's prestige to new heights.

So, this was the leader of the mountains whose forces swooped onto Georgia that summer day in 1854. He was a fanatic, a guerrilla genius, a performer and an administrator. He had crafted a system of government out of the Naqshbandi creed, and he imposed it mercilessly. His murids were his elite soldiers. Above them were his *naibs* – lieutenants who governed in his name. They ruled Dagestan – the bleak uplands with their deep valleys and rocky crags – and Chechnya, a lusher, softer land dominated by great beech forests. Chechnya has its high mountains, but much of the region is made of rolling hills, densely wooded, in which the Chechens could hide from the invaders.

Shamil looked out over these woods in upland Chechnya when the princesses were being brought in as captives.

On their miserable journey through the mountains, they had learned a lot about the hatred felt for the Russian government and its subjects. In one village, they were pelted with stones and sticks, and not one inhabitant would let them spend the night indoors. Their captors treated them brutally. Lydia, Prince David's infant daughter, had died early on when her mother was unable to hold onto her as she jolted along on the back of a horse.

Children were apparently deemed to be more or less disposable.

'Princess Baratoff observed one of the Georgian children, who had been separated from its mother, crying violently, to the great annoyance of the Lesghian who had taken charge of it. The mountaineer at last took the child by the legs, dashed its brains out against a rock, and threw it towards the abyss which received the stream somewhat lower down,' says a contemporary account of the affair written from the princesses' own testimony.

With twenty-two days of this misery on their journey, it is not surprising that they were apprehensive about appearing before the imam. He was a man with a cruel reputation, but he fascinated people throughout Russia and beyond. Who was this man who defied the might of the Russian empire? Many writers had imagined a character for him, sometimes with unwittingly comic results.

A German, for example, remarked – apparently without any source beyond his own imagination – on Shamil's 'aquiline nose, small mouth, blue eyes, blonde hair and beard, and delicate white skin'. All these qualities could only point to more of 'a Germanic than an eastern extraction', we learned, as if a guerrilla leader could not possibly have emerged from the Caucasus without an infusion of good north European blood.

Now, with the princesses' arrival, for the first time outsiders would have a chance of closely observing the imam and his household. On arriving at Shamil's home – a complex of buildings around a courtyard – they saw a figure in white looking down at them from a balcony. This was Shamil, and though they did not know it at the time his mind was likely to have been in turmoil as well.

Some fifteen years previously, the imam had suffered a grievous loss. Trapped by Russian troops in the mountain village of Akhulgo, he had been forced to give up his youngest son, the six-year-old Jamal-Edin, as a hostage for good behaviour. Ever since, he had been trying to get him back. The youngster had since become a Russian officer, and russified, but Shamil still dreamed of uniting his family. With these high-ranking new captives, perhaps he finally had hostages of his own that the Russians would be prepared to exchange for his son.

And while the negotiations dragged on – sometimes happily, sometimes painfully – the princesses would gain plentiful insights into the household of the Lion of Dagestan, as some of the more excitable newspapers had taken to calling him.

What they found resembled a soap opera, although the cast would have seemed far-fetched if it were fictional. Shamil had three wives: bitter, sharp-tongued Zeidat; sweet-natured, kind Shuanat; mischievous young Aminat, who delighted only in irritating Zeidat. He had two resident sons: noble Gazi-Muhammad, whose visits everyone looked forward to; delinquent Muhammad-Sheffi, who once almost set the whole complex on fire.

Zeidat's father Jamal-Edin, who was also Shamil's spiritual superior in the Sufi hierarchy, and his wife provided emotional support for the captives, while a steward, Hajio, was the target for merciless teasing.

Shamil's third wife Aminat, a seventeen-year-old girl from the Kist nation, which is closely related to the Chechens, was delighted to have the princesses to talk to. She constantly cooked up new schemes to keep everyone amused, including breaking into the imam's quarters, where he lived with a favourite cat.

'The captives accompanied her with fear and trembling; but curiosity overcame every other feeling. In Shamil's private room they saw some very rich carpets and a great number of books. Aminette also showed them some beautiful Georgian pistols mounted in silver, and pistol cases of cloth embroidered in silver and gold,' the account of their captivity says.

Aminat seems shortly after this to have incited one of the princesses to 'accidentally' bump into Hajio, a man who was rather enamoured of the princess. If an unbeliever touched him, he would have to wash himself ritually seven times, a fact that the princess then found out about and exploited mercilessly with regular accidental contacts. 'At last Hadjio avoided the young princess as if she had been fire, and went in a cautious and circuitous manner round every point where she was likely to make her appearance. He was moreover in a constant state of trepidation as long as he was in the same room with her, and was particularly amusing whenever she gave the least sign of approaching him.'

With diversions like this, time passed, although the princesses, their children and their servants remained desperately uncomfortable in a small room measuring just twenty-six shoe-lengths by twelve shoe-lengths. The major enemy was boredom, particularly when Shamil went away campaigning and they became targets for Zeidat's spitefulness. The senior wife appeared to derive pleasure from tormenting the women, and took the opportunity of her husband not being present to serve them scarcely edible food, and to dangle the prospect of death over them.

Shuanat, mindful of her Christian background as an Armenian's daughter and the possibility of rumours about her loyalty starting behind her back, was kind to them but had to be careful to visit them only rarely.

Only Aminat remained friendly and during the winter was their

only visitor. One evening, the princesses sat on their balcony enjoying the moonlight and the fresh air, and the young wife came to
see them. They all sat and looked out on the view, when Shamil
appeared wearing a white coat and walked to Aminat's chamber. It
was clear that he wanted to see his wife, but his wife – it transpired
– did not want to see him, since she dived under the princesses' bench
and hid there.

Shamil knocked, but there was no answer. So he waited, and
waited, and waited, and still his wife did not come. 'Thus, for a considerable time, the illustrious saint, the powerful Iman of Chechni
and Daghestan, waited freezing in the cold, like an ardent and not
particularly saintlike young man, for the sake of a love-meeting with
a girl of seventeen. At last the severity of the night, and the evident
inutility of waiting any longer, made him return to his own apart-
ments.'

While this peculiar family story unfolded, letters had been to taken
to St Petersburg, requesting that the imam's son be released. The tsar
agreed, as did the unfortunate Jamal-Edin, who now faced the prospect of setting up home in mountains he had not seen since he was a
child. Shamil demanded 40,000 silver roubles in ransom as well, and
the prince was forced to mortgage his land and seek loans from
elsewhere to redeem his family.

The outcome of the talks was probably never in doubt, although
Zeidat kept the princesses in a state of panic by occasionally saying
they would be sent as wives to Shamil's lieutenants if the ransom was
not larger than previously agreed. The distractions aside, however,
the handover was finally set for mid-March 1855, on the Michik river
not far from the town of Khasavyurt.

The two wives the captives had befriended were heartbroken to
see them go. 'Now you are going away you will forget us,' said Shuanat in a melancholy tone. 'When you get home, you will live as you
did before; but I – We had become fond of you; your presence here
occupied and interested us; and we were quite accustomed to you.'

Aminat could not speak for sadness, but Zeidat – true to form –
saw the opportunity and stole their samovar.

The handover is probably a unique occasion in the entire Caucasus war, when we have four separate accounts of one event, as well as the official Russian documents. It was a fascinating display, the highlanders and the Russians lined up opposite each other in force, with hostilities postponed for the day.

Madame Drancey, the governess, wrote of her joy in seeing the Russian troops lined up to receive the freed hostages, their ranks shining in the sun of a glorious spring day. When the Russians arrived, there were already some highlander units waiting for them, and these too made an impression on their foes. Jamal-Edin, the son whom Shamil had not seen for a decade and a half, was ready for the exchange.

A group of Russian soldiers escorted Jamal-Edin and the carts full of money to the place of exchange. His half-brother Gazi-Muhammad and an equivalent number of highlanders were already waiting to receive them, and to escort the princesses back to the Russian lines.

'All the poetical ideas which had been formed in Europe about Schamyl and his followers, the fallacy of which three years sojourn here has sufficiently proved to me, seemed at this moment to be more than justified. At the head of the troops rode Khasi-Mahoma, a young man of good though slender figure, but a pale expressionless face. His entirely white appearance – he was mounted on a beautiful white horse, wore a white tunic, and a white fur cap – gave me a very disagreeable impression of him, which was much strengthened by his pompous and affected manner,' wrote a Prussian serving as an officer in the Russian army and part of Jamal-Edin's escort.

'Behind him in two ranks appeared his 32 followers, all Murids, splendidly mounted, equipped and armed. There was a grace in their proud and military bearing which was enhanced by a dash of half-savage wildness. They carried their long guns cocked, and rested on their right thigh. Their stern dark faces and wiry forms, the richness of their arms, glittering with gold and silver, the beauty of their fiery little horses, combined with the background of the surrounding landscape, offered a coup d'oeil, the like of which I never remember to have witnessed.'

As Prince Chavchavadze rode forward, he heard one of his daughters call out: 'Look, mama! There is papa on a white horse!' It was then that he knew his family had finally been freed. Gazi-Muhammad sought to reassure him that the women had been well treated.

'The Imam gave me orders, prince, to inform you that he took as much care of your family as if it had been his own; and that if the captives suffered any discomfort with us it did not arise from any intention on our part to annoy them, but from our ignorance how to behave towards such women and from our want of means,' the young man said.

Jamal-Edin, still dressed in Russian uniform, embraced his brother, and the two sides separated once more. As the highlander party returned to the river, the excitement bubbled ever higher. Individuals dashed forward from the ranks to kiss the hands of Shamil's eldest son, freed from the clasp of the non-believers, then joyously joined the escort which swelled to hundreds of people.

'I have seldom seen, collected in one place, a body of more fine and more powerful men and horses,' wrote the Prussian officer, who accompanied Jamal-Edin on this last journey too.

But before the young man could be presented to the father who had waited for him now for sixteen years, he had to change into the clothing of his people, and to discard the uniform of his captors which he had worn for so long. Hajio walked forward and handed a bundle of clothing to him, upon which he was surrounded by his companions to screen him from sight. He changed, and emerged as a magnificent prince of the mountains, in tunic, fur hat and silver-gilt weapons.

He rode to his father, and dismounted, and Shamil took him in his arms, tears pouring down his face. The imam had won a great victory, and his son was restored to him. But, even now, he did not exult or show any crude emotion. He turned to his son's escort of Russian officers and thanked them for their kindness.

'I had, I know not why, formed to myself quite another idea of Schamyl,' the Prussian officer wrote, 'and his dignified exterior, his noble features, his graceful and distinguished, though somewhat shy deportment, surprised me in the highest degree, and made a deep impression on me. That such a man should be able to inspire a sentiment of enthusiastic devotion I can well understand.'

A hundred of the murids escorted the Russians back to their lines, and Jamal-Edin was led before his father's troops. 'They rejoiced in God's blessing and glory. They fired their weapons to show happiness and anger at [their] enemies. As for the imam, he sat under a tree – crying, humbling himself before God, thanking Him, and saying, "Praise God and exalt Him",' one of Shamil's closest allies later wrote.

The silver was handed out among those who had conducted the raid, with a fifth reserved for the imam. Shamil's army was rich. The troops could turn and go home, thinking themselves fit to take on the world. They had seized the imam's lost son from the coils of the Russian state. What could stop them now?

But, perhaps even then, Shamil may have seen the dangers that awaited him. The very same day he won back his beloved son, the tsar who had fought him all his adult life was being buried. The hide-bound, reactionary, unimaginative Nikolai was dead. His energetic son Alexander, the second tsar to bear that name, would be a far more deadly foe.

And yet, at that moment, the war was in the past and the future, and Imam Shamil could just revel in having his son back for a while.

21. Fire is Better Than Shame

Apollon Ivanovich Runovsky was an ordinary officer in the Russian army in the Caucasus. Born in 1823, he had not completed his science training when he was sent off as a cadet – the most junior of officer grades – to Dagestan in 1840. He served in the Caucasus for the next two decades, and was shot in the leg while fighting Shamil's forces; the bullet stayed there for the rest of his days.

He became an ensign in 1846, and an aide-de-camp a year later. By 1852, he had spent a year fighting the Circassians and become a lieutenant. After two more years had passed, he perhaps sensed that his talents lay more in administration than in battle and he asked to be named supervisor of the military hospital in Grozny. All in all, it was an undistinguished career, its chief point of interest being a minor blemish in 1857, when he was briefly dismissed for exploiting lower ranks in his own service.

But then, in 1859, everything changed for the 36-year-old, when his career was yanked spectacularly off course.

Shamil had been defeated.

When the end came, it came very quickly. Shamil might have seemed at the peak of his powers when he raided Georgia, carried off the two princesses and regained his son, but, in truth, that had been his last moment of triumph, and the delight of reuniting his family had held within it a tragedy more bitter even than the initial loss.

Jamal-Edin, the prince who had been welcomed back by the rapturous highlanders, had spent too long among the Russians. He was not ready for the harsh life of the mountains. Deprived of the Russian food he had grown accustomed to, praying five times a day, and subjected to the harsh discipline of his father, the handsome young man sickened and started to fade.

In February 1858, a messenger galloped into Khasavyurt, desperate to see the military commander. He came from Shamil, and begged that medicine be provided for Jamal-Edin, who was dying. It was clear to the doctor that the symptoms were those of tuberculosis. Medicines were given, and the messenger galloped away again. The Russian officers wondered if the medicines would arrive in time to save the young man, though in truth there was little that a nineteenth-century doctor could have done anyway.

What hopes they entertained must have all but vanished three months later, when the messenger returned and this time he wanted to take a doctor with him. The doctor agreed, and endured a relentless weeklong journey into the hills, his guides changing daily but never willing to talk to him or tell him how much further he must travel.

Arriving at last, he looked at his patient and realized there was nothing he could do. He stayed for three days, but Jamal-Edin was dying. His face drawn, his body emaciated, he died alone and uncomplaining, as he had lived those sorry last three years of his life.

Two months before his death, he had been taken to the village of Karata, where his brother Gazi-Muhammad ruled in the imam's name. Perhaps Shamil thought the climate there would be more suitable for a consumptive person, or perhaps he thought that the brother's care would be more amenable than the fierce regulation of his life elsewhere.

Jamal-Edin had loved reading, but he feared punishment from his father, and had hidden away his books – written in the proscribed Russian language – for as long as he could. Many of his 300 volumes had been obtained in exchange for freeing a Georgian prisoner of war given to him as a slave by Shamil. That fact alone must have shown Shamil that his son's heart was not in the fight.

His death was drawn-out and painful. Jamal-Edin – understanding that he had tuberculosis, and knowing enough about the disease to know it was incurable – predicted each stage of his decline. He was desperate to avoid rumours springing up around his untimely death. But the highlanders did not believe him, and the story told by the villagers was that he had been given a slow-acting poison when in Russian hands.

He tried repeatedly to persuade those nearest to him that the story was not true, that he was dying of a slow and fatal condition, since he felt a great debt of obligation to his former captors. He struggled to persuade his brothers that the Russians were not bad people and, they said, he died happy, believing he had convinced them. Perhaps indeed he had.

His death could have been an omen for Shamil that the end was near. The triumph of regaining his son had turned sour for the imam. This time there would be no miraculous escape, there would be no clambering down precipices, and no death-defying leaps over ranks of bayonets. The Russians were coming to finish the job.

For the Russians, humiliated in the Crimean War and energized by their new Tsar Alexander II, had re-adopted the plans laid out by Velyaminov forty years before. They would treat the Caucasus as a fortress, and its inhabitants as a garrison.

The Crimean War was taken as a signal for the highlanders as well. The sultan, in whom they had pinned their hopes for so long, had failed to crush the Russians, even though he was allied with the armies of England and France. In the Caucasus, the Russian capitulation and the humiliating conditions of the Treaty of Paris, which barred warships from the Black Sea, were seen as a victory for the tsar, since he had survived the onslaught of three sovereigns without capture.

A delegation of Chechens wrote to Shamil in 1856 asking him to sue for peace. Shamil, perhaps sharing their opinion, made no immediate reply. He must have sensed this was no time for a theatrical response, for fasting and flagellation. He asked only for a couple of months for the smoke to clear.

The end was near, but Russian overconfidence and instinctive brutality saved him for a while. A council in Stavropol decided that, to pacify the Caucasus, tribesmen who submitted must be moved to Manych – some vacant land on the plains to the north of the Caucasus. The effect on those who had not submitted was predictable enough. They would never willingly surrender their homeland, so all thoughts of suing for peace were forgotten, and the war went on.

'I could never invent such punishment for those Chechens who had betrayed us as their Russian masters did,' Shamil told the Chechen delegation. 'Do you want to go to Manych as well?'

But it was only a temporary reprieve. The Russians might have been politically inept, but they were militarily competent at last. The command had been reorganized along rational lines, and a steady pressure was exerted to squeeze Shamil's control of his heartland. The forests were felled in great strips either side of the roads, and new forts were built, meaning the highlanders could not even bring the Russians to fight any more. This new tactic proved more effective than any number of battles had been.

'The mountaineers could not be frightened by fighting. Constant warfare had given them such confidence, that a few score men would engage without fear a column several battalions strong, and returning one shot to our hundred would occasion us much more loss than we them. Fighting underlines equality between forces, and as long as the mountaineers could fight, they entertained no thought of submission,' said Prince Alexander Baryatinsky, the new and gifted commander of the Russian forces.

'But when, time after time, they found that they were not even given a chance to resist, their weapons started to fall from their hands. Defeated, they would have gathered again on the morrow. Circumvented and forced to disperse without fighting, while seeing their valleys occupied without opposition, they came in next day to offer their submission. Shamil's power was undermined by nothing so much as the gathering of useless hordes which had to disperse to their homes without anywhere offering serious resistance.'

In one last desperate roll of the dice, Shamil struck out of Chechnya towards Vladikavkaz, where the Ingush were revolting. Apparently he believed that Musa Kundukhov, a Muslim general in the Russian service whom we will hear of again, had promised him his cooperation. Nothing came of it, and by the end of 1858 Shamil had not only lost his son, but the best part of his territory.

The final assault came in July 1859. Russia's troops manoeuvred around the defences Shamil had set up, forcing the waiting army to disperse, and the last shreds of morale left with it. In a final indignity, Shamil's wagons and treasury were robbed by his former subjects, and he was abused and insulted as he headed for his last stronghold: the mountaintop village of Gunib.

Shamil despaired, and recited a poem as he rode to his last battle.

'I swore by my brothers, whom I considered my coats of armour, but they were armour only for my enemies. I considered them well-aimed arrows, but they were aimed only at my heart. They said "we have pure hearts" and they spoke the truth, but only of my love.'

As his miserable party laboured along the last stretch of road, he turned to his son-in-law and later chronicler Abdurakhman and asked him: 'If meat spoils, we treat it with salt. But what can we do if the salt spoils?'

Gunib, however, was a wonderful place to make a last stand. It is a natural fortress that, if only the defenders had enough men, could surely never be captured. It is ringed by cliffs, which rise sheer all around a bowl-shaped plateau. The plateau has fields, a stream, houses and trees, and its only exit is guarded by high walls, pierced by a single gate.

Now there is a prosperous village at the foot of the cliffs, but in Shamil's time the defenders were ensconced on the plateau, too far from the Russians to be harmed by artillery, and secure in the knowledge that they were impregnable.

Or, they would have been, if only there had been more of them. Shamil had commanded thousands just weeks before; now there were only 400 defenders, and even they were wavering in their loyalty.

The Russians wanted to take their enemy alive. They posted rewards for him in case he tried to flee, and held peace negotiations for two weeks, but that came to nothing.

According to one account, Shamil's envoys were sent with the message that the imam was prepared to surrender, if he was allowed to make the pilgrimage to the holy places with his family. 'If you release me, my family and my followers on the Haj, then between us will be peace and agreement. If not, then the sword is unsheathed and the hand is strong,' the imam's message said. The Russians' reply did not satisfy him, however, so the battle was on.

Before dawn on 6 September, the highlanders began to hear the Russian soldiers cheer as they made their advance. Some of Shamil's followers threw stones down the cliffs, hoping to knock out their assailants, but the resistance was hopeless in the dark. The Russians were swarming up the cliffs all around the village. The thin screen of defenders might be able to hold them for a while, but even the smallest toehold on the plateau would allow the Russians to push soldiers up the cliffs, and would leave the last few hundred people loyal to the imam outnumbered and outgunned.

Abdurakhman feared for his family and rushed back to the houses where they had been staying. 'When I got to where our families were, I found them in the house by the mosque. They looked like baby swallows held in the hand. They were crying from the horrors of the day.'

The defenders, having lost their hold on the clifftops, retreated down the slight slope towards the last pocket of resistance. Russians now held the heights, which dominate the bowl of the plateau from all sides, and poured fire down into the throng.

A Russian emissary called out to the last men left fighting: 'Save your ammunition, do not bring death upon yourselves. Do not spill your blood. Save your honour.'

The highlanders stopped firing and listened: was this the end? Some looked to the imam for a decision, but found no comfort. 'They did not speak to him about it, being afraid of the shame. As it is said, fire is better than shame. And the imam was quiet, saying nothing; he was fully determined to die and to fight until his sword was broken to pieces,' Abdurakhman recalled.

Shamil begged his followers to kill him: 'Is there no one among you who would kill me? I allow you to spill my blood, so the enemy does not see me.'

But they refused. Shamil then gave them permission to leave, and said he would die alone. Again, they refused. His son Gazi-Muhammad knelt before him and begged him to surrender: once, twice. On the third time the imam gave in. He could resist his son's entreaties no longer: the father's love had overcome the fanatic's zeal.

Accompanied by twelve of his followers, he rode towards the Russians – 'he looked not to the right, not to the left, only at the horse's mane' – and gave himself up. Ahead of him, seated on a small rock, was Baryatinsky. He welcomed the imam into captivity, and Shamil unbuckled his sword and handed it to his conqueror. Shamil's war was over.

Apollon Runovsky, meanwhile, was busy running his hospital in Khasavyurt, the job he received when he was allowed back into the army after his temporary disgrace. It must have been a relief for him to have any kind of job at all, and perhaps he felt he would be in the posting until the end of his career. If he did, however, he could not have been more wrong.

A new posting was on its way, and one that surely he did not expect. He was to live with Shamil.

'Live with Shamil! Take care of him! How could I ever have imagined such a thing? On the contrary, I well remember how during my long period of service in the Caucasus, I more than once thought that Shamil would be taking care of me, if the fortunes of war had left me as his prisoner,' Runovsky wrote.

As Shamil's *pristav* – the word means policeman or bailiff, but in this case he was more like an aide-de-camp – he was ordered to help the imam, while simultaneously keeping him under control. He had to watch him permanently, but without being intrusive. He could not interfere in Shamil's religious or family life, but must keep a diary of sayings, comments, conversations and events.

Shamil was to be honoured and feted as a worthy adversary, with Runovsky supplying his wants. It could have been a tough job for the hospital administrator, since no one knew if Shamil would turn out to be a savage, twisted by anger. But it did not turn out that way. The imam appreciated this rare display of magnanimity from the Russians – one that would never be repeated – and he came to love his captors as his son had done.

'When I decided to obey the wishes of my wives and children and surrender,' Shamil told Runovsky many months later, 'and when I walked to the meeting with your commander, I was convinced I would hear from him the words: "Well, pig, where's your sword that you suggested I should come and take from you?" The expectation of this meeting was so upsetting that I fully believed myself worthy of this insult, and decided that I would stab myself as soon as I heard it. But when the words of the commander were translated for me, and had only a friendly meaning, I at first did not believe my ears, and, not expecting anything like that, I could not give an answer, and when I spoke, I made so many mistakes that it seems I did not speak very well at all.'

Runovsky's diaries give a sometimes daily, sometimes weekly, sometimes monthly but always fascinating account of the imam's existence. They are the completest study of his character that we have, and illuminate this guerrilla warrior in unexpected and wonderful ways.

In one series of consecutive entries, for example, in February 1861, Shamil told Runovsky about highlanders who were in Russian service, then about the mountain beliefs concerning snakes, then about why boys and girls are born at different times (girls are conceived if the mother is well-fed, apparently), then about who in the mountains is best able to treat a scorpion sting. Elsewhere, Shamil discussed the laws he imposed, which of his lieutenants were most loyal, the appalling sexual habits of the Turks, and more.

Shamil, on his surrender, had been taken with his wives and children down to the plains. After a short rest, Shamil, his sons Gazi-Muhammad and Muhammad-Sheffi, and the follower called Hajio were separated from the others, and sent north into Russia.

According to a family anecdote related to me by one of his descendants, after a few days of rattling through the uninterrupted steppe, Shamil commented: 'If I had known Russia was so big, I would never have fought against it.' True or not, the remark is entirely in keeping with the imam's outlook on life, which turned out to be startlingly naive.

At times, I had to keep reminding myself that the man described in the hundreds of pages of diaries and recollections had resisted the mighty Russian army for two and a half decades. He seemed like someone who had never encountered the modern world before.

If Shamil feared the reaction of the Russians to his presence, he was again mistaken. He was greeted by cheering crowds at every stop he made on his journey and, on arrival in St Petersburg, he became a sensation. Giant throngs gathered outside his hotel, hoping for just a glimpse of his face, or outside buildings where he stopped as he was conducted around the city. He was amazed by all he saw, and particularly by the warmth of his welcome.

'Your people are very good to me in captivity; they are not angry with me, and do not wish me evil. This is very good, and it was not like this in my place. Our lads would throw rubbish at the prisoner and, if they could, they would even have killed him,' he told his translator.

The warm sentiment was one he felt for Emperor Alexander II as well. The tsar's father had cared for Shamil's son, and now it was the son's turn to treat Jamal-Edin's father with grace and generosity.

'Not only gratitude for your Majesty's magnanimity towards one who was your enemy, but also – I proclaim it again and again – a sincere and deliberate conviction compels me to be your subject. If there be a man upon earth worthy to represent God Almighty, that man, sire, is yourself. If a throne is grounded upon the hearts of men, that throne is yours. Sire, I wish it to be known everywhere, that if old Schamyl of Daghestan, who fought against your arms for thirty years, experiences a regret at the decline of his days, it is only that he cannot be born again to devote his whole life to the service of your empire,' the imam said, according to an account printed in the London *Times* in November 1859.

The compliments may have been expressed in the traditional forms of the Arabic-speaker, but they were clearly heartfelt. Imagine a captured Osama bin Laden expressing such gratitude to the American president, and you have some idea of the surprise that Shamil's words provoked in those who heard them.

And the Russians appreciated the dignity of their captive. Shamil's popularity was such that he appeared at times to possess the draw of an exotic specimen in a zoo, particularly for those officers who had fought against him, and finally had the chance to see their opponent in the flesh. Most of them were stunned by the gentleness of the man they saw in front of them, and the news of the dignity of his appearance made more officers desperate to see him.

For the crowd of ordinary Petersburgers, however, his popularity seems to have gone far beyond that. Perhaps they admired his resistance to the autocratic state, or perhaps they were simply welcoming him as a genuine hero, but they waited for him and cheered him everywhere he went.

It was at around this time that Shamil and his sons first met Runovsky. The imam's new minder had arrived in St Petersburg, and was introduced to Shamil by his first name, Apollon. They had not heard this name before, and tried, unsuccessfully, to pronounce it quietly to themselves: 'Aflon', 'Aflon', 'Afilon'.

Shamil, learning that Runovsky had spent twelve years in the Caucasus, asked what battles he had taken part in. As it happened, Runovsky had missed out on most of the major engagements, but had been involved in one desperate affair in 1843, perhaps the year when Shamil's influence was at its peak. The highlanders had taken several fortresses that autumn, and the Russian generals were penned up behind their ramparts while the soldiers starved and hoped for relief.

Runovsky had been a junior officer in a detachment trapped in a small fort in the village of Zyrani, deep in the mountains of central Dagestan. Highlanders held the high ground on all sides. In the context of the war that year, it was a small affair, and the tiny force only had to hold out for six weeks, so it barely makes it into even the most detailed histories. But, for some reason, a song written by the defenders became a popular ditty throughout the army at the time. It described their privations as they suffered in the siege and the cold of the mountain winter, and went something like this:

> So we came to eat our horses,
> Which we boiled and we baked.
> Lacking salt, we seasoned them
> With powder from our cartridges.
> We smoked hay in our pipes and
> Said farewell to tobacco.
> We were shabby, we were ragged,
> Our clothing fell down off our shoulders.
> We clothed ourselves in sacking
> Instead of cloaks or heavy coats.
> After eating all the horses
> We made shoes from their hide.

In an interesting sign of how much intercommunication there had been between the highlanders and the Russians, Shamil knew all about the affair, and may even have known the song, for his first question on learning that Runovsky had been in Zyrani was to ask with a smile if he had eaten horse. Runovsky replied that he had, and that it would have been tastier if they had had more salt.

'Well, that is bad,' said the imam. 'However, you held on there very strongly; my lads would not have held on.'

The encounter formed the basis of a firm friendship that grew up between them over the next two and half years. One night, Runovsky took Shamil to the theatre to watch a ballet about a sultan and his harem. This was the imam's second time at the theatre, so he did not examine the magic of the dimming lights as closely as he had before, but the performance was enough to amaze him none the less.

'On seeing the harem on stage, with all its attributes, Shamil became noticeably animated, but he immediately reconsidered and adopted a calm pose as befits the lord of a harem. In fact, for the whole show, he held himself like a true gentleman,' Runovsky wrote.

Nonetheless, his nonchalance notwithstanding, Shamil was clearly impressed, not least by the finale, when the harem inmates formed themselves into a human pyramid.

'The prophet promised us this only in heaven and I am very glad to be able to see it on earth,' the imam said.

It is clear, however, that the life he was living was wearing him down. He was missing his family and tired by the attention and the ceaseless round of receptions and visits. As they walked back from the theatre through the cold evening, Runovsky had to lend the shivering Shamil his jacket, and Gazi-Muhammad asked the officer – in the pidgin Turkic that the Russians and highlanders used to communicate – whether their wives and children could come to join them soon.

Other observers too noticed that Shamil seemed listless under the constant scrutiny.

On the morning of 24 September, for example, according to an account in a Scottish newspaper, twenty or thirty officers were waiting to see the imam before he had even got up. The officers, who included generals, were talking quietly among themselves to avoid disturbing their defeated enemy.

'What a quantity of tea he can take in,' said one subaltern, 'he would ruin his father and be the death of this mother, if they had a frugal turn of mind.'

'How is it with the imam?' asked a general at last when a servant appeared. 'I hope he will not keep us waiting the whole day long.'

When they were finally admitted to the imam's room, they found him seated under a portrait of the tsar. Shamil had been looking at a watch, carefully comparing its face with that of a clock, but he put it away in his pocket when they came in, and nodded in their direction. The officers approached, stood around two yards in front of him, and waited in silence, scrutinizing his appearance.

'Certainly, this was but a bad sample of an oriental hero, as far as exterior went,' the journalist wrote with heavy sarcasm. 'If the features could be trusted, this man was neither cruel nor ferocious, but mild, intelligent, and prudent.'

They waited and examined him for five minutes without a word, until Shamil turned aside and began to pray. The officers took this as a cue for them to speak, and discussed his appearance loudly.

'The majority were struck with admiration, and called him a lion with the gentleness of a lamb, a great warrior, a sagacious leader, with many other eulogistic expressions. However, there were some of the party who, having served in the Caucasus, recalled the many executions he had ordered, and insisted on terming him savage and fiend.'

When Shamil finished praying, he spoke for the first time, asking through an interpreter when he would be allowed to continue his journey to his final destination. A general said he would leave within a week if he so wished, which seemed to satisfy the imam, who then rose and left the room.

The audience was over for the generals, but it is a scene that was probably repeated for the imam time after time. It is little wonder that he was exhausted.

When the time finally did come for Shamil and his sons to leave St Petersburg, Runovsky was with them. The crowd outside the hotel was even denser for this last glimpse of the popular hero. They cried out to him, saying: 'Farewell, farewell', 'Stay here with us, Shamil' and 'Be our guest for a while longer.' But he would not stay. He was – no doubt with a feeling of relief – on his way to the train station.

As he sat on the train, the crowd thronged the platform. Shamil reached up and opened the curtain and the mob exploded with joy. Hats were thrown into the air, and Shamil – clearly moved – put his hand on his heart and nodded to them repeatedly for the half an hour that the carriage sat there. When the time came for the train to move out, the imam wished to make a small speech.

'Tell them, please, that I cannot express my feelings in words, they are too deep and sincere. Tell them only that their attention makes me full of happiness, and gives me the same satisfaction that I felt on receiving the news of the relief of Dargo in 1845, and that I received from the successes in Dagestan in 1843 ...'

But it was too late. The train had pulled out and there was no time for St Petersburg to hear Shamil's gratitude. That would be stored up for the residents of another town, for Shamil was on his way to a new life in Kaluga.

22. The Old Man Shamil

In every memoir written by someone who met Shamil in Kaluga, of which there were several, the captured imam always made a comment of some kind of about how the hills and countryside around the town reminded him of Chechnya.

These could only have been the remarks of a profoundly unhappy man. The vertical lines of the Russian pine forests, and the jagged but horizontal horizon of the central Russian plains have nothing in common with the rolling beech forests and soaring peaks of the Caucasus. Maybe, though, the little self-deception was a comfort of some kind for the old man, who had nothing left but his family, his books and his memories.

On one occasion, Shamil used a variation on the line, which was clearly something of a party piece that he dragged out to amuse his Russian guests, perhaps to assure them that he was not feeling homesick.

Runovsky, who seems to have genuinely won the imam's trust, asked him if anyone else in the Caucasus could rise up and take his place as a unifying leader of the Chechens and the Dagestanis. Shamil was silent for some time and just gazed at his questioner, with a look that Runovsky described as containing 'the past, which definitely was, and the future, which for him will never be'.

'No,' Shamil said at last. 'Now the Caucasus is in Kaluga.'

It took me several readings of that short passage to realize the depth of bitterness encased within it. His last months of warfare, when his armies had melted away faster than the snow on the hillsides and his allies had turned into robbers and spies, had permanently scarred his heart. The Caucasus had betrayed him, and no one there was worthy of bearing the name 'imam' and leading the tribes to war. If the Caucasus was now a land of turncoats and traitors then the true spirit of the mountains had deserted them.

Or perhaps I am being unfair to Shamil. Maybe he was reflecting the deep love he felt for his family members – they were to join him in the town three months after his own arrival – and was saying that the only people that made the Caucasus precious were in Kaluga with him. Hence for him the Caucasus was truly in this little town.

Or yet again, maybe he saw the spirit of the Caucasus as being something that was captured when the mountains were conquered. With the imam captured, so was the mountains' soul, and that was now trapped in the gilded cage of the little provincial town.

He was certainly troubled by his capture, and it is hard to see how he could not have been. He had exhorted thousands – possibly tens of thousands – of his followers to choose death over the dishonour of capture by infidels. Yet, here he was, living in comfortable exile while his soldiers' widows still mourned their loss, and their children grew up without fathers.

These questions that Shamil's personality still poses – the combination of simplicity and intelligence, of cunning and naivety – make him a fascinating man. Runovsky's papers give us the opportunity of examining that personality in some depth, and the results are extraordinary.

Runovsky was given money to pass on to Shamil, and he tried to encourage his charge to manage his own household expenses. But the imam refused to do so. He had no understanding of money, and it clearly upset him. Nevertheless, Runovsky finally wrote out a receipt for the imam to sign. The receipt ended with the signature: 'The Slave of God Shamil, Imam'.

Shamil objected to that, and refused to sign it, using words that are heartrending even today, coming as they did from such a strong man.

'What kind of imam am I? I could be in no way satisfactory to those who chose me as imam. What kind of imam am I?' he asked.

For no amount of comfort could take away from the imam the knowledge that he had failed, and failed catastrophically. He may have seen similarities between Kaluga and Chechnya, but he was still an impossible distance from his homeland, and had no chance of ever seeing it again.

Kaluga is 200 kilometres south of Moscow, and was then a pleasant little town, with a centre of Russian brick-and-stucco houses and outskirts of peasants' cabins, sited on the banks of the river Oka. The house that was assigned to the imam is still called 'Shamil's house' and is a handsome three-storey mansion of yellow stucco with white flourishes. It has a private garden surrounded by a fence in the local style, and bears a sombre plaque in the Russian language – 'In this house lived Shamil, Imam of Dagestan and Chechnya 1859 to 1868' – with a stylized portrait of Shamil wearing his turban and national dress.

It was around this time indeed that the first photographs of Shamil were taken. Writers had previously speculated about his appearance, but now they could see from the portraits from St Petersburg that he was a good-looking man, with a pale face and a dense black beard. His eyebrows are often drawn into a frown, giving him a look of stern concentration, and his shaggy hat is wrapped in the white turban of a Sufi sheikh.

In one photograph, he sits flanked by his two sons. All of them are dressed in the tunics of their homeland, and have daggers at their belts. Shamil clutches his sword in his left hand as he glowers at the photographer. Together they give out an air of wary readiness. They may have surrendered, but they were still on their guard.

After they arrived in Kaluga, Shamil retreated into himself. Runovsky left his charge alone, not wanting to impose on him. But the imam sought out his Russian officer and, via an interpreter, began to tell him a story of a nanny looking after an orphan child. Runovsky was not sure where the tale was going but listened to it attentively.

'I am an old man, but I am here in a strange land. I do not know your language or your customs, so I do not think of myself as the old man Shamil, but as this little child, who, by the will of God, has been left an orphan and needs a nanny to look after him,' Shamil said, with irresistible candour.

'The king has made you my minder. The colonel has told me about what you have orders to do, and now I think you are that very nanny that I need. I am sure that the king, in showing me so many kindnesses, wishes me well, therefore I will not ask you to be a "good" nanny, and just ask you to love me in the way that a normal nanny loves her child. And I promise that I will love you for this, not just how a child loves his nanny, but also in the way that the old man Shamil loves someone who does him a kindness.'

Runovsky then promised not only to love him, but to respect him too, but Shamil had not finished. The imam said he had watched Runovsky closely ever since they had first met, and was sure that they would have a close relationship.

'The old man Shamil has never made a mistake about a person he has observed for a long time, and I know I have not made a mistake this time.'

Shamil regularly retreated into his own quarters – the top floor of the house, which the younger men later nicknamed Akhulgo, after the fortress where Jamal-Edin was taken by the Russians – but he still appeared for tea and chats with Runovsky, sometimes one suggesting the topic of conversation, and sometimes the other.

The regular diary entries written by the Russian officer progressively build up a picture of Shamil that is surprising and rather lovely. In place of the fierce chieftain the Russians might have expected, they had a gentle and thoughtful old man who contemplated before speaking or acting, and lived by a moral code as unshakeable as it was peculiar.

One day, Shamil and Runovsky sat and ate lunch together. The officer did not record what the food was, merely that it was very bad. He pushed his plate away, saying he would complain to the cook. Shamil was shocked, and told him he must not do so.

'It is a great sin,' the imam told him.

'But is it not a sin for the cook to feed us with dreadful food?' replied Runovsky, perhaps in jest.

'Yes, it is a sin, but God will punish the cook for it himself,' said Shamil, with great simplicity. His answer did not satisfy Runovsky, who clearly preferred his rewards from God to be more immediate, and ideally to arrive before the next meal was scheduled.

'But if I do not tell the cook that he has cooked dreadful food then he, not knowing this, will always cook it the same way, thinking that maybe he is supposed to do it that way. It must be right to tell him that there is too much salt or that he has somehow spoiled the food,' the officer said.

Runovsky clearly felt he had won the day with this speech, but Shamil did not budge, so Runovsky went on the offensive once more.

'So is it also a sin to tell a person that he is ruining a valuable thing, that he interferes with your affairs, that he wants to change your customs, or that he harms your condition of life and forces you from happiness into unhappiness and need?'

Shamil was ready for this reply, however, and perhaps this was an argument he had been through in his own head. What followed was as complete a discourse on his own philosophy as anything Runovsky ever recorded. It is complete in itself, logically coherent, yet somehow alien and peculiar.

'A man must never express his dissatisfaction with anything at all. If someone gives me food that is not tasty or is over-salted, then I must not judge him. I must keep my silence, in the same way that I must if it is very good food. Above all I must not criticize a servant if he is to blame for something. If I start to scold him, then it is a great sin, that is what it says in the books. Therefore I am always content, content with everything, and I have no needs, and I must observe my customs when it is necessary for other people. If I do not do this it will be a great sin, it says so in the books.'

As Runovsky's acquaintance with Shamil and his family went on, he discovered that this philosophy informed much of their attitude to the outside world. The shoes they had bought in St Petersburg, for example, did not fit and were very uncomfortable. The imam did not mention it, however, since that would have been a sin, until it was too late to replace them. It was a pattern regularly repeated.

Runovsky became very frustrated by Shamil's insistence that what was 'written in books' was the only truth, but he failed to shift the imam from his beliefs, which admitted no hypocrisy or double standards. For example, Shamil would give out charity to all poor people as he walked through Kaluga, and would often force it upon people who had not even asked for it. Once, indeed, he apologized to a young child for not being able to give him anything. The child's reaction was not recorded.

Shamil did not himself carry the money, leaving it to his follower Hajio – the same man who was tormented by the captive princesses during their enforced stay in the mountains – to do so for him. Hajio was regularly instructed to distribute large sums, which were far greater than the household could afford. On one occasion he gave out 10 roubles – a huge amount by the standards of the time. Runovsky eventually took Shamil aside and warned him off the practice. He said most of the beggars did not deserve the money, and would spend it undesirably.

Shamil was having none of it. 'But it is no business of mine where the poor person takes his money,' he said.

'But you can't give out so much,' the ever-sensible Runovsky insisted.

'Well, how much can I give out?'

'One kopeck, two, three, maybe five,' was Runovsky's reply. But if the officer thought he had controlled this drain on Shamil's resources, he was wrong. The imam asked for an explanation, asked how many kopecks there were in a rouble, and asked how many someone would need to survive. Runovsky explained the cost of food, drink and accommodation, but failed to satisfy the old man.

'Well, what help is it to give one kopeck?' asked the baffled imam, having learned that a beggar could not live on such a small sum.

'You give, I give, a third person gives, thus the poor person gathers enough for his daily existence,' said Runovsky, giving a little summary of the principles of Western charity. But that, inevitably, did not satisfy Shamil.

'What need have I for others? If a poor person asks help of me then I must help him. If I give him too little, that means I am mocking him. And in books it says poor people must be helped and not mocked for their situation. Does it not say the same in your books?'

Even Runovsky had to recognize the logic in Shamil's position, and was forced to give in. Eventually, however, he had his way, by persuading Hajio that most of the supplicants went and spent the money on vodka, which was not good for them.

It is not surprising that this gentle and thoughtful old man was a giant success in Kaluga society. Shamil was perhaps the second most famous celebrity – behind only the tsar – in the empire, and having him in their midst was a huge coup. The imam was regularly invited to parties and balls, or to drink tea.

One woman, Maria Chichagova, saw the imam regularly, since her husband was in charge of his well-being for a while. She had the disarming habit of referring to the imam as the 'former terror of Dagestan and Chechnya' and said he liked nothing more than to play with children.

'Shamil very much loved children, and such a person cannot be evil,' she wrote, in her own – disappointingly uninformative – memoirs. 'On Shamil's departure, I realized that I had not once remembered his Caucasus cruelties. Nothing made him appear a soul-less, cruel, severe person. On the contrary, from first acquaintance, Shamil inspired sympathy in me. As a consequence I discovered that in this highlander's wild nature was hidden a divine spark of love for his neighbour.'

But, for these early months in Kaluga, Shamil was not happy. He hid it well, but he desperately missed his family. He worried that Shuanat, now she was back among her own people, might return to Christianity and be torn away from him. He should have trusted his beloved wife, who would have stayed with him through more than a few months' forced separation, but it worried away at him. Other perceived slights from his past now rose up and concerned him too.

He had a particular dislike for the Turks, since the sultan never wrote him a letter to ask how he was, and he expressed hatred for Daniel-Sultan, one of his former allies who had deserted him.

But in mid-January 1860 his depression vanished.

A rumbling from outside the window showed that a wagon was arriving. A messenger entered the receiving room, asking the imam what he would like done with his books. Most of his library, which he had lost in the last humiliating retreat to Gunib, had been recovered and here it was, ready for him to read again. The imam was delighted, and then overjoyed when he heard that his family was close behind. He clearly struggled to follow his own rule of hiding his feelings, and trembled with impatience before mastering himself. He also failed to stop himself criticizing a servant and swore at Hajio for only giving a 30-kopeck tip to the messenger. The bringer of such news deserved gold, Shamil said.

First up the stairs came Muhammad-Sheffi, Shamil's youngest

son. The imam walked to the head of the stairs to meet him, then reconsidered and went back to sit at the table, adopting an expression of indifference. His son, on entering the room, also looked like he wished to embrace his father, but instead calmly walked up and kissed his hand.

They prayed together while the remaining carriages arrived.

In quick succession entered Gazi-Muhammad, Shamil's oldest son, followed by the imam's oldest son-in-law (also, as it happened, the brother of his senior wife, the brother of Shamil's other son-in-law, and the son of the imam's spiritual leader). Then the women arrived, and stepped out of their carriages into the snow. The family went upstairs, kissed the imam's hand and prayed, before retreating upstairs for a week.

Shamil was no doubt relieved that his favourite wife, Shuanat, had come back to him, but the rest of the family were less pleased that the senior wife, Zeidat, had done so. Hajio had already, rather disloyally, suggested that it would not be a bad idea if someone thought of converting Zeidat to Christianity and leaving her in the Caucasus.

For now that Shamil's bossy senior wife was in Kaluga, life would be anything but relaxing. Politics, personal dislike and petty viciousness would transform the three-storey brick-and-stucco mansion into a little nest of problems.

Zeidat carried a host of political issues with her. No one had much of a good word to say for her, but that may well be because Runovsky's informants – Gazi-Muhammad, Hajio, Muhammad-Sheffi – were all in the opposing faction. They felt that Zeidat exploited her position as senior wife to make Shuanat's position hell, and to squeeze the rest of them out of any position of responsibility.

The third wife, Aminat, who had so loved the Georgian princesses, had been divorced and was nowhere to be seen. Most accounts hold that she was divorced for being infertile, but Hajio said she had been sent away because she was too mischievous. Her habit of making jokes against her older rival had backfired, and Zeidat had forced Shamil to dispense with her.

Shamil's sons' main ground of complaint against Zeidat was that, though their sisters – the children of Fatimat, a now dead wife – had been due to marry two of the imam's chief lieutenants in solid and sensible dynastic marriages, Zeidat, keen to increase her own influence, had forced the imam to marry the two girls to her own brothers. These brothers were hated by Shamil's sons, who were jealous of the weight they carried as the sons of Shamil's spiritual adviser.

By this stage, the three-storey building contained, besides Shamil, his two wives, his two sons, his five daughters, one granddaughter, his two sons-in-law, one daughter-in-law, a nanny, the nanny's son, a translator, a servant, two companions for his sons, a seventeen-year-old captured Ingush girl whose position was uncertain and a random Afghan dervish who seems to have adopted Shamil but to have served no discernible purpose.

The Afghan, who was an ally of Zeidat's, was engaged in lengthy and unsuccessful attempts to persuade Runovsky to give him a pension for unspecified services to Russia, related to the time of Shamil's surrender.

With so many people in such close proximity, it is unsurprising that conditions were insanitary. By June 1860, Abdurakhman – Shamil's son-in-law, one of Zeidat's brothers – had contracted a painful and irritating rash and Runovsky called in a doctor to treat him. The doctor advised him to wash more, and to change his underclothes more frequently, but Abdurakhman refused to, saying such things were unnecessary.

Runovsky, scared of contagion and angry that the young man risked infecting the whole household with his refusal to treat his rash, then declined to shake his hand. Abdurakhman exploited his connections, via his sister, and Shamil stopped speaking to Runovsky for a while.

It was a difficult game for Runovsky to play, since he was ever mindful of his order not to interfere with Shamil's family life.

Gazi-Muhammad returned to fetch his wife in the summer of 1860, leaving Abdurakhman in charge of the household. As a result, Shuanat and Muhammad-Sheffi did not receive money for food or medicine, and Runovsky was forced to subsidize them from his own pocket. Shamil, under the influence of his wife's family, demanded an oven be installed on the top floor and even rejected food cooked by Christians.

The situation looked like it could not get much worse, but in fact more trouble was around the corner.

Gazi-Muhammad's wife Keremet was the daughter of Daniel-Sultan, a lieutenant of Shamil's who the family believed had betrayed the cause. Shamil also – despite Runovsky's insistence that it was not the case – believed that Keremet had sent spies to help the Russians.

Shamil refused to live in one place with his daughter-in-law, while Keremet herself refused to live in the same house as Zeidat. A new house had to be found.

The tensions were surely heightened by the extreme boredom of their existence. They had nothing to do but scheme and walk, and – in winter – they could not even sit on the banks of the Oka and watch the river flow. The men of the family, used to ruling a country and waging war, suddenly had nothing to do, while the women were unable to go outside, fearful of being seen by infidels.

From Runovsky's account, it is clear that time passed almost imperceptibly, with feuds simmering for months and years. Abdurakhman also wrote an account of their life and completely blocked out their time in Kaluga, except for mentioning two visits that Runovsky organized to local factories. In his account, you get the impression the visits came on consecutive days, whereas from the diary it is clear they were seven months apart. It is terrible to think of these energetic and resourceful people reduced to squabbling and visiting sugar plants.

'This factory was just the same as the paper factory: wheels, ropes and boilers. There was no difference, except that this was significantly dirtier than the paper factory,' wrote Abdurakhman. Runovsky noted that Shamil refused henceforth to take sugar in his tea after seeing the dirt in the factory.

While this scheming and visiting was going on all around, Shamil studied his books and prepared for death. He arranged his room on the top floor so all his texts were accessible from where he sat, and he spent days sitting down and scrutinizing the scriptures. At one point, the doctor even told him he must take more exercise or risk serious problems with his legs.

'In our books it is written that the human span is limited by the Lord to sixty years. Only a few people live more than sixty years.

Prophet Muhammad lived to sixty. Gazi-Muhammad [the first imam] died before this age. I also do not have long to live. Therefore, now I must think as much as I can about what will happen after my death. All the details of this are written in my books, and apart from that there are so many good things that the more I read the more I want to read,' Shamil told Runovsky in October 1860.

But such a life of indolence was not enough for some of the younger men. Hajio and Muhammad-Sheffi in particular delighted in going into Kaluga society. Shamil's youngest son learned Russian very quickly, and Hajio also learned enough to compliment a lady on her looks.

Shamil only went to such parties rarely, but on one evening he attended a ball at the house of a local notable called Fyodor Shchukin, of whom he became very fond. He sat throughout the party with his host's young son on his knee, smiling and looking happy despite the music, the dancing and the ladies showing a lot of chest – all things that his strict personal code disapproved of. The revellers did not return home until two in the morning, and Shamil said he had had a good time.

'Thanks be to Allah, the ceiling did not fall on us, and we are still whole and unharmed,' said Hajio, with a degree of sarcasm that appears to have shocked even himself.

Shamil just looked at him steadily, with the light of the moon falling on his face and making him appear very imposing. Hajio shrivelled under the gaze and from then on the imam did not go out in the evenings, and devoted himself to his books.

Among all this chaos, the imam still found time to tell Runovsky about the people he used to rule, the laws he imposed, and the system he created. There are long sections in the diary detailing precise legal measures that Shamil used, and listing the lieutenants that he most relied upon.

He was brutally honest about what he thought were the qualities of his former subjects, and reserved particular bile for the mountain Chechens. His assessment of their baseness, in fact, would have been shocking in the mouth of a Russian leader, let alone their deposed ruler.

He said that until he imposed Islamic law on the people of Tadburty
– one of the regions of mountain Chechnya – they had lived by a
widespread belief that illegitimate children were of greater value
than legitimate ones. They would kidnap each other's wives and
daughters and hold them as hostages – something that was more than
acceptable to the wives themselves, who would gladly 'bring forth to
the world heroes and valiant warriors' by having illegitimate children
by their captors.

The mountain Chechens, according to the imam, lived in five-
storey towers, with the livestock at the bottom, then the stores, then
the family, then the family's property, and finally the kidnapped
women at the top. In smaller towers the women were often kept
alongside the legal family ('the sense of shame not being known to
these degenerates of humanity'). Shamil had, he said, managed to
impose Islamic rules on them, and to demolish many of their towers,
but not without years of effort.

'There is nothing worse than this trash in the whole world. The
Russians should say thank you to me that I corrected them a little.
Without this, you would have only one way to deal with them: shoot
them to the last man, as is done with harmful animals. In fact, I did
not just break the people of Tadburty, but those of Shatoi and Ichkeria too. I did not fight them for their loyalty to the Russians. You
know they never had that. I did it for their nasty character, and their
inclination to theft and banditry. I am speaking the truth, and I am
sure that you will now fight them, not for their loyalty to me, but
for the same inclination to banditry, which they do not want to
abandon,' the imam said, simply.

'I tell the truth that in softening the character of the highlanders
I employed harsh measures. A lot of people were killed at my orders,
but there was no other way to carry on. There is no other means for
this people. If you had been in my place, you would have done the
same thing, and I am not scared of answering for it before God.'

Whenever someone passed through – and all Russian officers passing through Kaluga had a standing order to call on Shamil to pay
their respects – and asked if he had any messages for the Caucasus,
Shamil always asked him to tell his former followers that he was

happy and comfortable in captivity. He also never missed an opportunity to tell Russian listeners of his gratitude to the tsar.

And the surprise that visitors might feel hearing these comments was counteracted on one occasion when soldiers from the nearby garrison who had been prisoners of war with Shamil, and forced to work as slaves, asked if they could visit him. The conditions endured by captive soldiers were proverbially uncomfortable and were one of the greatest charges levelled against Shamil during the war.

To Runovsky's surprise, though, the visiting soldiers chatted warmly with the imam about conditions in the mountains, and then, on leaving, one of them bent down and kissed his hand.

'Why did you kiss his hand?' asked Runovsky afterwards. 'In the mountains maybe you had to do this, but here, why did you do it?'

'Your eminence, we did not have to kiss Shamil's hand. We do it from the heart,' the soldier replied.

'He is a good man. The only prisoners who lived well were those where Shamil lived or those in places where he passed through. It was forbidden to complain about our bosses, but it happened, and if an appeal got through to him then he would take the prisoner away and keep him at his own place, and even punish the guilty party.'

Runovsky was surprised by the warmth of the former captive's praise for the imam.

'He was good, your eminence. In a word, he had a heart. He doesn't believe in Christ, but he's a good man.'

Exchanges such as this never ceased to delight Runovsky, who recorded them faithfully in his diary. Often Shamil's replies – like his comment about Kaluga resembling Chechnya – seemed to have a stock quality. They appear in almost identical forms in several different memoirs. He praises the tsar, he praises Russia, he praises his house. But on one occasion Runovsky asked him for his opinion about Russia as a whole, about St Petersburg and Kaluga, and the people he met.

The question seemed to flummox the imam, who clearly had not expected it. Runovsky said he could wait and prepare an answer if he preferred, and that he should not be shy of saying negative things. But no, he had not understood Shamil's pause. The imam was once again getting the words he wanted to say just right.

'Now I understand what my son Jamal-Edin died of,' he said at last.

Like many of Shamil's comments, it gains more meanings the more you think about it. Maybe he meant he could understand why his son had fallen in love with Russia, since he had too. Or maybe he meant that a Russian – living in the conditions of their life in Kaluga – could never survive the harsh life of the mountains.

I think he meant both of those things, but his main meaning – in my opinion – was that the gulf between Russians, in whose number he included his son, and highlanders was so wide that there could be no true mutual understanding.

His son pined away in the alien conditions of the mountains, just like he was pining away amid the dinner dances, petty intrigues and mansions of Kaluga.

23. People Should Not Return Ever

In May 1860, Shamil received a guest – Muhammad-Emin, his envoy to the Circassians, former lieutenant and friend. Muhammad-Emin led the Circassians before and during the Crimean War, but faced obstacle after obstacle in the Turkish political scene, which limited his ability to take the fight to the Russians.

When Shamil surrendered, he appealed to his comrade-in-arms to give in also. Muhammad-Emin did so, and he too was received in St Petersburg.

In May that year then, the two friends met for the first time in thirteen years.

It was a funny encounter, similar – from the way Runovsky described it – to any meeting between old and close friends who have not seen each other for a long time. During the three days of Muhammad-Emin's stay in Kaluga, the two old men reminisced about the war and filled each other in on the years when they had been at opposite ends of the mountains.

The customs of the Abadzekhs – the Circassian tribe that Muhammad-Emin led – were a particular source of amusement for them. When Shamil and his sons heard that an Abadzekh man could not visit his wife during the daylight hours, they fell about with mirth.

'Imagine having to go secretly to one's own wife,' one of the group said to much laughter.

The laughter reached new heights when Muhammad-Emin told the gathering about how the Abadzekhs count. He said that five, for the Abadzekhs, is 't'pfu', which was too close to the sound of someone spitting for the roomful to take it seriously. In a complex multi-linguistic joke, they started then using the word 'five' in one of the other Caucasus languages to express disgust with something. 'Abadzekh' rapidly became a synonym for 'bad', which delighted the group.

'Abadzekh-woman: five!' and 'Abadzekh-horse: five!' managed to amuse even Shamil, who joined in with a joke of his own, describing a drunkard visible through the window as an 'Abadzekh man'.

The picture is irresistibly reminiscent of a group of old empire hands, who served in Nigeria say, or India, getting together to make desperately politically incorrect jokes about the locals and about themselves, with the easy familiarity of old friendship.

But sadly they would never be able to do so again, for Muhammad-Emin was leaving for Turkey, going into an exile from which he would never return. At least he would not be lonely there, however, for increasing numbers of his fellow countrymen would be leaving soon too.

This was not the desperate rush into exile of the Circassians, whose national collapse drove them onto overloaded boats and to almost total destruction. It was a slower process whereby religious leaders and former lieutenants of Shamil decided they did not want to be ruled by non-believers, and that the Ottoman Empire – which was headed after all by the sultan, who, as caliph, was nominally head of all Muslims – was their natural home.

Shamil's son Gazi-Muhammad, on returning from a trip to the Caucasus in late 1861, told Runovsky that blood feuds – repressed under Shamil, who believed only the criminal should pay for a crime, not his family – had made a spectacular resurgence. He said of the 16,000 households in Chechnya, as many as 600 were in a state of blood feud of some kind. That is, almost 4 per cent of the whole population.

Shamil had recommended to the Russians that they crack down hard on his former subjects to prevent their reverting to their old lawless ways. 'Now, they are like sheep,' he had said. 'Wherever you drive them, they will go without objection. When they have looked about them, they will be harder to cope with.'

The Russians were paying the price for letting the tribesmen 'look about them'.

An intrepid British traveller ventured into Dagestan in 1861, perhaps attempting to blaze a trail for mass tourism, or perhaps driven only by a desire for adventure. He wandered right across Shamil's old domains. He recorded that even in Georgia it was considered unsafe to venture out of the house after dark, and the Dagestan he described was a land of constant upheaval.

One story he told was about the destruction of a group of Russian soldiers who had gone fishing.

'The Russians were all fine strong men, and though they were soon overpowered by numbers, made a determined resistance. But it was a hopeless fight, six of them were almost cut in pieces by the terrible khangiars [swords], the seventh rushed into the water and gained the opposite bank, and escaped by concealing himself in the underwood.'

The survivor managed to creep back towards the army camp. He 'staggered, naked, though the freezing night, up a difficult path to a spot whence he might perhaps even see the tents of his comrades – a few yards further and he might have lived – but though his brave heart had not failed him, cold and loss of blood dragged him down.'

It is clear from this account, and from others, that the land was far from calm and, as Gazi-Muhammad noted, the targets for the attacks were not only Russians but often those who, in Shamil's service, had been brutal in crushing the liberties of their countrymen. Such men, scared of revenge, had begun gathering up their belongings and leaving for the Ottoman Empire. Daniel-Sultan, Shamil's friend-turned-sworn-enemy, was one of them and many others went with him.

Such men genuinely could not reconcile themselves to what even an optimist knew must be the final conquest of their homeland by Russia. Among them, perversely, was Musa Kundukhov, the most prominent Caucasus tribesman in the Russian service.

Born in 1818 to a Muslim Ossetian family, Kundukhov was given while just a boy as a hostage to the Russians. It was standard practice for young highlanders – like Jamal-Edin – to be taken to St Petersburg or Moscow and there enrolled in a military academy, where they would learn the virtues of a Russian officer. The idea was an ingenious one. Their families would be too scared to rebel, since their son could pay the price, while the son and with him the new generation of potential rebels would be russified and thus less likely to reject the tsar.

Obviously, as in the case of Jamal-Edin, it did not always work in quelling their parents' rebellions. But, from the Russians' perspective, the case of Musa Kundukhov was more successful. He became a resourceful and respected officer, rising to be a general and military governor of Chechnya.

His service was never straightforward, however, since he lacked the accepting spirit of a young Russian aristocrat. Aged just nineteen, he was an interpreter for the tsar on his tour of the Caucasus, and – he later said – this insight into the governing style of the Russians left him disillusioned with their supposed civilizing mission. The tsar, according to Kundukhov, treated a Chechen delegation arrogantly, calling them ungrateful, and ruining any hopes of winning their trust and support.

Tsar Nikolai relied on the blunt instrument of General Pullo – who is famous above all for the inflammatory remark that 'now we have taken away their arms, we have only to take away their women's trousers' – to keep the Chechens intimidated, with disastrous results.

'I consider that it would be quite correct to name as the chief cause of the past twenty-five years' cruel struggle, i.e. the rising of the entire Eastern Caucasus, and the unlimited power there and in Chechnya of Shamil – the deaf ear Nikolai turned to the just petitions of the peaceable mountaineers into whom, instead of fear, he instilled the hatefulness of their position and strong enmity to himself,' Kundukhov wrote in his memoirs, which were published after his death.

He had personal experience of that hatred since two of his brothers rejected Russia, and fought alongside Shamil. Kundukhov, although he stayed in the Russian service, did not accept Russian values. He still engaged in blood feuds and, in one encounter, he shot dead a treacherous Chechen who dared to walk through society with his head held high.

He served in Poland – then a Russian province – and helped suppress the 1848 Hungarian revolution, which had shaken Vienna's power over central Europe. Although he declined to serve against Shamil, he bemoaned the advance of puritanical Islam in his homeland, and felt that both Shamil and the tsar brought nothing good.

'Every day, every hour of the day, in all the villages, the hapless inhabitants were waiting, gun in hand, for the onslaught of the foe who came after them with fire and the sword. And in the mosques, they prayed, to make removed and far from them the fear of death and so to steel themselves for unyielding resistance,' he wrote of a visit to the Caucasus in 1848, when he had attempted peace negotiations with Shamil.

'The usual folk songs have been replaced by this: "There is no God but God. O, God, we have no one to whom we can turn for help, no one whom we can trust, in thee only we put our trust. To thee only we pray. Save us from tyranny",' he added.

He was clearly no fanatic, and he had equal condemnation for Shamil's methods as well as for the cruelty and corruption with which Russia ruled the Caucasus after its victory. In 1860, after Shamil's surrender, he was made head of the Chechen district, which he attempted to govern fairly. He went round the villages, promising them that their lands would not be taken away from them, that they could be governed under their own laws, and that they would not be conscripted into the Russian army. But, shortly after he made these promises, the government decided to break them, by giving some of the Chechens' land to Cossacks. Kundukhov resented being made into a liar, and was furious.

This is not to say that he was a gentle man. He was merciless in his pursuit of those of Shamil's lieutenants who had not surrendered with their chief. A Chechen called Baisungur, for example, held out in the remotest parts of Chechnya and was the target of Kundukhov's ruthless military skills until his capture in 1860.

'On the land of Benoi, neither a single [person] who has not submitted, nor a single house, has remained. All the food stores have been destroyed,' he wrote in a report in January that year.

But he strongly objected to non-rebellious highlanders being punished along with the rebels. The government's plans to move peoples en masse into the interior of the country to make sure they would never rebel again particularly enraged him. Eventually, after a series of tyrannical actions of this kind, which convinced him that the Russians intended no good for the Caucasus, he decided to leave. He began to circulate among elders, persuading them of his plan, telling them that without a homeland the Muslims of the Caucasus risked becoming just another wandering people like the Jews of the Russian empire.

'These unhappy Jews do not have their own fatherland, they do not have anywhere to live, where they can be proud of themselves. This is why these unhappy people have been deprived of human dignity, why they have to live and work under the oppression of the people on whose territory they live,' he said.

He told the elders he spoke to that he did not believe his descendants would forgive him for having stayed in a land that had been conquered.

'Having looked at the desolation that is our fatherland, I find it unbearable, the air seems unbreathable, and this is why we have a duty, in the presence of two evils, to choose the lesser.'

His speeches found a receptive audience, and he knew he had a destination, having already visited Turkey, and found the government there willing to accept 5,000 families from the Caucasus every year.

He was not as successful in gathering emigrants as he had hoped, but he still collected a caravan of several thousand families – mainly Chechens and Ossetians – and received money from the government to pay for their transport expenses. The first caravan to depart in early summer included his family and his parents. They crossed over the chain of the mountains, and passed down to Tbilisi. Other caravans came later, until in July he too – having sold his lands, his orchard and his house – left his home for the last time and headed for the border.

Perhaps he believed he would return home one day, but he never did. He was just one more Caucasus emigrant to Turkey, albeit a distinguished one, and his convoy of families was dispersed around the country, where they could swell the Turkish labouring and military classes.

'I addressed to the Almighty an ardent prayer, asking him to give me the strength to return at the head of Turkish regular soldiers to deliver the Caucasus from this abhorrent government,' he wrote later, describing how he crossed the border.

As it happened, the first half of his prayer was granted. Turkey and Russia went to war again in 1877–8 – a war that lost the Turks their hold over the Balkans, and their last lands in the south Caucasus. Kundukhov led a cavalry division against his former comrades-in-arms. But, once again, the Turkish army was trounced on the battlefield, and the last conceivable chance of winning independence back for the Caucasus went with it.

The war was accompanied by an uprising in Chechnya and Dagestan. The rebels were widely popular, and for a time they held the mountainous districts. Russian repressions, which typically involved burning the villages of mutineers and executing prisoners, succeeded only in inspiring further uprisings. But the Russians were merciless, forcing out civilians and destroying houses. Once more, the rebels were isolated in Dagestan, where they were surrounded, betrayed and captured. By November 1877, the leaders were in jail and in March the next year most of them were executed.

The Russians knew what to do now. The highlanders had rebelled too many times.

'Our aim should be to pluck out all the untrustworthy people from the villages and to exile them and their families to Russia for ever. The taking of hostages should be merely a temporary measure. In general [we should] pluck out as many as possible and in the most oppressive manner. The entire population of Benoy and Zandak should be exiled to Siberia and if these rascals refuse, they should all be exterminated in the winter like cockroaches and starved to death,' wrote Adjutant-General Svistunov to his deputy.

'Under no pretext should they be untied on their way and in case of the smallest resistance by anyone, beat them all up. I must add: my strong wish is for the latter possibility to happen.'

Thousands of Chechens and Dagestanis were sent to Russia, where many of them simply pined to death. On their being pardoned three years later – when Tsar Alexander III took the throne in 1881 after his father's assassination – many of them left their homeland for ever, to become the second wave of emigration to the Ottoman Empire.

The Turkish village of Guneykoy, in the Yalova region south of Istanbul, was founded by such emigrants. At their head was the Naqshbandi sheikh Muhammad Madani, who was in his early sixties when he left his homeland in 1896. In truth, the Naqshbandi order had struggled to retain its pre-eminent position in society after Shamil's surrender and he was just one of many leaders who chose to start a new life abroad.

According to stories told in the village to this day, Muhammad Madani, who was born in one of the villages near Gunib where Shamil made his last stand, was offered a place to live in Istanbul. He refused it, telling the government he would seek his own residence.

The village is a cluster of red roofs around a white mosque, all overshadowed by wooded hills. This was a wasteland of forests and rocks until the Dagestanis came – attracted by a fresh water spring, which, according to local legend, sprang out of the rock at Muhammad Madani's call. Ties to Dagestan are still strong. The older generation speak Avar among themselves, and the women still wear the baggy pantaloons of the Caucasus. At least ten pictures of Imam Shamil adorn the walls of the 'Barkala' ('thanks' in Avar) café, along with the green Chechen flag, with its horizontal red and white stripes.

Muhammad Madani is the subject of dozens of local legends, which tell of his miracles and wisdom. According to one account, he was taken to Siberia after the failed uprising, but no amount of chains could contain him and he would always appear in the prison yard unencumbered and unmarked, where he would publicly pray, sit or read. Eventually, his Russian jailers were forced to let him go, since his imprisonment was making them a laughing stock.

I wondered if that was a garbled version of the real story, in which the Russian government was forced to allow the exiled Dagestanis to go home or to Turkey just to keep them alive. Many of the high-landers moved to the plains simply died of homesickness and disease. Some 429 of the 1,625 Dagestanis settled in the Novgorod region died in the first few months after their arrival. Russian officials may have endorsed cruelty to the highlanders at a distance, but they could not watch these poor people dropping at such a rate.

So, the tsar let them leave his realm. Muhammad Madani brought the first group of emigrants to the Turkish village he founded, and was then joined by another group under a second Naqshbandi sheikh, called Serafuddin, who was to become his son-in-law and principal follower.

'My father left Dagestan in the early 1900s, with Serafuddin,' said Hatice Sener, the 75-year-old great-aunt of a friend who took me to see the village. She told me some of the stories of the village, where fact and fiction mix together in confusing ways.

'This was before Nikolai [II] became tsar. They decided to emigrate because the tsar was very cruel. After the collapse of Imam Shamil there was pressure on Dagestanis. There was fear that the roads to Turkey would be closed. Muhammad Madani predicted that communism would bring big problems for religion. He said the roads would open for three months and then they would be closed by snow. He said those that left would go to Turkey, and those that did not leave would stay for ever and that it was a pity to live in Russia.'

The stories told about Muhammad Madani show him to have been an unusually gentle man.

In one legend, he was leading the *zikr* – the ecstatic prayer ritual of the Sufis – for the whole village, when he felt a small undercurrent of unhappiness which nagged at him. 'Everyone is doing zikr. All the animals are doing zikr with us. The worms are doing zikr with us. The birds are doing zikr. Every being in the village is doing zikr with us except one animal who is disconnected from his father and feeling depressed. Allah is not happy. The prophet is not happy, the saints are not happy,' the sheikh intoned.

It turned out that a small child was keeping a worm in a box, and the misery of the worm had upset God. 'From that, the people of the village understood and raised their children with an understanding that harming any creature, no matter how small, causes unhappiness and earns the displeasure of God, of the prophet, and of saints,' the story relates.

And the influence of the sheikh's teachings was still strong. As Hatice Sener sat there in a flowered top, a white headscarf and brown cardigan, she recounted tale after tale from her family's past. The husband of her great-aunt was in the leather trade and he stayed in Dagestan, and she had long dreamed of trying to find her family and seeing a land where everyone spoke Avar, but she said she would never do so.

'I never plan to go to Dagestan, because the sheikh said that Dagestan was a bad place and that people should not return ever,' she said.

Muhammad Madani passed leadership of the community on to Serafuddin, and the village became a refuge for many Dagestanis.

Although Serafuddin himself died in 1936, his house is still open to all supplicants, and his daughter-in-law – a tiny, wizened old lady who was watching television when I called – keeps it ready for prayer meetings and callers.

Those Dagestanis who made it to Guneykoy were the lucky ones. Most emigrants faced conditions far more extreme than those enjoyed in the Yalova region, which is nestled in the hills overlooking the Sea of Marmara.

Groups of Chechens were settled elsewhere in the Ottoman Empire, and many were forced to make their own way to the unforgiving lands of the Middle East. They arrived in what is now Jordan in 1901, and found a land of ruins and nomads.

'It was completely Arabs then, there was nothing in this place, just a few ruins,' said Abdul Baki Jamo, an 87-year-old who is now perhaps the most powerful Chechen in Jordan, having served in government or parliament more or less without interruption since 1956.

'We have preserved our culture because the people around here were living in a very tribal community. For this reason, the Chechens lived lives separate from the rest of the people.'

When I had driven up to his house, which is in a pure Chechen area of Zarqa, Jordan's second city, I saw how the Chechens were tied to their own identity. The guttural buzz of Chechen was the only language I heard on the streets, which were marked with graffiti telling incomers that this was no Arab neighbourhood.

'Warning Chechen area,' said an English-language inscription on one wall. Others were in Arabic writing, but made more or less the same point, while one or two were even in Cyrillic.

'The Chechens only really interacted with the Circassians, who had come here twenty years earlier. The Ottoman authorities did not have full authority over the tribes and for this reason the Chechens lived a double life, both agricultural to support themselves and a military life as well to protect themselves from the attacks of the Bedouin,' said Jamo.

Jamo, a small, dapper man with a white beard and a house full of books, said his father left the Caucasus at the end of 1899, as part of a group of Chechens. Apparently, their Sufi leader – identified by Jamo as Suleiman al-Gilani, although that may have been the founder of the whole Sufi order – prophesied that Islam would die out in the Caucasus, and the emigrants would have to preserve their faith so they could take it back to their homeland when the threat had passed.

The difference in the circumstances of their emigration had also helped the Chechens to preserve their culture and identity. Where the demoralized Circassians had fled the Caucasus as a starving rabble, the Chechens had left in discrete groups under the leadership of the Sufis.

'We preserved our language and traditions for the reason that we were always under the leadership of these Sufi sheikhs. The Sufi path helped us to preserve our culture more than the Circassians. And until now, we do not speak any language other than Chechen to our children. We interact with them according to our customs.'

The Caucasus community in Jordan is made up entirely of Circassians and Chechens, of whom there are 5,000–10,000, and they are treated together under tribal law. I met no Ossetians while I was there, and only one Dagestani.

But she was distinguished in a way that more than made up for the lack of a community. She was a relative of Imam Shamil.

Shamil's existence in Kaluga becomes less well-documented after 1862, when Runovsky stopped being his minder, and the replacement officer was both less scrupulous in keeping a diary and less friendly to his charge. One visitor, the black American actor Ira Aldridge, who was forced by racism in his homeland and in England to seek a living on tour in Europe, described Shamil as looking calm and happy.

'There is a decidedly benevolent expression in Schamyl's countenance, so much so, indeed, that he looks more like a placid Patriarch of old than a fierce mountain warrior. He is considerably above the middle height; I should say full six feet when standing erect. He wore on his head a large white turban, with a small red crown and tassel, and just below it an encircling band of beautiful black lambskin,' the actor wrote in a letter in January 1864 after a meeting with the imam.

'His face, which is of oval form, is of remarkably fair, almost delicate, complexion, his forehead high, broad, and unwrinkled, his nose aquiline and thin, and his mouth beautifully formed. His eyes are grey, deep-set, and expressive, and his teeth, which are somewhat large, are of pearl-like whiteness, seldom seen in a man of his age, for he is verging on seventy. His moustaches and long flowing beard are perfectly white – the latter extending to his chest – and his hands, which are small for so large a man, are as soft and delicate as a lady's.'

Shamil had, it would seem, not lost his ability to hide his feelings. His minder – a colonel of Polish origins – had made his life a misery, and personal losses had destroyed what peace of mind was left. The fact that his beard had turned completely white in just four years may, however, have been a sign of the stress he was under. In May 1862, Keremet – the wife of his son Gazi-Muhammad – died of a fever. Perhaps he did not mind that, since he hated her father, but her death was a foretaste of what was to come. His favourite daughter Nafisat died in 1865, shortly after the death of her son. Another grandson of Shamil's also died as an infant.

All told, seventeen members of Shamil's family and household would not survive the stay in Kaluga, and he mourned each one. After the death of Nafisat, it is said that he never smiled again, even when he finally rid himself of his hated minder. He left Kaluga in 1869, moving on to Kiev, before being allowed to make the pilgrimage to Mecca the next year. He was aged seventy-four.

In Turkey, he was received as a celebrity and cheered as wildly as he had been in St Petersburg.

The effect was the same when he arrived in Mecca, where the police had to assign special hours for his prayer to prevent public disturbances. Shamil, visibly ailing, lived a life of contemplation. His wife Zeidat died here, and only Shuanat was with him, for the Russians had not allowed Gazi-Muhammad to go into exile alongside his father. When Shamil's son was finally allowed to leave the tsar's empire, he was too late. Shamil died on 4 February 1871 without his favourite son by his side.

Although he surrendered to the Russians, and had governed with severity, he was mourned in the Caucasus, according to Baddeley, who quoted one of his guides as saying there had been one last miracle on the night of the imam's death.

'It was long ago – some thirty years – when I was a lad. I was out by night watching my sheep on yonder mountain; all at once the sky grew bright as fire and red as blood. I was afraid, for I knew not what it meant. Afterwards, when I returned to Shoura, news came of Shamil's death that night in Medina,' the guide told him.

Gazi-Muhammad lived on in Istanbul for a while, and even attempted to retake the Caucasus at the head of irregular cavalry in 1877–8. But he fell under suspicion from the Turkish government and was despatched to the Middle East a couple of years later, as was his young brother-in-law, Muhammad Fazil Daghistani.

Muhammad Fazil's father had been a follower of Shamil's but, accused of treachery in 1852, the family had been exiled to one of the most inaccessible of all the villages in Dagestan. Their lives were ruined, despite Gazi-Muhammad's struggles to clear the family's name – a struggle that introduced him to Fazil's sister, an educated, charming and devout woman.

When Keremet died, Gazi-Muhammad called for the woman he remembered as being so articulate and beautiful, and she travelled to Kaluga, where she married him and took the name Habibet, 'the beloved'. Her brother Fazil found a place in the Russian service, where he was an officer until he too went into exile. In Turkey, he and Gazi-Muhammad became close advisers of the sultan.

It was Muhammad Fazil's granddaughter I met in Amman. She did not know the Avar language of her ancestors, but she still retained enough of the Dagestani virtues to have surely won Shamil's approval, though her appearance and behaviour would most likely have shocked him.

Tamara Daghistani is a short-haired lady with an absurdly infectious laugh whose lovely limestone villa on the outskirts of Amman is packed with antique weapons, pictures and mementoes of her family's glorious past. When I arrived, her husband Nasser al-Sadoun was standing in a tree in the garden – he may have been pruning it but he looked more like he was levitating as I walked up the path – which set a suitably absurd tone for surely the jolliest interview I conducted during the entire time I spent researching this book.

She went to school in England, and still speaks perfect English. But she had the old-fashioned slang of a 1950s schoolgirl, which made her seem like an extra from an Ealing comedy. Imam Shamil, for example, was a 'toughie', as was her grandfather, who had, she said, at one point wrestled a lion back into its cage in the presence of the Turkish sultan himself.

After her grandfather was expelled from Istanbul, he went to Iraq – then a Turkish province – where he lived quietly until he came out of retirement to lead the Ottoman resistance to the British invasion of Iraq during the First World War.

'He went off to war, aged sixty-four. He did not have to but he did not want the English unbelievers to take Iraq. But he was killed by the English in 1915,' she said.

'The Turks retreated, but he did not retreat. He had a Chechen with him and they never retreat, those Chechens. He went on his horse with his followers, but a machine gun hit him and he fell from his horse. The horse was called Weder, she carried him home but she refused to eat and drink after he died, and she died too. The horse stood by his body until it was dark.'

Her husband had by this stage changed into non-gardening clothes, and had come into the living room to help tell the story. He could not resist chipping in with a blow-by-blow account of the battle, and the glorious role of his own ancestors, much to his wife's fury. He darted around the living room to evade her attempts to silence him, while keeping up his account of how an army controlled by one of his relatives had forced the British to retreat.

'Oh, why will you not retreat somewhere else?' she called out, as he moved on to how the British army became besieged in Kut.

'He is not interested, he must feel like he is besieged,' Tamara called out. But al-Sadoun could not be silenced, and continued with an account of the ransom that was paid to release certain British officers.

'Oh, he will be offering a ransom to get away from you in a minute,' was his wife's riposte.

By this stage, I was literally crying with my attempts not to laugh, and could not help reflecting inwardly on how funny the picture was compared to what I had expected.

I had imagined she would be a Dagestani woman in a headscarf, with a demure manner and a deferential attitude to her husband.

Instead, it was as if I had dropped into the house of a friend's eccentric, articulate and beloved grandparents.

Finally, Tamara had to enlist the help of her son – by telephone – to get the conversation back on track.

'Faisal, your father is causing a scandal. We have a terribly nice Englishman here who wants to talk about Dagestan and your father is forcing him to listen to an account of the First World War, please make him go to the office instead,' she said into the telephone.

'And make him put a different shirt on,' she added as an afterthought. Faced with opposition from wife and son, her husband was defeated. Tamara returned to talking about Dagestan, although she had to be alert to attempts by her husband to rejoin the conversation via a side-door and the window.

Her father was a small child when her grandfather was killed by the British, but he was still raised in the traditions of a Dagestani and taught the value of restraint and honour. They were values that Imam Shamil would have approved of, but Tamara herself said she could not stand the traditional customs of the Caucasus.

'They invited me to go and see a rehearsal of a Dagestani show in London. And the girls were sitting on one side and the men on the other, and even if they were married the man would go into the middle and the woman would come into the middle and they would talk. I asked if they would ever sit together and they said no,' she said, when I asked her if she would like to live in Dagestan.

'I am a tough cookie myself and it is important that women have rights, and these did not have rights. When Shamil had his lunch he would sit with his mother and his favourite cat and the others could go where they liked.'

Nevertheless, she was brought up with the traditional Caucasus values of bravery and forbearance, which have served her well in light of the history of Iraq for the last half-century.

'My grandfather was another Dagestani, he was a toughie. And we were all taught as children that we could not cry. Crying was not done. My aunt told me a story that when she was a little girl she was in the men's divan, and my grandfather loved animals so baby lions were wandering about. She said she was sitting near her father and a horse stuck its head through the window and puffed into her ear. She squeaked, so he said to her in Turkish: "You have shamed me, leave the room" and he did not speak to her for days.'

Later, Tamara's aunt was showing a seal in her father's menagerie to a friend, and the seal bit her hand. Although there was blood pouring from the wound, and her hand was still in the seal's mouth, she did not make a sound. 'You are now my daughter again,' her father, Tamara's grandfather, said.

Tamara was brought up with the same injunction to never show weakness, and it was a lesson forced into her when the Iraqi monarchy was overthrown in 1958. Her father, who was deputy chief-of-staff of the Iraqi army and named Gazi-Muhammad after his celebrated uncle, was arrested. Tamara said she was pressured into begging the country's new rulers to release her father, but she refused, saying it would shame him.

And the Dagestani conventions would serve her in even better stead during her life ahead. Her family fled to London in 1959 when she was twelve. She attended a British school and tried not to think of her father in prison. Homesick and worried, her weight ballooned from 45 to 120 kilograms, but she still did not cry, all the time until her father was released.

'Caucasus people are extremely loyal wherever they go, it is important to remember. I remember talking to my father about the revolution and to him it had been very disloyal. They had sworn loyalty to the king and the country, and to him that made them traitors and he despised them,' she said.

'You had to gain their respect and once you had it then you had it for life.'

24. This is All for the Sake of Allah

In March 1921, a Soviet official responsible for the hundreds of small nations scattered across the Bolsheviks' new state addressed the 10th Congress of the Communist Party.

In the four years since the revolution that brought down the tsars, he and his comrades had battled the old ruling classes, rival left-wingers, foreign armies, separatists, religious leaders, maniacs, democrats and monarchists for control of Russia.

Now, on 10 March, that battle was all but won. The foreign armies had either withdrawn or were about to. Internal opposition was continuing, but would soon be crushed. The Bolsheviks were looking about them and deciding how to build the perfect society.

The Soviet official, himself a Georgian from the southern flanks of the Caucasus mountains, said he sympathized with the ethnic minorities, whom he governed as Nationalities Commissar. They had been forced into the Russian state, he said, their land had been stolen and given to favoured groups like the rich peasants – 'kulaks' in Soviet speak. They had been driven to the verge of complete destruction.

'The old government, the landlords and the capitalists have left us as a heritage such browbeaten peoples as the Kirghiz, the Chechens and the Ossets, whose lands served as an object of colonisation by Cossacks and the kulak elements of Russia. These peoples were doomed to incredible suffering and extinction,' he said.

'The position of the Great-Russian nation, which was the dominant nation, has left its traces even on the Russian Communists, who are unable, or unwilling, to establish closer relations with the toiling native masses, to comprehend their needs, and to help them emerge from their backward and uncivilised state.'

He promised a new era for the minorities. He held out a hand of friendship to them. From now on, the Chechens and their neighbours

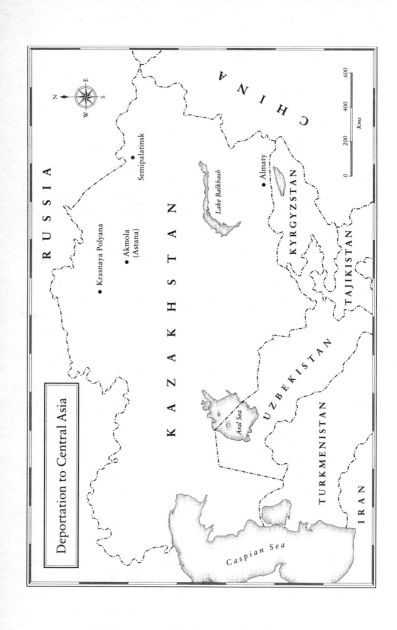

Deportation to Central Asia

RUSSIA

CHINA

KAZAKHSTAN

Semipalatinsk

Krasnaya Polyana

Akmola
(Astana)

Lake Balkhash

Almaty

KYRGYZSTAN

TAJIKISTAN

UZBEKISTAN

Aral Sea

TURKMENISTAN

IRAN

Caspian Sea

N
W E
S

0   200   400   600
Kms

would be trusted as full citizens. They would be helped to gain all the wonders of modern civilization.

'We must save the Kirghiz and the Bashkirs and certain of the Gortsi [highlander] tribes from extinction and provide them with necessary land at the expense of the kulak colonisers.'

It was a clear promise. From now on, the highlanders would live in peace and freedom. The official who made the promise would have plentiful opportunities to see that it was fulfilled, for his name was Joseph Stalin.

But he had made a giant miscalculation. Hidden within his promise and his pleasant words was a mistaken assumption, which would come back to haunt him when he gained supreme power. No matter what help the Russian communists gave the Chechens, it would not change much. The Chechens did not wish to emerge from their 'backward and uncivilised state'. In fact, they rather liked it.

Mazhmudin Samursky, a disillusioned communist from the North Caucasus, put it rather neatly in 1925. The legacy of hatred created in the wars of the nineteenth century was all but unconquerable, he said. Put simply, the Chechens and their neighbours in upland Dagestan did not want to be ruled by Russians, and that was all there was to it.

'Dislike of European civilisation, sanctified by religion, is more difficult to fight than religion itself. It is essential to avoid intimidation which would only confirm the clergy's preaching that European civilisation was always a weapon of oppression and enslavement of the Eastern peoples,' he said.

It is not clear where he had been living for the eight years since the revolution, for the 'intimidation' he was so desperate to avoid had been the major method of interaction between Chechens and Russians for most of them.

In 1919, a Chechen Naqshbandi sheikh, Uzun Haji, declared himself Imam, raised the banner of Shamil once more, and declared holy war on the Russian incomers. Thousands of Muslims trekked to his capital in the mountains of Chechnya, where they danced and prayed and honoured the new leader. He was to die – of natural causes – just after the Red Army entered Chechnya, but his followers resisted the Russians whichever flag they marched under.

For the Red Army, intoxicated by its own power, came not as a liberator but as a plunderer. It attacked 'patriarchal traditions and Islam', it relied on 'punitive raids, police denunciations, blackmail, settling of private feuds, plunder, confiscation of food supplies and fodder, forced conscription into Red regiments, requisitions and destruction of small trade'. It is hard to think of anything better guaranteed to enrage the Chechens.

The rebels and the Reds battled in the mountains of Dagestan. Some 10,000 people died on each side, before the last stronghold was seized.

By the time of Stalin's speech, the rebels were close to defeat as an organized force, and their last stronghold in Dagestan fell in May 1921.

For the next two decades, 'bandits' continued to haunt the mountains, hidden among the civilian population. They were hunted and sometimes they were caught. More often their civilian sympathizers were persecuted and killed. Stalin's brave new policy towards the Chechens had never been implemented. Almost every year brought a new sweep against anti-Soviet elements, sometimes whole Red Army regiments were wiped out before order was restored.

In 1931, by which time Stalin had secured near total control, more than 35,000 Chechens were arrested and most of them shot in a crackdown on religious leaders, nationalists and – ironically, considering what Stalin had said – 'kulaks'. In 1937, at the start of the truly giant purges, another 14,000 men were arrested, including the entire local Communist Party.

And what was the crime of these arrested communists? They were guilty of quoting the Bolshevik policy on nationalities and saying that their Russian comrades had to 'struggle even more resolutely against Great Russian chauvinism, against any oppressive attitude to the Chechens, to strongly and openly defend the necessity of a specially sensitive, specially cautious Russian attitude to a nation that had for decades been exposed to humiliating mockery and has therefore the right to be suspicious of the smallest manifestation of a similar oppressive attitude'.

The comments were a rephrasing of Stalin's own speech of 1921. But, sadly, the Chechens were sixteen years too late in making them, and they had signed their own death warrants by doing so. Inevitably – since the purges meant that now even the communists were not safe – more Chechens headed into the mountains, whence they struck out at Soviet targets. The pattern of intimidation and resistance was maintained all the way up to 1944, when Stalin decided to have done with these people. It had taken him twenty-three years to come round and realize – as the tsarist officers, and even Imam Shamil, had done – that inflicting 'incredible suffering and extinction', far from being a misguided policy, was the only way a foreign conqueror could impose his will on the Chechens.

That is not to say that Stalin approved of Imam Shamil. The imam, who had been treated so honourably by his tsarist conquerors, was re-examined by Stalin's pet historians, who made the belated discovery that he had not been a brave freedom fighter or a religious fanatic, but a foreign agent bent on sabotaging the friendship between the highlanders and the Russians.

Under Stalin, even the dead were not safe. In 1950, the standard school textbook of the *History of the USSR* condemned Shamil's resistance as 'a reactionary and nationalistic movement in the service of English capital and the Turkish sultan. It was directed against the true interests of the highland peoples.'

A couple of years later, another historian – N. A. Smirnov – took the counterintuitive position that the mountain peoples had actually been asking Russia for help during the Caucasus wars. 'They unhesitatingly reposed their trust in the Russians, hoping for protection from Shamil and from encroachment by external foes ... The policy of severing the Caucasus from Russia was deeply alien and repulsive to the Caucasus peoples.'

For ordinary Chechens, it was a confusing time.

Abubakar Utsiev grew up in this world of instability, conflicting policies, irrationality, violence and horror. Born in 1924, he lived in the very heart of the unruly mountains, near Itum-Kale – one of the most inaccessible of all the Chechen villages. For the Soviet government to impose its will on the highlanders in these hills, they had to come in force.

In 1942, when Utsiev was seventeen, he and his family were driven out of the hills and forced to settle on the plains. When the real deportation came two years later, he was all alone, separated from his relatives and without support or help.

When the train carrying him arrived in the Akmola region of Kazakhstan, he was just the kind of man chosen first by the collective farm bosses. He was young, he had no dependants, and he would not be a drain on the resources of the village. Consequently, it is something of a surprise that he was bagged by a farm as remote as Krasnaya Polyana – one of three closely connected collective farms – twenty kilometres or so from the tiny steppe town of Balkashino.

'They brought me here on an ox-cart,' he remembered when I visited him in 2008.

'There was snow and slush. There were children, old people, women crying, dying. You cannot understand. The people had no idea what was happening.'

He was right. When I arrived in Balkashino, it was literally impossible for me to understand the suffering those emigrants faced. The bus I took to get there from the city of Astana had come second-hand from somewhere in northern Europe – its labels were in English and German – and its windows sensibly were not made to open. In the climate of the Baltic countries, where any draught could freeze a passenger, closed windows would probably be a blessing.

In the flaying sunlight of a Kazakh summer, however, the bus became an oven. The tiniest breeze from the open skylight was as refreshing as a cool drink of water, as I sat and poured with sweat in my squalid seat. I kept falling asleep, then waking as if to a nightmare when the same view kept reappearing outside the window.

The land could not have been more different to the Caucasus, where the mountains are craggy, or snowy, or wooded, but never boring. This country was featureless. A dead-straight horizon dominated everything, imposing its absolute tyranny on buildings and factories alike. When people flicked by our windows, they looked puny and insubstantial in relation to this single, powerful line dividing the green of the wheat fields from the blue of the sky.

A telegraph pole, or a tractor, or a barn became the complete focus of the landscape. Strange tricks of perspective and scale could make buildings seem huge or tiny – sometimes both at the same time. At one moment of wakefulness that I remember, a small cluster of huts in the middle of a blank patch of grassland was signposted from the road as a 'Relaxation Zone'. I could not imagine how it would be possible to relax there. A few minutes further on, we stopped in a village. Its shop bore the label 'Everything for Everyone'. I wanted to buy some water, but it had run out.

The Akmola region was the most dreadful of all the terrible destinations for the deported North Caucasus nations. In the five years after 1944, 35 per cent of the Chechen and Ingush deportees, and 49 per cent of the Balkars, sent here died.

The deportees had no idea what was happening to them. Collective farm bosses treated them with contempt and hatred. KGB files of the period show that the Chechens often responded by refusing to work, or attempting to gain positions of responsibility where they could steal from the state for their own ends. KGB agents went among the population in the run-up to the elections of 1946. Bafflingly – in a manner reminiscent of Russia today – the government of the Soviet Union seemed to genuinely want the electorate to vote for it, even though the election was meaningless and the result rigged.

The authorities were apparently worried that the deportees would simply refuse en masse to vote, as if that might somehow endanger their legitimacy. Their spying revealed a degree of confusion among the Chechens about the true situation that must have disturbed Soviet officials, who were presumably already paranoid enough now the Cold War was starting.

'I won't participate in the polling, because the Soviet government did not send us here to live, but to die. I would vote for an Anglo-American government with pleasure, because it would be better than the Soviet,' said one Chechen man quoted in the KGB documents.

'After the elections we will return to the Caucasus, because England and America will help us restore our state. That is why we will not vote for Soviet candidates, we are going to vote in the Caucasus, for our candidates,' said another.

Utsiev was luckier than most. Being alone, he was billeted on local people, who turned out to be kind and looked after him.

'When we arrived, they distributed us among the buildings. I lived with a family, but most people lived in the barracks with the field brigades,' Utsiev remembered.

His brother had been in prison when he was deported, while his father was dead, and his mother and sister were sent to a different town. He had no relatives to help him find his way, and could have been forgiven for dropping his head and accepting defeat.

But he did not do so. He found the support that the Chechens have always found when times are tough: from the Sufis. Akmola became the centre of a Sufi revival. More than twenty groups were active there by the mid-1950s, but the most dramatic focus of all was in Krasnaya Polyana, where a holy man worked alongside Utsiev in the fields.

'In 1946, I managed to find my mother and sister, in Kostanay; I told them to come back with me, because there was a holy Chechen man and I had made friends with him,' he said.

'I studied under him, and my mother and sister finally moved here in autumn 1948.'

It was the beginning of an influx of Chechens that has transformed Krasnaya Polyana and the other two collective farms that neighbour it into a little Chechnya in Kazakhstan. Gradually, as the fame of the Sufis spread, so more Chechens moved here, squeezed out the other communities and created their own sanctuary in the midst of oppression.

Now, as I walked down the dusty main street, between the sky-blue single-storey houses, children with huge dark eyes called out to me in Chechen, then turned giggling to hide their shyness from my gaze. It was just like being in a Chechen village, except for the brutal, flat horizon that overshadowed everything.

Utsiev would not say the name of the holy man; none of the villagers would, in what seemed to be a mark of respect for his sanctity. But he was called Vis Haji. He was born in 1908, and studied the way of the Sufis in a brotherhood that arrived in the Caucasus around the time of Shamil's defeat, and which took the Naqshbandis' place as the movement of choice among tens of thousands of Chechens and Dagestanis.

Initially, the Qadiri movement – as it was known – had preached non-resistance to the tsars, just like the Naqshbandis had fifty years earlier. But it was a difficult position to maintain in the face of constant oppression, and within a couple of years it too allowed its followers to resist the Russians. Less intellectual than the Naqshbandi, it employed a loud, ecstatic prayer ritual – or zikr – and spread among less educated Chechens who did not have access to the Arabic texts or scriptures. The tsarist authorities, recognizing the power of the loud zikr in welding communities together, banned it. But the Chechens did not care. By the First World War, almost every Chechen or Ingush man was a member of one of the brotherhoods.

This was an exceptional development. Elsewhere in the Muslim world, official Islam of either a liberal or a strict stripe dominated. But in the Caucasus the mystical Sufi orders absorbed and swept over all other forms.

Vis Haji was, according to the stories told today, an exceptionally kind man. He would not sanction violence of any kind, or resistance to the state authorities. Believers should do what they are told, he preached, but not initiate cooperation.

'This man did not look for anything, he ate just a little,' said Utsiev. 'I studied with him, and learned from him. I looked for no honours, I worked honestly. I have a garden, livestock, and this has been my life's work.'

Vis Haji died at dusk on 17 May 1973, and Utsiev assumed his role as the leader of the community. He himself was too modest to say so, but it was clear from how the other men deferred to him that he was now the first man in the village.

I have a picture of Utsiev on my desk in front of me as I type. He is old now – eighty-four years old if his birth date in his passport is correct – and has the watery eyes and white beard that age brings. His eyes are hooded, but they have an intensity and a focus that seem to bore straight through you as you look at the photograph. Strangely, I do not remember his eyes being like that in the flesh. They were kind and careful, and always checked to see that I had everything I needed.

For the photographs, he wore a white fur hat, wrapped with the white cloth of a Sufi sheikh – the same cloth that marked out Imam

Shamil as a spiritual authority. The rest of the time he wore a little velvet skullcap of the kind typical of Chechnya.

He is one of just five men left alive who were Vis Haji's disciples. They are the keepers of the teachings of the holy man, whose life story has become the basis of village legend.

Abudadar Zagayev, a pale, round 42-year-old and the holy man's oldest son, told me of a miracle his father had performed when still a child.

'When my father was running along as a child he got a thorn in his foot. They did not have shoes in those days. This was still when they were in Alkhan Yurt [in Chechnya]. And a friend took the thorn out with his teeth. My father said to him if you live to a hundred you will not lose your teeth. This man died maybe seven or eight years ago and he still had all his teeth. That is a fact,' he said.

Lechi Birsanukayev, a local Chechen who had introduced me to the village, chipped in with a tale of his own. He said that Vis Haji had known the Koran intuitively, despite not having studied it.

'A few mullahs got together who knew the Koran and wanted to know what his father had, how he could get all these people together. His father said he could not read the Koran, he did not know Arabic, but everything he told them was in the Koran, when translated it was the same as the Koran,' he said.

Vis Haji was not disliked by the authorities, who probably liked the non-resistance doctrine that he preached, and individual state officials even respected him, according to the Chechens in Krasnaya Polyana today.

'There was a chairman of the collective farm, he was a Russian called Anatoly Popov who would not even smoke in front of the holy man, even though he was older than him. He earned their respect through his pure Muslim ideology. You cannot steal, you cannot cheat, you must be clean,' said Birsanukayev.

But that is not to say that Vis Haji preached collaboration with the Soviets. On the contrary, he believed everything should be approached in the same spirit of non-participation. He would not support the government, and he would not oppose it. He was indifferent to it. Perhaps his doctrine was an early expression of the Russian dissident mantra: 'Live as if you lived in a free country'.

'Even if a relative has been killed you have no right to interfere,' said Zagayev. 'One time three men escaped from prison and a person here wanted to turn them in but my father said he should not do this, they are saving their own souls and it is up to them.'

Perhaps because of this incident, or perhaps just through sheer suspicion, the Soviet secret police swooped on Krasnaya Polyana in 1977, four years after the holy man's death. His grave had become a pilgrimage site and, although the Chechen nation had been allowed to return home, more and more Chechens were moving to the village to be near his burial place.

Of the inhabitants of the village today, 1,100 are Chechen, the schoolmaster told me. They make up almost the entire population, with just thirty-six Russians, two Germans and one Kazakh interrupting their dominance. Only a dozen families are not part of the brotherhood.

The KGB wanted to find evidence of polygamy, which was practised by Vis Haji – who himself had four wives, according to Zagayev – as well as by other men in the village. They came up against a blank wall of non-cooperation, and it is difficult not to admire the locals in their stubborn insistence that they would obey their own rules and no one else's.

Ansar Ibayev, for example, is now the teacher in the school but he was a seven-year-old boy when the KGB came to the village to seek evidence of law-breaking. Since his mother was apparently a single woman with children – an impossible condition in a traditional Chechen community – it was obvious that she was someone's second wife.

'They asked me my name, I told them "Ansar". Then they asked who had bought the television, and I said Uncle Volodya,' remembered Ibayev. Saying 'Uncle Volodya' is a bit like saying 'Fred Bloggs', but it so happens that Volodya is the shortened form of Vladimir, which gave the investigating officials something to work with.

'What? Volodya? Like Vladimir Ilyich Lenin, they asked. I said yes, that's right. They said Lenin did not lie, and said he would not like it that I was lying. I said I did not know what they meant. They then asked me who bought the fuel. I said I did not know. They asked me if my uncle came to sleep in the house. I said I did not know. I was seven years old.'

The sheer frustration of the KGB men in being stymied – in a three-on-one interview – by a headstrong Chechen child must have been something to see. The boy did not reveal who his father was and that particular investigation was stillborn. The police did arrest one man for having two wives, but the rest of the villagers carried on as before.

Polygamy is still common in Krasnaya Polyana, and does not seem to cause friction with the authorities of now independent Kazakhstan. Or if it does, the Kazakhs are sensible enough not to try to break through the villagers' wall of non-cooperation. When I asked Ibayev to introduce me to a polygamous family, he said I had already met one. Zagayev has two wives, he said, before taking me to see a neighbour – Alavdi Shakhgeriev, who, since he was born in 1930, is one of the elders of the community.

Shakhgeriev barely spoke Russian, and every word he said to me was translated from Chechen. Most of the elders do not know Russian – a legacy of both their lack of schooling and their conscious rejection of the outside world – and his was the most limited I heard.

He said he was introduced to the movement when Vis Haji visited Karaganda, the town he had been deported to. (In a bleak example of Soviet jurisprudence, the fourteen-year-old Shakhgeriev was deported to Karaganda without trial, was left with his sisters to support and no money, but was not allowed to work in a coal mine – the only work in town – since it would have been a violation of a child's labour rights.) When the Chechens were permitted to move back to the Caucasus, he moved instead to Krasnaya Polyana, where he has lived ever since with his wives.

'I used to have three wives, but one of them died,' he said. He sat, stern, straight-backed and serious, and waited for his words to be translated. The perfect image of the patriarch that he presented was subverted by his wife Aminat, however.

She was wearing the long dress and headscarf of the dutiful woman, but had no intention of fulfilling the role of a meek and silent wife.

'He wants another wife now,' she said, before hooting with laughter.

Shakhgeriev ignored her interjection, and attempted to maintain his stern mien. 'The prophet allows us to have four wives, and no Muslim can disagree.'

Aminat, however, was not prepared to be quiet in the face of his disapproval. 'I was twenty-three when we got married in 1958. His other wife was about a hundred,' she said in bad Russian to make sure I understood, adding further hoots of laughter, which were beginning to be picked up by the children and younger men who had gathered to hear the story.

Shakhgeriev manfully continued with his tale and pretended not to have heard. 'It used to be two years in prison if you had a second wife, and they came and checked. But they asked her,' he said, gesturing to Aminat (who was now bubbling with mirth), 'if she had any complaints, and she said she did not complain. There was no law against mistresses so they had to stop.'

Aminat contradicted her husband, however. 'The prosecutors came and asked me if it was true that he had another wife. I should have handed him over to them so they could have imprisoned him.' The ripple of laughter took in almost the whole gathering, and I was finding it harder and harder not to join in myself.

Emboldened by the success of her joke, she then decided to take the initiative. 'He took his third wife at the start of the 1970s. I already did not care. I went with him to fetch the bride,' she said. I asked if she had been opposed to his marrying again, which set up a joke she simply could not resist.

'I was much less opposed than his new bride was,' she said, before dissolving into giggles, which were shared by everyone in the room. Even her husband looked at his troublesome wife and smiled fondly.

'I always wanted another wife but two years ago my health worsened and now I have changed my mind a little,' he said.

I had been promised another chat with Utsiev that evening, so I walked through the village to the cemetery, passing a ford in the stream where women were washing rugs and clothes. The heat had become more bearable now evening was coming. That morning as we drove through the fields, the heat haze had hemmed us in and disorientated us. Chunks of the sky broke off and floated along the fields, and combine harvesters trailed great plumes of dust – smoking islands of machine in a wavering blue sea.

Now the sun was lower, and I could walk without having to squint into the glare. As I strolled I wondered if Imam Shamil's relationship with his own wives had been as boisterous and loving and funny as the one I had just witnessed.

That evening, I returned to Utsiev's house, where he and three other old men sat and chatted in Chechen. The acoustics of the room, which was not large but seemed to have a strange resonance, made the sound run around the walls in whispers. Their words were incomprehensible to me, but the occasional mentions of the word 'Anglia' – 'England' in Russian – made me suspect I was the topic of conversation.

Eventually, their minds made up about something, three of them left, and Utsiev and I sat down to supper. We chatted for a while about the world, and he attempted to force food upon me with the good-natured but insistent hospitality of the Caucasus. Gradually, other men, many of them in their thirties and forties began to drift in. They were all wearing the same kind of baggy, long cotton shirts that Utsiev had worn all day, as well as skull caps. The shirts had bobbles of cotton instead of buttons, though I am not sure why.

There was an air of excitement in the house now, as more people piled in. I asked Utsiev what was happening, and he told me they were going to have a prayer ceremony – the ecstatic zikr that had been banned by the tsars and distrusted by the Soviets – for me to observe. I was overjoyed, since it is a rare privilege to see it, and I felt increasingly impatient as we waited for the participants to drift in.

Eventually, we rose and passed into the prayer room, and the men reached up to take drums down from the walls. The drums looked a little like Irish bodhráns, but were smaller and with a looser skin. The men sat down cross-legged on the wooden floor, and chatted and laughed with each other as they waited for latecomers to arrive. At this stage there were eight men in a circle, and one woman – Utsiev's daughter – sat outside it.

Utsiev suddenly – and unexpectedly, considering the spiritual air that had filled the room – addressed me in Russian. The language sounded harsh in this context, as if it was too large for his mouth, but he was keen to make sure I understood what he said.

'Allah is listening, he is speaking but not like people speak. This is his attribute. Allah never sleeps, Allah never forgets, he loves his slaves, he has fed them with everything alive. This world is not held in a balance, it is held up by his strength, by his will. And we are strengthless in this,' he said. 'But we believe in him and love him and appeal to him. This people has nothing else. They work with their hands honestly, and earn what they eat with their own labour. The sacrifices they make don't earn them any favours. This is all for the sake of Allah, for the sake of Allah.'

He stopped there, checked I had understood what he said, then looked around at his comrades. They exchanged a few words in Chechen, then he threw back his head and began to sing. He started with the single word 'Allah', then expanded it with more Arabic words. The other chanters added a complex harmony beneath his words, giving his old man's voice a purity it would not otherwise have possessed.

The song grew from nothing into a thrilling and full crescendo, full of spiritual longing and loneliness. It was, although delicate, imbued with a confidence that carried itself gently. There was no swagger here, but the irresistible power of a force of nature.

The chanters rose up onto their knees, and began to rock back and forth a little. The chant had not yet gained a rhythm, but it was clear one was on its way, and the men were feeling their way towards it. Three more men joined the circle after a minute or so, adding their voice to the swelling and intensely spiritual sound.

Two more women entered the room at this point, sitting outside the circle. I noticed to my astonishment that they were weeping, the tears clinging to their eyelashes. One woman's shoulders heaved with sobs. Utsiev slowly rose to his feet, raised his hands to the side of his face and chanted upwards. The change was immediate. The other chanters stood too, and the tempo began to become more insistent. More cries rose up above the background of the chant, and the men swayed back and forth.

When the first clapping came in after five minutes, it felt like an obvious progression. From a simple moan to an insistent rhythm had been a movement as natural as breathing. Within a minute of the clapping starting, the circle had unwound itself and re-formed in the neighbouring room. All the women now joined the circle, as the dancers started to follow each other round and round. Faster and faster they danced, and the rhythm became irresistible. Utsiev's hesitant old legs had become spry and nimble under the influence of the dance. Despite myself, I found my foot tapping along by itself, and had to deliberately stop it since it seemed somehow sacrilegious.

I noticed four children in the far corner of the room watching with wide-eyed amazement, and the circle moved faster still. The women were taking a full part in the ceremony – there were twelve men and four women – although one woman's shoulders heaved with sobs and she hid her face behind her hands. Her high female screams rose above the deep, bass chant, with the fierce urgency of childbirth or terror.

The clapping became faster, and faster, the dancers raised hands above their heads. And then they just stopped. The chanting slowed, swelled, subsided, coiled round itself, and came to a halt.

'Allah-h-h-h-h,' called out Utsiev once more, in a cry echoed around the circle. The sound gradually died away, and was replaced by silence disturbed only by sobs. The men and women turned to face each other, breathing heavily.

Utsiev talked to the group in Chechen, while the hysterical tears of one of the women too faded away of themselves.

The children, who had been watching the dancing, became bored by the talking and started to whisper to each other. Perhaps they had seen this ritual too many times for it to be interesting. One of the dancers surreptitiously handed one of them a telephone to play with, and turned his attention back to Utsiev.

For the next part of the ceremony, they returned to the first room, where they sat on the floor once more and chanted to the tunes of stringed instruments, which they called 'fiddles' and played with bows, but which looked nothing like any violin I've even seen.

As they played, I wondered to myself what chance a Soviet bureaucrat – raised on the certainties of Marxism and dialectical materialism, sure of the progression of history towards a future when the state would wither away, happy to take a bribe to make someone's life easier in the meantime – would have had if faced with these people.

They lived in a different world to the people who made the rules. They had no interest in imposing their values on anyone else, which might have made them seem soft. But they had survived torment, and emerged vibrant and strong, which is something the Soviet Union itself failed to do.

They worked, and they loved, and they danced. That was their life, and it was wonderful.

The ceremony over, I bid them farewell fondly and drove slowly back to my hotel in Balkashino with Birsanukayev. The stars were bright and huge overhead as we picked our way along the dust roads between the wheat fields. We turned off the headlights for a while, and sat just looking at the stars, which were peaceful and calm after the emotions of the evening.

I was overawed by what I had seen, at the little world that the Chechens had built for themselves in the midst of desolation, and struggled to answer Birsunukayev's good-natured questions about my impressions of his home village.

I thought back to supper, to a question Utsiev had asked me.

'Do you think I am wise?' he had asked.

Strong? Maybe. Kind? Definitely. But wise? It did not seem the right word somehow. I think perhaps English does not have the word to describe him.

25. Everyone was Scared of Them

The Chechens were obviously not the only people deported to Kazakhstan. Aside from the North Caucasus nations they were united in exile with ethnic minority deportees from Crimea, from Georgia, from the Far East and elsewhere. Political deportees joined them too, as the barren steppes of Central Asia became a giant dumping ground for those people that Stalin wanted to simply get rid of.

Among them was Alexander Solzhenitsyn, who was to become legendary as a dissident writer and would even win the Nobel Prize for Literature in 1970. As a young officer, he was caught making slightly facetious comments about Stalin, which was enough to condemn him to the camps.

In March 1953, at the end of his sentence – and, coincidentally, in the same month that Stalin died – he was exiled for life to the southern Kazakh village of Kok-Terek. There he taught in a school and observed first-hand how the Chechens lived in Central Asia – observations he wove into his giant indictment of Soviet rule *The Gulag Archipelago*. According to his account, the Chechens just refused en masse to compromise.

'After they were treacherously thrown out of their home, they believed in nothing ever again. They built themselves huts – low, dark, sad, such that you could almost destroy them with one kick. And all their life in exile was like that – for a day, a month, a year, without accumulating property, or reserves, without plans. They ate, drank, they clothed their young. Years went past, and they still had nothing like at the beginning,' Solzhenitsyn wrote.

'No Chechens ever tried to please or ingratiate themselves with the bosses. They were always haughty before them and even openly hostile.'

He recounted a story from his time in Kok-Terek which demonstrates the Chechens' sheer refusal to surrender better than any other

I have ever seen. His star pupil was a Chechen boy called Abdul Khu-daev, who was in the ninth year of school – hence, aged between thirteen and fifteen. Abdul did not ingratiate himself with anyone, being too proud, but he was respected for his sheer intelligence.

The boy lived with his elderly mother, and had no other close relatives except an uncle and an older brother. The brother had been imprisoned as a thief and a murderer, but had been released under amnesty. He returned to the village and got drunk for two days, then quarrelled with a local Chechen and attacked him with a knife. Before he could do his drinking partner any damage, however, an elderly Chechen woman stepped in to stop him.

By tradition, the brother would have stopped at this point, since no Chechen could ever harm an older woman. But he was too drunk and too fractious, and he killed her. He was not drunk enough to fail to realize what awaited him when the other Chechens heard what he had done, however, so he fled the village, turned himself in to the police and was sent to prison.

The Soviet legal system might have considered that to be an end to the affair, but the rules of blood had not been satisfied. In the absence of the brother, someone else from the family would have to pay for the murder. So Abdul, his mother and his uncle stocked up with food and water and barricaded themselves in their house, which was besieged by Chechens.

The whole community knew what was happening, but no one – not the Young Communist League, not the Party, not the police, not the teachers, not anyone – went to save this child from the threat of violent death.

'Before the revival of blood revenge these formidable organizations like the regional committee of the Party, and the regional executive committee, and the Interior Ministry komendatura and the police hid away like cowards. The barbaric savage ancient law had taken breath, and it seemed there was no Soviet rule in Kok-Terek,' Solzhenitsyn wrote.

The Chechen elders went to the police and asked them to hand over the brother, but the police refused. They left, discussed among themselves, and returned to the police to ask for there to be an open court case and that the brother be shot in their presence. Again, the police refused. So the elders summoned more elders – the most respected in the nation – from Almaty. They held a council and condemned the brother to death. Any Chechen, anywhere, was instructed to kill him on sight.

Honour was satisfied. Abdul was allowed to return to school, and everyone in the school hid their shame, and pretended nothing had happened.

It was an episode guaranteed to make sure that young Abdul realized the extent of his exile. He might be expected to conform with the Soviet laws, to join the institutions, but he would never receive the assistance from the law that he should have been given in return. From that day forth, if he did not realize it already, he would know that no matter how hard he worked, the Chechens lived outside the law.

It was a lesson drummed in throughout the exiled nation. In the 1950s, in the years after Stalin's death, the Soviet government initiated a project to try to increase food production by ploughing up the Kazakh steppes. They created the vast fields I saw on my trip to Krasnaya Polyana, and they brought in hundreds of thousands of idealistic young citizens keen to participate in what was called the Virgin Lands campaign.

These young settlers had been brought up to see the Chechens and other deportees as the worst kind of traitors, and when they realized they would be living next door to them, they reacted in fury. There were dozens of fights between the settlers and the deportees, often involving fifty or a hundred people.

Party officials and police paid little attention to these small battles, and once more the Chechens were cast back into defending themselves. Every cancelled police investigation, every biased court decision, was one step further to making the Chechens live outside the law.

Solzhenitsyn said the Chechens were not unique in being treated this way. Other nations had been deported too, and millions of people were imprisoned in the worst imaginable conditions for invented or insignificant crimes.

But, he said, the Chechens did not react like the others. Some, like the community at Krasnaya Polyana, retreated within themselves.

But most did the opposite. They refused to cooperate like the Sufis refused to cooperate, but they also fought back.

'There was one nation which completely refused to resign itself to its fate – not as individuals, not as rebels, but the whole nation as one. This was the Chechens,' Solzhenitsyn wrote. 'And the wonder is that everyone was scared of them. No one could stop them living like that. The government, which had already ruled this country for thirty years, could not force them to respect its laws.'

Every time I read those words I am irresistibly reminded of one of the Chechen men I became closest to on my travels.

His name was Khasan Bibulatov, but everyone called him 'Dedushka' (grandfather), since he was such a kindly old man. I spent many hours talking to Dedushka, who was sixty-five, in his ram-shackle house in a refugee camp in Istanbul, and it did not take me long to realize he was not a kindly old man at all, but an outrageous rogue, and he could easily have been the murdering, drunk brother in Solzhenitsyn's story, if only things had turned out differently.

He was deported as an infant, and knew nothing of his homeland but what his elders told him. His childhood was one long torment: not enough food, not enough clothing, abuse, disrespect. He fought back in the way he found easiest: with his fists.

It was hard to cast back to the events he was describing, as we sat in his little room with its kettle and its pictures of Chechen leaders on the walls. He seemed to consume only tea, cigarettes and perhaps bread. I never actually saw him eat bread, he just drank tea with sugar and chain-smoked, but he sometimes had a loaf on the table. Chechen children ran and played outside his hut, but inside – on visit after visit – we dissected how a young boy in a shack in Kazakhstan became an old man in a shack in Istanbul.

He grew up in the Chimkent region of Kazakhstan, in a town called Lenger – not far, as it happens, from where Solzhenitsyn taught Abdul in his school.

'I was small and I was always a scrapper. I was always fighting. These Kazakhs wanted to break us down, but we never let them. They wanted to beat the Germans too, and the Balkars, but we did not let them knock them down either. We are stronger than Kazakhs, if they see blood they run away. But we were real hooligans,' he said, with an irresistibly naughty grin in his white beard.

The time to go 'home' to the mountains he had no memory of came when he was sixteen. The whole nation was allowed to go back to the Caucasus, and most of them took advantage of the offer, some even digging up their dead relatives and taking them home for reburial. But they did not forget their ordeal, which affected them all in different ways.

'In 1959, my father came for me and took me home to the Caucasus. I lived there for a bit but I remained a scrapper and for these scraps, for using a knife, and for other things, they put me in prison,' said Dedushka.

As it turned out, 'they put me in prison' was something of an understatement.

Dedushka spent twenty-seven of the next thirty-five years in prison, becoming a genuine star of the Soviet criminal under-world. Chechens are famous in Russia for having run many of the Soviet-era mafia groups that control Moscow and the other cities. They are rumoured to be deliberately brutal. One former col-league of mine called Andrei worked as a student in a police photo lab during the 1980s and described developing forensic photo-graphs of murder scenes where the guts had been pulled out and rearranged to spell rude words on the floor. That, he told me, had been the Chechens.

If Dedushka had done anything like that, he did not tell me; he said his business had mainly been the classic mafia scam of protection rackets. But he delighted in shocking me with the coarsest of prison slang. Russian prisoners are so rude that they almost speak a different language, and employ the Russians' rich stock of obscenities to max-imum effect. On one occasion I amused myself by trying to directly translate one of Dedushka's anecdotes – it was about his relationships with his various wives, but moved on to the sexual habits of the Turks – into my notebook as he spoke.

It does not give a correct impression of the richness of his speech, since every Russian swearword can be twisted by the language's com-plex grammar into many different forms. But, even nannied into the dull handful of English swear words, I think the obsceneness of his speech comes across rather well.

'My bitches used to ask me where my money came from, because I never worked, but I'd tell them to fuck off. I'd give them money, I'd fuck them. They would go and work, that's how to treat a woman, not like these Turks, they are —' Here he used an obscenity so rude I had never heard it before, so I asked what it meant. He took a sip of tea from his glass, grinned, and gave a deliberately obscene explanation. 'Well, that means they do not fuck women. They will have a couple of children, then they stop fucking, they just lick them in the cunt. Imagine. For a Chechen, this is a load of cock.'

All his conversation was like that, and his eyes kept twinkling at me like a deranged Father Christmas to see how I was taking it. I have edited the rest of the comments he made, to exclude the swearing, but you should imagine it as a constant undertone to his words when we meet him again in the next chapter. In English it would have none of the humour of the Russian language though, so I decided to leave it out.

Although Dedushka would never say it, it is hard not to interpret his furious reaction to the world as a response to the horrors of his infancy. Growing up reviled, poor and dishonoured, he rejected the rules of his own society and Soviet society, and became a brutal man. The Chechen nation was allowed home in stages in the late 1950s, but the stain of their treatment did not leave them. Deportation – the injustice, the memory of the dead, the ill-treatment – would condition everything over the next three decades.

On returning home, it was hard for the Chechens to regain their old houses, but they were at last left alone for a while. The three decades or so that followed Dedushka's return to Chechnya – the three decades that he spent in prison and thus missed out on almost in their entirety, as it happens – were the only period in the last two centuries when Chechens lived in relative peace.

Many Chechens were not allowed to resettle in the mountain areas which had been their homes before the deportation. They were instead given houses in the lowlands, where they could be more easily watched and their hands would be kept busy in factories or on collective farms. Similarly, the local Russian-speakers were careful not to give the Chechens too many of the leading posts in government or industry.

Even Dedushka experienced this discrimination in his own unique way.

'Our group of lads,' he started, referring to the criminal gang he was part of, 'well, a lot of them did not know who I was or my nationality. They thought I was a Russian like them. And when you live among them, they tell you everything about how they think, and you will really find out how they hate non-Russians,' he said.

'I learned a lot, and understood that the majority of them are hypocrites. They say one thing and do another. When they find out you are not Russian they speak nice things until you leave.'

But still, while the Soviet state became ever more corrupt and sclerotic as the 1970s wore on, the Chechens began to work their way into the unofficial economy, and as criminal gangs like Dedushka's became powerful even in Moscow, that reflected on the position of Chechens in their homeland.

An extraordinary cultural awakening started, as Chechens began to write, perform and create in their own language for the first time.

Those Chechens who survived the deportation had children, and they told their sons and daughters about their homeland – the mountains, the forests, the rich land – and about the injustice that had been committed. Many of these children sensed the unfairness of their life as well, and dedicated themselves to trying to reverse it.

Sultan Yashurkayev, for example, who will play a big part in this story, remembered a one-armed old man called Nazhmuddin in his village in Kazakhstan who used to write to Stalin every week to explain the terrible mistake that had been made. The old man was convinced that had Stalin but known what had happened to the Chechens, he would not have allowed it.

Yashurkayev, who was deported aged two and who was separated from his parents during the deportation, grew up almost alone, since his grandmother and aunt died, and his uncles were forced to abandon him for days at a time while they went to work. He learned to write specifically so he could tell Stalin about his nation's troubles like Nazhmuddin was doing.

'If you were a Chechen, I could explain it to you in just a few words. There is the suffering and pain of the deportation of the Chechens, but it was not just those who were there that were deported but our children too, it has been passed on. I have written about this. The unborn were also deported, those who were born in 1980 or 1970,' he told me over an endless lunch one day in early 2009.

He was to grow up to write poems, but he was a little bit too old to take part in the true national movement. The awakening would belong to those who were too young to experience the raw horror of the Chechens' fate, but who heard at first hand the anger that it caused. These men – Zelimkhan Yandarbiyev, born 1952, Apti Bisultanov, born 1953, Akhmed Zakayev, born 1959, and others – would go on to lead the national movement. First, they would lead it with their voices, then with their pens, and then with their guns.

'The 1970s was like the beginning of the rebirth of national culture, mainly these were people who were born in Kazakhstan, or those who had just been born in Chechnya, and then were taken to Kazakhstan,' Zakayev recalled.

'They were educated in Kazakhstan, and their education was on the highest level. Meanwhile, all the Chechens' conversations for thirteen years were just about Chechnya, there was this melancholy and nostalgia for the homeland. "When will they let us go home?", "When will our problems be resolved?", all was about this, "When will we return home?", "When will we receive permission to go home?" Conversation, plans, everything was built around Chechnya, where we could not live. And this nostalgia for the fatherland assisted the surge in national culture – folklore, musical folklore, literature, prose, poetry.'

The young Chechens who were in their teens and early twenties in the 1970s felt increasingly able to express themselves, at first in private, and later in public, and thus to express the feelings of their people. They gathered in little cultural groups, which may sound like nothing much, but at the time these were brave attempts to push the boundaries of what was allowed.

'I remember when I was a child, in the 1960s, or the start of the 1970s. Let's say, in the 1960s, when I was with my contemporaries, aged nine or ten, and we found ourselves in Grozny, it was a big deal for us. But on public transport, if you spoke in Chechen you caused this wave of dissatisfaction among Russians. If you were a child, you'd definitely get a clip around the ear, and a reprimand. "Speak in a human language," they'd say. So our language was not even considered a human language,' Zakayev told me.

As a young man who loved his own language, he decided to become an actor, since the theatre was one of the few places where Chechen was publicly spoken. He studied to become an actor from 1977, first in Grozny and then in the Russian town of Voronezh. The young poets meanwhile were gathering in a group they called Prometheus.

'It is not that we were an elite, but we lived in our own world, all the cultural workers: writers, poets, actors, directors, dramatists. The theatre and this Prometheus group were interconnected and we knew each other. We held joint events, meetings that were official and non-official. We often met, just to discuss things that happened. We discussed questions about the deportation, the Caucasus war,' he said, with a sense of great excitement in what they had done, even three decades on.

This was still a time when dissidents were being locked up, or even put in psychiatric hospitals, so the risk they were taking was real.

'These writers, they had problems with publication, they could not publish what they wanted or write the truth, but in the theatre we could already speak out. And we discussed these problems too. And this all created a new generation with a new mentality. I would not call them nationalists, but this was an elite fighting against assimilation, fighting to preserve our national identity.'

The shows that Zakayev's theatre in Grozny put on in the 1980s had titles like *Freedom or Death* or *There is Only One God*, and these were to become slogans of the nationalist movement that was to explode at the end of the decade. The generation that the literary movement was to create would stand on the barricades with them.

Although the number of people involved in these groups was small – just a handful really, compared to the mass of the nation – their influence would be disproportionately large. When Gorbachev relaxed the restrictions on behaviour in the late 1980s, these poets and actors were young, energetic, motivated, handsome and organized. They seized control of the debate and pushed it in the direction they wanted it to go. And that is the direction that led to the Chechen National Congress of 1990, to the leadership of the renegade General Dzhokhar Dudayev with his spiv's moustache, and finally to confrontation with Russia.

Yashurkayev, who as a boy had learned his alphabet so he could write to Stalin, took part in the renaissance in a small way. He worked in the state prosecutor's office, then in the cultural bureaucracy, but he still wrote his poems and he knew and befriended the radical young men who were driving politics in the later 1980s. He was radical in his own way too, and worked for Zavgayev – the Chechen who became head of government in 1989 – as an adviser. But, when Zavgayev was overthrown, he refused to have anything more to do with government, and concentrated on raising calves and writing his poems in his house just outside Grozny.

That was where war found him when the Russian tanks pushed into Chechnya in 1994, and in him it would find its most compelling witness.

As the bombs fell, and the war surged around him, he wrote in a large notebook everything that he saw. He described the difficulties of feeding his cattle, and the nervousness of his dog Barsik. And passages of what he produced have the strength and power of the best war writing. Its very banality lifts it above attempts to intellectualize the fighting, and provides a bleak, funny and true tale.

'Today, 4 January 1995, under the howl of planes, which bomb the city without a break, I suddenly sat down and started these writings. When civilian houses fly into the air, like grey dust and do not return to earth, this may well be interesting. A plane has dropped a bomb or a rocket somewhere nearby and sent fifteen splinters into the house. All four windows on the side of the street are broken. One splinter broke the wall near the ceiling and knocked down the book shelf, the one that had books from the "Life in Art" series on,' he wrote.

'My mother and I at the time were in the cowshed. We have five head of cattle, two sheep, eleven chickens, one cat and a dog called Barsik. My mother says that animals cannot speak, so you can't just abandon them to their fate. Leaving my own home would also not be right. It is better to meet your fate where you are, than to run away from it.'

In his next few paragraphs, he speculates on the true source of wealth ('... a deep thick-walled basement, which we don't have ...'), and on the identity of the men fighting the Russians. He describes how his collection of books has stopped meaning anything to him, and – incidentally – the horrors of everyday existence.

'A Russian woman has been killed in one of these houses by a Russian shell from a Russian tank. She had bent down to look in a saucepan in her kitchen. Half of her head ended up in the dish. Her husband ran around the yard with this saucepan and its contents and asked everyone there what he should do. This "everyone" was a few old women, a drunken man and me, out looking for cigarettes.'

This combination of terror and black comedy is what makes his diary so extraordinary. As January and February progressed, and the Russian army's frustration at its inability to capture Grozny increased, the ferocity of its bombardment increased with it. But Yashurkayev remained primarily concerned with the fate of his neighbours, his livestock, his water supply and whether he could find enough cigarettes to keep himself sane among all this madness. 'I am particularly worried about Barsik, and what will happen if he wanders around and sees bodies. He might start eating them from hunger.'

The politics that was driving the war was scarcely relevant to him, and it is given no more space than any other aspect of his life, but the ironies of his situation scar every paragraph.

One day, for example, he found his yard full of dead doves, which he along with his neighbour Salavdi gathered for food. 'Yes, it would seem the Chechen doves have lost the war, and failed to become the doves of peace. And so far I haven't seen a single dead crow.'

And then a little later: 'Radio Liberty is reporting that fifteen shells are landing on Grozny every minute. I counted forty-seven and the minute had not even ended, and I did not count more. If the world was only listening to Radio "Russia", then it wouldn't hear a single explosion.'

As he wrote, he wove in his thoughts on the deportation, on the nineteenth-century war, on democracy and the Chechen leadership. His account seamlessly links what is happening in Grozny around him with everything that has happened in his homeland in the last two centuries. It is a very Chechen book.

'When the government in Chechnya became Chechen, it lost that aura that any government puts around itself. For a Chechen, it had ceased to be a government but was someone's son or brother who ended up in a good position when the Muscovites left. And, by what right? Why not me? How is his father better than mine?'

Barsik becomes an ever greater presence in the book, as the people around him die or are driven away. The dog's actions gradually allow the reader to picture his character. At one point, Barsik steals one of Yashurkayev's boots, and places it in front of the room in which Yashurkayev used to sleep before the war. Taking this as a sign of some kind, Yashurkayev decides to sleep in that room, although it was very cold and he normally chose to sleep elsewhere. In the morning, it turns out that a bomb had shattered the window in his normal room, and that most of the glass ended up on the bed and would have done him serious damage. From then on, he listens to Barsik's advice more carefully, and holds long, imaginary conversations with him.

The bombs that fell gutted apartment blocks, and shattered factories. The shoddily built five-storey buildings that housed workers all across the Soviet Union required little encouragement to fall down. When they collapsed, they buried anyone sheltering in the cellar under tonnes of concrete. Metal gates became shredded like doilies in the rain of shrapnel, and life in the city became ever more animal and basic.

Parallel with this, Yashurkayev's distant, ironic tone starts to become angrier, as he describes the murders of civilians all around him, how a shell landed by his house and miraculously failed to explode, how the roof of his barn is destroyed, and how Barsik is so scared he hides under the sideboard and refuses to come out.

The shelling starts to terrify him, and those of his neighbours who are left. One neighbour refuses to lend another a packet of cigarettes, since he would not get them back if his friend was killed. Relationships break down, but the neighbour is lucky because Yashurkayev was feeling light-headed that day and wanted to help everyone he saw.

As the months go by, the Russian soldiers inexplicably leave him in peace, perhaps because of his white beard, but their regular appearances terrify Barsik, who is becoming increasingly traumatized.

'It turns out my Barsik is a very clever dog. I never thought about this, I kept him just so he could bark in my yard. But when the shooting starts, he lowers his tail, and makes himself very small and prevails upon me to leave the building. If I refuse, he leaves me, looking both reproachful and guilty and runs to hide in his corner.'

Soon he has a new animal to worry about too. One of his cows gives birth to a calf he calls 'War'. As if as a counterpoint to this happy news, he follows it with a paragraph about Russian soldiers executing several young men in cold blood.

And so his life wore on: conversations with Barsik, feeding his livestock, survival, death and friendship. It was the life of a Chechen surrounded by a war that had been brought to him by others. Sometimes, the fighting slackens and sometimes he leaves Grozny to see family or friends elsewhere, but it never dies away completely.

And then suddenly the tale stops.

'I have decided to stop with that. For now, anyway. If these writings have not given anyone an impression of the tragedy of a people, and of its roots, if they have not included the whole depth of the events, everything that was unembraceable, inexplicable, then at least they have done one good thing. They have stopped one man from going mad ... Or at least, he hopes so.'

It is a profoundly disquieting finish. In the 200,000 words or so that he wrote to describe spring 1995 in Grozny, there is not a single paragraph that is not imbued with war. And the fact that it ends without resolution is the most upsetting element of all.

Excerpts of the diaries were broadcast on Radio Liberty/Radio Free Europe years later, and that is where I first came across them. The unresolved ending prompted me to find out where Yashurkayev was. Did the diary end because he was killed? Or just because he got tired of writing? Was he still in Chechnya?

As it happened, I found him in Belgium, living in a little provincial village in the rolling Flemish countryside. He had arrived here in 2000, after a Russian bomb destroyed the house he had lived in throughout the spring of 1995. The chaos in Chechnya had become more than he could bear, and he had chosen a second deportation: this one self-imposed.

Here, as if in mocking answer to the horrors described in his book, everything was neat and orderly. The trains were frequent and clean, the fields I looked out on from the train window were cropped and green. When I arrived at my destination, the cars were shiny and European. Stolid Belgian citizens ignored me as I sat outside the train station and waited for him to pick me up.

He arrived in a black Volkswagen, and smiled as I dashed through the traffic to his car. He was lean and hard-faced, with white hair and a firm jaw-line, but looked delighted to see me. He has now had his diaries translated into several European languages, but was pleased to talk more about them.

Over lunch – fish, potatoes, a vegetable stew, peppers, brandy and beer – we talked about the war, and the deportation, and why he had not left Grozny with his livestock before the fighting started.

'War is – well, you know, everyone expected it, but, well, everyone says there will be a third world war, but no one is taking their livestock anywhere at the moment. And such a large, insane, uncontrolled war was hard to imagine,' he said, trying to make sense of the danger that had engulfed his quiet life.

'I built my own house with my own hands, and a man who himself built his own house with his own hands, he somehow becomes very attached to it, Not in a material sense, but at the time I looked down on people who left.'

So he stayed and survived the war, and had only stopped writing for other, complicated reasons that he struggled to describe. I told him his diary was some of the most touching war writing I had ever read, and he thanked me. But, I said, I had one other question. What had happened to Barsik?

Yashurkayev looked down at his plate, and his son – who was sitting on the sofa – spoke across to me.

'He was killed. The Russians killed him,' he said.

26. My Sons were Killed

The savagery of the Russian assault on Grozny in 1994 drove wavering Chechens back squarely behind Dudayev, no matter how erratic his rule had been. Zakayev, the actor who helped lead the national revival, came home as soon as war looked inevitable. Dudayev made him culture minister, but he never really took up the post, going instead to his home town of Urus-Martan to help lead the resistance.

Nationalist poet Yandarbiyev was already installed in the heart of government, as Dudayev's deputy, and other cultural leaders were too. The war made them forget their differences, and unite to fight the invader. They fought in family groups, or friendship groups, taking advantage of their superior knowledge of the geography of Grozny and other towns to outflank and outwit the lumbering Russian tank columns.

The terrible bombardment of Grozny that Yashurkayev and his dog Barsik endured was born of the Russians' inability to take the centre of the city and the great edifice which had been the headquarters of the Party's Regional Committee, and which Dudayev called the Presidential Palace. Groups of Chechens moved into the centre to fight around the giant concrete hulk, which was ever more scarred and damaged.

Among them, perhaps inevitably, was Dedushka, my foul-mouthed friend.

Dedushka, on release from prison, had lived in Siberia, where his gang had its business interests. Krasnoyarsk, a city of aluminium smelters far from Moscow, epitomized the collapse of law and order in post-Soviet Russia. Here business disputes were settled with guns and bombs in what were known as the 'aluminium wars'. Reputations for hard business practices were made among the smelters, and small armies were employed by the bosses to keep their competitors and their employees in line. It was, I suspect, fertile ground for a man of Dedushka's talents.

He returned to Chechnya in autumn 1994, he said, along with two of his sons, to fetch his father to safety. War was inevitable, everyone knew, and he wanted to take his father back to Krasnoyarsk with him. He had seen the propaganda sweeping the country, in which Chechens were demonized, and he wanted nothing to do with the hostility being poured out.

'When I was going there, I heard how the Chechens were barbarous and sadists, and I knew it was not true,' he said.

He did not like being in Chechnya, and never had. The traditions were too strict for him, and he barely spoke the language after a lifetime in exile and in prison in Russia. But even this old cynic was swept up in the spirit of the times. Perhaps he saw this as a chance to get back at Moscow, which had ruined his life so comprehensively. Perhaps he was just having fun. Even he could not explain the fact that he and his sons then joined up with one of the groups fighting the invading army, and took up their positions on the edge of Grozny.

That was when the heaviest shelling came.

'My sons were killed,' he said. 'These sons that were killed, the oldest had two sons and a daughter. The youngest had two sons. And how can I go to my grandsons now, because they will ask what I did with their fathers. I would answer that they were killed in the war, but then they would ask why I was not killed too.'

I thought about that, and asked him why he had not been killed, and he paused for a while. Then he reached across and shut the door. He did not need to stand up to do so, since the room we were sitting in was only about the size of a small car. The door of his house was never normally shut, so two refugee children called out to him from outside, speaking in Chechen, but he ushered them away. And he began to tell his story.

'I said to my sons that they should not come with me, that they should stay in Krasnoyarsk, but they came with me, and we were under shellfire. I was concussed terribly, and I lost my memory. And I knew nothing, nothing. The Russians took me then, and they held me for 103 days,' he said.

He later told me that he had been stunned by the same Russian raid that killed senior commander Umalt Dashayev, which places it on 28 December 1994. He did not even manage to see in the New Year in Grozny. I had not expected this, and was taken aback by the bleakness of his tone. He had gone from twinkling patriarch to tortured old man in less than five minutes.

'See these teeth,' he said, reaching into his mouth and pulling out a plate of dentures. 'See them, they are not mine. These Russians, they got a file, you know what a file is, and they put it between my teeth, and they twisted it like this. Like this. And they snapped my teeth off. The roots were still there, but nothing else.'

I did not know what to say. He was looking down at the table now, with its oilcloth cover, and fumbling in his packet for another cigarette. Realizing he was still holding his old cigarette end, he dunked it in his cold tea and put it on the table, before lighting a new one.

'Then they took electric cables, they put one on my cock, and then put the other one on my ear, and they turned the power on. And they asked "What is your name, what is your name?", but I did not know. I could not tell them what my name was. Then they would strip me down until I was as naked as when I was born, and they threw me out of the train. They were keeping us in these wagons, and they made us sit in a row on the rails. It was twenty-seven degrees below zero, and we were just sitting on the bare iron of the rails. Anyone who could not stand up after that was shot and the train rolled over them, they were listed as "unknown".'

I wondered whether it was true that he had not been able to remember his name. For a man with a past like his, admitting his name would have led to life in prison. But I was not going to interrupt him. I'm not sure I could have stopped him talking anyway.

'I've never mentioned this before to anyone. I have never said a word of it. But my cock is two and a half centimetres shorter than it was. I could not go with a woman now and I am ashamed. People sympathize with me but they do not understand really.'

The torture, he said, became unbearable after a while. He lit the next cigarette before he told me what had happened. His hands were even shaking a little, which was shocking in such a proud man.

'When they were torturing me, I swore at them, using every word I could think of. I used prison slang, and normal slang, and all the other prisoners told me not to do it because it made them beat us harder, but I told them to help me swear, because then at least we would be shot,' he said. 'And then came the time for them to shoot us. They did not say they were going to shoot us, they said it would be the "liquidation" and that moment my heart began to beat so loud it was like the people in the first compartment could have heard it, and we were in the fifth compartment. And I was scared, scared for the first time. But when I took my first step, it calmed down. My heart calmed as if it had never beaten, and from that moment onwards I have never been afraid again.'

With Dedushka now even less cooperative after the fake execution, the Russian guards turned to ever more extreme methods. The train they were kept on was moved from place to place, but the prisoners were constantly kept in pain or suspense.

'When I was let out, I could hardly walk. They beat me on the feet. They would hang me upside down and beat me. You know, when you are beaten on the feet, you feel the pain in your head,' he said.

He was lucky as it turned out; a group of French journalists asked the Russian authorities for permission to see the train, and the pressure they put on the jailers freed the captives. After three months in the train carriage, Dedushka was allowed out.

'Some of the prisoners went back to Chechnya, and I went back to Chechnya with them and that was when I heard that my boys had been shot. What did I have left to do then? That was when I decided to go to Moscow to be treated by doctors. I could not even walk for ten or fifteen metres.'

While he was in Moscow, the war ground on, with desperate clashes in which the Chechen forces grew in confidence and the Russians became more mired in the mess they had created. As 1996 dawned, Yeltsin had elections coming up. The messy, costly war on Russia's southern flank had proved disastrous. The authorities were lying frantically about the human cost, but the people were not fooled. The adventure was ever more unpopular and the Kremlin had to get it over with.

Dudayev had been assassinated by now – a rocket had allegedly been fired down his satellite phone signal; either that or it was a car bomb – and Yandarbiyev the poet led the talks in Moscow, with Zakayev the actor by his side. They won a ceasefire, and a Russian withdrawal. Incredibly, the Chechens had won.

As I sat and talked to Dedushka, I became increasingly convinced that his life story was too perfect a mirror of Chechen history to be real. He had been deported as a blameless infant, mistreated, brutalized, and imprisoned. On release from prison, he had fought, been grievously wounded, and then set free in a ruined state to make the best of what had survived the war.

Likewise, the Chechen nation had been unfairly deported, abused in captivity, then allowed home but not given the rule of its own land. When it had finally achieved some freedom, it had been only the prelude to a new, dreadful war that left the capital city in ruins and the country strewn with mines.

As Dedushka had survived his terrible interrogation and been released, the Chechens as a whole had defeated Russia's brutality and won independence. Estimates of the cost of the fighting vary wildly, because of the nature of the war, and the fact that no one has made full lists. According to the best estimate from the most reliable sources, the two years of fighting in Chechnya killed at least 50,000 civilians, and probably more than 100,000. Around 15,000 Russian soldiers and perhaps 5,000 Chechen fighters also died.

It had been a terrible loss for every Chechen family. As Dedushka had lost two of his sons, others had lost parents, daughters, brothers and friends. Dedushka's punishment, I thought as I sat and listened to another one of his anecdotes about prison life, was his nation's punishment, and I could not resist asking him if he agreed that his life mirrored that of the Chechen people.

He shrugged, and changed the subject. 'Perhaps I will visit you in Europe,' he said, 'if I get married and my new wife wants to come.'

Would that be your fourth wife, I asked, trying to keep track of the marriages he had told me about.

'What are you talking about, my fourth?'

Well, perhaps it would be his sixth then, I ventured.

He just smiled and I wondered if I had understood him at all.

For, of course, his punishment did not end in 1996. I was talking to him after all in a refugee camp by the Bosphorus in Istanbul, and by that time the Chechen attempt to win independence had collapsed in the face of brutality as bad as anything the Caucasus had ever seen.

By the time Russian tanks returned to Grozny in 1999, fighters on both sides would have thrown away the last remnants of humanity, and were lashing out to kill without thought for the victims.

And that is where the story takes us next.

PART FOUR

Beslan, 2004

27. We Offer You Peace, and the Choice is Up to You

Hundreds of people stood outside the tall metal gates. White-faced and red-eyed from four days of worry, fear and no sleep, they were now waiting to find out if their lives would be ruined for ever. Occasionally, the gates would open a crack, and a couple of people – normally a man and a woman together, sometimes two women – would emerge, blank-faced and stunned. Then, another trickle of bystanders would be admitted through the gates.

The day was grey, and tiredness had rendered me stupid. Every now and then, a stray wisp of wind would push a putrid, sickly, over-ripe smell into the street. It was unpleasant, and seemed to cling in my nose. I was smelling it for the first time, or I would have known it at once. It was the smell that human bodies make when they rot.

Beyond the gates were the victims of the Beslan hostage tragedy – the worst hostage raid in Russian history. The chaos of the storming of the school, where 1,300 hostages had been kept without food or water for three days, had ended. But no one had any idea of the death toll, and I was hoping to get into the morgue in Vladikavkaz to count them. Russian officials had been lying to the press and the hostages' relatives all week. They had told us there were only 354 hostages. They had said the attackers had made no demands. They had lied again and again.

The dead bodies would not lie to me, and eventually I too gained admission to the morgue, where I would be able to find out the cost of the disaster for myself. Ahead of me was a straight stretch of road, twenty metres or so, then a left turn around the back of the morgue building. The smell was stronger here. It almost had a solid presence, and it felt like cheese or sickness in my throat.

I walked steadily, automatically almost, to the corner and, turning it, saw a vision of hell. To my right was a row of stretchers, with transparent plastic sheets covering bodies. The row receded for a few

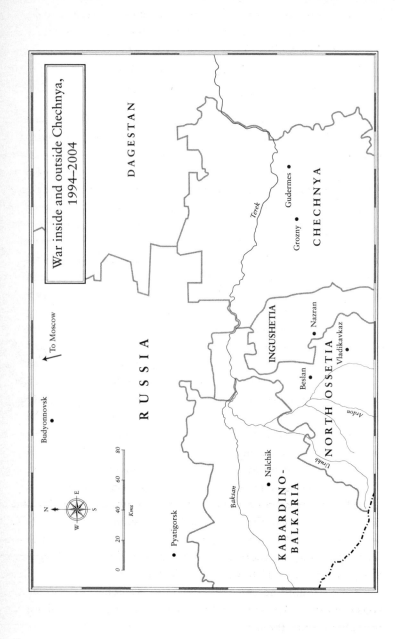

War inside and outside Chechnya, 1994–2004

metres to a broader courtyard where dense rows of stretchers held still more people: children, men, women, all mixed up together. At least a hundred bodies in all. And among them were the living, sleepwalking from body to body. They were searching for their children, their sisters, their mothers or their uncles among the army of the dead.

Two women, one of them with dyed red hair and clutching her face, stooped over a child's body, uncovered it, then pulled the plastic sheet back over its face and walked on along the row.

Many of the bodies were terribly burned and disfigured. In the furthest corner, a twist of gut emerged from a corpse's stomach like a spring bracken seedling turned rotten and vile. One or two bodies were just piles of pieces in bags, while others seemed unharmed. One boy's face is still with me. It was pale like a dairy product, with the same glistening surface as a cheap brand of cream cheese on sale all over Moscow. Freckles stood out on his face, unusually sharp against the pallid cheeks. His eyes were closed, and his long eyelashes fringed them rather beautifully. I had never examined a dead body this closely before. There was nothing obviously wrong with him, except that he was totally and unmistakably dead.

I spent perhaps twenty minutes in the morgue before I walked out, my clothes saturated with the smell of the dead. As I pushed my way through the gates, I saw Viktor, a photographer friend of mine, coming the other way.

'Wait for me, will you, I'll just take some pictures, then we can go and get some breakfast,' he said.

I was not sure I could eat breakfast, but I wanted company so I stood by the gate, lit a cigarette and waited for him to finish his work.

He was out again in thirty seconds, pale and stunned. He grabbed my arm for a second, then bent double and vomited into the roadway. This was a man who had documented the wars in Chechnya, Iraq, Afghanistan and the worst disasters Russia had thrown at him in a long career. This was the worst thing he had ever seen.

'I need a drink,' he said, as he stood up. We bought a bottle of vodka and two plastic cups, and finished it that morning, drinking toast after toast to the dead.

In total, 334 bodies would pass through that and other morgues before the victims of this terrible crime were all laid to rest in a new, giant graveyard that would come to dominate the approach to the little town of Beslan, which had once been known only for its vodka factories and its shabby airport. Now it has a hideous global fame that will stay with it for ever.

That morning, I had been awakened early. Perhaps, it was five o'clock, I did not know. The previous three days had blurred into each other in a single progression of gunfire and explosions and other people's grief. With the siege over, I was getting my first night's sleep all week, and was untroubled by nightmares or shakes. Then my phone rang.

President Vladimir Putin, who had refused to negotiate with the hostage-takers and who must have ordered the storm operation in which hundreds of people had died, had come to visit the survivors. At five in the morning, he had presumably had to wake them up to do so, and my editors wanted me to see his reaction to the horrors all around.

It was too late, Putin had gone. The Kremlin was too slick to allow the president to feel the popular wrath bubbling over against his government, so it had not announced his arrival until he had departed.

I was left to wander through the streets of Beslan, which for the first time in three days were free of the throngs of journalists and grieving relatives who had been waiting for the siege to end.

A police checkpoint tried to block my passage to the school building itself, but the police were sleepy and talking my way past them was easy. In the thin morning light, the school was a tired-looking rose-brick building, with two storeys.

It faced a railway line. Perhaps, in happier times, the children had looked out from boring lessons and counted the carriages on trains rattling by. I walked along the side of the rails towards the school, and was surprised to see a man sleeping against the corner of the wall, in the school gardens. He looked shabby, like the homeless men who slept rough in Moscow.

It was only when I saw that a couple of metres from him were four or five other men, all clumsily dropped into the pile they had formed when they had been shot and thrown out of the window, that I realized he was dead. These men had been murdered on the first day of the siege as it turned out, when the hostage-takers had feared they might form the kernel of resistance.

A little further was a gate passing from the railway into the school yard. Here children would have played in the grass and the beaten earth, but now there were rows and rows of body bags. Black plastic bags, numbering perhaps a hundred, stretched away from me almost to the end of the yard.

I felt blank as I looked at them. There was nothing inside me but despair. Overshadowing the whole scene, behind me, were three tanks. These were the tanks that the Russian forces had used to blast the hostage-takers out of their upstairs windows, despite the children that were still packed into the building. They had left huge star-burst blast marks on the bricks.

The sports hall where the hostages had been kept for their three-day nightmare was barely visible, but from what I could see the destruction was terrible. Blackened roof timbers lay mixed in with body parts on the floor where children had played basketball. The windows were blown out, and giant scars marked the walls, where the explosives and bullets of both sides had ripped up window ledges, plaster, bricks and concrete.

The scene in front of me encapsulated the horrors of the new Chechen war: the ruthlessness, the barbarity, the violence and the countless civilian casualties. The view behind me told another story: the three tanks summed up the brutal Russian response. Russia only had blunt tools for its job of crushing the Chechen people, and it did not care who got crushed along with them.

Of the 334 victims, 186 would be children, many of whom were going to Beslan's School No. 1 for the first time. September the 1st is a day of celebration in Russia – 'the Day of Learning', it marks the start of the school year – and they were wearing their best clothes. The hostage-takers had chosen the date for its resonance; they had declared war on children, and the demands they made were straightforward.

They had passed a shabby piece of paper to an intermediary, with a series of promises and suggestions, bizarrely detailed in the light of the horrific circumstances under which they were being proposed. Chechnya, they said, was prepared to keep the Russian currency, to enter the post-Soviet treaty organization, to remain neutral and to seek to prevent any violence against Moscow, if only Russia recognized its independence.

'The Chechen people is waging a national-liberation struggle for its own freedom and independence, for its survival, and not so as to destroy or demean Russia. Being free, we will be interested in having a strong neighbour. We offer you peace, and the choice is up to you,' it said.

The Chechens' 'national-liberation struggle' had come to this.

The warriors who defended Grozny so bravely and gloriously in 1994, who had somehow miraculously defeated Russia two years later, were now forcing children to drink their own urine in a packed sports hall so they could win their independence. A disaster for both the Russian and Chechen peoples, it was a descent into darkness and evil driven above all by one man: the man whose name stood at the top of the demands handed over in Beslan.

'From the Slave of Allah Shamil Basayev,' the heading said.

Basayev had learned his fighting as a volunteer in Abkhazia, a region within Soviet Georgia that broke free of central control in the early 1990s. During that war, he got very good at sending men and woman to detain, abuse and kill civilians. Taking his skills to Chechnya and beyond, he would be uniquely responsible both for prolonging the Chechens' ability to resist the invading Russian forces, and for blackening his nation's name in the eyes of the world. He himself admitted that he was a terrorist. Thanks to him, his whole nation was to be known as terrorists.

He was one of the most dynamic commanders in the Chechen forces in the 1994–6 war. But it was not warfare that made his name; it was a daring, ruthless and radical raid outside Chechnya in June 1995, when he and almost 150 men darted out of their homeland, pretending to be a convoy of military trucks full of coffins and loot. They battled police in the town of Budyonnovsk, and then, seeking a base to resist the heavy assault coming their way, they seized the town hospital and at least 1,000 hostages.

The siege that followed lasted from 14 to 19 June, and the Chechens beat off four attempts by Russian forces to storm the building. Russian heavy-handedness was broadcast around the world. Hostages waved white sheets out of windows in an attempt to stop the bombardment of the building, while Russian forces used snipers to try to take out the hostages so they could shoot the Chechens behind them.

In a crushing humiliation for the whole country, Russia was forced to negotiate. Television pictures of the prime minister, Viktor Chernomyrdin, talking to this bearded bandit from the south ('Shamil Basayev, speak louder! You are not audible' is the line that everyone remembers) seemed to confirm Russia's post-Soviet collapse. The ceasefire Basayev won allowed the Chechens to regroup, to breathe again, and eventually to win the war. Basayev and his men returned to their homes as heroes, and the hostage-taking raid was confirmed as a successful military tactic.

A deputy of Basayev's who was on the raid later justified the attack, saying what they had done was nothing compared to what Russia had unleashed on his home village of Shali.

'We analysed the tactics of the Russian troops on Chechen territory and concluded that only diamond cuts diamond. Therefore, we concluded that the only way to stop the war was to retaliate in the same way,' said Aslambek Abdulkhadzhiev.

'We did not make these plans except as a last resort. Why was the world silent when Shali was bombed, when some 400 people were killed and wounded? In fact, the evil we did in Budyonnovsk was not even 30 per cent of what they did in Shali.'

It was a dangerous and seductive philosophy. If the Russians were targeting civilians, why should the Chechens not target them too? Why should the Chechens not commit evil if a greater good should come from it? Basayev himself had lost eleven relatives in a Russian bombing attack just days before the raid on the hospital, so why should he not take revenge himself?

The trouble was that once he and his men abandoned the rules of natural justice, they found no stops. They had gained a great victory in Budyonnovsk, and they would try to do so again and again. But the philosophy is corrupting. A victory based on such violence is no real victory, as the Chechens learned to their cost.

After the Russians signed the ceasefire and pulled out in 1996, Chechnya sank into complete chaos. The man who succeeded Dudayev as leader, an army colonel called Aslan Maskhadov, lacked the strength of character to keep the feuding warlords under control. Arab jihadis who had come to help the Chechens waved their money around, drove around in shiny new vehicles, and attracted private armies of men keen to earn easy cash.

Less violent foreign sympathizers gradually were driven away from Chechnya by a wave of kidnapping that spread across the region. Most foreign charity workers pulled out after December 1996, when – in the worst deliberate attack in the history of the Red Cross – six foreign aid workers were murdered in their sleep, before Maskhadov was even elected.

The lack of alternative sources of income drove more and more men into the arms of Basayev's extremists. Maskhadov imposed aspects of sharia law, but Muslim puritans imposed their own executions on people they deemed to be criminals. The dreams of independence had collapsed into a lawless morass of murders, kidnappings and viciousness.

Russia sent troops back in 1999, provoked by bombings that destroyed apartment blocks in Moscow and Volgodonsk and killed almost 300 people. The Chechens denied involvement (and lingering doubts persist that the FSB security service organized them for its own ends), but since they followed shortly after an invasion of Dagestan by Basayev, the Russian people was in no mood to hear their denials. The authorities blamed the chaos in Chechnya for fostering a nest of killers, and the Russian nation wanted revenge.

In the terrible years of warfare that were to follow, Basayev remained single-minded in his pursuit of his goals: the goals that he was to express in Beslan. But he was to become ever more dreadful in the tactics he chose to pursue, taking the war to Moscow as he did so.

My own first taste of those tactics came in October 2002. Recently arrived in Moscow, I had gone to the theatre to work on a feature article about foreign-style musicals in the Russian capital. The angle was going to be something like 'American razzmatazz in the home of ballet', but I never got to write it. As I stepped backstage to interview the producer, I was told that Chechens had seized another theatre on the other side of town. I was out the door, and taking a taxi as soon as I could.

It was a wet, cold, rainy evening, and outside the theatre on Dubrovka street was chaos. Policemen unsure of what to do milled about, local residents and escaped theatre-goers mixed with them. A handful of journalists like me had made it there already and were looking for someone to tell them what was going on. In fact, there was no obvious sign that anything was wrong at all.

Disappointed in my quest for information, I set off towards the front door of the theatre, thinking that the situation might be more obvious the closer I got. The building was a concrete monstrosity, with a huge light-blue poster stretching across its entire façade advertising the musical *Nord-Ost* which the hostage-takers had interrupted that evening by running onto the stage with their Kalashnikovs.

In front of the theatre was a large car park, and I set off between the cars for the 200 metres that separated me from the front entrance. When I was about ten metres or so away, the glass doors opened and a man emerged into the night, lifted up his Kalashnikov and fired off a burst of shots over my head. I was stunned. I had never heard a gun fired in anger before, and it had paralysed me. I stood there looking at him for what felt like a minute, but was probably no more than a couple of seconds, before a policeman dived into me, knocking me to the ground.

It was the beginning of a long two days of standing around, waiting for things to happen, and wondering if the Russians would once again cave in, as they had in Budyonnovsk and halt their military actions in Chechnya and agree to negotiations. This time, the Chechens had fewer hostages – about 850 people in total – but they were right in the middle of the Russian capital. The embarrassment for Russia was even greater than it had been seven years earlier.

The Russians were in no mood to repeat their concessions, however. On the morning of 26 October, gunfire suddenly boomed around the theatre. The Chechens were firing in panic in all directions, as if they could see something the journalists could not. As it turned out, it was not what they could see that mattered, it was what they could smell.

The Russians had pumped gas into the building, in an operation so secret they did not even tell the doctors on hand what drug they had used. Soldiers carried unconscious hostages out of the theatre like sacks of vegetables, dumping them on the forecourt where I had stood that first evening, before returning for more.

The Chechens, unconscious in the theatre, had been executed where they sat. Television pictures showed black-clad women strapped with explosives slumped over in their chairs. Bearded men lay, shot dead, in corridors. A Russian soldier had placed a full bottle of cognac in one of the dead Chechens' hands: heavy-handed wit for such a sombre occasion.

For the operation had been, in human terms, a disaster. The Russian government had not been forced to stop its military operations in Chechnya, but 129 hostages had died. And all but one of them was killed by the gas pumped in to save them. Only one had died at the hands of the Chechens. Officials later justified their actions, saying they needed to gas the theatre to stop the Chechens blowing it up, but that was a nonsense. If the Chechens had wanted to explode their bombs and kill all their hostages, they had had plenty of time before they passed out. At the last moment, they had chosen not to wipe out all their hostages as they threatened, and they had died for their cause with little blood on their hands.

Nevertheless, the atmosphere in Moscow was one of fear. The funerals dragged on for days, and Muscovites wondered when the next strike would be. The threat was real for everyone, and tales of close escapes abounded. Months later, I learned that the hostage-takers in their quest for a suitable target had videoed the inside of two Moscow theatres. As it happened, they had decided to seize control of the theatre on Dubrovka, but they could easily have chosen the other one they filmed. Had they done so, I would have been one of the hostages.

Basayev blamed Putin for the deaths, and promised there would be no let-up in his terrible campaign. A series of suicide bombers struck in and around Chechnya, destroying a government building, a bus used by military pilots and other targets. The bombers were often women, who were videoed wearing black veils and saying they were on their way to heaven, before they were sent out to blow themselves up. They became known in the Russian media as the 'Black Widows'.

Moscow was struck again on 5 July 2003, a summer day, the kind of day when Moscow is at its most beautiful. It was a Saturday and I was shopping in a major electronics market on the edge of town when my phone rang. Reports had come in of a suicide bombing at a rock concert. Getting to the Tushino air field through the traffic was a struggle, but at last I was confronted with the grim reality of it: the crumpled heap of the bodies, the shrapnel from the explosive belts the two bombers had worn, and the continuing beat of the rock festival. Organizers had decided there was no need to end the party.

The two bombers killed fifteen young Muscovites, and injured many more. It turned out that only sharp-eyed security guards had stopped them entering the festival, where the carnage would have been even worse. The thought of two bombs in the heaving crowd was enough to make any festival organizer sick with worry.

And just four days later, another bomber was aimed at the capital: this time a young woman called Zarema Muzhakhoyeva was sent to explode herself against the plate glass window of a café, the idea being to kill all those inside with fragments of broken glass and shrapnel.

She later said she lost her nerve, and she was captured after she put down her bomb and surrendered to police. She was allowed to give an interview to the *Izvestia* newspaper from prison, and she told a story so bleak as to almost defy comprehension.

Her words showed how low Basayev has sunk in his quest to terrify the Russian people into peace. He was now not only targeting people whose only crime was to be in Moscow; he was actively recruiting vulnerable Chechen women to do it for him.

Muzhakhoyeva was just twenty-three when she was sent out into Moscow with a rucksack full of explosives by two men she knew as Igor and Andrei. Her background is so tragic, that it would be hard to condemn her at all, had the bomb she left behind not killed the sapper sent to defuse it.

Her mother abandoned her when she was just ten months old, and her father died while working as an unofficial labourer in Siberia seven years later. Living with her father's parents, she was regularly beaten and only saw her mother on special occasions. It was a loveless childhood, followed by a loveless marriage. She married in 1999, just before Putin sent the army back into Chechnya, but this impoverished orphan was no catch for a Chechen man and the man who stole her from her home – as is traditional in Chechnya – was an Ingush two decades older than her.

She got pregnant almost at once, but two months later her husband Khasan was shot, leaving her to carry his child alone in his family home, surrounded by his relatives, whom she hardly knew.

'I gave birth to a daughter, my husband's relatives called her Rashana, and I breastfed her for seven months. And then something had to be decided. A little girl without a father. My husband's relatives visited my grandparents, asked if they would take back their granddaughter and the child. They said they could not feed us,' she told the newspaper.

'Khasan's parents took my daughter from me and gave her to a different son, who had no children in his own marriage. And they sent me to my grandfather and grandmother to build my own life. By our traditions, that is a commonplace situation, it is always like that. It would have been fine, but I loved Rashana too much. I suffered a lot.'

Muzhakhoyeva, who was perhaps only then feeling human love for the first time, could not live without it.

'The last time I went to them, I bought different toys and clothes for Rashana. She was so zappy, she had begun to speak, although in Ingush. She was sitting in her aunt Lida's arms and said about me: "Mama, look what beautiful things the lady has brought me, let's go and show Daddy",' she said.

It was too much to bear, so she hatched a plan in her desperation. She stole jewellery from her grandmother and aunts and sold it at the market for $600. She planned to go and ask to take Rashana for a walk, then buy plane tickets for them both and fly to Moscow, where an aunt of hers lived, whom she barely knew. It was a desperate plan, and it was flawed from the start, because she left her grandmother a note saying what she had done.

'I wanted them not to worry about me, to be nice. What a fool! Six of my aunts stopped us in the airport. Four took me away, and two took Rashana back to Sleptsovsk.'

Her life had got even worse. She was beaten at home for the theft and for the disgrace she had brought to the family. Her aunts told her they wished she was dead. Eventually, they got tired of that, and her grandmother and aunts stopped even bothering to beat her. They just refused to acknowledge her. Even her mother had stopped coming to see her, and now her life felt completely worthless.

That was when she had her great idea. She would go to a woman she knew called Raisa who had connections to Basayev, who was deep underground by this stage, and she would volunteer to become a suicide bomber. She had heard that relatives of a bomber received $1,000. Her grandmother would get her money back and even make a profit on the deal.

'Of course, even if at the cost of my life I returned this money, then the disgrace would still remain, but I needed to take action. I always wanted to be good. And so I went to Raisa and said I wanted to sacrifice myself.'

She found it harder than she thought. The rebels had no use just then for a suicide bomber, despite her pleas. But eventually, they assigned her to an operation.

At first she was taken by the rebels to the town of Mozdok, armed with an explosive belt and told to blow up a bus full of pilots. She failed to do so. She just sat on a fence feeling worse and worse. A soldier even came up to her to check she was all right, perhaps thinking the bulge in her belly was a pregnancy.

She went to a phone booth and called Rustam Ganiyev, the man sending her to her death, and told him no bus had come. He picked her up, and she felt so ill they took her to hospital. Here, Ganiyev treated her well, they laughed and enjoyed each other's company. She later said she hoped she would never have to explode herself, but she had made her agreement and they had not forgotten. Soon they sent her to Moscow for another final journey.

She stayed outside the Russian capital with the two women who were to blow themselves up at the rock concert. One had been married to a rebel, had got pregnant, and the group leader had forced her to get an abortion. Shortly afterwards, her husband had been killed in battle, leaving her without a child or a husband, and she had decided to just kill herself.

The other woman's husband was still alive, but apparently he had sent her to her death, since a suicide bomber wife earned a man great praise among his fellows.

They departed on their mission to the rock concert, and did not return. Theirs had been two of the bodies crumpled up while the music thumped on. Days went by, during which she was taken around the city to get to know it, and to choose a target. Then Muzhakhoyeva was finally told it was time. She was dressed up like a fashionable Moscow girl, given a mobile phone and some money, and dropped off in the middle of town.

'Blue jeans, trainers, a T-shirt, a cardigan of a sandy orange colour. They also gave me beautiful dark glasses and a baseball cap, which went with the colour of the cardigan. I had never worn a baseball cap,' she said.

'When before my departure I looked in the mirror, I liked how I looked very much. I had never dressed that way. I was just happy for a few seconds. Good things, a mobile phone, more than a thousand roubles in my pocket. It's true that only Igor called me on the telephone, and I called no one, but all the same I loved my mobile. It was a Nokia, it was beautiful.'

She then took a taxi to the café she had been assigned to blow up, and took a seat on a table outside it. That was when her nerve failed her once more. She paced up and down. When people approached her, she walked away, then came back. Finally, when challenged, she told the three men who spoke to her that she had a suicide bomb. She waited for the police to come.

And so she was in prison when the *Izvestia* journalist spoke to her, and she was all alone. Her relatives did not come to see her, and she was left with nothing but dreams of her daughter.

'I of course want to see her. And I probably will some time. But it's unlikely she'll see me. And what do I have left? A young woman in Chechnya can't do much as it is, and a widow even less. I could only marry an old man or as a second or third wife. I had disgraced everyone. I had stolen from my aunt – disgrace. I had tried to kidnap the child – disgrace. I wanted to escape – disgrace. I left home – disgrace. I had not only left home, but I had gone to the Wahhabis [religious extremists] – disgrace. I wanted to blow up the Russians – disgrace. I failed to do that – disgrace.'

She had a photo of Rashana, but Igor took it away from her before she set off to kill herself. Now, she had nothing to remember the one person who had ever loved her by.

Two months after she gave the interview, on 8 April 2004, she was sentenced to twenty years in prison by a Moscow court. If she had hoped her decision not to cause mayhem would save her, then she was wrong.

'I had the possibility of running away, of doing something, but I did not do this. I put my hopes in you, I hoped that someone here would understand me,' she told the court. Her pleas went unanswered.

She argued at her appeal, a few months later, that surely it suited Russia to pardon her, to show damaged Chechens that they had protectors other than the men of jihad.

'I ask you to reduce my sentence. I could have walked away, leaving the bag, but I stood and waited for the police. No one teaches us to surrender, just to press the button,' she said. 'I did not press the button, and I think my example would be followed by other girls forced to this. They might do the same.'

The appeals court did not agree with her, upheld the sentence, and she is now in a prison near Moscow. Her lawyer has said she wants to become a doctor, but I have little hope for her. Two decades will not be enough to wipe out the stain of what she did, not for the Chechens, and not for the Russians.

After a decade of war in Chechnya, such people as Muzhakhoyeva are many. The trauma of the war, and the rape, and the death, had left a whole generation of people emotionally scarred, and Basayev and his rebels had rich pickings when they needed suicide bombers. Muzhakhoyeva's will to live, as it turned out, was so enormous that

it overcame everything that was thrown at her. But many others were
not so keen to survive.

Before Muzhakhoyeva was even sentenced, on 5 December 2003,
another woman blew herself up in central Moscow. It was a snowy,
crisp day, and I was sitting in the office when the call came in that a
bomb had gone off nearby. I swung on my coat and sprinted the 400
metres or so to the site of the blast, reaching it before the police had
set up an effective cordon. They had stopped traffic, but pedestrians
were milling around, unsure of what to do.

As I ran around a parked truck towards the National Hotel, where
the bomber had struck, I almost slipped on something in the snow.
Looking down I realized it was a piece of skin, mainly fatty tissue,
but pale and ghastly in the snow. Scattered all around me were more
pieces of flesh, some of them quite large – the size and colour of a
medium portion of chicken – others just flecks of bloody red on the
roadway.

Behind the trucks was the hotel façade, and the place where the
bomber chose to end her life. Chips of marble had been scarred off the
hotel by shrapnel, and the plate glass window shattered. At the foot of
the wall were the crumpled heaps of five ordinary Muscovites.

Perhaps they had been going shopping, or to study at the university building nearby, or to work in the hotel. Or perhaps they were
just out for a walk. Now, they had the same look as the boy in the
morgue in Beslan. Everything about them looked normal, except
that they were unquestionably and totally dead.

Slightly closer to the edge of the pavement than the heap of bodies was a woman's head, perfectly upright, with long blonde hair. It
was neatly severed and did not seem harmed in any way. It sat in the
snow as if it had been placed there. A briefcase stood nearby, and all
around was the terrible hail of flesh, skin, fat, bone and blood that
just fifteen minutes before had been a Chechen woman who met not
sympathy from her neighbours and relatives, but words of hate and
disgrace.

These attacks seemed pointless. There were no demands expressed,
or pattern, or justification. It was pure murder. It was rage, an instinctive desire to inflict pain. And they went on. The next summer, on

24 August 2004, two planes exploded simultaneously over southern Russia, killing eighty-nine people. Seven days later, another suicide bomber killed ten Muscovites outside a metro station.

I think I was getting numb to the attacks by then. My only memory of that last bombing is the Moscow mayor giving an impromptu press conference while a car burned, and dead bodies lay just ten metres or so behind him.

The next day, a group of thirty men and two women took over School No. 1 in Beslan.

What was driving Basayev by this stage? What could possibly justify the casual death he was handing out and the opprobrium he was bringing down onto his own people?

According to Andrei Babitsky, a remarkably brave Russian radio and television journalist whose contacts with the Chechen resistance are unrivalled, Basayev was suffering from a 'Budyonnovsk Complex'. The success of his raid on the hospital in Budyonnovsk, the fact that he won peace talks for his people and gained a famous victory, outweighed any harm he did to the lives of the civilians – both Chechen and non-Chechen – he exploited.

'Basayev believed that sooner or later he could repeat Budyonnovsk and put Putin on his knees. And he thought that children's lives would not be risked by anyone, that Putin would have to stop the war,' Babitsky told me one afternoon in his flat in Prague.

'But Putin disappointed him, there could now be no other terrorist act to make Putin stop. And I think this was a serious moment for Basayev. If you look at these terrorist activities before Beslan – the suicide bombers, the planes – then after, when there was nothing, then you will see that he stopped. Terrorism was designed to achieve a goal, and it stopped achieving anything.'

But there is no need to just take Babitsky's word for it. In the most spectacular journalistic coup of the entire Chechen war, he interviewed Basayev in his forest hide-out on 23 June 2005, thus having done what the entire Russian state apparatus had failed to do, and found the warlord.

The film he shot was fascinating. He pictured Basayev and fellow rebels in a little camp in the woods, heavily armed, praying, eating and relaxing. He conducted a long interview with Basayev, who clearly relished the chance once more to talk to the press – something he loved doing before there was a $10m price on his head.

Basayev was dressed all in black, and played constantly with a string of prayer beads. Strangely, considering the Islamic inspiration he had regularly trumpeted, he sounded just like he had ten years earlier. He did not talk of holy war or martyrs, but spoke in the language of a secular revolutionary.

'We are fighting for our liberation from colonial dependence, the result I see is of course freedom and independence for our people and our state,' he said.

'The most important thing is to protect our people from a repeat of the genocide of 1944, and of the past years, and the current genocide, to protect our people from the degradation that Russia brings with it.'

Babitsky sat next to Basayev as they spoke, holding a microphone, which was occasionally too far from Basayev's mouth for the Chechen's words to be audible. Sometimes Babitsky would check that the camera was still running, or look at his watch. It is a surprisingly amateur-looking film for such a respected and experienced journalist, but there was nothing amateur about his questions.

Babitsky asked how Basayev could possibly justify sending his people against the children in School No. 1. Basayev responded with a development of that same logical but horrific position expressed by his lieutenant after the attack on Budyonnovsk. Forty thousand children had died in Chechnya, he said, and no one cared about them.

'It is not the children that are responsible but the whole people of Russia which today with silent agreement gathers food and things for these aggressors in Chechnya. They pay their taxes, they approve of these actions, they are all responsible. Therefore, until war comes to all of them, it will not stop in Chechnya,' he said.

'You can ask why I did this, it was to stop the killing of thousands and thousands of Chechen children, Chechen women, Chechen old people ... I do not see a different way to stop the genocide of the Chechen people. Today there is a genocide of the Chechen people and to me the Chechen people is more valuable than the whole rest of the world. You understand? My own people is more valuable to me because it is my own.'

He was right when he talked about the horrors faced by Chechen children. The handful of psychologists working in Chechnya said a whole generation was traumatized by the terrible warfare that had waged around them for their whole lives. They had no schooling, no health care, and their families were ill-equipped to deal with their damaged offspring.

In early 2005, a few months before Basayev gave that interview, I visited a building in Grozny used as a home by hundreds of Chechens whose houses had been destroyed. The families there had lived in refugee camps outside Chechnya, but the Russian government, embarrassed by the camps and their silent reproof, had forced the inhabitants to go home.

In one room, Viskhan Siriyev lay on a bed, and writhed away from me as I walked in. He was sixteen, but was as small as someone half his age, and his thin arms barely covered his huge eyes as he tried to hide himself from the upsetting visit of a stranger. Five members of his family shared this one room, and they took it in turns to care for their brother, who had not spoken since a bomb destroyed his family's home ten years before.

He might be still alive, but he was as much a casualty of the Chechen war as anyone who had actually died. And, in a cruel irony, he could not go abroad to receive the treatment he needed since he could not get a passport. The reason he could not get a passport spoke volumes about the cruelty and indifference of the Russian adminis- tration. He had to be photographed by an authorized photographer for his passport to be valid. His family dared not take him out of the room, since it upset him too much.

The photographer was too arrogant to come to this room, even if it might have meant an easier life for a terrified and ruined child. As a result, he had no valid passport and no chance of treatment.

Across the other side of the town was the Republican Children's Hospital, where staff and patients were bundled into huge coats against the cold, and the only heating was naked gas flames in the corridors. Doctors and nurses were doing what they could but they lacked medicines, resources and equipment, and the health situation was disastrous.

Sultan Alimkhadzhiyev, the head doctor at the hospital, welcomed me to his office but had none of the exuberant Chechen hospitality when he described the horrors he dealt with every day.

'Almost all the children, probably 80 per cent, have psychological trauma. They have seen death, explosions. That's about 300,000 children,' he told me.

Infant mortality, he said, was probably 50 per 1,000 – double the level in the rest of Russia – and he guessed that every fourth or fifth child born had some kind of birth defect, reflecting the terrible state of their mothers.

While aid had been pouring into Beslan to help the children rebuild their shattered lives, he was left with just the hard-working staff of his hospital to try to reconstruct a whole country's future.

I could see why Chechens would be angered by what Russia had done to them. And it was that anger, caused by Russia's total destruction of Chechen society, that was driving Basayev's attacks on his enemies wherever he might find them. But it was enough to remember the morgue in Vladikavkaz, where the children were laid out like lengths of timber in a saw mill, to know that his response was wrong.

It did not help the children of Chechnya if the children of Beslan suffered, and no matter how horrible Basayev's response, the Russian state could withstand anything he threw at it.

No one mourned Basayev when he died in an explosion in July 2006, ending a chapter in Chechen history more terrible than anything before it.

When I think of his victims, I always remember first that boy in the morgue with the butter-pale face. The serenity of his features in that place of death was touching. I was holding cotton wool dipped in some strong-smelling liquid to my nose – it was being given out by medical assistants – to hide the smell, but there was no hiding from the horrors before my eyes. There had been no horror in his face though. It was whole and undamaged.

I do not know his name, but in my mind I imagine that he might have been Kazbek Bichegov-Begoshvili, a nine-year-old boy who died in the siege.

I became, during my repeated visits to Beslan, friendly with Kazbek's parents. By the time the first anniversary came round, they had a new baby. They called him Sarmat.

'I decided to have this child for my wife. She was crying all the time. And maybe I did it for myself as well, to make it easier for me. For my soul,' explained Roman, the baby's father, as we drank vodka on one of my many visits to the family in their home just a hundred metres from School No. 1.

Roman looked shattered, a decade at least older than his forty-two years. Most of the time he smoked, standing in the courtyard outside his single-storey home, and looked blankly into the distance. Sometimes we smoked together. Sometimes we talked, but most of the time we did not.

Sometimes we could hear Sarmat crying inside the house, a new life untouched by the siege. Perhaps he will grow up to be a man in a Caucasus without war.

'I want Sarmat's life to be happy, not just his life, but all our children's lives. We have to hope this new generation will be without grief,' said his mother Zarema as she held him in her arms.

But, with the heavy load of anger and deprivation weighing down a new generation growing up just a hundred kilometres away in Grozny, I fear the cycle of violence will not stop just because she wishes it.

28. I Cannot Even Raise My Eyes towards Them

The victims and bereaved relatives of Basayev's actions rarely got the chance to see their attackers face punishment for what they did. Suicide bombers did not survive to face justice, and the hostage-takers also tended to know they were on a one-way mission.

That was why the trial of Nurpashi Kulayev, a Chechen man born in 1980, was so extraordinary when it opened in May 2005 in the city of Vladikavkaz.

While gunfire had cracked overhead, and the rebels within the Beslan school building battled with special forces troops outside, he had been picked up by police trying to escape from the building.

He was not local, and he barely spoke Russian, so it did not take the police long to work out that he had been part of the group of hostage-takers. He was the only one that survived and so became a target for all the hatred and anger directed at the group of armed men who had brought death to School No. 1.

On the first day, as a prosecutor tried to read out the charges against Kulayev, the bereaved relatives packed into the tiny courtroom screamed and shouted at the defendant. Judge Tamerlan Aguzarov was forced to appeal to the crowd.

'Let's not make this process into a disgrace,' he said, but his words had little effect. He postponed the session to another day, and he was forced to order that Kulayev's head be shaved. The crowd was angry that the defendant's long dark hair was obscuring his face.

The start of the second session was much the same.

'I ask you all to calm down,' the judge said, but again with no response.

'He should be forced onto his knees,' a woman shouted from the crowd.

And so it continued throughout that whole second day. Kulayev remained standing – voluntarily, as it happened; he could have sat down – as the judge read out the long charge list, including a list of all the victims of the attack which alone took ten minutes to detail. The slim, dark-haired, dark-eyed, pale figure in the defendant's cage was charged with terrorism, hostage-taking, murder and more – a whole litany of charges that seemed to span the entire Russian criminal code. The women and men in the courtroom stared at him with hatred. At the end of that long day, he was asked whether he accepted his guilt.

'No,' he said, mumbling through his thick Chechen accent. He was asked to repeat himself, and to speak more loudly.

'You shouted well in the hall,' one woman yelled at him from the crowd.

'Not guilty,' he said. 'I was there because of my brother.'

His chances of persuading the court that he was not guilty seemed slim. The awesome moral force of the bereaved mothers of Beslan was already being felt by the Russian government. They demanded a full inquiry into the disaster, and received visits by some of Putin's top officials on a regular basis. It was impossible that a single judge would withstand their desire for vengeance and go easy on the defendant. Kulayev discovered this when he asked if he could have a translator.

'I am not agree. I without translator, I cannot completely. I badly understand in Russian. Without a translator I cannot, I have said. I do not know in Russian,' he said in broken and thickly accented Russian, but he won no sympathy from the judge.

'What? You don't understand Russian? You speak Russian beautifully,' the judge replied.

Even I could tell he did not speak Russian beautifully. His accent was so thick as to be almost incomprehensible, but his request was denied – the prosecutors weighed in as well to try to persuade him that having a translator was not in his interests, since it would make it difficult to ask questions – and the trial got under way.

The hearings were chaotic. Rows of women in black with headscarves packed the benches in the small hall on the first floor of the court building. Journalists sat downstairs, where a television link played a simultaneous recording of the events. Even from there it was obvious that the judge was failing to keep control.

Under Russian law, there are not just two sides to a case – the defence and prosecution – but also a side representing the victims. The victims now had the chance to question the defendant, the judge and the lawyers on almost any question they wanted. Regularly, they launched into long conversations with one of the other participants, or with each other. And since there were more than 1,000 victims – the former hostages or the killed hostages' bereaved relatives – the process threatened to last for ever.

Often, the judge had to call a halt to proceedings to calm down the angry women, who had organized themselves into a group called the Beslan Mothers. They had their own interests, and wanted a full inquiry into the events. They believed Kulayev could tell them more than he was being allowed to say, and regularly expressed sympathy for him.

But the majority of the victims and the witnesses had no such warm feelings. Hatred boiled out of people when they were asked to make any comments about him, regularly showing the amount of thought that had gone into fantasies of revenge.

'I have heard that Kulayev beat children with the butt of his rifle. Maybe he killed them, or not, but he beat them. And kicked them. Which children, I do not know. But that he abused children, that is certain. He is guilty just because he was in the band. And he should be tried on all articles of the law. He should be shot. Take him out on the square and shoot him. He should be lynched. Three hundred children have been killed, 330 people,' said one man at the start of a long, scarcely coherent rant against the defendant.

'There should not be just punishment. Shoot him! The highest form of punishment ... Mr Judge, I ask you, believe no one, he was in the band, that means he is already guilty on all counts. All. If I had been there, I also would have been shot. The highest form of punishment. Because I would already have been in a group. It was a common group. Common. This group came together to take the school. They all know well that he was going somewhere.'

With witnesses dissolving into such anger, it is not surprising that the trial failed to establish much in the way of evidence. Kulayev's attempts to defend himself – which we will come to – were ignored by almost everyone. Victims came and asked him the same questions over and over again. Why had he attacked their children? Why had he attacked them? Who had been his accomplices? And so it went on for sixty-one court sessions of grief and chaos.

Some witnesses, like the man quoted above, said Kulayev had beaten children, or shot in the air, but the majority said they had not seen him, and their evidence did nothing but complicate an already tangled mess of evidence. Some said he had been kind to them, and nicer than the other hostage-takers. But there did not seem any logic to the process. There was no attempt to establish which testimony was correct, or even to pretend the court was fair.

'Who taught you to fight, so as to kidnap small children? Why could you not have attacked a military base?' asked the judge at one point, leaving no doubt that he had already made up his own mind about Kulayev's guilt.

And, in truth, who could believe this man's protestations of innocence? Kulayev had been caught escaping from the school, he admitted having been inside. His claims not to have fired a gun and to have not killed a hostage seemed farcical. There was no doubt at all, from the very start, that he would be convicted. And he duly was.

The prosecutors asked for the death penalty – even though Russia has proclaimed a moratorium on its use – but the judge did not impose it. Sentencing Kulayev to death would have meant obliging Putin to pardon him, which would not have been a popular decision with the Kremlin, so Kulayev received life imprisonment. It appeared to be a fair end for an evil man.

Even his lawyer, a 25-year-old who had held a lawyer's licence for just a fortnight and who was only appointed to represent him ten days before the trial opened, clearly did not believe his client was innocent, and did not pretend to when appearing in court.

'Of course, I did not want to defend him, but it is hard to argue with the decision of the court,' he told one local journalist after the first session.

'Such cases cannot be examined without a lawyer in court. I was the duty lawyer at that time and I could not refuse,' he added, desperate to justify himself before his people, and to reassure them that he did not like or believe Kulayev.

'I do not think this will mark the death of my career. I think there is an understanding that the defence of Kulayev is an obligation.'

Although I am not saying the lawyer did not do his job as well as he could, it is hard to see how this attitude was in his client's interests. He even began his summing up of his client's defence with an apology.

'My position as lawyer of the accused Kulayev is very difficult, and internally contradictory,' he said.

'You must understand me, I am a lawyer. I am tied to the position of my defendant. The defendant has the right to choose, his lawyer does not. Today I am not defending the crime, I am defending the rights of my defendant.'

Without even the faith of his lawyer, it was hard to sympathize with Kulayev. But after the trial, the vision of the gaunt, hollow-eyed man in his cage stayed with me. I only attended three of the sixty-seven sessions – it took six sessions for the judge to read out the 120,000 words of the sentence and summing up – but twice while I was listening the defendant had said the same thing.

'I was there because of my brother,' he had said. I wondered for a while what he meant, then I forgot about it. A little while later, however, I discovered that a liberal activist keen on media freedom had paid for a secretary to type up a full record of all the court hearings, and had posted the transcripts on her website.

Having a spare few hours, I decided to go back and scan through the transcripts to find out what he had meant about his brother. I was interested in what would turn a normal human being into the kind of homicidal maniac who would abuse children to make a political point.

But I did not find any information to help me with that at all. The more of the transcripts I read, the more disturbed I became. Piecing together my own notes and the transcripts, I came to a worrying realization. Kulayev may not have been guilty at all. In fact, he may have been the unluckiest person to come out of School No. 1 alive.

No human rights groups or journalists have advocated for him. His cause, not surprisingly, has not proved popular with activists. Convicted terrorists are not prone to attracting sympathy. So I have no second opinion to back up my conclusions. But I approached the evidence with an open mind, something his own lawyer and the rest of the court failed to do. The result was startling.

In his summing up of the case, the judge rejected the defendant's not guilty plea in a few sentences. He specifically quoted two Chechen witnesses – Zarema Muzhakhoyeva, the failed suicide bomber whose story is detailed in the previous chapter, and Rustam Ganiyev, a captured Chechen rebel also mentioned in the previous chapter – as confirming that Kulayev had been a member of Shamil Basayev's group of militants and that his own claims not to have been a militant were a lie.

This was my first disturbing discovery, because, in saying that, the judge was wrong. Neither of the two Chechen witnesses said anything of the kind.

Ganiyev, it transpired, had lived in the same house as Kulayev and Kulayev's brother, a former comrade-in-arms, and he knew the defendant well.

'Did Nurpashi have relations to the rebels?' asked a prosecutor.

'He did not,' answered Ganiyev.

As if that was not sufficiently categorical a rejection to satisfy the judge, a little later Kulayev himself asked the witness to confirm the point again.

'Have you ever heard that I fought, or that I had weapons?' asked the defendant.

'You did not, I said, you did not. I know you, because I lived in your house and everything. I saw you there and everyone else from your family.'

It is possible of course that the Chechen was lying to defend a friend or a comrade, but it is strange that the judge should so completely misrepresent not only what he said, but also what the second Chechen witness would go on to say. Muzhakhoyeva had also, it transpired, lived in the same house as Kulayev and knew him and his wife well.

'Nurpashi Kulayev as far as I saw did not play any role. They never told him about any terrorist acts being prepared. He lived there with his wife Zhanna ... He could go out, and they'd say: "Go, buy bread, or milk." That's all. His wife never wore a veil even. He did not pray particularly. I related to him, let's say, like to a decent person, not like to the others.'

According to her testimony, there were four rooms in the house, but Kulayev as the least significant person was left to sleep in the corridor. As the evidence continued, it departed further and further from the judge's summary of it. She said she never saw Kulayev with weapons, and also that he did not follow the extreme Wahhabi strand of Islam favoured by the others.

'I never saw him make his wife wear a veil, like I or the other women had to. He never prayed together with these rebels,' she said.

Again, we might assume she was just trying to defend a friend of hers, but then she specifically said that she was not.

'You are for some reason separating him from the rebels,' remarked a prosecutor.

'I am not separating him out because I want to defend him. I would never defend him, nowhere and never, after what happened. I am just saying what was. Anyone who was with us, Ganiyev, or Kodzoyev, they all could confirm that his wife did not wear the veil, and he was separate from the others,' she said.

She herself condemned him for what had happened in the school, but the very words she used could not help but raise doubts about his guilt. This was particularly the case when she later described how she came back from her failed suicide mission to Mozdok.

'I was categorically banned from speaking to his wife, or from telling him who I was or where they were taking me. They did not trust him. This I can say. And on the last day, when they took me to Moscow, his wife ran up to me. She was hysterical and said: "Zarema, where are they taking you? You should stay with us." And when I told them where I was being taken, she was just in shock. I was completely banned from talking to him or his wife.'

It was impossible to conclude from the evidence of these two Chechen witnesses that Kulayev and his brother had 'both been members of an armed group headed by Shamil Basayev', as the judge had done. The judge clearly did not listen to their evidence very closely, but how exactly did the two Chechens' words tie in with Kulayev's own account? And what did he mean, when he said he was just there 'because of his brother'? That was a story he told on the first day of the trial.

He had, he said, moved in with his brother in 2003, because his brother had lost an arm in an explosion, and needed help to repair his house. On 31 August 2004 – the day before the attack on the school – he had left the house to go a shop, and he had been picked up by a group of rebels.

'They picked me up. Because of my brother. They asked about my brother. "Your brother, where does he live? We have looked for him two or three days",' said Kulayev, speaking in the short sentences used by Chechens who do not speak Russian well.

'Then I went home and told my brother, some, some person has come for you, you should go to this place to see him.'

His brother went out for twenty minutes, came back, then took Kulayev and an eighteen-year-old friend called Islam out with him. They all went together to a rebel base, just outside the village of Sagopshi. His brother argued with the rebels. It transpired they were suspicious that he had been allowed out of detention, where he had been kept for four or five months, and not charged. They thought he might have agreed to work for the Russians in exchange for his freedom. Kulayev and his friend Islam were left to sit around with nothing to do.

'They said to me and Islam, make something to eat. They said, you will sit here, until someone says what to do,' he said. His brother continued to argue with the group of armed men, of whom there were about eighteen. Two Ossetian men, one of whom had long hair, took Kulayev aside, and began to demand to know if he or his brother was working for the Russians.

'They said, we will cut you up anyway, tell the truth. I said, I have nothing to say, my brother is not working. Then this Ossetian and another one brought Islam. They said, wait, dig yourself a grave and then let's see. They gave us spades. Dig yourself graves, they said.'

That proved to be an empty threat, but it was enough to terrify Kulayev. His brother went up to him and said he was not being allowed to go home, since he had seen the rebels' base. His brother then went on to say they had somewhere to go that evening, and that Kulayev and Islam would be dropped off by the side of the road somewhere.

That evening, they were loaded onto the truck and driven over-night to Beslan. The two young men were the last to get out of the cab of the truck. By the time they had done so, children and adults were being driven screaming into the sports hall.

By his own account, he walked into the hall where the hostages were being gathered and stood there for just a few minutes. He was then placed in the cafeteria with Islam and remained there for almost the entire time of the siege. He was given a rifle only after the school had been seized. One of the guerrillas had been killed, and he said the leader of the group – whom he called the Colonel – gave it to him and told him to look after it.

For three days, he said he sat there with nothing to do or to eat, except for a Snickers chocolate bar. When the storm operation started, a tank began to shoot at his side of the building, and the grill over the window was ripped off. He jumped out of the window, so as to tell the soldiers not to shoot.

'I said, don't shoot, there are people, there are no rebels there. They detained me at once, they did not let me talk more. They took me somewhere. In some basement they began to interrogate me.'

And that, improbably enough, was his story. He enraged the prosecu-tors, who demanded that he recognize his guilt, but he continued to insist that he did not know Basayev, that he did not have a gun, that he had never fired at the hostages, that he had never killed anyone, that he did not take part in planning the raid, and that he was not guilty.

'We will assess your action. We need you to understand. We need you to know, you to say, what happened. That you were in an armed group, which attacked a school. That you held weapons in your hands, that there was an attack on policemen, on special forces. That this Colonel gave you orders. I am explaining it to you simply, what is not clear? And the next article, the taking of hostages. Did you take hostages? Did you gather them, and not let them go? Here is another point, article 206, 105, where you say you did not kill. Then how did it happen, that 330 people died in this tragedy?' demanded a prosecutor.

'I did not kill anyone,' replied Kulayev. 'I know that more than 300 people were killed. I understand these people. I have never killed anyone in my life. I have never taken part in anything, not in terrorist acts, nowhere. Is there just one bit of evidence that I was in a band or was seen with someone? I did not do this. How can I say that I did all this? I will accept responsibility for everything if there is just one bit of evidence that I was in a band. The only thing was we were taken to Beslan, forced to. If I knew where we were going, they could not have taken me there.'

And, by the end of the cross-examinations, they had failed to force him to admit to anything. And the extraordinary thing was that in the whole course of the case, he never did. Because of the strange format of the court, he was permanently being asked the same questions: why did he kill the children? How could he do such a thing? The questioners were people with anger and moral authority that it is hard to imagine, but he never once changed his story.

Even the way he carried himself seemed strange. He did not have the certainty of a committed rebel fighter, like Ganiyev, for example, who was combative when he talked to the prosecutors and arrogant in his answers.

Kulayev, who stood to hear the charges against him although he did not have to, always said that he was sorry for the bereaved relatives, and that he would never have allowed himself to be taken to the school had he known what was about to happen.

'Kulayev, all this evil happened with your participation,' said a prosecutor at one point.

'I know this,' he replied.

'That is why I ask. How do you relate to these actions? Now, before these victims, looking them in the eyes.'

'I cannot even raise my eyes towards them,' he said.

Again and again, he came back to the point that he would never have harmed children.

'I am sad for them, of course. A child is a child. To any Muslim, and I am a Muslim, of course I am sad for them. But what could I have done? A child before the age of seven is considered an angel, I know. I could not even raise my hand to a child, even if he was killing me,' he told one woman questioning him.

So how can we understand this? Was he just defending himself by a long and improbable lie? Was he so soul-less that he was prepared to not only kill children for a political cause, but also then lie about it?

Perhaps he was not lying at all, and it certainly looked that way from the testimony of Alik Tsagonov, one of the few hostages to have a clear recollection of Kulayev in the school. Tsagonov was forced into the cafeteria after the explosions that triggered the Russian assault to free the school. A group of hostages were made to sit on the floor while the rebels fired out of the windows over their heads. He admitted that he did not remember everything clearly, but he was certain that Kulayev was sitting among the hostages, not battling the army like the rest of the rebels.

'I did not see that he had weapons at that moment. When he sat among us, he had nothing in his hands. When he spoke, we understood that he was one of them. Sveta Bigaeva sat near us, she said to me: "He is reacting to what we are saying." And we were talking in Ossetian. I asked him: "Do you understand Ossetian?" He said to me: "I understand a little." These were the words that he said first: "I killed no one. I want to live",' the witness said.

Kulayev later had the chance to cross-examine the witness himself, and asked him if he remembered a fifteen-minute conversation they had about a man in Chechnya who might have been a mutual friend.

'Tell me, when I sat with you, do you remember how I told you how we were brought there, taken from our home? I explained to you. I of course could not speak well in Russian. Do you remember this?' Kulayev asked. He was talking to a man who had no cause to like him, or to defend him, but the witness backed him up.

'He said this as well. He said he was forced, that he did not want to go. But, how it was, it could not all be saved in my head. All his words,' Tsagonov said.

'Well, I said to you, when they started to fire from the tanks. Do you remember, I said, they will now shoot the ground and first floors. And then they will start shooting here. Therefore, whoever of us, let them jump out now. And then you said to me: "You jump out, and tell them there are children here." And then, when they fired from the tanks, when you said, there were explosions on the first floor, and the cage [from the window] fell. A rebel shot one lad, a child. And you said to me: "Jump out." And I jumped out,' said Kulayev, desperate to have his story at least a little confirmed.

The witness could not in fact support everything that Kulayev said, saying he could not remember, but he did say that Kulayev had been the second person to jump out of the window.

Other witnesses had vague memories of Kulayev running around with a gun, and terrorizing them, but Tsagonov's account is far more detailed, and at least raises doubts whether the defendant was the dedicated jihadi depicted in the charge sheet.

Be that as it may, the judge rejected Tsagonov's testimony in favour of the more numerous, but less specific, evidence of people who said they saw Kulayev in camouflage clothes shooting uncontrollably with an automatic rifle. (Kulayev himself insisted he was wearing the white clothes and trainers that he left his house in, and did not shoot at anyone.)

In his final summing up, the judge rejected also Kulayev's own testimony, and the elaborate story about his brother. The judge compared Kulayev's words to statements the defendant made in detention prior to the court hearing. In those statements, which bore the defendant's signature, Kulayev admitted many of the charges against him, including that of being part of an armed group.

But, taking into account Kulayev's own cross-examination, those documents themselves seem doubtful.

'Did you read them before you signed,' asked one of the lawyers.

'I did not read.'

'Why did you not read?'

'I do not know the Russian language,' replied Kulayev.

'From the moment of your detention, you were offered a lawyer. Were you always interrogated in the presence of a lawyer?'

'No, he was only there three times in five months, I think,' said Kulayev.

'But now you are being questioned in the presence of your lawyer. You and your lawyer sign the documents, after they have been read by you personally, and you write that you personally read it at the end of the document. What can you say now?'

'In these months, I only saw my lawyer twice. Where they told me to sign, I signed.'

The judge ignored this testimony, instead using the circular argument that Kulayev must have voluntarily signed the documents – documents the defendant said he had not read, or agreed to, and only signed because he was beaten – since he had also signed a statement declaring he had voluntarily signed the documents.

So, that was the judge's argument. The testimony of the two Chechen witnesses was rewritten to support the prosecution case. Kulayev's own testimony was rejected in favour of earlier testimony that the defendant said had been beaten out of him. And testimony by hostages that could have been used to support Kulayev was ignored.

It was hardly a model trial, but that was no surprise. Trials in Russia rarely are. But the most important thing is: was Kulayev really guilty? Just because the trial was a farce, does that mean he was not guilty?

And here, obviously, it is harder to judge without spending months traipsing from house to house in Chechnya and Beslan compiling information about a convicted terrorist who has already failed his appeal. This is not a job for the faint-hearted, since it would attract police interest within minutes, and I confess it is one I am not brave enough to undertake.

And yet to my mind, his story that he shot no one in the school makes sense, if only because of the vagueness of the testimony against him and the consistency of his denial of having done any of it. His story somehow seems too unlikely not to be true. True jihadis boasted about what they had done, or tried to justify it. They did not flatly deny it.

And what about the beginning? Is it really possible that he had been picked up by rebels and forced to go with them just because his brother was suspected of having changed sides and gone over to the Russians? And here, there are problems, since, frankly, the story does not make much sense.

Why would the rebels who took his brother take him too? What did it matter to them that he came with them? This is the only bit of the story that does not seem logically coherent.

And this is where the chaotic, disorganized and biased nature of the trial is most frustrating, because on three occasions he gave out hints – or even firm comments – that there was more to it than he had at first said. If only more-insistent lawyers had been present, they would have followed up on what he said in passing.

Questioned as he was by non-skilful interrogators who did not in any case care very much, crucial hints were missed that could have explained why he was taken to the school in the first place. And once you see the hints, his whole story makes sense.

The first time he dropped one of his hints was right at the beginning, during his own lawyer's cross-examination of him. If he had had a competent lawyer – or perhaps a lawyer who wanted to defend him – it is surely impossible that what he said could have been missed.

When the rebels first picked him up, when he was on his way to the shop, and said they were looking for his brother, they took Kulayev 'away somewhere', he had said. While there they asked him about his brother, but they also asked him if he worked for Ramzan Kadyrov, a rebel who changed sides to succeed his father as the Kremlin-backed president of the region.

'Do you work for Ramzan Kadyrov? I have documents. They took them off me, questioned me. Then they said to me, let your brother, let him come, we will wait for him where the roads cross,' Kulayev said.

It is hard to figure out exactly what he meant in those comments, since his Russian grammar is so mangled it could be several different things, but it looks very likely that he had some kind of documents, which fingered him as being in the employ of Ramzan Kadyrov, the sworn enemy of Shamil Basayev and the separatist rebels. Kadyrov – and another group of Chechens from the Yamadayev family – was the prop of Russia's control of Chechnya, and was hated by the rebels. If Kulayev had been working for him, they would have taken him away immediately and punished him as a traitor.

Kulayev let slip the next clue when Ganiyev was on the witness stand. Although Ganiyev was technically the one giving evidence, the complexity of the trial structure meant that Kulayev regularly spoke as well. At one point, he yet again insisted that he had nothing to do with the raid, and that he had been taken along against his will.

'What, you were taken as a translator?' asked the judge with heavy sarcasm, in light of Kulayev's bad Russian.

'No, I was taken, I said, because of my brother. I had been with Yamadayev, I had my documents with me. Later also the Kadyrov documents. Because of this they did not let me go. I was for three months a guard for Yamadayev, the general. When my brother was with Basayev, I was with him [Yamadayev] there. Because of this they brought me here,' he said.

This time, his story is far clearer. He had been initially picked up by rebels looking for his brother, but when they searched him they found the documents incriminating him as a foot-soldier for the other side and took him with them.

The final and most convincing clue came from the other Chechen witness: from the failed suicide bomber Muzhakhoyeva. She was cross-examined by the prosecutors, and the defence lawyer, and the judge, and the defendant, but it took someone with more presence than any of them to get to the bottom of the case.

Susanna Dudiyeva, who led the Beslan Mothers group, appears to have been the only participant to have picked up on Kulayev's remarks that he had worked for the pro-Moscow forces in Chechnya, and she asked Muzhakhoyeva about it.

'Nurpashi said that he was part of the guard of Kadyrov. He could be killed for this. And for this, he was taken there, to the terrorist act. Does this mean that Ganiyev and the others knew that he had joined Kadyrov's forces?' asked Dudiyeva, who is remarkably articulate and intelligent.

'You know,' replied Muzhakhoyeva, 'I have not said this before. But his wife told me all about this. And I told her: "Take your husband and leave." Because he had already been there [with Kadyrov], sooner or later they would either kill him or send him somewhere.'

'So he was in Kadyrov's forces?' asked Dudiyeva, who should have been a lawyer herself.

'Probably, yes. That is what his wife said.'

So perhaps this was Kulayev's great secret. The reason he was detained and taken to the school was that he had served in the forces fighting against the separatists. But then the question remains, surely he could have used this information to save himself? Could he not have called in one of the pro-Moscow Chechen leaders to testify in his defence?

Who can say why he did not do this? To find out, I would need to ask him myself, and he will not be available to speak to reporters any time soon. Perhaps, in fact, he was not able to bring witnesses to the trial. It is unlikely that his lawyer expended much energy in that direction.

Looking at my notebooks and the trial transcripts, I do not think he should have been found guilty of any of the crimes he was accused of on the evidence that was presented at his trial.

Perhaps he could be condemned for failing to stop the hostage-takers, or for not fighting them when he had the chance, but does that merit life imprisonment? Would either of those failures to take action even constitute a criminal act? Even if it did, no information was presented to justify such charges.

Guilty or not, though, his story is a sad one, and he was as much a victim of the violence as the people he was convicted of fighting against. For this new Chechen war that Moscow launched in 1999 turned Chechen against Chechen. Brother against brother. The savagery which both sides unleashed was enough to divide families, and to ruin a nation.

29. It was All for Nothing

The Chechens' national unity forged in the 1994–6 war did not last long, although at first there was broad agreement, after the Russians pulled out, that the Chechen state should be a democracy with elements of Islamic law.

Akhmad Kadyrov had been elected as *mufti* – the leading figure among Chechnya's Muslims – in the midst of the war in 1995 and called for jihad against the invaders. There is an extraordinary video clip on the internet in which Basayev and Kadyrov sit side by side – the warrior of Islam and the spiritual leader, united on one path – while Basayev lectures a room full of journalists about the Russian cities he will conquer.

'We will fight further. We will take, if it works out, we will take Vladivostok, we will take Khabarovsk and Moscow. We will fight till the end, and no one except Allah can stop us on this road,' shouts Basayev, pumping his fist, as the mufti sits stony-faced beside him.

Both men retained great influence in peacetime. They were going to build a state based on the principles of Islam. In February 1997, Kadyrov announced that women employed by the state would have to cover themselves up, showing only their face, hands and feet. Later that year, Aslan Maskhadov – elected president of the Chechens in January 1997 – introduced elements of Islamic law into the region.

But, beneath the surface, disputes were brewing. The puritan forms of Islam introduced to Chechnya by Arab volunteers and Saudi emissaries were loathed by the more easy-going Sufis like Kadyrov, who dominated traditional Islam in Chechnya and saw the new arrivals as a threat to their positions. The actual theological differences can seem slight, and often they consisted only of minor differences in praying posture, but they masked major disagreements in the path believers wanted to follow.

The Wahhabis, as the puritans were known, were often young people, flush with Saudi money, inspired by their military experiences, and keen for their influential wartime positions to persist in peacetime. At their head was, of course, Basayev, who had returned from his hostage-taking raid on the hospital in Budyonnovsk as a hero. He had allied himself with a Saudi jihadi called Khattab, who had access to Arab money. Between them they attracted a substantial private army, and threatened to destabilize a people already traumatized by war.

Kadyrov put himself at the head of those Chechens opposing the Wahhabis, and sought to block the spread of the energetic, aggressive Islam these young men preferred. He wanted to keep Chechen society in its former shape, to keep the influence of the older generation and the Qadiri sect that he belonged to. He saw the Wahhabis as a divisive influence bent on destroying the traditions and customs of the Chechen people.

There were probably only a few dozen foreign Muslim volunteers in the country, but their influence was disproportionately large. Kadyrov regularly campaigned against them, saying they should be expelled now that the war was won. He almost paid for it with his life in October 1998 when a bomb gutted his car and injured his driver. The dispute had become personal. Chechnya was already plagued by kidnappings and bombings – legacies of mass unemployment and the high number of weapons-trained men left with nothing much to do. Now the clashes became more organized, and Maskhadov – a decent man, even his enemies concede, but no politician – was fearful of cracking down, not wishing to take sides against the former comrades who made up both sides of the bitter dispute.

Kadyrov urged the president to organize an armed force of Sufis – a return to the days of Imam Shamil and the nineteenth century – to oppose the military wing of the puritans, as he sought to mobilize Chechen society behind his vision of the future. Maskhadov dithered.

Then, in August 1999, the divide became a gulf. Basayev and Khattab sent their fighters into Dagestan, which still remained a Russian region, to help their religious allies in the mountains break free from Russian rule. Whatever way you look at it, it was a stupid thing to do. It was an aggressive violation of the peace deal signed between Chechnya and Russia, and most Chechens thought it was unjustified and unnecessary.

There have since been dark rumours about how Russia – keen for an excuse to enter Chechnya once more – encouraged the raid by pulling back its border guards, but there can be no excuse for the actions of Basayev and his allies. They made a terrible strategic error. Russian special forces battled in the mountains, bombing villages controlled by the religious puritans, and using helicopters to strafe rebel positions. War had returned to the Caucasus after just three years.

Then came a series of devastating apartment bombings – in the Dagestani town of Buynaksk, in Moscow, and in the Russian town of Volgodonsk in September – which killed almost 300 sleeping civilians. The bombings were unforgivable, and Basayev was quick to deny any responsibility. But the prime minister, an ex-KGB man called Vladimir Putin who was almost unknown to the Russian public, was not listening to such denials. He declared that Chechens were behind the attacks and that his government had to move back into the republic to restore order.

As troops poured into Chechnya –100,000 of them or more, a far more serious invasion than that of 1994 – Maskhadov's and Basayev's forces united to defend Grozny. Their differences could be resolved another time. Like 1994, this was a war for national survival and surely all Chechens would take up arms once more against the common enemy. That did not happen. For the first time, Chechens did not rally together when attacked. Kadyrov had other plans.

He and his allies – including the Yamadayev clan, which would also become influential in the years ahead – gave up the town of Gudermes without a fight. The rebel fighters were asked to leave, and Russian troops were invited to occupy the town peacefully.

Kadyrov then travelled to Moscow to meet Putin, who probably could not believe his luck. That such a senior and respected Chechen leader was prepared to break ranks with his comrades, betray the national cause, and change sides with hardly any pressure being applied was a coup worth delaying a cabinet meeting for.

And on 18 November that is exactly what Putin did. He apologized to his ministers for keeping them waiting. 'We had an unexpected event in connection to the arrival of Akhmad Kadyrov, mufti of the Chechen republic, who at the request of the residents of

Gudermes came to Moscow, to the government, and unexpectedly asked for a meeting,' Putin said.

That a private individual could arrange such a meeting spontaneously was extraordinary, but Kadyrov was no ordinary person. He was offering to effectively split the Chechen people, something which had been Moscow's long-term dream. To him, the threat of the puritans was so serious that it trumped the threat of the Russians.

'Their only goal is to seize power under the cover of Islam,' he told Russian television, as he explained why he had appealed to the Russians for assistance against his former comrades. 'The people are against this terrorism and force. It is just necessary to help this people a bit, to support them. As the prime minister said, to find some kind of option so as to stop the killings, to stop the war. To find some kind of option, so as to move onto a different track.'

I met Kadyrov many times, and always thought he was a decent and honest man, but it is hard not to conclude that he was fooled here. He seems to have genuinely thought Putin wanted to avoid war, or that perhaps only a little bit of fighting would be required to dislodge the Wahhabis. Perhaps he thought the rest of the armed resistance would come round to his way of thinking as soon as he spoke out. They did not, and the Russians were not in the mood to wait for them to change their minds.

The onslaught that Putin launched on Grozny that winter of 1999–2000 was as bad as anything Chechnya had seen five years earlier. The splits in the nation hardened and crystallized. Maskhadov declared Kadyrov to be a traitor, and the penalty for a traitor in wartime would surely be death. Kadyrov meanwhile said he would not rest until Basayev, Khattab and the other 'kidnappers and murderers' were dead.

Before peace of a kind returned to Chechnya, Basayev and Khattab would indeed be killed. But Kadyrov and Maskhadov would be dead too. And more than 25,000 of their countrymen would die alongside them, while maybe 200,000 or more Chechens – 20 per cent of the total population – would flee into exile. It was a heavy price to pay for this handful of men's failure to reach agreement. And they are all to blame for that.

For Russia would not repeat its mistakes of the 1994–6 war this time. There were no tanks sent into built-up areas, until those areas were definitively pacified. There would be no handicapping of troops by any insistence on obeying human rights regulations. This was going to be a war of complete savagery.

It started with the taking of Grozny. In the 1994–6 war, Russia had lost thousands of men trying to fight its way into the city centre. Tanks without infantry support are extremely vulnerable to rocket-propelled grenades, especially if they are fired from the tower blocks that lined the roads into the Chechen capital. As the Russian forces edged into Chechnya, the rebels in Grozny prepared to meet them once more.

Among the rebels was Apti Bisultanov, the poet who led the nation's cultural reawakening in the 1970s and 1980s. Now he was deputy prime minister in Maskhadov's government, and one of the commanders trying to coordinate resistance to the Russian troops.

It was a task that he found all but impossible. The Russians had no intention of battling among the ruins of Grozny. They parked their missile launchers and artillery pieces on the hills around the capital and started to demolish it block by block. The rebels could do little but hide underground.

'Every unit had its headquarters in a basement, I knew every basement, who lived where, how many refugees were there, I knew every point,' Bisultanov told me one evening eight years later in a café in Berlin.

It was terrifying for the resistance fighters. The few television pictures taken from inside Grozny – mainly by the brave journalist Andrei Babitsky – showed trees with branches ripped off and scattered. Apartment blocks were chewed and gnawed, their corners rounded, their balconies shattered. The smaller private houses – single-storey dwellings that ringed the city centre – were shredded. Every basement held refugees or fighters.

The Russians were merciless. On 21 October, a rocket hit the central market, and Babitsky's images showed a mass of twisted metal. Perhaps as many as 140 civilians died, but the Russians brushed off criticism. The market, they said, had been used to trade weapons, as if that justified the horror they had unleashed.

It was a campaign to terrorize the population, and it worked. Hundreds of thousands of Chechens fled for neighbouring regions, where they were herded through filtration points, and all men between their teens and pensionable age were separated off for interrogation and detention.

And the fighters could do nothing. Just like Imam Shamil's forces before their final surrender, these men were being denied the chance to confront the enemy with their grenades and Kalashnikovs, and morale slipped away amid this constant attrition. The destruction of Grozny may not have brought glory to the Russian forces, but it was effective.

'It was complete anarchy. There was a plan for the defence of the city and I went to see these groups that were defending different parts. Some had stayed, and some had gone. The whole city, the civilian population, was underground. And the fighters were also down in the basements,' Babitsky remembered years later in his flat in Prague.

Fierce fighting continued around Grozny, but the Chechens were outnumbered and outgunned, and the capital was surrounded by December. The Chechens held out in their basements until February, resisting Russian advances via a complex network of defences, but they had realized they had to get out if they were not to die where they sat.

They prepared a corridor through the minefields to one of the villages outside the capital, but they knew casualties would be heavy.

Bisultanov was one of the desperate men trying to escape the disintegrating city.

'It was like this, the corridor,' he said, holding his hands thirty centimetres apart, 'and 5,000 men went along this corridor. One step aside would have been death. There were forty people in my group, which was called the special detachment because we were all educated. We had a political strategist, whom we had to leave behind because he was injured near Alkhankala. He could not stand, his back was ruined. There was a journalist who lost an eye.'

The Chechens had always prided themselves on recovering their wounded, but this death march in February 2000 defeated them. With artillery pounding around them, landmines on all sides, and in freezing temperatures, they left maybe 500 men dead and dying in the fields. Many of the top commanders were killed, and Basayev himself lost a foot to a landmine.

'Basayev blew up before my eyes,' remembered Bisultanov, shaking his head.

The rebel fighters were battered, tired and demoralized when they trudged into the village of Alkhankala. Medics treated their wounded, and the rest of the guerrillas reflected on their defeat.

'It was all for nothing,' one Chechen commander told a French journalist who witnessed the retreat and met the rebels in Alkhankala.

'I'm ashamed, ashamed to be here in this village, ashamed to put its residents in danger. But I'm especially ashamed to have lost so many young men in an unsuccessful campaign. Now I must go to their parents. What am I going to say to them?'

And even here, when all the men were united in their grief and shame, the split in the nation could be felt.

'I've had enough of these politicians and of these Wahhabis I've been fighting the last few years. Now we're condemned to fight on to the last. I told Shamil [Basayev] not to go to Dagestan. He never listens to anybody … Behind us, we've left so many dead bodies, not only our own men but also civilians. There's nobody left to bury them.'

The French journalist Anne Nivat wrote in her book *Chienne de guerre* how she saw Basayev himself in the hospital as doctors operated on his mangled leg. The other fighters shouldered their weapons and moved on out. Grozny was lost. It was around now that Putin announced for the first time that the war was over.

As for Bisultanov, he was unharmed, but he was exhausted by what had happened. He and thousands more of the survivors waited – stunned – in Komsomolskoye, just outside Grozny. Then came the disaster that the rebels had avoided in Grozny. The Russians surrounded the village with tanks and shattered it. For more than two weeks, the Russians bombed and shelled the houses of the village. Hundreds of the rebels died. Organized resistance was crushed.

The Chechens would fight on, but as guerrillas. This would not be a war of frontlines any more.

And behind the Russian troops came the policemen and the interrogators. In the Grozny suburb of Aldy on 5 February, civilians paid the price for the army's failure to destroy the group of fighters leaving the capital. Soldiers rampaged through Aldy, executing civilians at point-blank range, throwing grenades into cellars, and stealing valuables. It was a campaign of terror, deliberately designed to stop normal Chechens from supporting Maskhadov's forces.

Such operations as that in Aldy – called by the Russians 'cleansings' – became common in Chechen villages. Troops would close off streets and go from house to house, checking passports, and taking away men who matched their profile of rebels. These men would vanish into the system of 'filtration camps', and often never be seen again.

Khadzhimurat Yandiyev was one such man. A bearded young fighter, he was detained by Russian troops in early 2000, and came face to face with a general. As it happened, a television crew from the CNN channel was present, and it is a remarkable sign of the impunity with which Russian officers felt they could operate that General Alexander Baranov was able to order his troops to kill him while being filmed.

'Get him the heck out of here,' the general shouted, according to CNN's rather prim translation of far cruder Russian words. 'Rub him out, kill him, damn it. That's your entire order. Get him over there. Rub him out. Shoot him.'

Yandiyev was never seen in public again, and it looked like a clear case of murder. The Russian authorities did not agree, however. Prosecutors closed their criminal case into his disappearance in 2004, citing a lack of evidence – a scarcely credible decision in the circumstances.

Yandiyev's mother wanted justice, however, and took the case to Strasbourg, to the European Court of Human Rights, which ruled in July 2006 that the Russian state had violated Yandiyev's 'right to life'. In short, he had been murdered by the government. The Russian government claims to take human rights seriously, but it is necessary only to look at the career of General Baranov – the man who issued the order to murder Yandiyev – to see that it does not. By May 2008, he had risen to be commander of the North Caucasus Military District, with responsibility for all of southern Russia.

The Strasbourg court's ruling has been followed by others like it, but most Chechens are unable to win such high-profile assessments of their plight. For most of the estimated 5,000 disappearances that have taken place in Chechnya since 1999, there is no evidence to produce in court except for the continuing absence of a human being as mute proof of the horrors of the war.

Despite the overwhelming force used by the Russians, the Chechens continued to resist, and abuses of civilians have become commonplace on both sides. Brave human rights activists gather details, but they are largely ignored by the Russian authorities and by the world's media, which has got bored of this dirty little war.

Every month, people vanished and people died, winning Chechnya a position as one of only three places in the world with the maximum score of 5 on the United Nations assessment of danger. What became commonplace in Chechnya would have been enough to cause panic in many other countries.

Taking one month at random – this is the first month I have got records for in my notes – here is a summary of the human rights abuses in Chechnya in September 2002, as compiled by the umbrella group the Union of Non-governmental Organizations.

An eighteen-year-old vanished, after being detained by the Russians. Artillery was fired at the village of Avturi, killing cattle. A young man was detained by the Russians, and only released after a ransom was paid. An explosion hit the village of Achkhoi-Martan. A pro-Moscow Chechen's house was robbed. A human arm was found in the forest. 'Cleansings' took place in mountainous areas. Artillery struck mountainous areas. A court bailiff was murdered. A pro-Moscow administrator's cousin was murdered. A Chechen man was paraded on television as a terrorist, after being severely beaten. Security measures were tightened. Soldiers searched houses. The village of Prigorodnoye underwent a 'cleansing'. An administration building was burned down. A family was killed by artillery. A pro-Moscow Chechen was shot dead. Chechen refugees were forced home. More 'cleansings' were conducted in Prigorodnoye. A mass grave of Chechens who had previously been taken by the Russians was found, six of them identified with names and dates of birth. A policeman was killed. Soldiers detained farmers, and killed a calf for their lunch. Four men were detained in Grozny. A local official was arrested for links with the rebels. Russian troops stole things when conducting a 'cleansing'. Eleven men were detained in a 'cleansing'. Two men and a child were detained in a 'cleansing'. A body was found. There was another 'cleansing'. Eleven people were killed and twenty-two injured when a bus was blown up in Grozny. Drunken soldiers murdered three security guards at Grozny market (their heads were delivered to the hospital, their bodies dumped). Artillery and aerial bombing was deployed against mountainous regions. A policeman was killed. Soldiers searched a home, wounded the owner, and left. A holy site was bombed. There were air raids. Four men were killed when a Russian armoured vehicle drove over the top of a car.

And so it went on, month after month. Chechnya was terrifyingly dangerous.

That danger was one of the reasons that the media did not report on the daily horrors that Chechens were living through. It was extremely difficult to ensure safety in the region, plus strict Russian restrictions on reporting made it hard to remain inside the law. Foreign journalists were only supposed to visit the region on specially organized trips, in which we would be taken to see pro-Kremlin youth groups, or a restored school, and kept safely isolated from anyone who might tell us what was really going on.

Often the only chance we had to get a real picture of what was happening was by talking to the Russian soldiers whose barracks we slept in. They were always happy to drink vodka at our expense, and their drunken boasts of battles and firefights were in marked contrast to the official line that all was calm.

This official image of Chechnya as a tranquil little backwater was supported by the army's daily press releases, which detailed how many rebels had been killed, and how little support the rebels had from the local population. I remember one weekend when the rebels raided Grozny, and the distortion in the Kremlin's press tactics became amusingly clear. The rebels had established checkpoints in the middle of the city in the evening, and stopped all cars driving past. Anyone with papers from the pro-Moscow administration was summarily executed. Dozens were killed. It was a dramatic demonstration of their continuing presence.

'Grozny was quiet this weekend. City transport was working, and people went to cafés and little shops,' said the press release on the Monday morning.

The Russian media meanwhile seemed more than happy to follow the Kremlin's line, although there were some notable exceptions – among whom, inevitably, was Andrei Babitsky, the daring reporter who was later to interview Basayev.

Babitsky was in Grozny for most of that terrible autumn and winter in 1999–2000. He filmed the bombardment of Grozny, and his images – some of which featured dead Russian soldiers, and thus contradicted official denials of casualties – enraged the Kremlin. Obviously, it could be difficult for him to phone his wife or his office in the circumstances, but he tried to keep in contact as often as he could. His broadcasts on the US-funded Radio Free Europe (called Radio Liberty in Russia) were the only independent view of what was happening inside the besieged city.

'In November 1999, I had gone in with a group of journalists. But in January 2000, I was on my own, and I did not know the city, it was so changed. Eventually I decided to leave. I am Russian with accreditation, and I thought there could be no objections to me,' Babitsky remembered.

'But they detained me immediately as a suspicious person.'

Babitsky was picked up by the Russian army, and was about to learn that the Kremlin viewed investigative journalists as enemy combatants. The film he had shot in November had made some Kremlin officials link him to Basayev, and they were not going to allow him to escape and damage their cause with more footage. They confiscated his tapes and took him to their military base outside Grozny. He received no explanation as to why he had been detained, but on 18 January he was moved on to the prison of Chernokozovo, the most notorious of the Kremlin's 'filtration camps'.

'They treated us like livestock. Some official told a journalist that I had been detained as a vagrant even though this was not true because I had documents. They told me nothing, I was just in a cell in Chernokozovo. They also told journalists I had been helping the illegal armed forces,' he said.

At first, he was confined in a cell with fifteen other people with just a dirty mattress to lie on, and a hole in the floor to use as a toilet. There was only one other Russian – a tramp the army had picked up – and the rest were Chechens.

He spent three days in that cell, and all around were the sounds of the inmates being beaten. There was screaming twenty-four hours a day. At one point, a woman screamed for two hours straight. He personally was lucky, and was only hit with a truncheon a few times. It hurt for two days though, he said.

'There was one fighter there, all the other lads were just village boys. This one man they thought was a fighter they beat in the most appalling ways, they would take him away. For those first three days, the sound of beating used to go on all the time,' Babitsky said.

His wife Lyudmila had no idea where he had got to, and her fears increased on 21 January when agents from the FSB – one of the security forces in charge of running the 'filtration camps' – came to demand negatives Babitsky had left with her last time he was in Moscow. Eventually, on 25 January, Radio Free Europe broadcast an announcement that its journalist was missing. Worried, the station's editor met one of Putin's advisers, was told Babitsky was in Russian custody and won a promise that his journalist would be released. But there was a twist.

Babitsky, it transpired, was not being flown back to Moscow to his wife and colleagues at all, but was being exchanged with the rebels for two captured Russians, as if he was a prisoner of war. It was a telling sign of how the Kremlin regarded the press.

Putin was asked how he could justify handing over a Russian citizen to people he himself had dubbed bandits. 'For me it was more important to return these two Russian soldiers who were fighting on our side,' Putin, who would shortly be elected president, was quoted as saying by the Russian press.

The Kremlin's story was not even true. The handover was a sham set up for the cameras. Babitsky was not being handed to the rebels at all, but to some Russian allies who could look convincingly Chechen for the cameras.

The FSB had been on hand to film the encounter, and the grainy footage showed an unshaven Babitsky, wearing a patterned sweater, being led forward and handed over to two men in masks. He was clearly reluctant to go with them, but he looked weary and stunned.

The man to whom Babitsky was handed was not a member of the resistance at all, but a bandit with connections to the Russian police who kept him locked in a room in the village of Avturi, to the east of Grozny. 'It was particularly scary in Avturi,' Babitsky remembered. 'I thought they could kill me at any time. I thought they were just waiting for the signal to liquidate me. I was just kept in a house. I sat from morning to evening with two guards. I was convinced they would kill me, it was a very unpleasant time.'

Eventually, on 23 February, the Chechen man decided to get rid of his annoyingly well-known captive. American officials, including the Secretary of State, had begun to ask questions about his fate, and he was more trouble than he was worth. So the captor took him to Dagestan, where he tried to make Babitsky cross the border to Azerbaijan, and even provided him with a false passport. But Babitsky refused to play along, and doubled back to the nearest Russian city. On 24 February, he rang a colleague and said where he was. Although he would subsequently be charged with possession of the false passport he had been given, effectively his ordeal was over.

If it was designed to scare him off reporting on Chechnya, it did not work. Babitsky being Babitsky, he still reports on the North Caucasus although he lives in Prague, but it was a useful message from the Kremlin to all other Russian journalists. If they dared to film from the unofficial side of the conflict, they would be treated as the enemy, whether they were a citizen or not.

It was a lesson they have learned well. Very few journalists have taken the risks Babitsky took to uncover the true face of the war, which has in turn helped the government sell the brutal conflict to the Russian people as a necessary and limited anti-terrorist operation.

Some Russian journalists have been brave enough to look behind the Kremlin's propaganda, but they have been rare exceptions in a craven profession. And the silence from the majority has made it easy to convince the rest of the world that Chechnya is nothing to worry about.

30. The Hard Shackles of Evil

As Russian tanks rumbled across the planes of northern Chechnya in October 1999, the Chechen president, Aslan Maskhadov, made a desperate appeal to NATO for help. It sounds absurd. NATO intervene in Russia? But it was not as peculiar an appeal as it now sounds. Just six months earlier, Western warplanes had bombed Serbian targets in support of the Kosovo Albanians, starting the process that would eventually lead to Kosovo's independence.

The position of the Chechens looked very similar. Like the Albanians, they were being targeted with indiscriminate attacks by a larger neighbour, and like the Kosovo Albanians, they were fleeing their homeland in huge columns of refugees.

But Maskhadov's hopes were stillborn. NATO would not support the Chechens. On 26 October, the secretary-general told reporters Chechnya 'is not the business of NATO at the present moment'. That can hardly have been a surprise for Maskhadov, since just two weeks earlier that same secretary-general gave an interview saying that rebuilding ties with Russia – which had objected strongly to the bombing of its Serb allies – must be his top priority. The Chechens were victims of global politics.

This was hardly a new position for them to be in.

In January 1995, when Yashurkayev was just beginning his diary describing how he and his dog Barsik survived the bombs raining onto Grozny, the US State Department made clear its full support for Russia in dealing with this 'difficult domestic matter'. It even compared the slaughter in Grozny to the American Civil War, as if the Chechens were a bunch of slave-owning secessionists who could not tolerate the human rights ideals of some Russian Abraham Lincoln.

Just a year later, the Council of Europe – which is normally described as 'Europe's leading human rights organization' – admitted Russia as a member despite the Chechen bloodbath.

'This is a decision which gives post-1989 Europe its full dimension,' said the organization's secretary-general. 'It averts the danger of a redivided Europe and it contributes to European stability.'

The Chechens had been sacrificed to the political desires of Western states desperate to keep the new Russia on their side.

In the circumstances of 1999, however, when Russia was once more demolishing Grozny with bombs and shells, perhaps the Council of Europe might do something? NATO was not planning to take action, but that was a military alliance, not a human rights coalition. After all, just three years previously Russia had agreed to uphold basic values on its territory, and demolishing Grozny from the air surely went contrary to that.

Initial signs were positive for the Chechens. The Council of Europe's secretary-general announced that the war was a 'violation of human rights in itself' in December that year. It was hardly a speedy response to a crisis that was already three months old, but it was something. What was more, the organization appointed a special envoy to investigate crimes committed against civilians in Chechnya. Perhaps the Chechens might receive some kind of international champion?

Time went by.

Eventually, in June 2000, six months of bitter fighting having passed since the envoy's appointment was announced, foreign ministers of the Council of Europe's member states convened to announce the action they would take against Russia. And their decision was: to do nothing.

They could not, they said, expel or suspend Russia from their organization because then they would not have any positive influence over it. The implication was that they were having some kind of positive influence at the time, which made their statement almost comic.

By this stage, the Chechens were likely to have known they were on their own. The Russian network of 'filtration camps', the 'cleansings', the bombings, the arrests, the disappearances had created a climate of horror in their homeland that no amount of hypocritical statement from Western powers could begin to outweigh.

In the months since the war started, perhaps because of the way the violence had spread to Dagestan, police had become increasingly vigilant all across the North Caucasus. Foreign Muslim preachers were asked to leave, journalists found themselves being harassed, and many foreign Circassians lost their residence permits.

Young Muslims, frustrated by official corruption, angry about probes into their religious leaders, chafed against the restrictions. One of these men was Rasul Kudayev, who turned twenty-two in January 2000. He was an athletic young man, having won the youth wrestling competition of his home region – Kabardino-Balkaria – when he was eighteen. Since then, he had failed to get ahead in life. He had done odd jobs in a factory, but had failed to buy his way into the police force. Anyone who has spent time in Russia will have realized that being a policeman is a lucrative job, and the entry bribe was too much for Kudayev.

He did not come from a wealthy background. His mother had left his father when he was just ten, and now she raised him and his older half-brother on their own in the village of Khasanya, just outside the city of Nalchik.

In the same month that the Council of Europe would decide not to censure Russia for its murderous conduct in Chechnya, Kudayev decided he wanted to seek a better life elsewhere. Perhaps he could succeed in sport somewhere else? He travelled to Uzbekistan, one of the former Soviet states in Central Asia, to work on his wrestling. It was a logical choice, since he is a Balkar – one of the mountain Turk peoples – and the Uzbek language and his own are very similar. Balkars, the minority people in his home region, are discriminated against, and he felt he might get a fairer hearing in a foreign land.

'He was not interested in religion then, he did not even pray,' remembered his mother, Fatima Tekayeva, eight years later.

'He was angry though that as a Balkar he could not move upwards. He had finished school, and then just worked in a textile factory. He decided to leave, he wanted success in sport. He left because of sport, but I did not know where he was going. He was offended by his trainer, I know this. The trainer was a Balkar initially, but I do not know after that.'

Her parents were ill at the time, and she was working to support her family, and she had no time to keep her sporty son at his studies.

She did not want him to wrestle at all; she wanted him to work hard and study more. Perhaps they argued about this, and that is why he left. It was a subject she did not want to talk about.

Tekayeva is a small, compact woman, with a forceful face under her headscarf. We met in the park in central Nalchik, a city in the foothills some hundred kilometres west of Chechnya. It was a sign of the paranoia we both felt that, on meeting, we spontaneously took the batteries out of our phones. We had clearly both heard the rumours that the FSB can use a phone as a listening device even if it is turned off.

She had brought along a pile of photos of her son, and she handed them to me as natural punctuation during the course of his story. She passed the first one to me at this point. It showed a young man, cocksure and handsome, laughing with a face full of glee. He had short dark hair, and the olive complexion of the Balkars.

The next one showed him at his most athletic. Stripped to the waist, he is making a jokey bodybuilder pose by straining his arms across his body to force the muscles of his chest and stomach to stand out in relief.

Tekayeva kept sniffing as she spoke. At first, I thought she was trying not to cry, but she explained that in fact she had been kicked in the face while milking the neighbours' cow. The cow, it transpired, hated men and it had seen a man passing and just lashed out. It had connected full in the face, but she had come to see me anyway. I looked at her with new respect after that.

Although she was not crying, she now regrets not having kept a closer eye on her son, because a crucial two-year period was starting that would not just see his wrestling career but his entire life permanently ruined, as a result of events two continents away.

Version one – his own version – is that he was trying to get to Iran.

'I left Russia to go to Iran, I wanted to study at university there. I travelled through Afghanistan, but before I could leave I was arrested by the Taliban in Herat. They thought I was a Russian spy and they imprisoned me,' he later told a lawyer from the British legal charity Reprieve.

Version two comes from a Russian television station, which interviewed him in 2005, and presumably got the facts from him.

According to the television channel, he was heading for an Islamic school in Pakistan, and was passing through Afghanistan to get there.

A third version, which has been repeated in a number of newspapers and which appears to originate at another Russian television channel, has it that he spent time in Saudi Arabia, then came to Afghanistan, via Iran.

Whichever version is true, no one disputes that Kudayev crossed the border into Afghanistan around the beginning of 2001. He was picked up by the Taliban militia, which was at that point ruling the country and giving asylum to Osama bin Laden. On 11 September of that year, suicide jihadis crashed four planes in the United States, killing nearly 3,000 people. Afghanistan was about to become a very uncomfortable place for anyone who had fought for the Taliban or its allies.

A Russian prosecutor who spoke to Kudayev in 2002 said he had been part of the Islamic Movement of Uzbekistan, a violent group seeking to overthrow the dictatorial government in that country, although this appears to have been pure speculation on the part of the prosecutor, since he also said Kudayev personally denied having been involved.

But that was academic. In 2001, no one was spending much time checking evidence on whether foreigners in Afghanistan actually had fought for the Taliban or not. Kudayev was rounded up along with hundreds of Taliban prisoners and dumped into the Qala-i-Jangi fortress in northern Afghanistan. The fortress was crammed with prisoners, many of whom had been able to keep their weapons. They rose up, killed their guards and an American interrogator, who was to be the first US casualty in Afghanistan, and took the fort.

Between 25 November and 1 December 2001, the prisoners battled Afghan and foreign troops for control of the prison. It was brutal. The attackers at one point poured burning oil into the basement where the prisoners were sheltering, and dropped bombs onto their positions. Less than a third of the prisoners survived, and many of them – including Kudayev, who took a bullet in the hip – were permanently maimed.

There could surely be no doubt of the young man's guilt now. Only the toughest Taliban prisoners had been in the fortress, and only the toughest of the toughest could possibly have survived the battle. He was packed off on a journey that went through a couple of American bases, before ending up in Guantanamo Bay, Cuba.

It is a measure of the hatred Kudayev feels for the Afghans who handed him over to the Americans that he has called his dog after their leader: General Dostum. Tekayeva handed me a photo of the dog too, and insisted I write the name 'Dostum' on the back, so as not to miss the joke.

This is not really the place to detail the abuse he suffered at the hands of the Americans, although he told his lawyer about regular beatings, denials of medical treatment, having to take strange pills, sleep deprivation and being forced into stress positions for long periods. It was a continuation of the nightmare, and has come to dominate his life. He has never been convicted of a crime, but that initial arrest by the Taliban has been enough to sentence him first to three years in American detention, and now to four years in a Russian prison.

He appears to have become more serious about his religion during his time in Afghanistan. He identified himself to his American captors as Abdullah Kafkas – Abdullah meaning 'servant of God' in Arabic, and Kafkas meaning Caucasus – and it took some time before anyone realized who he really was. That came when in 2002 he was visited in Guantanamo by a Russian prosecutor, who was able to check records of residence in Nalchik. The prosecutor was in no doubt of the young man's guilt, although it did not appear that Kudayev was puritan in his religious beliefs, judging by the fact that he smoked.

'He immediately asked me for a cigarette, and started to ask how everything was in Nalchik,' the prosecutor told a Russian newspaper on his return from Guantanamo.

'But in relation to Russia, he was very negative. He said he did not want to return. He asked to be sent to Saudi Arabia, or to Afghanistan. He said he would also happily remain in America. As if anyone wants him there!'

Either way, he did not get his wish. Despite his desire not to be sent back to Russia, the American authorities announced on 1 March

2004 that they had handed him over to their Russian counterparts. This was not a simple deportation, however, in which the ex-prisoners would be sent home and allowed to live their lives. A statement released by the US State Department said he and six other Russian nationals in the camp would 'face criminal charges relating to their terrorist activities during an armed conflict. The transfer is the result of discussions between our two governments over the past year, including assurances that the individuals will be detained, investigated and prosecuted, as appropriate, under Russian law and will be treated humanely in accordance with Russian law and obligations'.

Among those obligations were those Russia had signed up to on joining the toothless Council of Europe, including allowing due legal process and refraining from torture.

For Muslims in Kudayev's home town of Nalchik, those assurances would have seemed like a joke. Since the outbreak of the war in Chechnya, rebels had consistently tried to stir up the Muslims in neighbouring regions. In response, Russian police closely monitored religious congregations, particularly those that sought to distance themselves from the official state-backed Muslim communities. It became a vicious circle, with Muslims angered by police surveillance, and police following them more closely because of their anger. Basayev's rebels kept a close eye on everything, keen to exploit other people's despair for their own ends.

In the circumstances, the law became almost entirely irrelevant. At one point, ten Chechen women doctors were put on the Russian wanted list as would-be suicide bombers. Their photos and names were posted around Russian towns, and police were told to look out for them. Their crime? An internal document featuring their names and pictures printed by their employer – the US aid group International Medical Corps – had been found by police. There appeared to be no other proof. The document was even written in the Latin script, making it abundantly clear that it had originated in a foreign company, but the police's first reaction on discovering the pictures of the women had been to think they could only be suicide bombers.

The doctors were lucky they did not get picked up before the mistake was uncovered. Russian courts did not require much evidence before convicting Chechens of terrorism. Zara Murtazaliyeva, for example, a student in Moscow, was convicted on the basis of transcripts of slightly anti-Russian telephone conversations. The judge ruled she had a 'negative attitude towards the state' and found her guilty. If she did not have a negative attitude before her trial, she is almost certain to have had one after she was sentenced to nine years' imprisonment.

So this is the situation – one of tension, illegality and violence – that Kudayev was brought back to. He was kept in prison while the authorities looked for a crime to try him for. They failed to find one and he was eventually released from custody in June 2004. For Fatima Tekayeva, his mother, it was a terrible shock.

'He had changed completely,' she explained. 'He was changed, he was a real nutcase. He ate badly, he slept badly, he did not talk to anyone. Even if people came to see him, he would sit in his own room. He was not himself. He had been such a joyful lad but he came back from there completely different.

'He had had so many friends in childhood. I could not sit down at home even. They were mainly Balkars, but even a Russian who adopted Islam came too,' she said. 'As time passed, he became a bit better, but he did not talk to anyone but me and his brother, and even if he spoke to us his head hurt. He would go into his room and say: "Do not talk to me, I have to relax."'

He needed medical treatment as well. He had terrible trouble with his liver, and the bullet was still in his hip. The whites of his eyes had turned yellow during his captivity, and he was weak. The wrestler had returned as a cripple. But he could not go to a doctor, since he lacked the internal passport that is the key to all the Russian state's services. Without documentation, you are effectively not a human being.

In the absence of medical care, the only thing that might have improved his condition was rest, but he did not even get that, because the police came and interrogated him any time they felt like it.

'Rasul was at home between June 2004 and October 2005, and during this time they took him from our home in masks four times. They did not even say why they were doing this. One time they had him from nine in the morning until six in the evening, and we had to call an ambulance afterwards because he did not get his medicine. The ambulance took him to hospital and they treated him all evening, but I refused to leave him in hospital because I was scared, so I took him and treated him at home,' remembered Tekayeva.

Kudayev was taken to the police station and questioned on 23 May 2005. He was summoned again on 28 May and told a new case would be opened against him for alleged falsification of documents. On 19 June, he was visited by prosecutors, but was too ill to speak. In July, he was questioned by the FSB, then on 16 August he was abducted from home, and questioned for five hours about Guantanamo and Afghanistan.

It was a horrific time, but the next photograph Tekayeva showed me was rather lovely. It showed her son having finally gained his passport. He is grinning, showing a mouth of white, firm teeth, and his hair is brushed down over his forehead. He is wearing a grey jacket, and a dark T-shirt, both of which enhance his good looks. Through an open door behind him, you can see Tekayeva doing the washing up in the kitchen.

By this stage, Tekayeva had lost touch with all her other relatives, and was having to cope with just her sons for company.

'If these relatives came to me and asked how Rasul was, then they would be visited and searched too. Since that time I have hardly talked to my relations so my problems would not affect them too,' she said.

But then, on 13 October 2005, the problems became worse. A group of possibly a hundred men, most of them local Muslims radicalized by the violence they faced from the police, attacked buildings belonging to security forces in the city. It is hard to know what they were trying to achieve. They did not publish any coherent demands; nor did they take a significant number of hostages. They just opened fire on state targets, apparently more or less at random.

Basayev, the Chechen warlord, inevitably got involved, issuing statements on his website about the insurgents' links to the Chechen resistance. But those links were tenuous, since the men in Nalchik lacked the skill of the Chechens, and were rapidly and comprehensively defeated. The uprising had been a murderous expression of rage by a marginalized generation.

Tekayeva left home that morning unaware of what was happening, and reached her workplace – a clinic where she worked as a
cleaner – at around 11 a.m. The fighting had been going on for two
hours by now, but she, Kudayev and her other son, Arsen, were
completely unaware of it.

'At work they all ran up to me and asked me why had I come to
work. They said war had started in the town. They told me to go
home and sit down with my sons and not to let them go anywhere.
Arsen had driven me to work, but he had already left, so one ambulance agreed to take me home, because it was going nearby,' she said.

'I walked the 300 metres home and Arsen had not even got back
yet. He was just getting back when I walked up. I asked him where
Rasul was, and whether he was awake yet, and Arsen said that he was
still asleep.'

The three of them sat, appalled, and watched the news – all burning buildings and dead bodies – for a while, before deciding that they
needed to establish alibis, so the neighbours could testify that they
had not taken any part in the attacks. So, they went and stood in the
courtyard several times where everyone could see them.

Kudayev even spoke to Russian television after the attacks, telling
them that he had no connection to the attacks, and had no idea who
had carried them out. 'Some people say it was Chechens, some people
say it was Muslims, and some people even say it was an Orange Revolution,' he said, referring to the colour adopted by the peaceful
revolutionaries in Ukraine the year before. That last comment was
surely a joke, but it was not one the police appreciated.

For the police had a very clear idea of who was to blame. They
blamed a Wahhabi underground organization bent on destabilizing
Nalchik and establishing an Islamic state in the Caucasus. In the circumstances, it was inevitable that the police would think a former
Guantanamo inmate had to have something to do with this illegal
movement. Tekayeva at this point understood the logic of the authorities as well as anyone, and tried desperately to protect her son.

'We never left Rasul alone at home. Arsen would either go to work
or I would, but we basically guarded him at all times. On the 23rd
[of October] Arsen went to work, and I sat and chopped tomatoes.

Rasul slept. And suddenly ... well, I have no idea where the cars came from, jeeps, cars, they surrounded the house. I asked what was going on. They told me to be still but I shouted to the neighbours to watch that they did not plant weapons or bullets on me. They took Rasul from his bed, they put him in handcuffs. I told them they should put me in handcuffs, but they shouted at me, swore at me. I called my other son, and he came home, but they would not let him in, they searched him, they took his phone,' she said.

'They had already taken Rasul out into the yard, they turned everything upside down in the house, I have no idea what they were looking for. Arsen told them to take him too, but they said they wanted the Guantanamo man ... They took Rasul to the UBOP [the Department for the Fight against Organized Crime], and I waited there until about six. They had come to our house about nine or ten, and left about 13.30. I waited at the gates of the UBOP and saw how they were bringing young lads, how they beat them, what condition they were in, how they pushed their faces into the mud.'

Kudayev and the fifty-seven others detained that day have not been freed since, and those who got in to see them in the UBOP building were appalled by what they saw. A lawyer, Irina Komissarova, managed to gain access to him on 24 October, the day after his detention.

'Upon arrival at the Sixth Department I saw Kudaev R. V., who was sitting on a stool, in a contorted position, holding his stomach. There were a large bruise and many scratches on the right side of his face near the eye,' she wrote in a complaint to prosecutors and other officials, as obtained by the activist group Human Rights Watch.

'Kudayev R. V. told me that he had been tortured and beaten after he was brought to the Sixth Department. The testimony in the interrogation record was not his, it had been made up, and it was not correct ... When Kudayev R. V. informed the investigator that he would not sign the interrogation record ... all hell broke loose!!! From all sides people in the office gathered around (by the way, none introduced themselves) and everyone started issuing threats at Kudayev R. V. In the end, he could no longer stand it and said that he would sign the interrogation record because he was afraid that after I left they would beat him again. Someone in the room told me, "You are free to go, we don't need your services any more."'

Medical records show that an ambulance was called to treat Kulayev that night. He was diagnosed as having 'psycho-motor excitement, hypertension in the arteries, and numerous bruises'.

Komissarova saw him again on 26 October, when his physical condition was even worse.

'They almost carried him in because he could not walk without outside help. In my conversation with him, he told me that he had been subjected to physical violence. That is, he was beaten when he was delivered to the building of the UBOP,' she wrote.

'He was beaten in the area of the lower back and on the heels. One could see that he could not straighten out because of the pain, the leg that he could not stand on twitched, there were bruises on his face.'

More proof of his mistreatment emerged when the Russian security forces leaked a whole series of pictures of the fifty-eight men they had detained in their sweep through Nalchik that October. Some of the prisoners are holding up prison blackboards identifying them, but Kudayev is not. As a result, he is virtually unrecognizable, with only his eyes looking the same.

Tekayeva handed me this next photograph with a grimace. Her son's lower face and jaw area were swollen to almost twice their normal size, and the eye sockets were bruised and discoloured. The smiling man who had posed with his passport just a few weeks earlier was long gone.

So, this was the result of Russia's promises to the Americans that the Guantanamo detainees would be 'treated humanely'. The evidence of what was happening to him was available to the Americans, but they did not complain.

In the photo taken after his beating, Kudayev's eyes are hard and direct. They look straight at the lens with rage and resignation. Unlike some of the other men detained, whose photos show them to be scared, he knew about being beaten and being detained, and he was ready for it.

There seemed to be a deliberate government ploy to release pictures of the detainees and the dead attackers. I visited Nalchik around this time, and was shown a film recorded on a mobile phone inside the morgue used to store the dead bodies. The naked men were piled up like cordwood, their limbs twisted back, and their heads lolling down. One mouth was open in a grotesque yawn.

Under Russian anti-terrorist legislation, relatives do not receive the body of a terrorist for burial. It is a cruel rule, since the dead men had never been tried for terrorism, and were just assumed to be terrorists after their death. The law is intended to punish terrorists for their crimes, but it has the double effect of stopping any independent investigation into the cause of death. As a result, the security forces were free to do anything they wanted.

Komissarova was forced off Kudayev's case after she complained, but if the authorities thought that would mean no more trouble from Kudayev they were mistaken. Kudayev now has another lawyer: a Chechen called Magomed Abubakarov. Abubakarov is a typical Chechen, all flash and fire. But he combines his rage with a passion for the law, which he has turned to Kudayev's account.

'The detention centre administration has a serious problem with Rasul. The more he is tortured, the stronger he becomes. He writes a lot, and now some people write about him. He has a book now as well showing what he can do by law,' Abubakarov said as we sat in his car one afternoon.

Now that Kudayev had started complaining, all of the inmates had started complaining too. He was organizing and mobilizing his comrades, and the authorities seemed powerless to stop it. I asked him what Kudayev's current mood was. Abubakarov grinned and answered in one word.

'Militant,' he said.

Tekayeva had shown me three more photos of her son, taken through the bars of the detention centre at visiting time. The fresh-faced young wrestler is gone now, and the bruises of his beating have faded. Kudayev's hair is longer. It parts in the middle, and waves down behind his ears. A beard covers his cheeks, and his cheekbones seem more defined. The face is finer, though his good looks have not gone. His eyes, however, have changed permanently. They do not laugh any more. They have the same look as in the photo taken after his torture. He looks, in a word, militant.

I asked Tekayeva what her son was writing about in the detention centre and, after long negotiations, she managed to persuade him to let me see some of his poems. Here are two of the verses she sent me. They are not always grammatically correct – in one of them, he writes:

> I have no talent to write poetry
> But I can express my thoughts on paper.
> I have not studied science at superior schools

– and are scrawled in large handwriting on normal squared school paper, but they are from the heart.

They show, perhaps, that Abubakarov was not correct in calling him militant. He has gone beyond anger, to a realm of faith:

> Oh mother, I see you in my dreams again.
> I can feel your aching heart.
> I remember and see your kindness.
> My heart is aching that I am not near you,
> That I had to part from you
> On that autumn day in October.
> I was taken away from you, by filthy hands.
> And you were told that your son had been killed,
> Even though you yourself, with your own eyes,
> Saw me departing that day.
> You were preparing your home for a big funeral,
> But your mother's heart was beating with the thought
> That he is alive, your son is alive.
> Because is that what filth and evil wanted!!?
> To bury your son!
> But that is not what Allah wanted,
> What the Almighty wanted!!!
> To bury your son.
> Although in my misery and pain I have asked Allah,
> O Allah!!! Stop my heart!!!
> I don't have the power,
> I don't have the strength any more.

I have asked for a martyr's death.
But I did not deserve that grace, and remained alive.
But still, hoping for your grace,
I am alive again, O Allah, Almighty.
I am asking a blessing for mothers.
Give them patience and heart,
Strengthen them with faith.
O Allah, Almighty,
Give mothers the strength of spirit,
And feed them with the sweetness of faith.
And grant them satisfaction in both worlds,
And forgive all of our sins.
Amen.

Other poems recall more of the pleasures he has lost, and address the comforts of faith. The young athlete who tried his luck abroad aged twenty-two – just like I did, just like young men and women all over the world have done for centuries – has become a broken man because he was denied justice by the world. It is no way to win a war.

31. I Have Become No One

On 24 April 2008, I was a long way from the Caucasus, but it did not feel like it.

I was standing among the cigarette ends on the platform of the sad concrete building that is the Terespol train station, on Poland's – and the European Union's – eastern border. The railway line stretched off to my right and, in a few kilometres, would cross into Belarus, before stretching unbroken throughout the old Soviet Empire: to Kiev, to Rostov, and, eventually, to Grozny.

Waiting with me on the platform were five Chechen men. They were speaking Russian for my sake, and the thick Chechen accent was conjuring up a vision of the mountain peaks that would be visible if I were to hop on a train here, travel for two or three days across the plains of Belarus, Ukraine and Russia, and finally see the sheer wall of rock and snow rising out of the steppes.

Now, though, none of us were planning to take a train; we were meeting one. A group of thirty Chechens had arrived here this morning, and their refugee papers were being processed. Their train had come in at 6 a.m. It was now 7.23 p.m., and the border guards had still not finished with them.

All the same, my companions were not impatient. One of them, called Magomed, I had met before. When I walked onto the platform, I had recognized his red beard, his cap and the shoulder satchel that he wore. He is a friendly man and he introduced me extravagantly to the others who stood around calmly smoking, chatting and laughing on the platform.

Suddenly, the conversation ceased. A middle-aged woman in a floral dress emerged from the office. We all looked towards her – slightly to her alarm – before we realized she was not one of the arriving Chechens. She was just a cleaning lady going off shift.

More cigarettes were lit, and one of the group started to engage a

Pole nearby in conversation with an anecdote about a car. The Pole probably understood less of his conversation than I did, since his version of Polish sounded more like deliberately non-grammatical Russian than anything else. Either way, none of us got to hear the end of the story, because, suddenly, an elderly woman appeared in the doorway with a flash of gold teeth.

She vanished into the embrace of her son Vakha – one of the men who had been waiting – and behind her came others: women in headscarves, men with black jackets and worn faces, girls, boys. They pushed past her, as she hung on to her son's shoulders. She crooned to him, and laughed. She rocked backwards and forwards, crying with purest happiness. They were united after a year apart.

As I stood watching the group of laughing people, I could not help smiling. A little girl in her best party dress caught my eye and made an elegant little skip of a dance before hiding to peek around her mother's skirts with a shy smile.

My friend Magomed brought over his sister for me to meet. They had not seen each other for six months and she was beaming across her face. Magomed, himself not a man to hide a smile, was practically jumping up and down. I shook Magomed's hand and smiled too, their joy contagious.

My eyes strayed back though to the old woman. Her son was busy with her luggage, while she was staring around at the crumbling walls and rotten concrete of the station. She looked along the platform, then through the grimy windows into the ticket hall. It was not, I realized suddenly, much of an advertisement for the European Union, but she did not seem to mind. Her look was one of unrestrained delight. Her gold teeth lit up the evening. As she walked past, I could not help myself.

'Welcome to Europe,' I said. She dropped a curtsey, laughed, and I was rewarded with a grin.

And then, within just five minutes, they were gone. The waiting men quickly organized the new arrivals into groups, loaded them into cars, and drove off for Warsaw. Magomed packed up his sister, her husband, a teenage boy and two infants into his Volkswagen. He smiled and waved at me as they drove away.

The taxi drivers who had circled the group hopefully like grey-haired sharks went back to smoking on their bench, and the excitement was over. If I had arrived late, I would have seen nothing. Within ten minutes, Terespol had gone back to being just a normal provincial Polish town, with a sluggish trade over the border to Belarus.

You had to see a train arrive to realize what it really is: the gateway through which Chechens are pouring into Europe.

As I stood there, I did a little sum in my head. If 24 April was a typical day, and I saw no reason why it should not be, then thirty Chechens were arriving in Poland daily. Multiplied by 365, that made more than 10,000 refugees a year. It is generally considered that a million Chechens live in the world, so this little town was welcoming one per cent of the total Chechen population every year.

This was the response of the Chechens to the Russian pacification of their homeland. They were voting with their feet, and seeking a life away from the mountains, in a continent where they could be protected by a fair legal system. In 1944, Moscow had to force the Chechens out of Chechnya. Now they were leaving of their own accord.

In fact, as it turned out, my estimate was slightly too high. In 2008, Poland received 6,647 asylum applications from Russian citizens, almost all of them being Chechens. To put that into context, it received just 216 asylum applications from all the world's other countries put together.

A recent surge in the numbers of Chechen asylum seekers in Poland – and almost all Poland's asylum seekers are Chechens – had tailed off by the time I was in Terespol. Chechens are well-informed on European immigration legislation and there had been concern that Poland's entry into the Schengen Agreement, which removed visa regulation between EU states but toughened entry regulations, might make it hard for Chechens to enter the country.

Some 1,148 Chechens claimed asylum in Poland the previous November, and 2,275 did so in December. That was up from just 225 in July of the year before. Now, numbers were back to the steady few hundred a month that was normal.

According to these statistics, which are compiled by the United Nations, that number has stayed stubbornly constant for years. The governments do not list Chechens as a separate category, but experts agree that almost all Russian asylum seekers are in fact Chechens.

In 2000, there were almost 17,500 Chechen asylum seekers in the industrialized world, a figure that jumped to more than 33,000 in 2003, before falling back to 21,000 by 2005. The number of applicants has stayed between 15,000 and 20,000 a year ever since. In 2008, the year in which I watched the train arrive in Terespol, there was a total of 19,483 – of whom thirty were the Chechens I saw arrive on 24 April.

Asylum figures can prove hard to analyse, because sometimes a single person can register an application in more than one country. However, under European rules, that is not possible in the European Union. Since almost all Chechens are claiming asylum in the EU, a rough estimate of the number who have arrived over time can be gained by just adding all those numbers together. Taken together, since the beginning of 2000, when Russia was pulverizing Grozny with artillery, bombs and rockets, more than 190,000 people – almost 20 per cent of the Chechen population – had applied for asylum in the West. And a further analysis of the figures shows just how catastrophic the situation really is.

In 2008, Russian citizens – i.e. Chechens – were the third largest group of asylum seekers in the industrialized world, behind only Iraqis and Somalis. And the Chechens were forming discrete communities. Taken together, two-thirds of them were going to just three countries – Poland, Austria and France. As I had seen with sons greeting mothers, and brothers greeting sisters in Terespol, when communities form they act as magnets.

This is not just a movement, it is an exodus.

The destination of the arriving Chechens was always a holding centre, where they would be registered, and then shipped on to another refugee camp elsewhere. In Austria, the camp is in a suburb of Vienna called Traiskirchen, accessible by a suburban train or a regional bus. When I visited it, I took the wrong bus, however, and was left to trek through the small provincial town to find the building I was looking for. It was an enlightening experience.

I wandered through street after perfectly clean street of two-storey houses in pastel shades. At one point, two houses in succession had large dogs that threw themselves at the wire fence as I walked past. A grey-haired man turned and watched me out of sight with a neutral expression.

Eventually, I found the train tracks and followed them to the station. Here, the picture was very different. A group of African men squatted outside the station building, talking in their own language. Two Austrian women hurried past, pursing their lips. Three Chechen women saw my surprise at the Austrians' reaction and called me over. They were happy to point me in the direction of the holding camp.

'Do you want to give yourself up,' one of them asked in all seriousness. New arrivals must be a regular event here, and they had assumed I was a Russian. The camp was not far, just a couple of hundred metres round the corner. It was a large yellow building surrounded by a spiky black fence.

Here too were Chechens – dozens of men – standing along the street or squatting in the dust. The distrust of the Austrians had clearly rubbed off on them, however. They refused to talk to me when I addressed them in Russian.

I gave up trying to make conversation and walked back to the station. A young Chechen man was checking the timetable as I handed over a ten-euro note for my train fare. The ticket-seller, a plump, pink man with dark hair scraped over his scalp, made shooing gestures at the young Chechen. I failed to understand what he was doing, and eventually he pointed at the Chechen, pointed at his eye, then made a ticking gesture with his finger. He was clearly trying to warn me about the young man's intentions. I hoped the Chechen might be able to compensate for my lack of German, so I asked him what the ticket-seller was trying to tell me.

'Oh, he's just fucked up,' the Chechen replied with a grin.

It was easy to see that relations between Chechens and Austrians were not easy, and in fact they have not been for some time. Clashes have flared up in the past which populist politicians have exploited for their own ends. Jorg Haider, the far-right ex-governor of the province of Carinthia, deported eighteen Chechens from his region after an outbreak of violence on New Year's Eve 2007–8.

In an action of dubious legality, he threw out three families that he claimed were connected to an attack by young Chechens on a seventeen-year-old and his sixteen-year-old girlfriend. The three families were sent back to Traiskirchen, where in a previous incident in 2003 a Chechen was killed in a fight with a group of Moldovans. The next year, more than 20,000 Austrians in Traiskirchen signed a petition calling for the camp to be closed, and a nightly curfew imposed on camp residents.

In protest meetings, they held up signs saying they did not object to receiving victims of persecution, but did not want to host criminals or economic migrants.

As I stood on the platform waiting for the train back to Vienna, I watched a group of teenage Chechens who had been leaning against the wall stand up as a slightly older, blonde Austrian girl walked past. They stopped talking and followed her with their eyes. One of them finally got up the nerve to address a few words in German to her.

She turned round and raised her middle finger at him, lifted her chin and stomped away. The boys grinned.

The train pulled up, and I climbed on board. As I sat down I pondered the difficulties of integrating Chechens into traditional Austrian society. I had already seen how Chechens steadfastly refused to integrate in Kazakhstan, in Russia and in Jordan, and I failed to see how they would do so here. If they truly were economic migrants, rather than fleeing persecution, it would make it all the more unlikely that Austria would welcome them warmly.

As I looked out the window, I realized I was being spoken to. A man across the aisle was asking me a question in German. He was middle-aged, sharply dressed in a pinstripe suit and a trilby, with dark glasses and very shiny, pointed shoes. In short, he looked like a Chechen, so I replied in Russian, and we struck up a conversation.

This, I discovered, was Khozhbaudi Denisultanov, aged forty-four, and if anyone was likely to give the Chechens a bad name for seeking wealth, not safety, it was him. The train journey was a short one, and he seemed to have a lot to say, so he invited me to visit him the next day. It was to prove an eye-opening experience.

He lived with a couple of younger cousins in a flat on the edge of Vienna. It smelt of cigarette smoke and fried food, and had the bare, functional look of a temporary refuge where only men live. Here, Denisultanov told me his business plan, and tried to persuade me to invest in his dream.

He had got the idea, he said, from watching television on 11 September 2001, when people trapped in the World Trade Center by the flames were forced to throw themselves out of the windows. While the world was appalled by the carnage, Denisultanov saw an opportunity. Could these poor people not have been saved by a simple and efficient device? He set to work and designed a harness that people could use to lower themselves out of windows too high for the fire brigade to reach.

He even had a prototype under the bed to show potential investors – such as me. It featured coils of nylon rope and a harness inside a rather smart metal box. Professional-looking drawings showed a man casually descending away from harm. The idea seemed flawed to me – surely the flames would burn through the nylon rope, let alone the descending escapee – but I was more stunned by the colossal cheek of his thinking he should qualify as a refugee.

He had lived in St Petersburg, he said, and although he had faced problems from the police, these did not seem in any way out of the ordinary for any Russian citizen. He had earned a perfectly decent living in a law firm. But he had become fixated on his plan to make escape kits, and wanted a better business environment to do it in.

'The economic situation in Russia makes it impossible to realize myself,' he said grandly.

I asked him if he thought that the problems in Russia, where corruption can make it difficult to open a business, should qualify him for refugee status. He openly said they should not, and not only that, he knew the Austrians would not give it to him. He had previously become convinced he was about to be refused leave to remain, so he cancelled his application, left the country, flew to Ukraine, dashed back into Belarus, Poland and the Czech Republic, and returned to Austria, where he had applied for asylum again.

Under European law, an asylum seeker must ask for refuge in the first safe country he visits. He would seem to have disqualified himself from seeking asylum in Austria by visiting Poland and Prague, but Denisultanov insisted he knew better. He was a lawyer, he said, and had figured out a loophole in the system. Perhaps he had. I did not know enough about European immigration regulations to argue with him, but I knew I did not envy the official who would have to process his case. Just like the Chechens who had defeated the bureaucrats of Kazakhstan, Denisultanov and – no doubt – thousands of others like him were opening a new front against the regulations of the European Union.

Austrian officials have been left baffled by how to accommodate the Chechen arrivals into the economy. Unlike most asylum seekers, Chechens arrive in families, with their wives and children. The women often find work, but, according to Klaus Neumann, an Austrian who works with Chechen refugees, men can be very hard to accommodate.

'Often the men are not prepared to work under a woman, or else they have no training and will not work in a restaurant or something,' he said, and he noticed me smiling at the thought of a Chechen man working in a restaurant. It was an unlikely image.

In response, he asked me what I thought Chechen men could do to earn a living, saying he had been asked by the government to suggest jobs for them and was looking for ideas. I was stumped, and suggested he could employ Chechens as mechanics.

'Most of these Chechens are not trained at all,' he objected. 'Many of them say they want to be truck drivers, but this is difficult for them. Most of them don't learn German very well, and I have a feeling that most of them communicate only within their Chechen culture. It will be interesting to see what happens to them over the next ten years, because we have no history of Chechen immigration.'

He lamented the fact that the Chechen community had no one leader. It is fragmented into family and social groups, and is very hard to deal with as a united body. This was a very different exodus to the one that took place after the Russians defeated Imam Shamil in 1859, when the people's spiritual leaders led them into the Ottoman Empire. This new departure was happening in dribs and drabs, one family at a time. Many of the parents bringing their children to safety had had no proper education during the fourteen years of war in Chechnya, and precious little in the chaos before that, so they were bringing few of the skills demanded by employers in a Western society.

And even educated men were finding it hard to integrate into a society so profoundly different to their own. The law-abiding, orderly Austrian system could not be more alien to a Chechen man raised on the concept that ripping off the state was a duty and a pleasure. Visita Ibragimov was one such man. He had been one of the leaders of the Chechen political awakening in the late 1980s, an ally of the poet Yandarbiyev in his goal of winning the Chechens their own state.

Now, he was a lonely man in a flat in Austria, reduced to welcoming a wandering British journalist into his home to talk about the past.

He pulled down Yandarbiyev's autobiography to show me details of the protests that engulfed Chechnya in 1991. Instead of a history lesson, however, his account became a macabre recital of how his world had changed. He started reading out a list of the leaders of the demonstrations, wanting to tell me their personal qualities, but his voice changed as he realized what had happened to them. He sounded stunned, as if he had never before noticed the extent of the catastrophe that had engulfed his generation.

'This one was killed ... this one is dead ... this one is dead ... this one was killed ... this one I do not know what happened to him ... that one was old, he is probably dead ... this one is dead,' he intoned, as he stared into the gulf of his past. The list went on like that for several minutes.

'I tried to build a state, but I lost everything instead. My wife wants a good husband, my children want a good father and here I am. I am always running here and there, trying to organize this and that,' he said.

'I said to my son, he's a teenager, he's fifteen and he wanted some jeans, I said to him that I had no money but when he grew up he would be proud that his father was a patriot. He replied that it would be better if I were a traitor, at least then we'd have some money.'

Ibragimov had got out a bottle of vodka by now, and we sat drinking shots and eating snacks throughout the rest of the morning and the afternoon. He became increasingly morose as the drink took effect, his face became blotchy and his stories became sadder. Curiously, though, he became more active in his gestures.

'It is beautiful to say I am a patriot, but that word has required me to sacrifice all those who are close to me, this word causes problems for everyone. There is no longer a war between Russia and Chechnya. There are people in the resistance, there are people making money, there are people killing, there are other people. And I cannot take part in this, but it is hard to explain to my family that my moral principle means that I must cause them harm.'

He kept talking and talking, about how he had warned Basayev against his raid on Dagestan, about how he had escaped Grozny in winter 1999–2000, about his own quarrels with the religious extremists. But he said nothing about his life in Austria. It was like being transported back to Imam Shamil's exile, when the group of former rulers lived completely in the past. He dissected the events of his life in great detail, but could come to no conclusions.

'This time in Austria is the most comfortable I have ever known. I live here. I do nothing. I receive money. It is socially speaking the best period of my life. But the happiest time was in 1996–9, the period between the two wars. I had no money, there were no salaries, but we were happy,' he said.

Former separatist politicians like him are scattered all across Europe. Akhmed Zakayev is in London. Apti Bisultanov is in Germany. Others are in Norway, in Belgium, in France and in Italy. And perhaps the hardest thing to bear for them is their complete irrelevance to the lives of Chechens today. These men once led the independence struggle, but the Chechens refuse to group under their banners in exile. Once again, the Chechens are proving impossible to organize at anything but a family level.

But those families were keeping a close eye on their members. As I saw at the Terespol train station, Chechens told their relatives when they were arriving and those relatives would come to the border to pick them up and take them to Warsaw, where they would be processed. For the Poles have a single holding centre too. All arriving asylum seekers had to report to a former barracks in a forest outside Warsaw called Debak.

The situation here was very different to that in Austria. This was not a large building in the middle of a prosperous town; it was a ramshackle complex surrounded by a tall fence, with trees in every direction. Once again, though, like everywhere I went in those weeks, Chechen men stood or squatted outside the gates, chatting away in their guttural language.

There was not much to do in the depths of this wood, so they welcomed me as a pleasant distraction when I wandered up and greeted them in Russian. They were insistent that I needed to see inside the centre though, to appreciate the size of the challenge that had over-whelmed the Polish authorities. There were, they said, at least double the number of people inside than the centre was designed for.

I tried arguing that I was not allowed in the centre – in truth, I was slightly nervous – but my resistance crumbled in the face of good-humoured insistence from my new friends. Smuggling a British jour-nalist into a detention centre was the kind of thing that might amuse them for an hour or two, and eventually I went along with the joke.

We set off, in a line of four, into the trees and made a big loop around the compound. At the far end, two of the pieces of metal that made up the fence had been pushed aside. I squeezed through and walked into the centre: the first port of call for Chechens in the Euro-pean Union. A clump of crumbling buildings, once painted yellow ochre, were to my left, and a boy was kicking a football against a wall. Ahead was a long, low, building, with women in headscarves hang-ing out washing, and men sitting around and chatting to each other.

We ducked through one of the doors, and the scale of the influx became immediately apparent. Camp beds lined the corridors, and every room held four or five people. Women looked out of the doors curiously as I passed. A girl smiled at me as she sat and watched her mother mopping the floor.

Ahead of me was the entrance hall. It was a spacious room, with windows and a higher ceiling, and must once have been rather pleas-ant. It was probably designed as a place where inmates could gather and watch television, but here were beds too: perhaps as many as thirty, all clumped together in the middle of the floor, with just a narrow walkway around the side. The centre was bursting at the seams. Now, all the inmates were outside in the spring warmth, but I shuddered to imagine what it was like in winter.

The noise in here at night must have been frightful too, but I had no chance to find out, since my illegal invasion of the refugee centre had come to a sudden end. A porky security guard appeared from nowhere, demanded my documents, and marched off with them towards the command post at the front gate.

His bosses were, not surprisingly, worried to have found me there. The overcrowding in the centre could probably have made a story for a Polish journalist looking for a scoop. They asked if I was a journalist, I replied that I was a tourist. This ridiculous explanation failed to satisfy them for a second, so they seized my camera and started to scroll through the pictures.

As it happened, I had not had time to take any pictures in the centre, and all the photos on the memory card were from a recent holiday in Africa. The first image was of my girlfriend swimming, then there was an elephant, followed by a giraffe, then by a warthog. The security guards were stumped. Perhaps I was a tourist after all. They told me to wait, speaking in broken Russian, and I tried to keep a straight face as my new Chechen friends – who had not had this much fun in weeks – jumped up and down outside the window, pulled faces and tried to make me laugh.

By the time the guards released me, I had become something of a hero in the camp, and I was greeted with sarcastic cheers. Musa – one of the men I had spoken to earlier – volunteered to drive me around all the Chechen sites in Warsaw, as long as I provided the petrol. It was a perfect offer, for both of us. I got to see how Chechens live, and Musa got to conquer his boredom for a little while.

'We sit here, then maybe we go and sit over there, then we go to the shop if we have any money, which we normally don't,' Musa had said earlier, explaining the ritual of a normal day.

I examined him as we walked to his car. He had grizzled stubble, a scarred cheek and dark hair falling forward over his eyes. He gave me a roguish grin as he unlocked the car. He lived in the car as it happened – it being more comfortable than the accommodation provided – but he did not normally have enough money to fill it with petrol.

As we drove off through the forest, he slipped a tape of Chechen music into the stereo, and I tapped my fingers on the roof. It felt like being in Chechnya for a minute or two, until we passed a Catholic church and I realized how far we were from Musa's home.

He told me about his life in little chunks of information, which all added up to a typical Chechen story of loss and horror. He had left Chechnya after being harassed by the police, following an accident between his car and a Russian armoured vehicle. He had lost his documents, which made him an easy target for arrest whenever the police needed a suspect. They had beaten him, and abused him, until he could take it no more and had left the country.

He had arrived in Poland the previous February and then, frustrated by the slow pace of his asylum application, left for Belgium nine months later. He was picked up there though and, under European law, he had to be sent back to Poland, where now he was in limbo again.

'When I was young I used to talk about what I would be: a doctor, a farmer. And look, I have become no one. Look at me, I'm no one, this is not what I imagined when I was seven,' he said at one point as we drove through the countryside.

But his bad moods never lasted long. He changed the tape to the Bee Gees – 'How Deep is Your Love?' – and started joking about Chechens who came to claim asylum saying they were former rebels when they did not even know the smallest thing about weapons. He took his hands off the wheel to make his point.

'They think you hold a grenade launcher like this,' he said, with a shout of laughter, clutching his hands to his stomach. The car lurched sickeningly into the opposite lane, and we faced the oncoming traffic for a worrying half-second before he swung the car back to safety.

'Ha,' he shouted, with a flash of gold teeth. 'Idiots.'

He, on the other hand, was sure his application would be approved. He had listed the beatings he had received, the harassment he had endured as the cousin of a famous rebel commander, and the difficulties he had faced just living in his homeland.

He took me on a tour of the hostels where Chechens live. At the first one, the atmosphere was tense and no one wanted to talk. The police had been there that morning, and taken eight of the refugees away in handcuffs. Women stood on the balconies amid the washing lines and looked at me until I went away. It was a bleak place: an old hotel, overshadowed by a factory chimney striped like a rugby player's jersey.

The second hostel was a more welcoming experience. Here men stood around in the sunshine, and they welcomed me into their circle. They too had nothing else to do.

'My profession is war,' explained one man, who called himself Zaur. 'I did not even finish school. The war started when I was just fifteen years old. What could I do but defend my homeland?

'We are military people, it is all we know. If Poland asked us to fight, we would fight for Poland. We would fight for England. We would fight for you like we fight for our own country. We no longer have a country, you see.'

The other men in the group nodded their agreement. They were soldiers without weapons, without a cause and without a country. It was desperately sad. They all had similar stories to tell me, and I could have stayed there in the dust all day, but we had to hurry. Musa had plans. He wanted to show me the office building where Chechens have to file their application requests. It was in central Warsaw, and we had a long drive if we were to make it there before it closed at 2 p.m. We roared away from the group of men with a flamboyant wheel spin in the dirt.

In Poland, Chechens have the chance to receive asylum, which gives them the right to work, to education and to state benefits. If they receive the coveted card, they are also allowed to travel throughout the European Union. More common, however, was the *pobyt tolerowany*, the right to remain in Poland but without state protection. Of applications, about half received this 'pobyt', as the Chechens called it. They none of them wanted it, but it was better than having your application turned down altogether, in which case you could be deported.

Chechens tended to receive a pobyt, unless they could prove they were a former rebel or somehow discriminated against. Just being a Chechen was not enough. Normally, therefore, they needed to produce media reports that identified them by name, which – in a

war that had had little media coverage – could prove hard. Musa was
not worried about that though. He had evidence, he said, of the
suffering he had undergone.

Musa told me that the system was slow and bureaucratic, and that
the officials were stupid. He decided it would be funny if I imperson-
ated him at the processing centre and took his identity card up to the
front desk to ask if there was any change in his condition. After the
joke of having me detained earlier in the day, this would be a new
way of amusing himself.

I refused to play along, although the photograph was of such bad
quality that it could just as well be my face as Musa's on the card. If
nothing else, I told him, it might prejudice his application if he played
too many games with the authorities in one day.

'All right,' he said, 'but you have to stand next to me while I talk
to her, so you can hear how rude they are. It won't make any difference anyway, they won't have made a decision yet.'

We arrived just before the centre was due to close, and walked
straight to the only open window, where two women sat, one of
them filing a tall pile of asylum applications, each with a passport
photo clipped to it. They looked weary, and Musa had to speak quite
loudly before one of them decided to notice we were there.

She looked up Musa's details in the computer, which took a while.
Musa filled in the gap by explaining a new plan he had concocted.
Apparently, the guards at the reception centre were less alert after
4 p.m. so I could get in there again, and we could all have a party. The
guards might even come along. Before I managed to think up an
excuse, the Polish woman broke into his prattle, telling him in her
strange, Polish-accented Russian that his application had been refused,
and the papers were in the post. That was that.

He could fill in a new form to appeal, and a decision would be due
in six weeks, she added before turning back to her screen.

She was not exactly unkind when she said it, but it was clear she
had told so many people these same words that all the edges were
rubbed off them. She was a study in bureaucratic indifference.

Musa was stunned. 'If you'd left me in Belgium, I wouldn't need a
pobyt or anything,' he snapped.

She kept looking at her computer screen, and did not respond.

I have never seen a man change so quickly. The cocksure, jocular man who had tried to incite me into impersonating him was gone. Suddenly he looked old. His hopes of getting asylum were done. He did not even have the despised pobyt. That would have to wait for the appeal. He had nothing. He was suddenly an illegal alien in Poland, and could be deported at any time.

It was terrible.

'I thought I'd get a status as a refugee, I really did,' he said, as we sat once more in the car. 'They give refugees 1,000 zlotys a month, and now I will get nothing. Even if I get this pobyt, they won't give me anything. I think they did this because I went to Belgium. I've lost my mood now, I'm sorry.'

He was rambling. Earlier I had told him the British superstition about how seeing a single magpie was bad luck, and I felt guilty as he brought this up in his disappointment.

'If only we'd seen a second magpie, I'd have got it,' he said.

When we had driven up to the office building, the stereo had been playing Boney M at full volume – 'Rasputin' – but now there was just Musa's voice, bitter and broken.

'I only came here to this centre to show you what it was like. I did not expect an answer. I won't appeal it, what's the point? It's not just in Chechnya or Russia that there's no justice. There's none here either,' he said.

He sat quietly in the car for a while as we waited at the traffic lights and then, when they turned green, he pulled over to the side of the road.

'I'm sorry, I've lost my mood,' he said. 'Can you go now? This is the will of the Almighty. Positive, negative, pobyt, it's not down to me to decide. But I've lost my mood. I'm going to drive away. Can you go now?'

I climbed out of the car. He did not even glance at me while I did so. He sat there motionless, and I watched him wait for a gap to pull out into Warsaw's traffic. His grin had vanished, his eyes were bleak and his face was grey. The gap came at last, and he pulled out steadily, without the tyre spins he had delighted in just ten minutes earlier. He pulled into the outside lane. From his silhouette I could see that his shoulders were still slumped.

He was on his way to the clearing in the forest where he would park his car and sleep that night. And after that? He had said he might go to Turkey. Or perhaps he will try his luck in western Europe again. Whatever he chooses – and I never even found out his surname, so I will never know – it would be even further from what he dreamed of as a boy.

Had he not been a Chechen, I would have called him a broken man.

32. There is No Need for This Any More

While I was writing the previous chapter, a headline popped up on the news that Russia had finally ended its war in Chechnya. The anti-terrorist rules imposed there since 1999 had been cancelled, Chechens would be ruled under the same constitution as the rest of the country, and the rebels – if they emerged again – would be dealt with through normal procedures.

The war, in short, was won.

Ramzan Kadyrov, who rules Chechnya on behalf of Russia, exulted in the news.

'The nest of terrorism has been crushed, illegal armed groups have been neutralized, and militant leaders on whose conscience lay the grief and suffering of thousands of people have been destroyed, detained and brought to court,' he said, according to one Russian news agency.

Leaving aside the question of whether Kadyrov, who was barely literate when I first met him in 2003, could actually construct such a complicated sentence, the fact was impressive. He took over from his father, the mufti Akhmad Kadyrov, who disliked the Wahhabi fighters so strongly as to side with Russia, when his father died in a bombing in 2004.

Since then, he has established a brutally personal form of government that has little in common with the liberal values that still underpin Russia's constitution. Rivals to his rule have been brushed aside. The Yamadayev clan, for example, which allied with his father in helping the Russians in 1999 but became a rival for power, has been sidelined. Two of the brothers were assassinated in unsolved killings within six months of each other in 2008 and 2009. Their surviving brother blamed Kadyrov, but he denied involvement.

A week after the announcement that the war was over, as if the rebels wished to put their hands up and point out that they still existed, they killed three Russian soldiers. So much for the war being over.

In truth, though, the legal changes would have made almost no difference on the ground anyway. The violence in Chechnya has spread to Ingushetia and Dagestan. Policemen, civilians and soldiers will continue to die sporadically for the foreseeable future. The war may have lost its intensity, but it has spread out and it will take years to vanish altogether.

Still, be that as it may, the Russians are right. There is no doubt that militarily speaking they have won. Kadyrov, a man professing loyalty to Moscow, is in charge. The rebels are marginalized and hunted. The most energetic opponents of Russian rule are almost all dead, and more of those who are not are in exile in Europe or elsewhere.

I have to admit though that the Russian announcement made me smile. Just a few weeks before it was made, I had been sitting and chatting with an exiled former rebel leader – he does not like to be identified, to protect himself from retaliation – who made completely the opposite point.

'Chechens have effectively won independence,' he said.

'Now the Russians have almost no influence in Chechnya. I remember a period when I could not speak in Chechen in the bus. We were slapped for this, and now day after day you don't hear a Russian speaking in Chechnya ... I remember the speeches of the Russians. "This is Russian land, this is our land. If they want to build a state, let them build it somewhere else, this is our city, it was us who built it." This is what the Russians said. And now, let them try. In Kadyrov's Chechnya, let some Russian say it is Russian land.'

I was surprised by his apparent endorsement of Kadyrov, whom he considered a traitor, and surprised still further when he told me he would no longer encourage young Chechens to 'go into the mountains' and join the groups resisting Moscow's rule.

He was still a firm believer in his people's cause, he told me, and did not regret having spent much of his adult life fighting the Russians. On the contrary, he exulted in it. But now was the time to sit tight and repair their damaged society. The Russians who once dominated Grozny have left, so the Chechens have the space to rebuild their country in their own way.

'We have won, the people won. There is no need for this any more,' he said.

So, who is right? Who has won? The Chechens, as the rebel leader with his fierce eyes and dark beard told me, or the Russians, as the Kremlin had insisted?

Perhaps they are both right. If both sides of a war have won, then both sides have lost, and that seems far more important than crowing about victory. Just as the Russians have won militarily, there can be no doubt that they have lost in every other way. The former rebel commander was right. The last time I was in Grozny I did not see a single Russian out of uniform. Young people on the street barely spoke the state's language, and my cosmopolitan Chechen friends, educated in the Soviet Union, despaired of the uneducated generation growing up.

The city, which had been so shattered on my earlier visits, had been tidied up and rebuilt. New façades made old buildings look new, and new shops and parks gave Grozny a pleasant air. A new and handsome mosque with minarets and extensive gardens laid out in the middle of town added a suitably Middle Eastern look, only added to by the portraits of Kadyrov on every lamp post and major building. These could have been posters celebrating an Arab dictator.

Kadyrov, though he pays lip service to the Kremlin, has a style of government far removed from the nominal democracy in Russia proper. He has imposed elements of sharia law just like the rebel government before him. I was in Grozny in Ramadan, and alcohol was – for people without connections – impossible to find. Gambling had been banned, and women working for the government had to wear headscarves.

The Russians who lived in Grozny before 1994, the Russians who sheltered with Yashurkayev and his dog Barsik when the bombs rained down, are gone. They live to the north now, in the heartland of the Russian state. The peripheries have been reclaimed by the nations – the Chechens, the Ingush, the Dagestanis – that the Russians tried so hard to displace.

And without ethnic Russians on the ground, the influence of the central government has slipped. In a farcical series of events in February 2009, Moscow tried to impose a new head of the government's tax department in Dagestan. His candidature was unacceptable to the locals because, quite simply, he was a Russian.

Mass protests followed his appointment, and when he arrived in Dagestan in spite of the popular opposition, he was kidnapped and threatened with murder. Not surprisingly, he decided not to take up the post. This is hardly the iron hand that the Kremlin is supposed to wield.

Just a few weeks later Kadyrov, in an interview with the Russian government's own newspaper, made it clear the reason why so many Chechens have now changed sides to support the Kremlin. They want its money.

Asked if he would like to lead an independent Chechnya, he said: 'I will tell you why I don't need sovereignty. We have a small country, not much room to sow and plough, and the birth rate is high. The oil will finish, and then what will I do as a separate state? Who do I turn to?'

With such cupboard loyalty, the Russian government has no reason to congratulate itself on bringing up a new generation of Chechens dedicated to Moscow. Who knows where they will turn when the Russian money runs out?

And yet, if the Russians have not won, then the Chechens certainly have not either. For the 190,000 Chechens or so who have sought asylum in the West, there is the pain of homesickness, and the bureaucratic complications of life in a foreign country. For the Chechens who have chosen to remain at home there is a lack of education, a homeland strewn with mines, a destroyed economy and, still, the risk of arbitrary arrest and death. And though Kadyrov might have brought stability, he has not brought law.

Umar Israilov found this out in the most direct way in 2003, when he was just twenty-one. According to his own account, which he told me over a long afternoon in a Vienna flat, he had helped out the rebels in a small way ever since Russian troops returned to Chechnya in 1999. He had been considered too young to take a direct role in the fighting, he said, but he had done what he could.

'I stored their weapons, I helped them. I lived with a couple of comrades on the edge of Belgatoi,' he said, referring to a village south-east of Grozny. 'And we were ambushed one night when we went into the village for food. They took us first to Argun, they kept us for a couple of days in a basement. Then they took us to Kadyrov's sports club in Gudermes to show us to Ramzan.'

I knew that sports club. A shiny building on a side street, it has a boxing ring and training facilities. Kadyrov has an office upstairs, and likes to welcome foreign journalists there. After being shown to Kadyrov, Israilov and his comrades were moved to Kadyrov's home village of Tsentoroi, where Kadyrov and his father then lived in a large brick compound guarded by grim-faced, bearded men who watched you when you approached.

It was another place that Kadyrov liked to show off to the press, but, according to Israilov, all this time it had a secondary function.

'They had a list of seventeen or eighteen people that they wanted me to sign. They wanted me to admit that I'd killed them. I asked how I could have killed them, so they beat me for two or three days. Then they probably got fed up so they appealed to Ramzan,' Israilov told me.

'I said to Ramzan: "Take your dogs off me or kill me." After that they started to beat me a bit less. Different people came to beat me though, then Ramzan himself. They knew I had stored weapons and wanted to know where they were. I could not stand it. After two weeks I admitted where they were. There were probably ten machine guns, mortars too, I do not remember exactly.'

After that, things got more terrifying. He was still kept in the basement of the big brick compound where I used to be treated to tea during interviews, but now he was just beaten for fun. At one point, an old man was brought in who had sheltered the rebel leader for a couple of days.

'They beat him so badly, even a beast could not have beaten that old man like that. They asked why he had fed Maskhadov, and the old man replied that Maskhadov was a guest and so he had fed him. They called him a dog and beat him for two or three days.'

Eventually, the guards got bored of Israilov, and put him through an amnesty system that allowed former rebel fighters to return to ordinary life. Thousands of separatist foot-soldiers took advantage of the scheme to join Kadyrov's own private army, and Israilov was one of them, though he kept the little kernel of rebellion in his heart.

'I spent three or four months in their base in Tsentoroi, and then Ramzan had me working as his personal bodyguard for a year, maybe for a year and a half, then he let me go and sent me to my village. At that time, my documents were all ready and I immediately went to Poland.'

Although he had reached freedom from his tormentors, in some ways his nightmare was only now beginning. He was sitting in McDonald's in Warsaw, eating a burger, he said, when his phone rang. It was Kadyrov, whose voice he recognized immediately. He had no idea how Kadyrov had got his number, and pretended to be someone else.

'He asked for Umar. I said I did not know an Umar, and that I had just bought the phone. He then told me that I should tell Umar that he had arrested Umar's father and Umar's father's wife, and that he would kill them if I did not come back.'

Kadyrov rang back every day, and eventually Israilov admitted that it was him, and told Kadyrov to just kill his father because he was never coming home. Israilov stuck to his word, and Kadyrov illegally held and tortured his father for ten months, before releasing him too. His father is now a refugee in Europe as well. His story tallies with his son's.

Israilov finally applied for asylum in Austria, and received it in September 2005. He was still only just putting a life together when I spoke to him. We were sitting in the flat of a mutual friend, and Israilov was trying to find a place for himself to live. At the time, he, his wife and his three children were living about a hundred kilometres from Vienna, and he wanted to be nearer to the centre of things, but it was proving hard.

'There are flats but when I phone up and say I have three children, well, I have an accent and when I phone up they ask who I am and I say I am from Russia so they ask if I have children, and I say I have three and they say they cannot help me. I think I have looked at every flat in the paper,' he said.

'Poles are more friendly. At least, they look at you with a smile, but these Austrians won't even look at you.'

He finished phoning up the numbers for flats in the paper, and moved on to a property website. He must have called ten different houses with the same result. Although his German was as good as any I had heard spoken by a Chechen, as soon as he opened his mouth and introduced himself, the landlord put the phone down.

This went on all through the long afternoon, and after a few hours he laid the phone aside and came to sit with me on the sofa. He put his head in his hands. 'This is the fourth month I have been looking for a flat,' he said, 'and nothing.'

Israilov had kept himself busy throughout his time in Austria. He had learnt German, and had submitted papers to the European Court of Human Rights to try to win recompense for his suffering. He had given evidence to activist groups, and he had even spoken to another journalist or two. But none of it helped the fact that he was living in a far-off country, and could not fit in no matter how hard he tried.

I parted from him sadly. I had enjoyed talking to him, and I was hopeful about his future. He seemed to be an energetic, intelligent man, keen to become involved in European life, who could go far if only he could get a little help. But I did not really think about him again until the next year, when a headline appeared on an internet news service: 'Austrian police probe political link in Chechen's killing'. For some reason, I knew immediately it was about Israilov.

I opened the story, and sure enough he had been killed. On 13 January 2009, he had left his Vienna flat – he must have found one at last, not that it did him much good – to buy yoghurt. Two men were waiting for him. He ran zig-zagging through the traffic to get away, but stumbled and fell after his pursuers fired four times. As he lay on the ground, they fired two shots into his head. He died instantly.

The killing gained a surprising profile in the international media. Obviously, a Chechen being killed in Vienna was far more interesting than Chechens being killed in Chechnya, but still it was strange to see how much more interested the world was in this bright, abused young man now he was dead. A suspect picked up by Austrian police was quoted saying that Israilov had 'deserved to die', since he had changed sides, which allowed the newspapers to speculate on death squads roaming the streets of Europe's capitals.

And perhaps they were right, for Israilov's death was part of a worrying trend. Three Chechens had been killed in Istanbul in the previous few months, and Sulim Yamadayev – the most prominent pro-Russian Chechen after Kadyrov – was assassinated in Dubai in March 2009, just six months after his brother was killed in Moscow.

Chechens dying abroad is not a new thing. Two Chechens were killed in London as early as 1993, while the poet Yandarbiyev was killed by Russian agents in Qatar in 2004.

But the latest wave of killings seems far more extensive, and far more politically driven.

The world has ignored the horrors and killings in Chechnya these last years, but with an ever-growing Chechen population outside Russia, and no sign that Moscow is prepared to compromise on its heavy-handed approach to Chechens' dreams of independence, perhaps we will find more Chechens being killed on European streets. And that would surely be impossible to ignore.

Postscript
The Boy Who Chose an Orange, Not a Gun

In the depths of winter, in early 2003, my editor sent me out of Moscow to a little town where the central heating had broken down. Russian towns often still possess these Soviet-era heating systems, when a whole block or suburb gets its hot water from a single factory.

In this case, the factory had halted its work briefly. That meant the water in the pipes had stopped moving, had frozen and had exploded out in extraordinary frozen waterfalls of rusty ice. It was the kind of slow-news-day story that journalists have to do sometimes. It would barely be noticed in the slew of interesting articles from other places.

The excitement for me was that Adlan Khasanov, Reuters' Chechen photographer, was coming with me. I had been trying to learn enough to report properly on Chechnya for months and this, it seemed, would be the perfect time to learn a few details about the fighting, the people and the culture. I would have a real-life Chechen to myself for the whole four-hour drive there, and the four hours back, and reckoned I would learn as much from him as I had from all the books I had read.

It did not turn out that way.

Adlan had no interest in talking about war. He wanted to talk about my home in Wales, about music, about concerts, about vodka and about girls. We gossiped all the way there, and laughed our way around the story. The unfortunate people we were meeting, whose houses were so cold there was ice on the light bulbs, were welcoming and jolly in the face of his charm. One family was from Grozny. As Russian emigrants, I expected they would loathe their Chechen visitor, but Adlan made friends with them too. They gave us tea and biscuits and thawed us out in their warm house, where they mocked their neighbours who had not had the brains to install a private heating system.

So, my plan was a failure, and I found out nothing about the war. But I gained a new friend, and Adlan proved a ray of light into the often dark job of covering the Chechen war.

I can picture him now, striding down the open-plan Reuters office: long, dark hair; handsome, wide face with a grin of welcome; big, laughing voice.

'Oliver, you have become so fat' was a common opening to our conversations. If I had not seen him come in, he would sneak up behind me and grab the side of my stomach to prove the point that, as I got closer to thirty years old, I was indeed getting fatter.

He spent much of his time in Grozny, whence he would send photos of refugees, soldiers and poverty. But his pictures often missed the standard war clichés – tanks, guns, soldiers – in favour of children, or weddings, or sports practice, or prayers. In short, he documented how Chechens kept living while the bombs exploded around them, while the politicians failed to save them.

When he came to Moscow, he became playful. He took daft photos at the zoo, including a whole series depicting monkeys with bottles in their mouths; and touching shots of a polar bear cub with its mother. A favourite game was to swipe the most impressive-looking cameras from the cupboard and shoot close-up pictures of the models at the fashion shows held downstairs in our office building. Adlan loved girls, and these girls loved him: tall, dark, good-looking and a photographer.

Adlan and I went out for beers, and he taught me a bit about his homeland, when he wasn't talking about the subjects that really interested him. I had an insatiable appetite for war gossip, since this was a time when Reuters did not let its staff travel to Chechnya without an official escort. But most of his chat was about his friends, or his parties. He talked about them with such life that eventually I learned that war isn't about politicians anyway, it's about the people caught up in it.

Even when we covered events together in Chechnya, he didn't much want to talk about what we were doing. I can remember standing with him outside the polling station in the village of Tsentoroi on 5 October 2003, waiting for Akhmad Kadyrov, the former Chechen mufti who changed sides to become Moscow's man in Chechnya, to come out and talk to us. I was so excited to be there I could hardly stand still. Adlan wanted to talk about a film he'd seen.

After that, whenever I wrote something about Kadyrov and the convoluted loyalties of Chechnya, I would imagine Adlan, his eyes glistening with merriment, ducking through the crowds at the polling station, sidestepping men with guns to get the shot he needed so he could finish for the day, and get stuck into the real business.

At the time, I had been mystified. How could he not have been fascinated by these changes in his homeland? I learned later how completely I had misjudged him. He had spent the night before huddled with a friend in the corner of his courtyard as the bullets flew overhead.

It was a useful image to have, because Russia is so large that it is easy to forget that history and politics are not about enormous social forces, or economic interest groups, but about the people who are trying to live their lives. Having a teacher with a life-force as strong as Adlan's, it was impossible to overlook the fact that Chechens were not pawns being moved around a battlefield by generals or terrorists, but individuals whose lives had been turned upside down by a war they had not wanted.

And it is an image I have kept in my head when writing this book, to avoid the world view of the Russian rulers who have imposed their own pictures on the Caucasus for too long. I hope readers will have seen that the history of Russia's conquest is one of tragedy for the people of the mountains. The Circassians, the mountain Turks, the Ingush and the Chechens have all suffered horribly just so the map of Russia could be the shape the tsars, the general secretaries and the presidents wanted it to be.

Sadly, that suffering is not well-known in Russia, perhaps because Russians themselves have suffered so terribly that they prefer not to remember the horrors they have imposed on others. Joseph Stalin is supposed to have once said: 'One death is a tragedy, a million deaths is a statistic.' It is a proverb that fits Russia's policies in the Caucasus like a Cossack fits his boots.

'Russia for centuries has played in this region of the world, in the Caucasus as a whole, a positive, stabilizing role, has been a guarantor of security, cooperation and progress in this region, and it will behave in the future as it has in the past. Let no one doubt this,' Vladimir Putin, once again prime minister, told Russian television viewers on 9 August 2008, as he prepared them for the Russian–Georgian war.

I am not defending Georgia's attack on South Ossetia, which killed hundreds of people who should not have died, but Putin's comment was so far removed from the actual experiences of people living in the Caucasus as to appear to be describing a completely different part of the world. Putin actually seemed to believe that the brutal conquest of the mountains, the destruction of the Circassians, the mountain Turks, the Chechens and the Ingush, along with the corruption and the violence that Russia brought, came under the heading of 'security, cooperation and progress'.

Or perhaps, more worryingly still, he did not even know about the massacres, the deportations and the destruction.

In June 2007, Putin, then still president, met a group of history and humanities teachers at his official residence just outside Moscow. The teachers expressed their concerns about their jobs and their wishes for the future. One history teacher, Vladislav Golovanov, from the remote Siberian region of Yakutia, was appalled by revisionist approaches to the past, by attempts to introduce a bit of balance to Soviet hagiography, as exemplified by a pupil who claimed to have read a book saying that Soviet forces had killed their own comrades in the Second World War.

For real historians, this is not a contentious point. Execution was a crucial element in steeling discipline against the German invasion, and special units were created to scour behind the Soviet lines, to find deserters and to kill them. Many veterans of the Red Army, particularly those who were freed from German prison camps by Soviet soldiers, can testify to it and it is an accepted fact in standard histories of the Second World War.

For Golovanov, however, it was blasphemy.

'Our history is not a cause for self-flagellation,' he exploded.

'For me personally our history is always successful: it is successful per se, together with all its difficulties, maybe it is successful particularly with its difficulties. The importance of success is that a child wants to be in a successful team, do you understand? They demand to be in a successful team, they want, they delight in the successes of our history.'

It is perhaps worrying for residents of Yakutia that Golovanov sees history not as a record of the past, which can teach children about the world, about how they got where they are, but rather as a tool of propaganda, a list of 'successes' to turn his pupils into cheerleading Russian patriots. But, essentially, that is not too surprising a comment from a provincial teacher in a country that was, after all, communist just sixteen years before.

Far more worrying is Putin's response to his little rant, which I will quote at length, just because it is so revealing of his mentality and, by extension, the mentality of the whole ruling class of modern Russia.

'Yes, there are problematic pages in our history, in just the same way as there are in the history of every state and every people! And we had a lot fewer than some others. And ours were not so terrible as those of others. Yes, we had scary pages: let's remember the events starting in 1937, let's not forget about this. But in other countries there were no fewer, and there were many scarier. In any case, we did not use atomic bombs against a civilian population. We did not pour chemicals on thousands of kilometres, and did not drop onto a little country seven times more bombs than were used in all the Second World War, as occurred in Vietnam for example. We did not have other black pages, like Nazism for example,' Putin said, in a rant of his own.

'And it must not be allowed that we are forced to feel a sense of guilt. Let them think about themselves.'

It is true that Moscow did not drop atomic bombs on civilians; nor did it attack Vietnam; nor was it Nazi. But, for all that, Putin is profoundly wrong. As I hope this book has demonstrated, Russia's actions in the Caucasus – independent of the politics or beliefs of its rulers over the centuries – have been destructive, murderous, brutal and cruel. A history that only portrays the successes of the Russian nation cannot accommodate the experiences of minority peoples that were oppressed in altogether non-glorious episodes.

A glorious narrative of the nineteenth century can have no place for the genocide of the Circassians in 1864. A glorious narrative of the Second World War cannot include massive crimes like the deportations of the Chechens, the Ingush and the mountain Turks, let alone squalid little massacres like that in the Cherek valley in 1942. A glorious narrative of the post-Soviet years can find no place for the tactics of murder, destruction and robbery used to crush the Chechens, nor for the mass exodus that has been the Chechens' response.

And it can have no place for the character of someone like my friend Adlan, who will never fit any historian's theories.

In the winter of 1999–2000, Adlan and a friend were driving back from Georgia, where they had been delivering pictures they had taken of the bombardment in Chechnya.

Just forty kilometres from Grozny, their car stalled when crossing a river, where it was a perfect target for the roaming Russian jets. The terrified driver vanished, and the two friends desperately pushed the car off the bridge, nervously scanning the skies. His friend later recalled that Adlan shouted throughout: 'I hate war. I don't like people with guns. I am a peaceful man. This is not for me.'

And he had always been like that. As a child, his father once offered him an orange with one hand and a gun with the other. The stereotypical Chechen boy, the trainee bandit of the Russian newspaper reports, should have reached out for the gun. Adlan took the orange.

In early May – or perhaps late April – 2004, I was working in the office, when Adlan walked up to my desk. He was leaving for the day. I was doing some administrative tasks, but they were not important as such, so I stopped what I was doing to have a chat.

'Let's go and have a beer,' he said after a while. 'We can go to the Chechen bar.' The Chechen bar was a café near the office run by a woman from Grozny who, like Adlan, now spent much of her time in Moscow.

'I can't,' I replied, gesturing to the various bits of paper I had pulled out of the chaos of my desk. 'I've got to get this stuff done. Let's have a drink tomorrow.'

He said he was going back to the Caucasus in the morning, and we agreed to have that drink as soon as he got back. He made a couple of jokes about the size of my stomach, shook my hand and left to find another drinking partner.

He was killed by a bomb in a Grozny stadium a few days later, on 9 May 2004, in the same attack that killed Akhmad Kadyrov.

Pictures of my friend's body – twisted and ungainly as it sprawled on the grass of the stadium, lacking all the grace and lightness he possessed as he bounced through life – decorated Russian newspapers for the next few days. The Moscow papers lack the squeamishness of Western titles when it comes to graphic pictures of death, and every time I saw him it was like another blow of grief.

I saw him at night too. At first, the dreams were urgent and ugly. He had something to tell me, and I could not make it out. Time passed, the grief faded, and the dreams became less frequent. Now, when I see him, he is his old funny self again. Before my last trip to Chechnya, he popped up to counsel me to buy a ruinously expensive camera lens I had been coveting for months.

'What are you waiting for?' he asked me, with that same old grin. 'You'll regret it if you don't get it and you won't regret it if you do.'

He was right too. I haven't regretted it for a moment.

I had that lens in my bag when I visited his grave a few months ago. It is marked by a tall slab of concrete, painted white, with his name and dates set into it. The earth is piled high over his body, and the friends who were with me prayed, passing their hands over their faces in the graceful Muslim ritual, while I stood with my head bowed.

Since his burial four years previously, another 300 or so gravestones had been erected in this little cemetery, on the edge of the village of Starye Atagi, just a few kilometres south of Grozny, where the plain slopes into the wooded foothills, which in turn soar upwards until they become the high, white peaks. Every person in that graveyard had been – like Adlan had been for me – a friend, or a father, or a sister, or a daughter. And every death was one more tragedy. Stalin was wrong. If you add a million of them together, you don't get a statistic, you just get a million tragedies.

That evening, although it was Ramadan, I raised a glass of beer to him in a café in Grozny, and made sure to take leave of my friends properly, and to tell them how much they meant to me.

Very early the next morning, they came to see me off when I departed from the dusty square where minibuses pick up loads of passengers, squeeze them in next to large, checked nylon bags tied up with string, and drive off to the other cities of the North Caucasus: Vladikavkaz, Makhachkala, Nalchik, Pyatigorsk, further still.

As dawn lightened, we were climbing one of the many ridges that score the rolling plains of northern Chechnya on the road towards Mozdok, a garrison town of dirty, low-rise red-brick buildings that had been my staging point on the way out of Chechnya so many times.

The rising sun had burned off the fog and, as we topped the long ridge, the mountains suddenly loomed up to the left of us: impossibly grand in the pink light of the morning. There was Kazbek, with its sloped shoulders like a monk in white. Then there was the jagged chain running away from it, far into the west, higher and higher to the sharp peak of Dykhtau, which rears above the Cherek valley. And that solid loom on the horizon was Elbrus, the double-headed giant of the central Caucasus, emblem of the land of the mountain Turks.

The peaks, despite their bulk, floated in the buttery morning light with a grace the harsh noon glare never allows them. Blue pockets of the sky hung in the shadows where the light did not reach. I gazed entranced as the light changed, and the mountains shifted and altered with it.

The minibus slowed down. It was time to concentrate again. Ahead was the ugly gatehouse of a Russian checkpoint, a temporary structure that had over time become permanent, surrounded by vicious tangles of barbed wire. The soldiers, bored after their night on guard, scanned our van with casual arrogance and waved us through.

The passengers around me relaxed a little, as we sped away from the wire and the warning signs. I was tired, leaned my head on the window and dozed. The mountains melted into the morning haze as we jolted through Mozdok, and were invisible long before we arrived at the old spa town of Pyatigorsk, where Lermontov died in his senseless duel. There I paid a bribe to a policeman who questioned my passport and he, perhaps out of gratitude, found me another bus. This one took me through Cherkessk, Maikop and Krasnodar, before we arrived by the sea, in Sochi, where I had plans.

The roads I followed in that bumpy twenty-four-hour bus ride were laid down more than two centuries before as tracks linking Cossack villages to Russian forts. They solidified into post roads, the nerves of empire, before becoming the tarmac arteries that they are today.

I sat in Sochi, drank a cup of tea and watched the tourists in their shorts and bikinis. I wondered if even one of them knew that this stretch of balmy coastline once belonged to the Circassians, or that Circassians had died on these very beaches as they waited for Turkish boats to take them into an exile from which their nation never returned.

Few if any of these Russian holidaymakers would know at what cost their country had purchased the clean air and sun of the south. The Circassians still remember; as do the Chechens, the mountain Turks, the Ingush and the others. But the Russians have not preserved the memory of their wars for the Caucasus, and the ghosts of their victims will haunt them till they do.

Sources

As is obvious from the text, much of this book is based on personal reminiscences from people I met during my travels. Almost all of them agreed to be identified, and I am very grateful to them for it.

I also used books in Russian, English and French (many of which were only available in the British Library, which provided an excellent service for which I am very grateful) as sources of ideas and information.

The best overall book for the conquest of the Caucasus and for a general history of the region is John F. Baddeley's *Russian Conquest of the Caucasus*, which, although it was published in 1908, is still superb. The more recent *Muslim Resistance to the Tsar*, by Moshe Gammar (London, 1994), is also excellent.

Sadly, both of these books largely ignore the Circassian war, and the mass deportation that followed it. This has never been properly dealt with by historians.

Charles King attempted the impossible in his *The Ghost of Freedom, a History of the Caucasus* (Oxford, 2008). His book is interesting, and useful, but the lack of detail is sometimes infuriating.

An excellent atlas of the history, demographics and geography of the Caucasus was written by Artur Tsutsiyev and published in Moscow in 2006 under the name *Atlas etnopoliticheskoi istorii kavkaza* (*Atlas of the Ethnopolitical History of the Caucasus*).

More specifically, here are the main sources used for each section of the book.

1783

The main source for this section is the imperial Russian historian Vasily Potto's *Kavkazskaya Voina v otdelnykh ocherkakh, epizodakh, legendakh i biografiyakh* (*The Caucasus War in Separate Essays, Episodes,*

Legends and Biographies, published in 1889), which was also used as a
source by Baddeley.

Baddeley, like seemingly all writers in English, wrongly located
the battle at the town of Yeisk, rather than at Yei Ukreplenie nearby.
Some other details on the Nogais are taken from *Vorontsov, Osnovatel
goroda Yeiska* (*Vorontsov, the Founder of the City of Yeisk*) (Yeisk, 2006) by
Yevgeny Kotenko; from Philip Longworth's *Russia's Empires* (London, 2006); and from *Russia's Steppe Frontier* by Mikhail Khodarkovsky (Bloomington, Ind., 2004).

The 'English traveller' was J. A. Longworth in the second volume
of his *A Year among the Circassians* (London, 1840, and reissued in
facsimile by Elibron Classics in 2005), which is an invaluable account
of how the Circassians lived before their destruction.

The 'let our fame be great' story is from the magnificent selection
of Caucasus folk tales compiled and translated by John Colarusso,
under the title *Nart Sagas from the Caucasus* (Princeton, NJ, 2002).

1864

Chapters 1 and 2

There has been very little research into the Circassian diaspora, but useful
articles include 'Some Notes on the Settlement of Northern Caucasians
in Eastern Anatolia' by Georgy Chochiev (*Journal of Asian History*, 40/1,
2006) and 'Some Aspects of the Social Integration of the North Caucasian Immigrants', also by Georgy Chochiev, http://www.circassianworld.
com/pdf/G_Chochiev_Immigrants_Applications.pdf.

Chen Bram is probably the best researcher into the subject, and specializes in Israel's Circassians. He has written 'Muslim Revivalism and
the Emergence of Civic Society, a Case Study of an Israeli-Circassian
Community' (*Central Asian Survey*, March 2003) and 'Circassian
Re-Emigration to the Caucasus' (in *Roots and Routes: Emigration in a Global Perspective*, Jerusalem, 1999). He is also a very interesting lecturer.

The www.circassianworld.com website has a good selection of articles on Circassian subjects, including 'From Immigrants to Diaspora:
Influence of the North Caucasian Diaspora in Turkey' by Mitat

Elikpala; 'Emigrations from the Russian Empire to the Ottoman Empire: An Analysis in the Light of the New Archival Materials' by Berat Yildiz; and 'The First "Circassian Exodus" to the Ottoman Empire (1858–1867), and the Ottoman Response, Based on the Accounts of Contemporary British Observers' by Sarah Rosser-Owen.

The Circassians (Richmond, 2001) by Amjad Jaimoukha is also a useful book, although it is expensive and focused on the Circassians to the exclusion of all context.

Chapter 3

This chapter is primarily based on J. A. Longworth's journal *A Year among the Circassians*, as well as on James Stanislaus Bell's two-volume *Journal of a Residence in Circassia* (London, 1840, and reissued in facsimile by Elibron Classics in 2005). Edmund Spencer's *Travels in Circassia, Krim Tartary, etc* (London, 1838, and reissued in facsimile by Elibron Classics in 2005) was also helpful.

Tornau's own volume of memoirs, *Vospominaniya Kavkazskogo Ofitsera* (*Memoirs of a Caucasus Officer*), was first published in Moscow in 1864, and since 1991 has been printed several more times. John Shelton Curtiss's *The Russian Army under Nicholas I* (Durham, NC, 1965) is magnificent.

The Alexandre Dumas anecdote is from *Adventures in the Caucasus* (published in English in London, 1962). Xavier Hommaire de Hell's *Travels in the Steppes of the Caspian Sea, the Crimea, the Caucasus, etc.* (London, 1847) was also useful. Nikolai Ivanovich Lorer's memoirs were published in the Soviet Union as *Zapiski Dekabrista* (*Notes of a Decembrist*) in 1931 and are moving and wonderful.

George Leighton Ditson's *Circassia, or a Tour to the Caucasus* (New York, 1850) was not very helpful, and neither was G. Poulett Cameron's *Personal Adventures and Excursions in Georgia, Circassia and Russia* (London, 1845); nor was *Notes of a Half-Pay in Search of Health; or Russia, Circassia and the Crimea in 1839* (London, 1841). I will not be reading any of them again.

David Urquhart has attracted the interest of several historians, but sadly his only biographer has been Gertrude Robinson, whose *David Urquhart: Some Chapters in the Life of a Victorian Knight Errant of Justice and Liberty* (my version was published in New York in 1970, but it was originally published in 1920) is not a triumph. He is a man who would be a wonderful subject for a proper biography.

Other details can be found in David Urquhart's *England, France, Russia and Turkey* (published in 1835); in *British Diplomacy as Illustrated in the Affair of the 'Vixen'* by 'An old Diplomatic Servant' (viz. Urquhart), a pamphlet published in 1838; and in a speech by Urquhart published as a pamphlet in 1863 under the title *The Flag of Circassia*.

'David Urquhart and the Eastern Question 1833–37' by G. H. Bolsover (*The Journal of Modern History*, VIII, 1936) was useful, while 'Urquhart, Ponsonby, and Palmerston' by Charles Webster (*English Historical Review*, LXII, 1947) gives the crucial insight that Urquhart was mad. Also interesting is *Imagining Circassia: David Urquhart and the Making of North Caucasus Nationalism* by Charles King (*The Russian Review*, vol. 66, issue 2). *The Genesis of Russophobia in Great Britain* by John Howes Gleason (Cambridge, Mass., 1950) has an excellent chapter on Urquhart.

Chapter 4

Much of the information on Muhammad-Emin and the Crimean War comes from Longworth's report in the UK Foreign Office archives in Kew, London. On the slave trade, Dumas's travel notes and Moritz Wagner's *Travels in Persia, Georgia and Koordistan* (London, 1856) were useful, but the best source was Ehud R. Toledano's *The Ottoman Slave Trade and Its Suppression* (Princeton, NJ, 1982).

Chapter 5

The major sources for this chapter are of course the books themselves: Lermontov's *A Hero of Our Time* (English translation by Vladimir Nabokov, New York, 2002); Pushkin's *Prisoner in the Caucasus* is found in *Eugene Onegin and Four Tales from Russia's Southern Frontier*, translated by Roger Clarke (Ware, 2005) and *Journey to Arzrum* (translated by Birgitta Ingemanson, Ann Arbor, 1974); Bestuzhev's *Ammalat Bek* (there is a section in English in *Blackwood's Magazine*, published in Edinburgh in May 1843 and available online); Grace Walton's *Schamyl, or the Wild Woman of Circassia* (London, 1856); and Alexandre Dumas's *Adventures in the Caucasus* and *The Snow on Shah-Dagh and Ammalet Bey* (London, 1899, in a translated form that credits Bestuzhev-Marlinsky).

The best summary of the criticism is Susan Layton's *Russian Literature and Empire* (Cambridge, 1994).

Other useful books were Lauren G. Leighton's *Alexander Bestuzhev-Marlinsky* (Boston, 1975), Lewis Bagby's *Alexander Bestuzhev-Marlinsky and Russian Byronism* (University Park, Pa., 1995), Elaine Feinstein's *Pushkin* (London, 1998), Laurence Kelly's spectacularly good *Lermontov: Tragedy in the Caucasus* (London, 2003), Harsha Ram's 'Pushkin and the Caucasus' in *The Pushkin Handbook* (Madison, Wis., 2005) and T. J. Binyon's *Pushkin* (London, 2002).

Chapter 6

The 'extermination alone' quote is from George Leighton Ditson's memoirs. This was rather an own goal, since he was attempting to repair the damage done to Russia's image by other foreign visitors.

The Foreign Office documents are available in the UK government's record office in Kew, which is a great place full of very helpful people. Arthur de Fonvielle's account was originally published in the imperial Russian magazine *Russky Invalid* (*Russian Invalid*, 1865), but has been reprinted in pamphlet form as *Posledny god voiny Cherkesii za nezavisimost 1863–1864* (*The Last Year of Circassia's War for Independence 1863–4*). The complete version was published in Kiev in 1991, and the bowdlerized version was published in Nalchik in the same year.

The historical newspaper quotes here, and throughout the book, come from copies held either digitally or on microfilm in the British Library, which is a magnificent institution.

Chapters 7 and 8

There is not much on the modern history of what was once Circassia, but books covering the development of elite and mass tourism include

Sochi, stranitsy proshlogo i nastoyashechego (*Sochi, Pages of the Past and the Present*) (published in 2007 by the Sochi history museum); *Bolshoi Sochi* (*Greater Sochi*) by Sergei Shumov and Alexander Andreyev (Moscow, 2008); *Kurorty Chernomorya i severnogo kavkaza* (*Resorts of the Black Sea Coast and the North Caucasus*) (published in 1924); as well as modern guidebooks such as *100 Chudes u Chernogo Morya* (*100 Wonders of the Black Sea*) (Krasnodar, 2007).

Chapter 9

Berzegov's plight has been ignored by mainstream media organizations, but has occasionally been covered by the Regnum news agency and the Caucasian Knot (www.kavkaz.memo.ru) human rights website.

1943–4

The best book on the deportations is Robert Conquest's *The Nation Killers* (London, 1970). Aleksandr Nekrich's *The Punished Peoples* (New York, 1978) also has some good information, as does Anne Applebaum's magnificent *Gulag* (London, 2003). *Against Their Will: The History and Geography of Forced Migrations in the USSR* by Pavel Polian (Budapest, 2003) has also been useful.

Chapter 10

This chapter is based on the unpublished manuscript *U menya byl dom Rodnoi* (*I Had a Home*) by Osman Korkmazov and on my conversations with the author.

Chapter 11

Details in this chapter are taken from some of the many books written about Chechnya. The massacre in the Chechen village of Khaybakh is well described in Carlotta Gall and Thomas de Waal's excellent *Chechnya: A Small Victorious War* (London, 1997). Michaela Pohl's superb research was published as two papers called 'It Cannot be That Our Graves Will be Here' (www.chechnyaadvocacy.org/history/Graves%20-%20MPohl.pdf) and 'From the Chechen People' (http://www.chechnyaadvocacy.org/history/From%20the%20Chechen%20people%20-%20MPohl.pdf).

Chapter 12

Figures and documents in this chapter are taken from *Balkartsy: Vyselenie i Vozvrashchenie* (*The Balkars: Deportation and Return*) by Kh.-A. M. Sabanchiyev (Nalchik, 2008); from *Byli soslani navechno* (*They were Sent Away for Ever*) (Nalchik, 2004) by the same author; and from *Pravda o Vyselenii balkartsev* (*The Truth about the Deportation of the Balkars*) by D. V. Shabayev (Nalchik, 1992).

Chapter 13

This chapter is based on Douglas Freshfield's *The Exploration of the Caucasus* (London, 1896); on his *Travels in the Central Caucasus and Bashan* (London, 1869); and on F. C. Grove's *The Frosty Caucasus* (London, 1875). The account of the 1829 expedition to Elbrus is from Prince Golitsyn's *Zhizneopisannie Generela ot Kavalerii Emanuelya* (*Life-Sketches of the Cavalry General Emanuel*) (published 1851 and Moscow, 2004).

Credit for the conquest of Elbrus is too often assigned for nationalist reasons. British writers tend to assign it to Freshfield (see *From a Tramp's Wallet: A Life of Douglas William Freshfield* by Hervey Fisher (Norfolk, 2001)), whereas Circassians or Russians assign it to a local (such as in Amjad Jaimoukha's *The Circassians*). I tried to be fair, and assigned it to neither of them.

The details on turn-of-the-century conditions in the high Caucasus come from J. F. Baddeley's magnificent two-volume labour of love *The Rugged Flanks of the Caucasus* (Oxford, 1940), which is full of treasure for anyone interested in the region, and also from Zhilyabi Kalmykov's very competent *Ustanovlenie Russkoi Administratsii v Kabarde i Balkarii* (*The Establishment of Russian Administration in Kabarda and Balkaria*) (Nalchik, 1995).

Chapter 14

The 'sardonic journalist' observing the collapse of white rule in southern Russia in 1920 was C. E. Bechhofer, whose *In Denikin's Russia and the Caucasus* (London, 1921) is unjustifiably forgotten. Richard Douglas King's *Sergei Kirov and the Struggle for Soviet Power in the Terek Region 1917–18* (New York, 1987) was also useful.

Most of the details on Khutai's life come from conversations with elderly Balkars, but articles from the magazine *Balkaria* and the website www.balkaria.info were useful pointers towards what questions to ask.

Chapter 15

Most of the detail in this chapter comes from the extraordinary book *Cherekskaya Tragediya* (*The Cherek Tragedy*) by K. G. Azamatov, M. O. Temirzhanov, B. B. Temukuev, A. I. Tetuev and I. M. Chechenov (Nalchik, 1994), which cuts through the official versions to detail the facts about the massacre in 1942. I cannot praise this book enough.

To create the narrative of the massacre, I have mixed the conversations I had with survivors with the book's tales of the Cherek valley massacre, which were gathered from survivors in the early 1990s. The book is now unfindable except with extreme good luck, although parts of it are available in Russian on the internet.

In the absence of the book, O. O. Aishaev's *Genotsida mirnykh zhitelei balkarskikh sel v noyabre-dekabre 1942 goda* (*The Genocide of the Civilian Residents of Balkar Villages in November to December 1942*) (Nalchik, 2007) has a good account of the massacre, and is based on the same materials.

Chapter 16

The information on the deported Balkars comes from *Pravda o Vyselenii balkartsev* (*The Truth about the Deportation of the Balkars*), *Byli soslani navechno* (*They were Sent Away for Ever*) and from *Balkartsy: Vyselenie i vozvrashchenie* (*The Balkars: Deportation and Return*).

Chapter 17

Much of this chapter is based on court documents given to me by Iskhak Kuchukov. Ali Misirov's tale is detailed in *Cherekskaya Tragediya* (*The Cherek Tragedy*), and his acting career is testified to in, among other places, the closing credits of *Khrustalyov, Mashinu*, the film described in the chapter.

1995

The best general book on relations between the Chechens and the Russian government is Moshe Gammer's *The Lone Wolf and the Bear* (Pittsburgh, 2006).

The North Caucasus Barrier, edited by Marie Bennigsen-Broxup (London, 1992), has several articles on different aspects of the mountains, but is perhaps best on the Chechens.

Chapter 18

Several journalists who covered the 1994–6 Chechen war wrote books about their experiences. Some of the best of these are Sebastian Smith's *Allah's Mountains* (London, 1998), Gall and de Waal's *Chechnya: A Small Victorious War* and Vanora Bennett's *Crying Wolf* (London, 1998).

Details on the discrimination suffered by Chechens in pre-1991 Chechnya are from an interesting article in the *Central Asian Survey* (vol. 10, no. 1/2, 1991).

The collection of Chechen state documents *Ternisty Put K Svobode* (*The Thorny Path to Freedom*) was published in Vilnius in 1993.

Some of the details on relations with Russia come from Tony Wood's *Chechnya: A Case for Independence* (London, 2007).

The collapse of the Russian state, and the rise of criminal gangs after 1991, is fascinatingly documented in *Comrade Criminal* (New Haven, Conn., 1995) by Stephen Handelman.

Chapter 19

The details on Peter the Great's expedition come from Gammer and Baddeley.

The stories from Dagestan were told to me on my travels in the Caucasus. Other anecdotes are taken from Baddeley's *Rugged Flanks of the Caucasus*, and from *Skazaniya Narodov Dagestana o Kavkazskoi Voine* (*Sayings of the Peoples of Dagestan about the Caucasus War*), which was published in 1997 in Makhachkala under the editorship of M. M. Kurbanov.

Accounts of Sheikh Mansur's life are very vague. Gammar's 'A Preliminary to Decolonising the Historiography of Sheikh Mansur' (*Middle Eastern Studies*, 32, 1, January 1996) is a bit incomprehensible, while other accounts are unreliable. The main biography is by 'Nart' – supposedly a descendant of Mansur. This was written in 1924, and published in the *Central Asian Survey* (vol. 10, no. 1/2, 1991). Other details come from the account of the last days of Imam Shamil in *Dnevnik Runovskogo* (*Runovsky's Diary*) in the twelfth tome of the *Akty Kavkazskoi Arkheograficheskoi komissii* (*Acts of the Caucasus Archeographical Commission*) (Tbilisi, 1866 onwards).

The best book on the arrival of Naqshbandi Islam in the Caucasus is Anna Zelkina's *In Quest for God and Freedom* (London, 2000). Slightly older, but almost equally interesting, is *Mystics and Commissars: Sufism in the Soviet Union* by Alexandre Bennigsen and S. Enders Wimbush (Berkeley, Calif. Press, 1985).

Also useful was *Islam in Post-Soviet Russia*, edited by Hilary Pilkington (London, 2003).

Timur Mutsurayev albums are hard to find these days, although his return to Chechnya may change that. The song 'Sheikh Mansur' is on his album *12 tysyach Modzhakhedov* (*12,000 Mujahedin*).

Chapter 20

The events surrounding Imam Shamil's raid on Georgia and the princesses' captivity are most notably told in Lesley Blanch's *Sabres of Paradise* (my edition was published in New York in 1995), in which she gives the impression she would like nothing more than to be swept off by a wild horseman herself.

Other useful sources were Anne Drancey's *Captive des Tchetchenes* (Paris, 2006); E. A. Verderevsky's *Captivity of Two Russian Princesses in the Caucasus* (London, 1857, although I have a reprint by Kessinger Publishing); and the anonymous Prussian officer's *A Visit to Schamyl* (London, 1857). Shamil's former scribe Muhammad Tahir al-Qarakhi wrote his own account, called 'The Shining of Dagestani Swords in Certain Campaigns of Shamil', which is included in *Russian–Muslim Confrontation in the Caucasus* (edited by Thomas Sanders, Ernest Tucker and Gary Hamburg, London, 2004).

Other useful snippets on Shamil came from *A Campaign with the Turks in Asia* by Charles Duncan (London, 1855); and from J. Milton Mackie's *Life of Schamyl* (Boston, 1856, although I have a University of Michigan reprint).

Chapter 21

Runovsky's biography comes from his *Dnevnik Runovskogo* (*Runovsky's Diary*) in the twelfth tome of the *Akty Kavkazskoi Arkheograficheskoi komissii* (*Acts of the Caucasus Archeographical Commission*); and from his *Zapiski o Shamilya* (*Notes about Shamil*) (St Petersburg, 1860), as do many of the details about the sad end of Jamal-Edin. The story about the end of Shamil's resistance at Gunib comes from Abdurakhman's *Kratkoe Islozhenie podrobnogo opisaniya del imam Shamilya* (*A Brief Exposition of a Minute Account of the Affairs of Imam Shamil*), which was reprinted in Arabic and Russian in Moscow in 2002.

The details about eating horses come from the Dagestani magazine *Akhulgo*, and the song is well-known to folklorists, featuring for example in I. F. Varayev's *Pesni Kazakov Kubani* (*Songs of the Kuban Cossacks*) (Krasnodar, 1966), as well as in Shapi Ganiyev's history *Imam Shamil* (2001).

Baron August von Haxthausen's *The Tribes of the Caucasus* (London, 1855) amusingly shows how Shamil was all things to all men.

Chapter 22

Details on Shamil come from Runovsky's two books; from Maria Chichagova's *Shamil na Kavkaze i v Rossii* (*Shamil in the Caucasus and in Russia*) (St Petersburg, 1889) and from Abdurakhman.

Chapter 23

Continuing instability in the Caucasus after Shamil's surrender can be seen in the second chapter of *Vacation Tourists and Notes of Travel in 1861*, edited by Francis Galton (London, 1862), as well as in Arthur Thurlowe Cunynghame's *Travels in the Eastern Caucasus, on the Caspian and Black Seas, Especially in Daghestan and on the Frontiers of Persia and Turkey during the Summer of 1871* (London, 1872).

Kundukhov's autobiography can be found in *The Caucasian Quarterly*, between April and September 1938. Annoyingly, however, this publication then apparently disappeared, and from Chapter 6 onwards the autobiography is only available in French in the sister journal *Le Caucase*.

Biographies of the Sufi leaders who left the Caucasus can be found in *The Naqshbandi Sufi Way: History and Guidebook of the Saints of the Golden Chain* by Muhammad Hisham Kabbani (Chicago, 1995). These are also available on www.naqshbandi.org.

Chapter 24

Stalin's comments from his speech at the 10th Congress of the Russian Communist Party can be found in his *Marxism and the National and Colonial Question* (London, 1936). The kind of craven work Soviet historians produced under his rule can be seen in *Borba gortsev za nezavisimost pod rukovodstvom Shamilya* (*The Highlanders' Fight for Independence under the Leadership of Shamil*) by S. K. Bushuev (Moscow, 1939), which opens and closes with quotes from Stalin.

M. I. Quandour's *Muridizm* (Nalchik, 1996) has a chapter called 'The Treatment of Shamil and Muridism' by Soviet historians which nicely details the steps communist writers took to show Shamil in a bad light.

I first heard about the Chechens of Krasnaya Polyana from Michaela Pohl's research.

Chapter 25

Alexander Solzhenitsyn's *Gulag Archipelago* has been published in abridged and full versions. The information here is from the full Russian-language edition. Sultan Yashurkayev's diaries have been published in several European languages, but sadly not in English or Russian. He helpfully gave me a copy of the Russian manuscript, large chunks of which can also be found on the internet.

Chapter 26

The best books on the war are the general ones mentioned under Chapter 18, although a lot more work needs to be done.

2004

Chapter 27

Timothy Phillips's *Beslan: The Tragedy of School No. 1* (London, 2007) tells the story of the siege.

I have concentrated on the home-grown origin of Basayev's tactics and Chechen extremism in general, because I think that is overwhelmingly the most important element. Others, however, prefer to stress the Arab and international links. For a completely different viewpoint to my own, you could try reading *Chechen Jihad* by Yossef Bodansky (New York, 2007), which appears to be exclusively based on the viewpoints of the security services. Even if you do not like the book, it is interesting to see how so much information can be married to so little insight.

Chapter 28

Transcripts of Kulayev's trials are available on www.pravdabeslana.ru, which also includes huge volumes of material on the siege, compiled by locals angry about the government's failure to investigate it fully. A lot of it looks like conspiracy theories, but some is disquieting. Marina Litvinovich deserves commendation for putting the site together.

Chapter 29

Some of the best work on Russian brutality was conducted by the legendary Anna Politkovskaya, whose book *A Dirty War* (London,

2001) is a terrifying picture of what happened. Elsewhere, Andrew Meier's *Chechnya: To the Heart of a Conflict* (New York, 2005) is superb. Anne Nivat's *Chienne de guerre* (New York, 2001) is a good account of the destruction of Chechen resistance.

The documentary *Babitsky's War*, directed by Paul Yule, chronicles Andrei Babitsky's attempts to show what was happening in Grozny in 1999–2000 and is available on the internet. I strongly recommend watching it.

Chapter 30

Kudayev has won assistance from Reprieve, the British legal charity, which worked hard to win justice for the men being held at Guantanamo Bay. Reprieve provided me with copies of his papers, and I am very grateful to them, particularly to Saadiya Chaudary, who gave up a lot of her time to talk to me. The excellent book *Bad Men* (London, 2007) by Clive Stafford Smith, the director of Reprieve, does not deal with Kudayev, but shows the kind of problems he faced in legal limbo.

Human Rights Watch made him one of the three primary subjects of its *Stamp of Guantanamo* report, which uncovered the abuse he received on his return to Russia.

Kudayev's mother allowed me to use his poems, and thanks to Maria Golovnina for her help in translating them.

Chapters 31 and 32

The figures on asylum applications are taken from the UNHCR's *Asylum Levels and Trends in Industrialised Countries* reports, which can be found in the publications section of its website www.unhcr.org.

Postscript

Putin's comments are available on www.kremlin.org, which is a surprisingly good website.

Acknowledgements

Thanks first of all to my family. To Jenny and Willy, for making me who I am. To Tom, for making me laugh and making me think. And to Rosie, for making everything perfect.

Thanks to Helen Conford at Penguin, for agreeing that this book might be a good idea and for being a thoughtful editor and a patient listener, and thanks too to Abbie for introducing me to her. Thanks to Mike Morrogh and David Gee for being bright lights in a dark place, and to Geoffrey Ellis for the encouragement and help.

This book has involved lots of travelling, and I am very grateful to the Winston Churchill Memorial Trust for paying for so much of that. I recommend that anyone reading this who is keen to travel the world should look into asking WCMT for help (www.wcmt.org. uk). Thanks also to staff members at the British Library and at the National Archives in Kew.

I have shamelessly exploited the hospitality of people I met while travelling. I have been bought drinks, snacks and meals, and have been taken to weddings, meetings, commemorations and parties despite my travel-stained appearance. Thanks to everyone who helped me, and thanks to those who shared their recollections with me too.

In Moscow, thanks to German Tom for his hospitality, his good company, his inspiring photos and his financial assistance, without which I would have been ruined. In Grozny, thanks to Aslanbek, Arbi and Asya for many good times, and for all your help. In Almaty, thanks to Marusya for fun and a long walk. Thanks also to everyone in Krasnaya Polyana, and above all to Atlan. In Bishkek, thanks to Ivar and Elina for letting me come to your wedding; I wish you happiness together. In Turkey, thanks to Zeynel Besleney, for introducing me to the Circassians. Thanks to Emma for making me feel at home in Istanbul, and thanks also to Aytek in Kayseri, to Ergun, Okan and Setanay in Istanbul, and to Murat in Ankara. In

Jordan, thanks to Zaina for introducing me to everyone I could have hoped to meet, and to Amjad Jaimoukha for his help. In Israel, thanks to Kujan for showing me around, and to everyone in Kfar-Kama. Thanks also to Mark Mackinnon in Jerusalem for teaching me how to play the guitar. In the Czech Republic, thanks to Andrei Babitsky for taking time off to help me out, and for allowing me to see his video. In Dagestan, thanks to Abu-Talib, for being brilliant. In Austria, thanks to Joachim for putting me up. In Belgrade, thanks to Ellie for being great.

Some of my material dates back to the time I worked as a journalist in Moscow, when I was blessed with my colleagues.

At Reuters, thanks to Maria Golovnina, Meg Clothier, Tom Miles, Tom Peter, Ron Popeski, Richard Balmforth, Olga Petrova, Kolya Pavlov, Dima Madorsky, Nino Ivanishvili, Sog Afdjei, Viktor Korotayev, Sergei Karpukhin, Eduard Korniyenko, Kazbek Basayev, Maka Antidze and Niko Mchledishvili. And, outside Reuters, thanks above all to Yana Dlugy and Simon Ostrovsky. I wish all competitors could be like them.

This book is for Adlan Khasanov, who deserved to live for ever. Rest in Peace, my friend.

Index

Page numbers in *italics* refer to maps.